Baedeker

Portugal

www.baedeker.com

Verlag Karl Baedeker

SIGHTSEEING HIGHLIGHTS ✶ ✶

Beautiful coasts and marvellous beaches await visitors to Portugal, but that's not all. There is also a variety of sights to see: castles, palaces and cathedrals, and the »white city on the Tagus« – Portugal's capital. In addition to this Portugal boasts uniquely beautiful landscapes, in which pretty villages, still unknown to tourists, are to be found. By way of introduction, here is an overview of the destinations that should on no account be missed!

1 Peneda-Gerês
National Park
2 Citânia de Briteiros
3 Guimarães
4 Porto
5 Douro Valley
6 Vale do Côa
7 Buçaco National Park
8 Serra da Estrela
9 Coimbra
10 Conímbriga
11 Batalha
12 Tomar
13 Alcobaça
14 Castelo de Vide
15 Óbidos
16 Marvão
17 Mafra
18 Sintra
19 Lisboa
20 Serra da Arrábida
21 Évora
22 Algarve
23 Cabo de São Vicente

©Baedeker

1 ✶ ✶ Peneda-Gerês National Park
Superb mountain scenery on the Spanish-Portuguese border ▶ page 423

2 ✶ ✶ Citânia de Briteiros
Legacy of the Celtiberians: Portugal's oldest settlement ▶ page 338

3 ✶ ✶ Guimarães
The »cradle of the nation« is under the protection of UNESCO. ▶ page 334

4 ✶ ✶ Porto
Portugal's second largest city is considered by some to be the most interesting. ▶ page 441

5 ✶ ✶ Douro Valley
On the slopes grow the grapes for the famous port. ▶ page 297

6 ✶ ✶ Vale do Côa
20,000-year-old cave drawings first discovered in the 1990s ▶ page 516

7 ✶ ✶ Buçaco National Park
Fairy-tale woodland with 400 indigenous and 300 exotic species of plant ▶ page 255

8 ✶ ✶ Serra da Estrela
Portugal's highest mountains – where you can even ski! ▶ page 479

9 ✶ ✶ Coimbra
Old university city with a mixture of tradition and student flair ▶ page 273

Porto
The seaport on the Douro. The large port lodges are on the other side of the river.

BAEDEKER'S BEST TIPS

As an introduction, here is a selection from the Baedeker tips in this book which are particularly interesting or useful. Experience and enjoy the best that Portugal has to offer!

◼ O melhor de Amália
The best of Amália Rodrigues: CD with fado classics sung by Portugal's greatest fadista ▶ **page 93**

◼ Hiking in the Algarve
Explore the lesser known corners of Portugal's most popular holiday region on foot – preferably with competent guides or on footpaths chosen by the locals ▶ **page 212**

◼ Passeios na Ria
Get to know the flat lagoon at the gates of Aveiro on a boat trip ▶ **page 225**

◼ Café Santa Cruz
Enjoy a cup of coffee in the monastery rooms – the café in Convento de Santa Cruz in Coimbra ▶ **page 276**

◼ Fado »à capella«
Coimbra fado in a special location: performances every evening in a small chapel in the old town ▶ **page 278**

◼ Kayaking on the Mondego
Enjoy the landscape from a kayak – between Coimbra and Penacova ▶ **page 288**

◼ By train through the Douro Valley
The line runs right beside the river in the region where port grapes grow. ▶ **page 299**

◼ The legendary 28
No longer a secret tip: rumble through Lisbon's historic centre on the old tram. ▶ **page 365**

The memorial
The monastery palace of Mafra – the conditions under which the superlative building was created are described by José Saramago.

Café Majestic
Old established coffee house in Porto. Pure unadulterated Art Nouveau

■ »A Brasileira« – The Brazilian Girl
Once a meeting place for artists and writers and still worth a visit
► page 373

■ Memorial do Convento
The book to go with the monastery – written by José Saramago, winner of the Nobel Prize in Literature ► page 397

■ Mina de São Domingos
A closed-down copper mine in the Alentejo. Industrial landscape and unusual accommodation in the middle of nowhere ► page 402

■ Do as the »tripeiros« do?
The inhabitants of Porto were known as »tripeiros« – go ahead and try their alleged favourite dish! ► page 441

■ Café Majestic
Coffee in real Art Nouveau surroundings
► page 453

■ Enjoy a glass or two of port in a pleasant atmosphere
Approximately 200 ports to try!
► page 454

■ Dolphin watching
Tours cast off from Setúbal and head into a nature reserve to spot dolphins
► page 488

The legendary 28
A tram journey through Lisbon

How much port is produced on average per year?
▶ **page 34**

PRACTICALITIES

BACKGROUND

PRICE CATEGORIES

▶ **Hotels (double room per night)**
Luxury: double room from € 180/£ 120
Mid-range: double room € 90 – 180/£60 – 120
Budget: double room up to € 90/£ 60

▶ **Restaurants (for a main course)**
Expensive: over € 25/£ 17
Moderate: € 10 – 25/£ 7 – 17
Inexpensive: less than € 10/£ 7

TOURS

Aveiro, the »Little Venice« on Portugal's Atlantic coast
▶ **page 225**

SIGHTS FROM A to Z

One of the country's main sights: Batalha Abbey with the unfinished funerary chapels in Manueline style
► **page 236**

Background

THINGS WORTH KNOWING ABOUT
THE COUNTRY IN EUROPE'S
SOUTH-WEST, ABOUT ITS COAST AND
THE SEA, ITS SEAFARERS AND CONQUERORS,
ABOUT FIGO, FADO AND SAUDADE, THE
UBIQUITOUS DRIED COD AND SWEET PORT:
A BRIEF PORTRAIT.

PORTO
SANDEMAN

A JOURNEY OF DISCOVERY

»Bem-vindo« to Europe's south-west! With its gorgeous beaches and idyllic rocky bays, its picturesque fishing villages and endless sunshine, Portugal's Atlantic coast really hits the spot when it comes to relaxing beach holidays; though the great variety of water sports also attract those who like to be active on holiday.

There is a lot more than sea and sand to discover in Portugal, however. Few tourists know the stunning landscapes of the interior. Even confirmed Portugal fans are often only familiar with the coast of southern Portugal and the capital Lisbon, and perhaps with the north Portuguese city of Porto. But once visitors begin to explore the interior of Europe's most south-westerly country, they return again

and again. Just try two weeks in northern Portugal! The high mountains of the Minho and the Trás-os-Montes with its ancient granite villages have a timeless beauty, as does the sunny Douro Valley, on whose hillsides grapes for the world famous port wine ripen. There are small, unspoilt towns to discover, and lovely river valleys. Or how about a tour heading south from Lisbon? In the Alentejo region a delightful landscape of rolling hills covered in cork oaks and olive groves charms – and in spring it is covered in scented flowering meadows. And the Algarve? Of course the most beautiful beaches are here, but a completely

Lisbon
Emblem of the capital: the tower of Belém on the bank of the Tagus

different Algarve can be experienced in the interior: a quiet, gently rolling landscape with sleepy villages, a world away from the noisy glitz of the coastal towns.

Cultural Treasures on the Edge of Europe

Those interested in art history will notice that the country's most significant epoch, the Golden Age of the 15th and 16th centuries, still makes itself felt everywhere. In that era, brave seafarers set off from Portugal's coast to discover and conquer new continents and their treasures. Old Lusitania glowed in its new wealth and the buildings of Belém, Tomar, Batalha and Alcobaça reflect the adventure of seafaring, the sea and other distant cultures in their extravagant stone

Fantastic beaches
The coast of the Algarve has idyllic bays between the cliffs. But with 850km/530mi of coastline you can be sure that long stretches of sandy beach are to be found elsewhere.

Blue-and-white azulejos
Both inner and outer walls are totally covered with tile pictures.

Fried balls of dried cod
Bacalhau, otherwise known as dried cod, is the Portuguese national fish dish. There are said to be 360 different recipes.

Painted boats
Typical of the small town of Aveiro: the colourful sailing boats of the kelp fishermen

Full-bodied tipple
The grapes thrive on the sunny slopes of the Douro Valley; the liquid goods are stored in Vila Nova de Gaia near Porto.

Baroque palaces
Typical 18th-century architecture. The Solar de Mateu is known to many from the label of the rosé wine wh is produced here and in large part exported.

decorations. But other cultural highlights, less well-known but just as beautiful, also deserve attention: in the Alentejo, towards the Spanish border, there are unique fortified medieval white villages built on hilltops. In the north, a very special cultural sensation awaits; in fact, it has been there for some time, though it was only discovered at the end of the 20th century: the 20,000 year old cave paintings in the river valley known as the Vale do Côa.

A Country with Several Time Zones

After the flowering of Portugal's Golden Age, during which the country enjoyed a definite leading role in world events, it disappeared into obscurity for centuries and it was as if time had stood still. During the 20th century and the time of the dictatorship Portugal slumbered like a regular sleeping beauty, but since the Carnation Revolution, and especially since its membership of the European Union, the country has been hurrying towards the here and now. Progress is not across the board, however. While modern Portugal can be seen forging ahead energetically in Lisbon – with the country's second city of Porto close on its heels – the old Portugal can still be found in the countryside. In the wide expanses of the Alentejo and in the mountains of the north, the way of life can seem really archaic. Even remote towns often give a strange impression of another era, such as the university town of Coimbra, the religious Braga and Évora, the »Pearl of the Alentejo«.

Porto
North Portuguese metropolis on the banks of the Douro

Port, Fado and Saudade

Time is needed! Not only for travelling around, but also for the extended hours in bars and cafés, perhaps for a little glass of port or a cool Vinho Verde with some good fresh fish. Time is also needed for a long Fado evening, not least to soak up the atmosphere of the music and to get a sense of the »saudade« that is expressed in it. Once you have got an idea of this fundamentally Portuguese emotion you can truly say you have arrived in Portugal.

Facts

Portugal is oriented to the water. Its location by the sea in Europe's extreme south-west has defined the country and its fate: seafaring, fishing and beach tourism continue to play decisive roles. But of course there is also another Portugal: an urban and rural one, and life here looks very different to that on the coast.

Landscapes and Nature

Mainland Portugal's present day borders have remained unchanged for more than eight centuries, a fact that is largely based on its geography. As a marginal country away from the main thoroughfares, Portugal did not play a central role in the warring exchanges of European states after its foundation in the 12th century. Military efforts were directed solely towards the consolidation of national borders, at first against the repelled Moors, and later against the colonial ambitions of Spain. Most of the **Spanish-Portuguese border follows the great Iberian rivers** – the Minho (Span. Miño) in the north, the Douro (Span. Duero) in the north-east, and the Guadiana in the south-east; otherwise, it follows the **winding mountain ridges** in the north of the country. Those border regions easily reached and not characterized by natural barriers have become clearly demarcated as such by fortifications and depopulation. Almost half of the territorial border runs along the **Atlantic Ocean**; this explains why all of Portugal, including the interior, has had a definite focus towards the sea throughout its history and a noticeable tendency to differentiate itself both culturally and economically from its Spanish neighbour.

Geography as national borders

Numerous rivers wind throughout Portugal, defining the country's climate and flora, and in recent times they have also become of interest for energy provision. Only a few larger rivers – the Minho, Douro, Tagus, Sado, and Guadiana – are navigable in their lower reaches and there are no significant inland ports. Two rivers originating in Spain, the **Douro** and the **Tagus** more or less naturally divide Portugal into three parts: northern, central and southern regions.

Rivers

Northern Portugal is encompassed by the border river of Minho in the north, and the Douro in the south. There are several mountain ranges in the region that almost reach 2,000m/6,562ft. It is a country of hills and mountains, known as »**Montanhas**«, especially in the region of the Serra do Soajo, the Serra da Peneda, and the Serra do Gerês, which is wildly rugged and forms a uniquely beautiful landscape of great touristic interest, not least in the Peneda-Gerês National Park. The same can be said for the **Douro Valley**. The sides of the Douro Valley have been terraced and here, in the »**Pais do Vinho**« (wine country), the grapes for the world famous port wine ripen. It is then stored and shipped from Vila Nova de Gaia, the Douro's harbour near Porto.

Northern Portugal

South of the Douro, the Serra da Estrela rises as the western outcrop of the Castilian border mountains. Heavily marked by erosion, its

Central Portugal

← *Portugal's 850km/530mi coastline has always been a source of profit.*

Rivers and Mountains

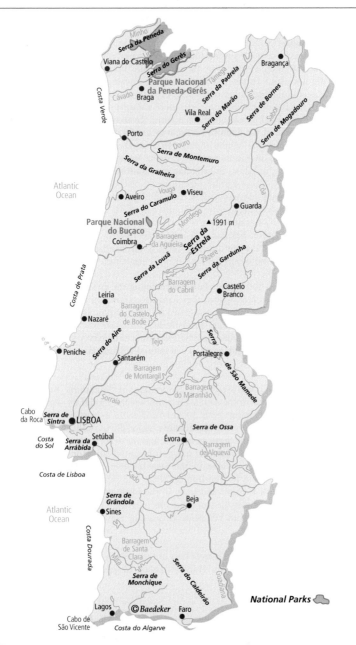

highest point and Portugal's highest mountain is the **Torre, which is 1,991m/6,532ft** high. The Serra da Estrela is the country's only significant winter sports region. To the south-west, it continues into Estremadura, a landscape of medium-sized mountains with a mild climate and fertile earth. The western reaches of this range go all the way to the coast and form the foothills of the **Cabo da Roca**, the **western tip of the European continent**.

However, central Portugal is only partly a mountain landscape. In the region of the Ribatejo and the mouth of the Sado there are fertile **lowlands** – which even today still suffer from earthquakes – that are enriched by river sediment and a high humidity, and also have numerous thermal springs. The valley of the lower Tagus (Span. Tajo) widens almost to an inland lake shortly before it flows into the Atlantic, providing the country's capital city of Lisbon with a giant natural harbour.

Southern Portugal

The **Alentejo**, a broad, partly hilly, partly flat plateau dotted with occasional small mountains that reach up to 700m/2,296ft, extends south of the Tagus. It is a landscape characterized by immense arable fields and lone olive trees and cork oaks. To the south it is bordered by the **Serra de Monchique**. This mountain chain, which reaches heights of up to 902m/2,959ft, forms a protective wall for the **Algarve** on the southern coast against cold temperatures from the north, and that along with its many streams makes for the region's sub-tropical vegetation.

Coastal landscapes

The Iberian landmass continues underwater for approximately another 15km/9.3mi to 20km/12.5mi before suddenly dropping off to a depth of 300m/984ft. Along the entire coast a band of limestone rock can be seen, left by the sea which once reached further inland, and which has been pushed up during the course of the earth's history. Today it forms the famous and exceedingly picturesque steep cliff faces and towering rocks under which the most beautiful beaches stretch along bays and niches – particularly lovely along the so-called **Rocky Algarve**. In the region known as the **Sand Algarve**, around the mouths of the rivers Douro, Tagus and Guadiana, the limestone has been severely eroded to become a landscape of dunes and lagoons.

Flora and Fauna

Forests

Portugal was originally thinly forested, but centuries of thoughtless cultivation policies have severely decimated the country's forests. Today primary forest can only be found in inaccessible mountain areas and in order to avoid desertification, reforestation programmes have been put in place; most recently in coastal dune areas in paticular, as well as in the mountains in the north. In northern Portugal primarily summer-green deciduous forests are seen, with pine forests at higher elevations. In the south, evergreen tree species predominate and Nordic pines cover the dunes along the coast.

Pine trees

It is impossible to imagine the Portuguese landscape without the Italian stone pine (pinus pinea) which stands alone or in groups, and only occasionally forms small forests. The seeds of the large round cones are edible and have a hazelnut flavour.

While Italian stone pineshave relatively specific needs, the **maritime pine** (pinus pinaster) can grow even on dry and nutrient-poor ground. The young pines grow quite quickly and are commonly harvested for resin which drips into containers fixed under small incisions in the bark.

Cypress trees also belong to the characteristic flora of Portugal (cupressus sempervirens). They were given the name semper virens (eternally alive), because they can live for up to 2,000 years. Cypresses are well adapted to the local climate due to their pillar form, which prevents excessive light damage.

Deciduous trees

In the rougher climate of the north, chestnut trees, lime trees, maples, poplars and birch are common. Further south, as in the rest of the Mediterranean, **olive trees** are widespread (Olea europea). The best growing conditions for them are found in the Alentejo, but

On the cliffs of the Rocky Algarve: pines can also grow here.

there are also olive trees in the north. The tree's fruit need a long, dry summer and relatively low winter temperatures for their development. In May and June insignificant white and yellow blossoms form, and the harvest lasts from November to March. Depending on their ripeness, the colour of the olives changes from green to black.

Portugal is the world's largest producer of cork (►Economy and Baedeker Special, p.208), which is why large areas of **cork oaks** (quercus suber) can be found in central and southern Portugal. The tree forms a cork layer composed of dead cells which regulates temperature changes and inhibits water loss. When it is peeled from the tree, care must be taken not to damage the fibre and bark that carries the sap essential for survival. After peeling, the trunk is at first a pinkish yellow and later turns to red-brown. Another cork oak variety especially prevalent in northern Portugal is the quercus occidentalis, which produces significantly less cork.

In the Peneda-Gerês National Park in particular, there are still significant stocks of **holly oak** (quercus ilex). This species of evergreen oak has dark green, leathery leaves that have a whitish fuzz on their underside.

Eucalyptus trees (eucalyptus globulus) were only introduced to Portugal a few decades ago. They grow extremely quickly and therefore play an important role in forestry, though they do need a great deal of water (►Environmental Problems). Young trees and shoots have round leaves, while older ones have gently curved, lancet-shaped leaves. Eucalyptus trees can turn their leaves to a north-south position to protect themselves from receiving too much light, the sun's rays only reaching the narrow edges of the leaves. A noticeable feature is the bark, which is often shed in long strips, revealing a smooth, shiny green trunk underneath.

On occasion there is criticism that palms, as non-native species, are depriving native plants of their habitat. The only native palms in Portugal are the **dwarf palms** (chamaerops humilis), usually the type without a trunk that only has shoots. In addition, especially in gardens and parks, the **Canary date palm** (phoenix canariensis) is common, which is a close relation of the north African and Arabic date palm, though it has a thicker trunk and has a more decorative, fuller crown.

Palms

The undergrowth of the damp north-west is home to **gorse** and calluna heathers; while the south and east have a **macchia** of aromatic herbs and shrubs, such as broom, cistus, rosemary, thyme, lavender and bulbiferous plants. Parks and gardens provide a magnificent display of blossoms in the spring and summer, including **oleander**, **camellias** and **hibiscus**.

Shrubs, herbs

Portugal's fauna is similar to that of Central Europe. Deer, chamois, fox, and the occasional lynx live in the richly forested northern

Fauna

Flamingos are among the bird life to be seen in the flat coastal lagoons.

mountains, along with **feral horses**, game, and even **wolves**. Rare animal species are protected by a total hunting ban in the Peneda-Gerês National Park, yet stocks of some species in Portugal are highly endangered. The number of wolves for example is estimated at no more than one or two hundred. Small game is widespread and vigorously hunted. The coastal lagoons are the favoured territory of numerous water fowl, including **flamingos**. In the spring there also are a significant number of storks here, who even venture into the cities to build their nests. The many rivers and dams are extremely rich in trout, pike, salmon, carp and eels.

Nature Conservancy • Environmental Problems

Protected areas

In addition to the Peneda-Gerês National Park and the Buçaco National Park, Portugal has twelve nature parks. The largest are the Parque Montesinho in the extreme north-east, and the Serra da Estrela. There are also nine protected areas and three nature reserves. Thus approximately 6.3% of the Portuguese mainland is officially under nature protection.

Environmental problems

Increasing industrialization and the use of chemicals in farming, the far-reaching impact of tourism, annual forest fires and an increasing water shortage in southern parts of the country are all serious environmental threats for Portugal. Winter rains have often failed to appear in the south, and the result is an acute **water shortage**. There is insufficient water all over the county during the summer and autumn months, and in addition the **monoculture of eucalyptus** is contributing to a drying out of the ground. Imported from Australia, eucalyptus draw substantially more water from the ground than other trees. However, since they are planted for the paper industry and play a role in one of the most lucrative branches of agriculture, new plantations continue to be planted. Thanks to this policy the Minho region is now one of the most heavily forested areas of the Iberian peninsula. The impact of the diminishing level of ground water is, however, a matter of intense debate.

The whole of Portugal regularly suffers from uncontrollable **forest and wild fires** in the summer and autumn months. Next to the total drying out of the ground due to failed rains and the uncontrolled incineration of rubbish, the monocultivation of principally eucalyptus and pine trees is increasing the risk of forest fires. In addition, fires are often laid on purpose to clear areas for eucalyptus planting or for the creation of new pastures. The fires often last several weeks. Efforts are made to stem the fires with water-carrying aeroplanes. It takes up to two years for shrub growth to recover in affected areas.

In the Algarve especially, the impact of **tourism** is a very serious problem. Right up until the 1950s, the coast was more or less undeveloped. However, in the following decades vast areas of the coastal stretch were concreted over, with the result that the natural habitat of numerous flora and fauna species was destroyed and the landscape changed within the shortest of periods. The annual rush of holidaymakers creates enormous seasonal pressures on the environment and water facilities.

For a long time, awareness of environmental problems was severely lacking in Portugal. Large areas of the country were or seemed to be undamaged and no one paid attention to ecological questions, but the impact of tourism, among other things, has contributed to a change in attitude.

Environmental awareness

Joining the European Union in 1986 also resulted in a sea change, because although funds were made available for industrial development and road building, the European Union also demanded the implementation of strict laws aimed at protecting the environment. Portugal passed a basic environmental protection law for the first time in 1987. A national environmental office was founded in 1989, and a ministry for the environment in 1990. The Portuguese media continue to give environmental issues and scandals relatively limited coverage and the job of increasing the population's awareness is left to non-governmental environmental organizations, such as »Amigos da Terra«, QUERCUS (»oak«) or the LPN (Liga para a Protecção da Natureza), which was founded back in 1948.

Population • Politics • Economy

Industrial conurbations and rural flight

Portugal has slightly less than ten million inhabitants, unevenly spread throughout the country (see map p.25). With an average population density of 108 inhabitants per sq km (280 per sq mi), the figures for Portugal are below the comparable values for other European states. Around 35% of the total population is concentrated into the extremely densely inhabited conurbations of Lisbon and Porto. In contrast, the population density of the Trás-os-Montes area of the north-east and the Portalegre, Évora and Beja districts of the Alentejo is very low and rural flight to the developing industrial regions continues to increase. Rural poverty in the Alentejo is so serious that the Red Cross has had to send food aid several times over the years. **Young people are deserting the countryside** in droves, in search of employment in the cities, and an **ageing population** is the result. In several villages of the Alentejo, the average age is already over fifty. In recent years the birth rate has stood at an average of 0.13%, which compares with the rates in other European countries. Traditionally, however, Portugal is **a country of emigrants** and about three million Portuguese live abroad today: mostly in the USA, Canada, France, Brazil and Germany.

? DID YOU KNOW ...?

- It is not only rural areas which suffer from a lack of young people. 25% of the population of Lisbon is of pensionable age, which puts the capital in 9th place among 258 European cities where the ageing population was studied. Younger people prefer to move into newer residential areas away from city centres.

Iberian Celts, Romans, Suevi and Moors

Celts were the first to settle in Portugal, and from an early stage, particularly in coastal regions, they mixed with seafaring and trading **Phoenicians**, Carthaginians and Greeks. The six centuries of **Roman** overlordship not only had an ethnic impact, but also significantly influenced the development of the **Portuguese language**. The impact of the comparatively short presence of the **Suevi and Visigoths** is still noticeable **in the north of the country**, where there are occasionally tall, light-skinned people, and where the heavily parcelled land use in agriculture still harks back to their era. The **Moors** have left their mark on the people and their culture **in the south** of the country. An unknown number of arrived in Portugal in the early Middle Ages, expelled from Spain by the Inquisition; they were again persecuted in their new land until they accepted the Christian faith. In this way, and due to the contiguous isolation from Spain and the other European countries, the mixing of newly arrived peoples and religious groups over thousands of years created a more or less ethnically and culturally homogenous and independent society. The **African minorities** are either descendants of slaves or come from the former African colonies.

Portugal Administrative Districts and Population Density

District borders
more than 600
180-250
90-180
60-90
30-60
less than 30
Inhabitants per square kilometre

VIANA DO CASTELO
● Viana do Castelo
BRAGA
● Braga
Bragança ●
VILA REAL
● Vila Real
BRAGANÇA
PORTO
● Porto
AVEIRO
VISEU
● Viseu
GUARDA
● Aveiro
● Guarda
Coimbra ●
COIMBRA
CASTELO BRANCO
LEIRIA
Leiria ●
Castelo Branco ●
● Nazaré
SANTARÉM
● Peniche
Portalegre ●
● Santarém
PORTALEGRE
© Baedeker
LISBOA
LISBOA
Setúbal ●
Évora ●
ÉVORA
SETÚBAL
● Beja
● Sines
BEJA
FARO
Lagos ●
Faro ●

Women at a market in Lisbon

Predominantly Catholic 94.5% of Portugal's population is Roman Catholic. The rest are estimated to be Protestants (0.6%), Muslims (15,000) and Jews (2,000). According to the law **state and church are separate**. Church taxes are not levied, so pastors have to be financed by the community. Fees are charged for marriages, baptisms and funerals. The Catholic Church is bureaucratically structured into three provinces: Lisbon (which includes the Azores and Madeira), Braga, and Évora.

Employment The **average income** lies at approximately €804.22 per month (2007), with **a minimum wage** set at €403. The average **cost of living** is around 25% less than in the UK, though there are large differences between urban and rural areas. In Porto and Lisbon the cost of living is relatively high. The working week ranges between 36 and 45 hours, and there are usually four weeks paid holidays. The **unemployment rate** between the autumn of 2002 and 2005 rose by 6.9%. Many workers only have seasonal employment and permanent contracts are the exception rather than the rule. Although the **employment of children** under the age of 14 is illegal, these regulations are regularly flouted. How many children – sometimes including children as young as six years old – are illegally employed can only be guessed at: the figures are between 50,000 and 110,000, which represents between 5% and 13% of the ten to 14-year-old age group.

According to the statistics almost every second Portuguese family lives below the poverty line and approximately 25% of the population must survive on the minimum wage. This is due to low wages and the limited provision of social services. There is no social security and income support is only available for the very few. About 75% of all unemployed people receive no help at all. Many businesses fail to pay wages for months at a time or fail to pay the full amount, but due to fear of losing their jobs, most employees are too frightened to do anything about the catastrophic working conditions.

Standard of living

Lisbon and Porto are bursting at the seams. Cities in general and Lisbon in particular are spreading their tentacles into the surrounding countryside and **satellite towns** have sprung up everywhere. Around Lisbon and Porto especially, so-called »bairros da lata« could be seen until the end of the 1990s: shack settlements of wood and corrugated iron, populated predominantly by old people and families from the provinces and the Cape Verde islands looking for a better life and working conditions. In the meantime, the inhabitants of these »bairros da lata« have been relocated to new housing areas and housed in satellite towns. A change in the **Landlord and Tenant Act** in 1985 caused the housing market to spin totally out of control. Until that year, rents could only be increased when there was a change of tenants, with the result that flats remained in the same families for generations. Even today, there are still numerous long-term residents who are living in their flats at knock-down rents. The new law was intended to encourage landlords to invest in their properties and maintain the value of housing stock. On the other hand, it also caused an explosion of rental costs, esp. in the cities, to such a degree that they are practically unaffordable for families on low incomes.

Accommodation

While several generations often live together in the countryside, **families with one or two children** predominate in Lisbon and Porto. The position of women in modern Portugal is very much defined by history. According to the Salazar Constitution of 1933, women were excluded from the equal rights granted to all citizens on the grounds of their different natures and to preserve the family. Women were only granted suffrage in 1968; they were not given the right to vote in local elections until 1974. Since the 1976 constitution men and women now have equal rights. However, in practice traditional gender roles often prevail. Many women are less well educated and have noticeably lower job qualifications than men. On the other hand, women from wealthy families who can afford a good education have good career prospects. Many women have become more independent through having careers, but housework – in addition to their jobs – remains almost exclusively their responsibility. While there are women in better paid, more authoritative professions, well over half of the women's work force is at the lower end of the pay scale and wotks in unskilled, service or agricultural jobs.

Family life

School class in Lisbon – the conditions for pupils are best in the capital.

Education is a matter of money

Nine-year compulsory schooling has been in place in Portugal since 1987. Until the mid-1960s it was four years, and later it was six. School is free for the first nine years, but further education must be paid for. A little over 10% of all school children continue on to university. There are **universities and technical colleges** in Coimbra, Lisbon, Porto, Évora, Braga, and several smaller towns. However, 20% of all children of compulsory school age do not attend school at all, or drop out before completing their sixth year. Rural areas, in particular, continue to have inadequate school and teacher provision, and the training and payment of teachers is often totally unsatisfactory. But in addition to failures within the educational system, there are other reasons why schooling is not exactly top of many families' lists: financial considerations. Many parents are dependent on their **children's income** due to their economic situation, even if child labour is illegal. The **illiteracy rate** is certainly alarming. In the male population the illiteracy rate lies at 5%, and in the female population it is 10%, though it can be significantly higher in the interior of the country compared with industrial and coastal regions. By comparison, the illiteracy statistics for Romania lie at 1–3%, and those for Hungary are below 5%. The figures for Portugal have only improved marginally in recent years, despite the increase in the length of compulsory education: the illiteracy rate still stood at 20% in the 1980s. A solution is being sought, for example, by a loosening of the state monopoly on education in favour of private providers, and by establishing continuous quality control of educational establishments which is intended to foster competition.

The national language is Portuguese (português, pronounced: purtugéhsh), an independent Latin language. It is also spoken in the Azores and Madeira, and is still in common use today in the former Portuguese colonies of Africa, India, Indonesia and Macau (South China Sea). A variation of Portuguese is the official language for the roughly 150 million inhabitants of Brazil, while the **Galician** spoken in the extreme north-west of Spain is also related to Portuguese. Altogether more than 170 million people speak Portuguese worldwide. The language evolved directly from **Lusitanian Latin**, and among the Romance languages it is most closely related to Spanish. The differences between individual Portuguese dialects are not as marked as in other western Romance languages. The vocabulary is predominantly Latin Romance based, with just a few Basque and Germanic elements, the latter usually of Visigoth origin. **Arab derivations** are less numerous than in Castilian, since the Moors' predominance lasted much longer in Spain. Words that begin with the »al-« syllable, such as Alfama and Algarve, hark back to Arabic origins. In Brazilian Portuguese, meanwhile, the indigenous Indian and African tongues (of slaves) can be recognized in the language. Written Portuguese and standard pronunciation was significantly shaped by the language of the educated of Coimbra and Lisbon, and early on adopted French, Italian and Spanish details.

Portuguese language

Facts and Figures Portugal

The Portuguese flag displays an armillary sphere, a navigational instrument of great significance to Portuguese seafaring during its exploration of the world's oceans in the 15th and 16th centuries, when it was also seen as a colonial symbol. The state coat of arms with five blue shields (»escudos«) can be seen in the middle of the armillary sphere, presumably recalling the victory of Alfonso Henriques over the five Moorish kings at the Battle of Ourique, in the year 1139. The five shields are arranged in a cross formation and the five dots symbolize the wounds of Christ. The seven castles in the red frame show the seven fortifications that Alfonso Henriques captured before he was finally able to found the Portuguese kingdom. The flag's red symbolizes the Republican revolution, and the green comes from flags used in the 15th and 17th centuries.

Geographical statistics
▶ In the south-west of the Iberian Peninsula
▶ Europe's most south-westerly country
▶ 42° 9' – 36° 58' northerly latitude
▶ 6° 11' – 9° 30' westerly longitude

Area
▶ 92,345 sq km/35,654 sq mi
▶ of which the Azores and Madeira are: 3,041 sq km/1,174 sq mi
▶ Length from north to south: 550km/343.7mi
▶ Breadth from west to east: on average 150km/93.7mi
▶ Coastline: approx. 850 km/531mi

Capital
▶ Lisbon

Language
▶ Portuguese

Population
▶ 9.8 million (UK: 60.8 million)

Population density
▶ 108 per sq km/280 per sq mi (UK: 246 per sq km/637 per sq mi)
▶ Three largest cities: Lisbon (main conurbation approx. 2.5 million), Porto (main conurbation approx. 1.6 million), Braga (approx. 164,000)

State
▶ Republic (República Portuguesa)
▶ State President: Anibal Cavaco Silva
▶ Prime Minister: José Socrates
▶ Administration: 22 districts (of which four are in the Azores and Madeira)
▶ districts are divided into »conselhos« which are divided into »municípios«.

Economy
▶ Gross domestic product per capita: 22,677 euros (2006)
▶ Average per capita income: 804 euros
▶ Economic structure: service industry: 56%; industry: 39%; agriculture: 5%
▶ Unemployment: 8.4% (2007)

©Baedeker

Portugal

State and Society

The Portuguese **constitution** of 1933 was dissolved as a result of the Carnation Revolution, and a new constitution that remains valid today replaced it on 25 April 1976. According to this constitution the Portuguese Republic (República Portuguesa) is based on a parliamentary democracy. Original socialist tendencies were weakened by a change in the constitution in November 1982, and a re-privatization law that came into force in 1990 finally wiped them out altogether. For the moment, the last change in the constitution took place in 2001.

República Portuguesa

The head of state is the **State President**, elected for a period of five years. Since 2006, this has been **Anibal Cavaco Silva** of the liberal conservative PSD. 230 members of parliament and four representatives of foreign-born Portuguese belong to the **parliament** (Assembleia Nacional), which is re-elected every four years. Depending on the election results, the State President nominates the **Prime Minister** who, since February 2005, has been **José Sócrates** of the social democratic PS.

The two largest parties are the **PSD (Partido Social Democrático)**, founded in 1974, and the **PS (Partido Socialista)**. Both names are misleading. The PSD is not a social democratic party; rather it follows liberal conservative lines. The PS party, founded by Mário Soares during his exile in Germany, follows social democratic lines. In addition there exist several smaller parties. The **PP** (Partido Popular), founded in 1974, grew out of the Christian democratic **CDS**, and counts as a nationalistic party with an emphasis on traditional values. Furthermore, there are the **communist PCP** (Partido Comunista Português) and the ecologically focused **Green Party, Partido Ecologista Os Verdes** or Partido Verde. Bloco de Esquerda, made up of a left wing block of intellectuals and former communists, is of little significance. The CDU (Coligação Democrática Unitária) is a communist coalition.

Political Parties

Portugal is a member of the United Nations (UN), the North Atlantic Treaty Organization (NATO), the Organization for Economic Co-operation and Development (OECD), the European Union (EU), the West European Union (WEU) and the Organization for European Security and Co-operation (OSZE).

International organizations

For administrative purposes, Portugal is divided into 22 districts (distritos), of which 18 are on the mainland (see map p.25) and four in the Azores and Madeira. The districts are divided into administrative districts (concelhos), that in turn are structured into municipalities (municípios) or municipal districts (freguesias). The eleven historical provinces (províncias; see map p.32) no longer have any political significance.

Government

Portugal Historical Provinces

Border of historical province

District border

Economy

After joining the European Union in 1986, Portugal experienced a notable economic upturn, succeeding in making the jump **from an agrarian to an industrial country**. Between 1985 and 1995, the country achieved an average economic growth rate of 3.17% (in the European Union the average was 2.29%); and in 2001 Portuguese economic growth stood at 2.8%. In the 1990's, inflation was 5.3%. The official **unemployment rate** has been rising in recent years, and in 2007 stood at 8.4%, the highest rate since 1987. In addition, a hidden joblessness continues to exist. It has been possible to significantly increase **per capita income**, yet at €804 per month (2007) it still only just reaches 70% of the average for Europe. Around 74% of imports and approximately 80% of exports are traded with European Union member states.

The economic position after EU membership

The liberal conservative government of economics professor Anibal Cavaco Silva is credited with the economic upturn at the end of the 1980s and beginning of the 1990s. His programme, »more growth and less state«,, was promoted by generous structural assistance funding from the European Union. Foreign investment also contributed to the positive economic development of the country. Its low wages and employment costs make Portugal an **attractive production base** for British, American, French, Spanish and German businesses.

Portugal has significantly changed in the past 15 years. New roads have been built and infrastructure has been greatly improved. In the place of small shops there are now giant shopping centres. Overall, the cities have taken on a more modern look. Yet the country continues to be characterized by great contrasts. Modernization has completely passed some regions of the interior by, and any initial euphoria has largely evaporated. Portugal, the country that managed economic and monetary union with such bravura, is meanwhile in danger of **falling behind the mainstream** within the EU. The country's economic deficit and inflation rate are amongst the highest in the EU, and talk of a recession has been going on since 2002. Since the EU's **expansion east**, Portugal has had to compete with countries that have lower employment costs, but in part offer a better qualified workforce.

Joining the EU has had an in part very negative impact on agriculture in Portugal. Fruit and vegetables from Portugal do not always match norms set by the European Union, and moreover agriculture is not helped by bad soil, antiquated cultivation methods and uneconomical working practices. The EU's agrarian policy often limits itself to rewarding fields lying fallow and early retirement regulations for which, however, many small farmers do not even fulfil the basic requirements. The additional problem of an ageing population will probably only make itself felt in the coming years. Only 8.6% of

Agriculture

those working in agriculture are under 35, while 25% are **over 65 years old**, and a shortage of workers means that future agricultural production can no longer be guaranteed. The percentage of the workforce active in agriculture has already declined drastically in recent years. At present it lies at 13% of all those employed.

A significant reason for the poor condition of Portugal's agriculture can also be found in the old-fashioned forms of ownership. **Rural smallholdings** predominate by far. Of approximately 420,000 concerns just 2% have more than 100ha/247ac; the average size lies at just 9ha/22ac – the average in the EU is 18.5ha/46ac. The splitting up of properties no longer allows for profitable production, especially in northern Portugal. Only in the south is a different division of property found: here, 45% of farming businesses have more than 100ha/247ac. The differing ownership conditions between north and south Portugal can be traced back to their different historical roots. The parcelling up of large agricultural areas in northern Portugal goes back to the time of the Suevi. In the south, by contrast, which the Suevi never penetrated, the large Roman properties survived intact.

Approximately 28.2% of Portugal's countryside is given over to agricultural production. 24% of fields are irrigated. Portugal's most important agricultural regions lie **between the Douro and Tagus** rivers. Wine grapes, apricots, figs, almonds, wheat, rye, oats, barley and rice grow in the sun-warmed river valleys. The most important cereals are grown in the south, in particular; maize and potatoes are predominantly grown in the north.

Producers of fruit and citrus fruit still depend heavily on the **domestic market**. Olives are also predominantly consumed within the country, though increasingly tangerines, cherries, almonds, olives, new potatoes and onions are reaching **export markets**. Tomatoes have been produced for the export market for some time, the majority being sold abroad as puree.

Vineyards are common all over Portugal, though the main wine-growing regions are in the north. The most famous wine is port. The average annual production in Portugal reaches 8.5 million hectolitres.

Animal husbandry is significant in the north of the country, in particular, where predominantly cows are bred, which also requires a sufficient production of fodder. Milk production is also primarily located in the north, but numerous dairy farms with intensive feeding programmes are also located in the Lisbon area. The breeding of milk cows takes place mostly on small farm holdings. All too often, farms only have one cow, and only 3% of all farms own more than five cows.

Forestry The use of **eucalyptus trees** is very important and entire hills continue to be planted with young trees. Their wood is used for the production of cellulose. The ecologically questionable cellulose industry has developed a strong presence in Portugal – especially along the

Wine-growing Regions

1 Vinhos Verdes
2 Chaves
3 Valpaços
4 Planalto Mirandês
5 Douro
6 Varosa
7 Encostas da Nave
8 Pinhel
9 Castelo Rodrigo
10 Lafões
11 Bairrada
12 Dão
13 Cova da Beira
14 Encostas de Aire
15 Alcobaça
16 Tomar
17 Óbidos
18 Santarém
19 Chamusca
20 Portalegre
21 Torres Vedras
22 Alenquer
23 Cartaxo
24 Almeirim
25 Colares
26 Bucelas
27 Arruda
28 Coruche
29 Borba
30 Carcavelos
31 Arrábida
32 Moscatel
   de Setúbal
33 Palmela
34 Évora
35 Redondo
36 Reguengos
37 Granja/Amareleja
38 Vidigueira
39 Moura
40 Lagos
41 Portimão
42 Lagoa
43 Tavira

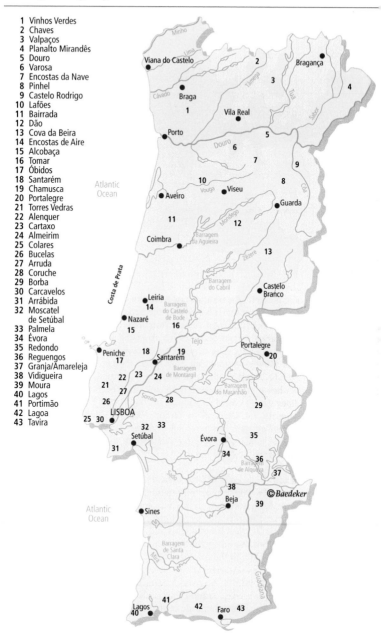

In Nazaré teams of oxen pulled the fishing boats on land.

Tagus river – because of the relatively lax environmental protection policies here. But it is not only the paper mills that are causing great environmental strain. The plantations of fast-growing eucalyptus trees draw a great deal of water from the ground and thereby dry it out excessively. The production of **cork oaks**, meanwhile, plays an increasingly insignificant role. Even though Portugal remains the world's largest producer of cork, cork production has declined greatly since bottle corks have more and more been replaced by synthetic equivalents (▶Baedeker Special, p.208). **Forest fires** have been a great problem for Portugal in recent years. In 2003 alone, 400,000ha/988,400ac were destroyed by fire. The damage caused considerable impact not just on forestry, but also on the related cork and paper industries.

Fishing Traditionally, the fishing industry is very important to Portugal. About 230,000 tons of fish are caught from the sea each year, a third of which is **sardines**. In this way enough sardines are caught for the domestic market, but in part other fish have to be imported. Portugal's fishing fleet is antiquated and cannot compete with other European fleets, especially the Spanish. The majority of fishermen can only work close to the coast due to inadequately equipped boats.

Saltworks At the mouths of the rivers Vouga, Tagus, and Sado, as well as along the Algarve coast around Faro, salt is produced which is used for conserving in the domestic canning industry.

Portugal has evolved from an agrarian country into an industrial **Industry** one. In the meantime, industry accounts for 36% of gross domestic product, and 35% of all employees work in this sector.

The **decentralization of industry** was begun under Salazar, so that next to the industrial base of Lisbon, Porto, Setúbal, Aveiro and Braga now also play a relatively significant role. Nevertheless, due to its port and advantageous transport connections, Lisbon is still the leading industrial base.

Traditionally, labour intensive **branches of industry**, such as the textile, clothing and leatherware industries predominate. In addition there are industries that make use of internally produced primary products. They produce, among other things, building materials such as concrete, tiles and glass, or work with wood producing paper. Cork exploitation continues to play a role, as does the food and luxury food industries. Branches of the metal working industry play a comparatively insignificant role and focus on products for the building, agricultural and textile sectors. Since 1994, there has been a limousine factory near Palmela, south of Lisbon, initially a joint project between Ford and VW; since 1998, it has been run by VW alone. The electrical industry produces mostly radios and televisions, as well as electrical motors. The chemical industry is represented, among others, by pharmaceuticals and agro-chemicals.

For a long time tourism was an economic sector with a rising trajec- **Tourism** tory. After a few dips in the early 1990s, optimism took hold once more at the turn of the 21st century. Not counting the many short-term visitors from Spain, six million people visited the country in 1999 alone. In 2006/2007 it is estimated that 2 million Britons visited Portugal.

However, Portugal's tourism industry suffered after the 11 September 2001 terrorist attacks: though many of the world's tourism destinations enjoyed renewed holiday traffic by 2004, the **Algarve** recorded its worst figures in about ten years. About 50% of all tourists to Portugal spend their holidays on the Algarve. Only about 25% spend their holidays in Lisbon and the surrounding area, and the rest go to northern Portugal and islands that belong to the country. About two million holidaymakers visit the Algarve each year. 50% of Algarve tourists are British, approximately 22% are German, and almost 20% are Dutch. To these figures the large number of day trippers from Spain must be added.

Mass tourism, such as has developed on the Algarve in recent decades, does not exist to the same extent in the rest of Portugal. Tourism is only of great importance around Lisbon, near Figueira da Foz, and in Nazaré. Excessive building on the Algarve has prompted repeated criticism over the past few years, and in future the intention is to focus on quality tourism, a sector for which there are high hopes due to the variety of landscapes, the flora and fauna, and the many nature reserves.

History

Portugal experienced a short Golden Age during the 15th and 16th centuries. Other continents were discovered and conquered, the world was changed. But the wealth that flowed into the country was squandered. Portugal came under Spanish rule, an earthquake destroyed the capital, and to this day, Portugal hankers a little after the time when it was a colonial power.

The history of the Portuguese nation begins in the year 1143, when the county of Portucale was recognized as an independent kingdom by neighbouring rulers. The little country had an important pioneering role among European states: Portugal was the first European national state, initiated the voyages of discovery of the modern age, and it is also Europe's oldest and most enduring colonial power. The first civil revolution of the old world occurred in Portugal, and an agreement with England, made at the end of the 14th century, is the oldest surviving contract in Europe.

A pioneering role in Europe

Kaleidoscope of Peoples

from 2200 BC	Iberians settle the south of the Iberian Peninsula
from 1000 BC	Phoenicians found trading posts on the Portuguese coast
from 700 BC	Celtic tribes arrive on the Iberian Peninsula from the north
from 500 BC	Greeks trade on the Portuguese coast

From the second millennium before Christ, Portugal was an important melting pot of various peoples. Thus, after 2000 BC, the **Iberians** arrived on the Pyrenean peninsula, probably from North Africa. After 1000 BC, the first trading agreements were made between Mediterranean peoples. Phoenicians from present-day Lebanon founded trading posts on the Portuguese coast, in search of silver, copper and tin, to be traded further with England, Ireland and north-west France (Brittany). They were followed by Greeks, Carthaginians and Romans.

From 700 BC, **Celtic tribes** settled in Portugal and evolved with the Iberians into the Celtiberians, who mixed with other indigenous inhabitants, among others with the Ligurian population in the south of the present country. Around 30 Celtiberian tribes, who were later called **Lusitanians** by the Romans, and who also gave the region its name of Lusitania, settled in the north of present-day Portugal, where they built strongly fortified, high settlements. These »castros« or »citânias« - such as Citânia de Briteiros and Castro de Sabroso near Braga, were usually collections of circular stone huts built on easily defended elevations.

After 500 BC, Greek traders reached the Portuguese coast and founded trading posts.

← *Over centuries Portugal's kings decided the fate of the south-west European country.*

Roman Lusitania

2nd century BC	Lusitania falls to the Roman province of »Hispania ulterior«
27 BC	»Hispania ulterior« is divided into the two provinces of Baetica and Lusitania
3rd century BC	Early Christianization of Lusitania

Around 450 BC, **Carthage** spread its sphere of influence from North Africa to include the Iberian Peninsula. The conflict between Carthage and Rome was now also carried out here, and the **Romans** began conquering the Iberian Peninsula at the end of the third century BC. During the Second Punic War (218-201 BC) they fought primarily against the Carthaginians, though they also tried to secure borders against the Celtiberians in the north and the Lusitanians in the west of the peninsula. The peace accord of 201 BC, between Carthage and Rome, sealed Roman pre-eminence in Iberia and they divided the peninsula into the provinces of **»Hispania ulterior«** in the south-west and »Hispania citerior« in the north-east. At the end of the Celtiberian War (197–179 BC), in which Romans fought against Lusitanians, Lusitania fell to the province of »Hispania ulterior«.

The man with the armband

The Lusitanians offered strong resistance against Roman occupation between 147 and 139 BC, impelled by the Lusitanian **Viriatus**, »the man with the armband«, who the Portuguese later celebrated as a national hero in poetry and art. After his murder in 139 BC – presumably on the orders of Rome – in the region of Viseu, Lusitanian resistance temporarily faded.

The birth of Lusitania

In 45 BC, **Julius Caesar** became sole ruler of the Roman Empire and thus also over the province of Hispania ulterior. In 27 BC, Augustus split Hispania ulterior into the two Roman provinces of **Lusitania** and Baetica, whose territory more or less matched present-day Andalusia. Lusitania, which was only a marginal province in the Roman Empire, encompassed all Portuguese regions south of the Douro, as well as the Spanish region of Estremadura and the modern Spanish province of Salamanca. The capital of the Lusitanian province was Augusta Emerita, present-day Mérida in Spain.

Impact of the Romans

Though the Romans destroyed the old castros, they did sponsor the **development of towns**, such as Bracara Augusta (Braga), Portus Cale (Porto), Aeminium / Conímbriga (Coimbra), Felicitas Iulia / Olisipo (Lisbon), Pax Iulia (Beja) and Scallabis (Santarém). As in all conquered regions, the Romans also immediately implemented their **system of government and economy** in the Iberian peninsula, and developed a **road network**. However, the territory of modern Portugal was not as intensively colonized as the eastern regions of the peninsula, which is why there is very little left of Roman architecture. Nevertheless, the Portuguese have the Romans to thank for several things: its first system of state, which lasted over five hundred years, its Classical Mediterranean culture and, its most enduring legacy, the **Portuguese language** which evolved out of Roman Latin, spoken all over the Roman Empire. Christianity also arrived in western regions of the Iberian Peninsula with the Romans. **Christianization** is said to have started very early in the province of Lusitania, but Christian communities, such as the bishoprics of Braga and Évora, can only be traced from the third century AD.

Teutons and Moors

from 411	Invasion of the Suevi, Alans and Vandals
418	Visigoths penetrate as far as southern Portugal
from 711	Arabs and Moors conquer large parts of Iberia. Portugal falls to the emirate of Córdoba.
1035–1065	The Reconquista commences under Fernando I of Castile and León

Roman rule of the Iberian peninsula came to an end in the year 411, during the population migrations of the Suevi and the invasion of Germanic armies. Suevis penetrated northern Galicia, Vandals entered the southern area and Alans entered Lusitania. Of these peoples only the **Suevi** settled and founded a kingdom that encompassed Galicia and the area between Minho, Douro and Tagus. The heart of this kingdom was Braga. Around 414–418 **Visigoths** invaded the peninsula and conquered both the Alans and the Vandals, who retreated to southern Spain before later escaping to North Africa. The Suevi kingdom, on the other hand, was only conquered by the Visigoths under King Liuvigild in the year 585, when he amalgamated it with the mighty Visigoth empire of Toledo.

Christianization of the Iberian peoples really took off in a big way under Gothic rule. In the year 589, **King Roderic**, and therefore the Visigoths, accepted the Catholic faith in place of the Arianic, and shortly afterwards the religiously motivated persecution of the Jews commenced, inspired and led by the Catholic Church. Little survived of Visigoth culture. The ruling class was far too small and quickly mixed with the original population.

Christianization

The Visigoth empire came to an end in the year 711. Arabs, largely Moors (**Islamic Berber peoples with Arabic culture** from north-west

The Moors and their culture

Africa), invaded the Iberian peninsular via the Strait of Gibraltar and conquered Roderic, the last Visigoth king, in the battle at the Guadalete river. With the exception of the northern mountain regions, they occupied the entire Iberian peninsula from 713 to 718. The territory of present-day Portugal also fell to the Arab emirate (later caliphate) of Córdoba. The rule of the Arabs had a greater impact on the society and economy of the Iberian regions than that of the Germanic tribes. For the first time since the collapse of the Roman Empire, large parts of the Iberian peninsula were once again ruled by a superior civilization. **Business and trade revived**, and many communities achieved wealth. Agriculture profited from Moorish artificial irrigation techniques and from newly imported economically useful plants. The Arabs were far in advance of Christians in cultural and scientific areas, among others **art** and **medicine**. Furthermore, although they demanded total submission from the population, their rule did not include religious oppression. In fact, Christians and Jews enjoyed **extensive religious freedom**.

Moorish influence today? Today the Moorish influence can hardly be seen in Portugal, unlike in neighbouring Spain. Impressive architectural evidence from the Moor era has not survived, not even in the country's south, in the Algarve, where Moorish rule survived for the longest time while northern areas of modern Portugal were gradually re-conquered by Christians. The recovery of Arab occupied regions by Christians emanating from the Visigoth kingdom of Asturia, the so-called Reconquista which had already begun in 717, initially resulted in a severe setback for social and economic life. Not only were large areas of the countryside devastated, but also a formerly differentiated social order was forced to give way to a much more primitive and rural social structure.

Reconquista From 722 the Kingdom of Asturias, which was at the northern edge of the Iberian peninsula, succeeded in winning back the region between the Minho and the Douro by recapturing the Portus Cale fortification – present-day Porto. The actual Reconquista of Portugal, however, did not begin until after the establishment of new kingdoms in the Christian territories, and truly started with King Ferdinand I of Castile and León, who was able to re-take Coimbra in 1064. Jews and Arabs were driven out or enslaved and only a few Arab artists and craftsmen could remain working and living in the countryside as **Mudéjars**. The Arab agricultural system was adopted and the Portuguese also profited from the Arabs' scientific knowledge during the subsequent era. Ferdinand was succeeded by his sons Alfonso VI (León) and Sancho II (Castile). Jealousy drove them to war. Alfonso was defeated and exiled to the Muslim court in Toledo. But their sister Urraca instigated a rebellion in León ans saw to it that Sancho was killed. Thereupon Alofonso returned from his exile and took both principalities.

Portugal is Born

1139–1385	The Burgundy dynasty
1095	Founding of the County of Portucalia
1139	Afonso Henriques has himself crowned as the first king of Portugal
around 1250	The Reconquista ends with the recapture of the Algarve cities
1256	Lisbon becomes the capital
1279–1325	Fresh impetus under the rule of Dinis I

Portugal's national state history begins in 1095, when Alfonso VI of Castile and León (1065/72–1109) founded the **County of Portucalia** between the Douro and the Mondego. It was named after the city of Portucale, now Porto, and granted in fief to Alfons's son-in-law, Count **Henry of Burgundy** (1066–1112), in return for military services during the Reconquista. After the death of his father-in-law in 1109, Henry settled in Guimarães, continuing his rule as self-proclaimed Count and Ruler of all Portugal. With this the independently minded Burgundian gave a clear rebuttal to the claims to power from the Castilian overlords.

Birth of a nation

But it was his son, Afonso Henriques (►Famous People) who completed the break with Castile-León, when he proclaimed himself King Afonso I, after a glittering victory over the Moors at Ourique (near Beja in the Alentejo) in 1139. This was followed by military confrontations between Portugal and Castile-León that ended with the Treaty of Zamora, in which the Castilian monarch recognized the Kingdom of Portugal.

Break with Castile-León

Legitimization by the Pope was still required for full state recognition, and although Afonso I made himself a vassal of the Pope in the same year, paying tribute to the Curia, the title of king for him and his descendants was only recognized by the Vatican 36 years later – in 1179 – after a four-fold increase in the tribute.

By this time Afonso Henriques had already confirmed his initially contested power through victories in the south. Among others, for example, Lisbon had been re-conquered in 1147, during the Second Crusade, thanks to help from German, Belgian and British crusaders. Around one hundred years later, Afonso III (1245–1279) conquered the Province of Algarve in the south, completing the Portuguese Reconquista; the Guadiana river now became the border with Castile. With this victory Portugal became the first European country to achieve a territorial expansion which has survived almost unchanged to this day, and in 1256, Lisbon replaced Coimbra as the country's capital city.

Consolidation of the State and Crises

After Afonso Henriques, the second most noteworthy personality of the first Portuguese dynasty of Burgundy (Borgonha), which lasted until 1383, was **Dinis I** (1279–1325). He dedicated himself energetically to the internal development of the country and thereby gave Portugal a significant **economic and cultural boost** and encouraged agriculture – the reason he is known as Dinis the Farmer – as well as trade, mining, afforestation and seafaring. He reduced the influence of the Church and nobility and, following the tradition of his forebears, increased the power of civil society. **Portuguese became the official language** under his rule, and in 1290 the **first Portuguese university** was founded in Lisbon, which was transferred to Coimbra in 1307. He also succeeded in ensuring the Pope did not confiscate the assets of the Knights Templar, disbanded by him in 1312, but instead ensured they went to the newly founded Knights of Christ, which were directly subject to the orders of the Crown and which were later to co-finance the voyages of exploration. The death of Dinis was followed by several serious crises. Afonso IV (1325–1357) led ruinous wars against neighbouring Castile. He also ordered the murder of his son and heir's secret fiancée, the lady-in-waiting Inês de Castro, which caused a war between the father and his son Pedro (► Baedeker Special, p.284).

At the Battle of Ourique, Afonso Henriques won Portugal's independence from Castile-León and had himself crowned king.

The Rise and Fall of a World Power

1385–1580	The Aviz dynasty: great voyages of discovery and conquest and Portugal's Golden Age
1485–1521	Manuel I: Portugal at the height of its economic and cultural flowering
1521–1557	Decline sets in under João III
1580–1640	Spanish interregnum

Great problems arose for Portugal when Fernando I died in 1383 without producing a son and heir. Fernando's daughter Beatriz was married to the Castilian king Juan I. In order to prevent the return of Portugal to Castile after the male line of the House of Burgundy died out, the Portuguese assembly of the estates (known as the Cortes) pronounced Pedro I's illegitimate son, who was the **Grand Master of the Aviz Order,** King of Portugal. He became **João I** (1383/1385–1433). The election of João as Portuguese king was a provocation to Castile, and in 1385 it resulted in war, but with the help of English archers the Portuguese comprehensively beat the numerically superior Castilian invaders at the **Battle of Aljubarrota**. A year later, in 1386, Portugal and England made a treaty – the Treaty of Windsor – which is still valid today, and is therefore the longest running alliance of the post-medieval era. With the victory at Aljubarrota, in whose honour João had the **Abbey of Batalha** built (Batalha means battle), Portugal's independence was secured and the country could set its sights on new goals. The sponsorship of voyages of discovery commenced under João I, enabling Portugal to become Western Europe's leading maritime and colonial power.

The dynasties of Burgundy and Aviz

The period from 1383–1385, which marked the transition from the Burgundy to Aviz dynasties, is also referred to as the time of the **first civil revolution in Europe**. By no means all of Portugal backed João; his support lay in civil society, which feared a loss of power under Castilian rule, as well as with the lower orders, minor nobles and several representatives of the clerical orders.

Europe's first civil revolution

The high nobility and Princes of the Church, on the other hand, supported the annexation of Portugal by Castile in hopes of regaining some of their lost power. Representatives of civil society did not just vote against the church and nobility during the election of João as Portuguese king in 1385, they also took to arms in order to ensure their own political views prevailed and to ensure the country's independence from the external threat that had military support from the high nobility.

Discoveries and rise to world power

The real initiator of the voyages of discovery undertaken from the beginning of the 15th century was a son of João I, the Infant Henrique »o Navegador«, **Henry the Navigator** (▶Famous People and Baedeker Special, p.469). He won **Ceuta** near the Strait of Gibraltar – still a Spanish enclave on the Moroccan coast today – from the Moors in 1415, thus securing a colony for Portugal and making it the first colonial power of post-medieval Europe. From 1418, Henrique sponsored voyages of discovery along the West African coast and

Portuguese Voyages of Discovery

→ Scientific centre at Sagres
Capture of Ceuta 1415; Madeira 1419;
Azores 1427; Gil Eanes rounds
Cape Bojador 1434.

⇢ Sea route to India:
Álvaro Fernandez and Diniz Diaz discover
the mouth of the Senegal River in 1444.
Diogo Cão reaches the mouth of the
Congo River in 1492. Bartolomeu Dias
rounds the Cape of Good Hope in 1488.
Pedro Álvares Cabral reaches Brazil in 1500.
Starting out in 1497 from Belém near
Lisbon, Vasco da Gama sails aound the
Cape of Good Hope, reaches Mozambique
in south-east Africa in 1498 and in the same
year reaches India (Calicut).

⇢ Gaspar Corte Real reaches Newfoundland in 1501.

⇢ In 1519, in the service of the Spanish, Fernão de
Magelhães sails from Sanlúcar de Barrameda
across the southern Atlantic, passes through the
Strait of Magellan at the southern tip of
South America in the Pacific Ocean in 1520,
and is killed in 1522 on Mactan in the
Philippines in a battle with the indigenous
people there. One of his ships returns to
Europe across the Indian and southern
Atlantic Oceans to become the first to sail
around the world.

→ In 1660, David Melgueiro sets out on a
Dutch ship from Japan and sails north
around Asia and northern Europe to Portugal.

in the Atlantic, using the purpose-built scientific centre at Sagres as a base. At first the goals of these voyages were to discover a **sea route to India** and to establish **trading routes** with this country, rich as it was in spices. It was not possible to reach India overland since the mainland routes were under the control of the expanding Ottoman Empire, non-Christian and therefore an enemy. The Africans caught along the way, which were sold at the European slave markets, also promised wealth. The **fight against Islam** also provided a significant impetus for Henry's seafaring expeditions, as did the search for the legendary Christian empire of Prester John, assumed to be in Ethiopia and from which there were hopes of help in fighting the infidels. From 1419 to 1457 the islands of Madeira, the Azores, and the Cape Verde Islands were discovered and colonized. This was also the time when **the black African slave trade** began, a trade that was only legally banned in 1850. In 1482, a Portuguese expedition reached the mouth of the Congo; **Vasco da Gama** (▶ Famous People) rounded the Cape of Good Hope in 1497/1498 to become the first European to reach **India** via the sea route.

Portuguese and Spanish spheres of influence were laid down in the **Treaty of Tordesillas** in the year 1494. All territories remaining undiscovered west of a line running approximately 370 nautical miles west of the Azores were to be the domain of the Spanish, while Portugal was to be entitled to all those territories yet to be discovered to the east of that line. It was on the basis of this treaty that Lisbon laid claim to regions of present-day **Brazil**, which **Pedro Álvares Cabral** reached in 1500.

Two decades later, between 1519 and 1522, an expedition led by **Fernão de Magalhães** was the **first to sail around the world**, though the captain himself died in the Philippines. **King Manuel I** established the Portuguese trading empire with posts in East India, East Asia, South Africa and Brazil, and thus Lisbon became the centre of global trade. From 1510, the Viceroys of India, Francisco de Almeida and Afonso de Albuquerque established trading posts in India and Southeast Asia (among others Goa in

Portuguese caravels with the cross of the Order of the Knights of Christ on great voyages across the world's oceans

1510, Malacca in 1511, Hormus in 1514, and Diu) and for a certain time achieved a **monopoly in the global spice trade**. In 1557, the Portuguese founded the first European trading post on Chinese soil on Macau. The Crown, nobility and merchants attained unimaginable wealth and, apart from Spain, 16th-century Portugal was the richest European country and one of the most powerful nations in the world. Under Manuel I (▶Famous Perople) – also known as Manuel the Fortunate because of his successful rule – master builders created the country's greatest treasures and developed a unique style known as Manueline architecture (▶ Baedeker Special, p.388).

Decline
The amazing colonial expansion put great strain on the Portuguese population, however. Many young Portuguese emigrated to the colonies, and entire ship's crews died of scurvy and infectious diseases during long journeys, or drowned in shipwrecks. Within a short space of time, the population declined by a third, and the **domestic economy almost came to a standstill**, though it was also destroyed by the stream of immense colonial wealth: the easy import of foodstuffs from abroad resulted in a decline of agriculture, and it also had a negative impact on the trades. In the glittering capital of Lisbon hardly any inhabitants were still occupied in productive employment. In addition, **income streaming in from abroad was no longer invested**, but instead recklessly spent by the Crown and nobility. Yet the **costs of maintaining and running the overseas colonies increased** due to growing piracy.

When prices for once expensive spices and luxury goods fell due to a flooding of the market, bringing less and less money in for the state, the Crown was forced to take out loans with German and Flemish merchants. Economic collapse also had negative results for once powerful civil society, which was increasingly excluded from big business by a newly empowered nobility. Also, foreigners increasingly controlled business in Portuguese trade centres and part of civil society became the victim of the **Inquisition**: the Jews, who represented about 10% of the Portuguese population were persecuted from around 1496. Those who did not wish to undergo compulsory baptism had to leave the country, and in countless cases even those who did convert to Christianity ended up being burnt at the stake in an inquisition that followed the Spanish example. The Portuguese Inquisition also kept a strict eye on the Counter Reformation of the 16th century.

The death of **the last Aviz king**, the young **Sebastião**, who died during a Morocco expedition in 1578, showed that Portuguese civil society was no longer the same as during the revolution of 1383–1385 (see above). As he died without issue, Spain's King Philip II was able to claim the Portuguese Crown through his mother's lineage by being a grandchild of Manuel I. Some anti-Spanish sections of society tried to mount a rebellion, but they lacked the revolutionary self confidence of their predecessors in 1385 and Philip II was able to don the Portuguese Crown and take possession of the neighbouring country without any significant resistance in 1580.

From 1580, Portugal was ruled in union with Spain by the Spanish Crown – an era still viewed as shameful by the modern Portuguese. The administration of Portugal and her colonies remained under national control. However, the **former world power lost part of its colonial territory** to the Netherlands during Spanish rule. The Moluccas, Ceylon and the north-east of Brazil were lost after Spanish maritime defeats, and could only be retaken in 1654. Spanish rule of Portugal ended in the year 1640, when the people – pressurized by high taxation to finance the Spanish wars and also provoked by French agents – were driven to a rebellion in Lisbon. The rebellion was eventually successful, and the **Duke of Braganza**, whose grandmother came from an ancient royal line, became King of Portugal as **João IV** (1640–1656).

Under Spanish rule

The Braganza Dynasty

1706–1750	Portugal increasingly dwindles under the wasteful rule of João V
1755	A heavy earthquake rocks the land
1807	Napoleonic troops occupy Portugal
1832–1834	Liberal Wars between Liberals and Absolutists
1908	Carlos I and his heir Luís Filipe are murdered in Lisbon

With João IV, the House of Braganza came to power, and was to rule Portugal until 1910. In order to protect itself from a renewed claim by Spain, Portugal signed a friendship and trading treaty with England in 1642. Spain only recognized Portuguese independence at the Peace of Lisbon signed in 1668, and was given Ceuta in return. Fear of its Spanish neighbour led Portugal into an ever more dependent relationship with England (Protection Treaty of 1661). In 1703, Lisbon and London signed the **Methuen Treaty** – named after the English ambassador in Lisbon – which was a trading agreement that guaranteed the exchange of British textiles for Portuguese wine and had the long-term effect of creating Portuguese dependence on England (▶Baedeker Special, p.457). Even though discoveries of gold and diamonds in Brazil ended the financial crisis at the end of the 17th century, this wealth, too, was squandered in the same manner as that from East Asia in the 16th century. While the absolutist kings and high nobility lived in pomp and style, the rural population remained

Era of absolutism

desperately poor. **Pompous representative architecture**, such as the Mafra monastery cost shocking sums and, at the same time, the once thriving Portuguese wool industry was destroyed by English textile imports, initially also destroying early attempts to develop a domestic textile industry. Thus Portugal had to use Brazilian gold to pay for English imports, which exceeded exports to its trading partner by two to three times.

On **1 November 1755**, an **earthquake** rocked Lisbon and the south of the country, costing tens of thousands of lives and destroying countless buildings. At this time the **Marques de Pombal** (►Famous People), José I's Prime Minister, was in power; for him, escape from England's economic hegemony was an important goal. In the spirit of Enlightenment and mercantilism, Pombal instituted many reforms, including the promotion of manufacturing and trading companies, a re-organization of the tax and financial system as well as of the army, the establishment of a new law book, and the secularization of the education system. After José I's death, the authoritarian Minister of State Pombal had to go into exile and most of his reforms were revoked and his enlightened ideas quashed with the help of the **Inquisition**. Pombal, therefore, left little that endured. Most of the newly founded factories collapsed, and court and nobility dedica-

Borstellung und Beschreibung des gantz erschröcklichen Erdbebens, wodurch die Königl. Portugiesische Residenz-Stadt Lissabon samt dem grösten Theil der Einwohnern zu grunde gegangen.

On 1 November 1755 an earthquake reduced Lisbon to rubble and caused turmoil in the whole of Europe. A leaflet from Augsburg reports on the disaster.

ted themselves to a life of luxury once more. Only the lower part of Lisbon, which Pombal had built after the devastating earthquake of 1755, recalls the drive of this man.

As a traditional ally of the English, Portugal was occupied by Napoleon – England's greatest enemy – in 1807. Now, however, the alliance with London proved its worth and the royal family succeeded in escaping to Brazil under the protection of the British fleet. In the following war of independence, a British expeditionary corps helped to free the country of the Napoleonic yoke by 1811. After that, officially in the name of the Prince Regent and later King João VI (1816–1826), who had no thought of returning from Brazil as yet, the British established themselves as the new rulers of Portugal. In his absence, the Cortes of Lisbon convened in 1821 and devised a Liberal constitution that demanded conversion to a constitutional monarchy. After the civil council succeeded in persuading **João VI** to return to Portugal, he confirmed the new liberal constitution, in doing so **ending the era of absolutism**. But the desire of the Liberal members of the Cortes to re-establish Portugal's full control over Brazil accelerated the break between the colony and the mother country. In 1822 Pedro, the son of João who had remained in Rio de Janeiro, declared Brazil's independence and shortly afterwards had himself crowned as Emperor Pedro I of Brazil (1822–1831).

Napoleonic invasion and liberal constitution

João VI died in 1826 without his succession having been established. As João's son, **Pedro I of Brazil**, was not permitted to reunite his empire with Portugal, he abdicated in favour of his seven-year-old daughter Maria II da Glória, passed a watered-down constitution and declared his **younger brother Miguel as Regent**. He, however, annulled the constitution after the counter-revolution of 1828, and had himself declared king by the Cortes, as Miguel I. With this event an era of brutal dictatorship commenced, which was to last six years and bring Pedro I of Brazil back into the fray. He returned to Europe as **Pedro IV of Portugal**, having renounced the Brazilian Crown in favour of his son, Pedro II, in 1831, in order to defend the rights of his daughter Maria. He was able to triumph over Miguel I's regime with British help during the so-called Liberal Wars, and Miguel I was forced to leave the country.

Collapse of the monarchy

After the death of her father, **Maria II da Glória** became ruler in 1834. She married Duke Ferdinand of Saxe-Coburg and Gotha in 1836, and thereby founded the **Sachse-Coburg-Braganza dynasty**. However, the queen was unable to contain the party battles between the Conservatives and the Liberals, and the constitutional conflicts and short-lived depositions lasted until the middle of the 19th century. Changes of power between the rival political parties without major disturbances in public life only became possible in the second half of the 19th century, thanks to the Crown's focus on the politics of balance.

However, towards the end of the 19th century the **Republican move-ment** gained in strength. This was due to an increasing dissatisfaction: despite the influx of funds from the African colonies of Mozambique and Angola as well as the construction of railway lines, roads, bridges and the laying of telecommunication cables, a successful and independent economic production base failed to become established. Railway companies and banks were predominantly controlled by foreign business and Portugal, undermined by economic and financial crises, became ever more impoverished and remained an old-fashioned agrarian country. The Portuguese finally lost all faith in their monarchy when it failed to prevail against British colonial interests and allowed itself to be dictated to by London, forcing it to recall an expeditionary force that had already been sent to Africa to explore regions between Angola and Mozambique, which they were to claim for Portugal, thereby creating a land connection between its two colonies.

Death of Carlos I   The extent to which **anti-monarchist groups** were prepared to use violence became obvious in 1908, when King Carlos I and the heir to his throne, Luís Filipe were assassinated in Lisbon. With the death of Carlos I, the monarchy was practically at an end, and even an amnesty and further smaller concessions offered by his younger son, Manuel II, could no longer save it. Two years later, in 1910, Manuel II was forced to abdicate and sent into exile to Britain.

Republics and Dictatorship

1910	The republic is proclaimed
1933	Salazar proclaims the »Estado Novo«
1974	The dictatorship is ended by the Carnation Revolution

Changing governments and military dictatorships   Portugal's newly proclaimed republic was, however, no more capable of solving the country's problems. Due to party political strife, no effective reforms were instituted, which would have been especially needed in the agrarian sector, and Portugal therefore found itself in a prolonged internal political crisis. The new government was unable to stabilize. In the era between 1911 and 1926, the country experienced 44 governments under eight presidents. After the First World War (1914–1918), which under pressure from Britain Portugal had joined on the side of the Allies from 1915, the economic and social problems increased. In 1926, the military took power in a coup, and in 1928 **General Carmona** proclaimed Portugal's Second Republic and had himself installed as State President in a fixed election, a position he retained until 1951.

António Salazar proclaimed the authoritarian »Estado Novo« in 1933.

In 1928, a man then appeared on the political stage who was to go on to hold the true reins of state power for four decades: **António de Oliveira Salazar** (▶ Famous People). He was elected Finance Minister by Carmona that year, and in 1932 Salazar became President, a post he retained until 1968. In 1933 he proclaimed the **»Estado Novo«** (new state), which took its inspiration from the German National Socialists and fascist Italy, and installed himself as absolute ruler. Diminished civil rights, press censorship, spying, arrest and torture, as well as a secret police modelled on the Gestapo (the PVDE, which was renamed the **PIDE** in 1945) were the instruments of power in the new state.

During the **Spanish Civil War** (1936–1939), Portugal officially remained neutral, though it effectively supported Franco. During the **Second World War** (1939–1945) Salazar also maintained Portugal's neutrality, though he allowed Britain and America to use bases in the Azores in 1943 and 1944. Diplomatic relations with Germany were broken off on 6 May 1943. Salazar had solved the financial crisis that existed when he came to power. However, particularly after the Second World War, his authoritarian dictatorship – associated with fascism – and his inflexible **colonial politics** resulted in the country's widespread political isolation within the United Nations and also – despite its membership of Nato from 1949 – within the group of Western States.

By the early 1960s there was **disquiet in the colonies**. India annexed Portugal's possessions of Goa, Damão and Diu in 1961. In the same year freedom fighters took up armed resistance against the colonial power in Angola, followed by Guinea-Bissau in 1963, and Mozambique in 1964. The prolonged colonial wars eventually used up 40% of Portugal's budget at a time when it was known as Europe's poorhouse due to its backward economic structure. When Salazar had to stand down in 1968, for health reasons, **Marcelo Caetano**, lawyer and long-term Salazar associate, became his successor. The new leader tried to pursue a more liberal course for only a very short time; in the end he was neither interested in change nor was he capable of solving the colonial question. Eventually opposition developed and more and more officers opposed the dictatorship due to its pointless and expensive colonial wars in Africa. On 25 April 1974 the »**Carnation Revolution**« (► Baedeker Special, p.55) broke out in Lisbon, a military coup largely supported by the population which ended the dictatorship. The almost bloodless revolution ended a dictatorship that had endured a total of 48 years.

26 April 1974: soldiers celebrate the successful and largely peaceful military coup of the day before, the legendary Carnation Revolution.

CARNATION REVOLUTION

In the early morning of 25 April 1974, a coup d'etat ended the decades of hated dictatorship in Portugal. Triggered by the military and welcomed by the people, the »Carnation Revolution« was a peaceful coup which brought the country democracy.

On the evening of 24 April 1974, 5,000 soldiers stood ready for action, but barley 1,000 of them were informed that a coup was planned. Shortly after midnight the catholic radio station, Radio Renascença, broadcast the banned song *Grândola Vila Morena* by the member of the opposition and singer José Afonso, who – undeterred and unbroken by bans, imprisonment and torture – was a much-respected figure in the resistance against the dictatorship. A commando unit of the Portuguese army had captured the radio station and this song, which tells of Grândola, a small agricultural town in the Alentejo, the »dark town ruled by the people«, was broadcast at the arranged time. Only a few individuals heard the song on the radio, but those in the know were informed: it was the signal to start. The units waiting outside Lisbon made their move. Approach roads, government buildings, public squares, barracks, radio stations and the airport were taken by the revolutionary troops with no resistance to speak of. The rebels

had prepared their attack well: by three in the morning the centre of Lisbon was completely under their control. In other parts of Portugal, too, army units had directly taken the strategically important centres. At the beginning large parts of the population couldn't make sense of who the rebels were. Was it young left-wing officers who wanted to destroy the dictatorship, or right-wing military leaders who intended to seize political power for themselves?

The carnation becomes a symbol

The Portuguese writer José Cardoso Pires, as he later wrote, was at any rate called by an unknown person at 5 o'clock in the morning who – with very few words so as not to fall into hands of the police phone tappers – warned him that he should flee because the hunt for democratically minded citizens had begun. The man of letters eventually ended up roaming the city with friends who knew as little as he did. The streets were almost empty; the buses carried

Charismatic leader in the struggle against the dictatorship and a Portuguese legend: Álvaro Cunhal, general secretary of the communist party, was held in the notorious prison in Peniche for eleven years. In 1960 he escaped.

virtually no passengers. The closer to the city centre the men came, the more troops and armoured reconnaissance vehicles they saw at the junctions. Then they saw something astounding: Lisbonites rushing up to

> »It was loud but peaceful …
> The people stuck carnations into
> the muzzles of the soldiers' guns..«

the soldiers, embracing them or slapping them on the shoulder. Everywhere there were enthusiastic mass demonstrations: the streets were full of people cheering the army. On the Praça do Comércio, where the ministries were based, during the siege of the government buildings civilians came to the aid of soldiers and witnessed the first of those in power giving themselves up. Further up in Chiado, tanks aimed their guns at the headquarters of the Republican Guard, whose members were notorious for their methods of oppression and were now entrenched behind barricaded doors. The Carmo barracks on Largo do Carmo, the seat of the government, were surrounded by the insurgent military demanding surrender with megaphones, as well as a vast crowd of people. It was loud,

but non-violent. People sounded their car horns in chorus, shared cigarettes with the liberators, climbed onto the tanks, sang, and stuck red carnations into the barrels of the guns. Military police directed the traffic with carnations in their hands. Cardoso Pires tells of how the blooms were obtained from the markets at the banks of the Tagus; the harvest of carnations had been especially good that year and the flowers were correspondingly cheap – which is why they were chosen. The carnation became the symbol of the coup, and for the dawning of a new age. The revolution had its name.

»Movement of the armed forces«

During the course of 25 April it slowly became clear who was behind the coup: the MFA (Movimento das Forças Armadas), the »movement of the armed forces«, was a resistance movement founded in 1973 by left-wing officers, itself structured democratically. From the early 1970s opposition to the war in the African colonies Angola, Guinea and Mozambique had gradually formed amongst the Portuguese military leaders. They recognized that this war was no longer winnable because of the vehe-

After the Carnation Revolution, Mário Soares returned to Portugal from exile in France. From 1986 to 1996 he was Portugal's president.

mently increasing pressure from the freedom movements in Africa; they knew that time was working against Portugal and that political solutions had to be found. In February 1974 Spínola, the recently elected acting chief of staff published his book, entitled *Portugal and the Future*, with the approval of his superior Costa Gomes, in which he called for a political dialogue with the colonies. The book immediately triggered hot debate; Spínola and Costa Gomes were removed from their posts. The MFA were becoming increasingly popular, and that fact did not escape the notice of the Portuguese secret service (PIDE); in March 1974 many MFA members were imprisoned. The MFA had to react before it was too late.

The »young officers«, as they were also known, struck on 25 April 1974 at 12.30am. They knew that most Portuguese harboured a silent hate for the dictatorial regime and were sure they would find support from the Portuguese people. Added to that, they had the unspoken agreement of Spínola and Costa Gomes.

Bloodless coup

It was an almost bloodless revolution. Troops not yet involved broke their oath and joined the rebels. Surrounded, police and soldiers still true to the regime laid down their arms and surrendered. President Caetano, abandoned by his people and his troops, eventually came to the telephone and declared his unconditional capitulation; in a tank, he was escorted to a plane which flew him to Brazil.

Three young men died as agents of the hated secret police, the PIDE, who had barricaded themselves in their headquarters, randomly opened fire into the crowd. The political prisoners were set free, the PIDE chief imprisoned and the former rulers exiled. Several agents of the secret police were able to flee to Spain. Major industrialists and bankers tried to get their money out of the country; several suitcases full of escudos were confiscated at the airport. The people in contrast breathed a sigh of relief. The walls of Lisbon were covered with hundreds of political slogans – each person wrote what he hoped for the future. These revolutionary paintings became famous; though in the three decades that have passed in the meantime, they have disappeared.

Portugal after 1974 and today

1974–1976	Portuguese colonies become independent
1974–1987	There are 14 changes of government with different coalitions
1986	Portugal joins the EU

A new political order

During the transitional military government, opposition politicians returned from exile abroad. Parties and unions were permitted and the colonial wars were ended. Exactly one year after the Carnation Revolution, free and fair elections were held. Overall, however, the state's new political order was very problematic due to the negative foreign relations and economic and social difficulties caused by the colonial wars. Differences between parties of the Left and Right hampered the formation of a stable government. The period up until 1987 was characterized by **frequent changes in government**, which totalled 14, and was notable for its changeable and various coalition constellations. The major parties did, however, increasingly share fundamental values: they were **pro-West** and pro-Europe, though it had initially appeared that Portugal might be the first west European country to follow socialist lines. Agricultural land, banks, insurance and large industrial companies were nationalized, but later returned into private hands. The economic situation remained difficult. Portugal accepted hundreds of thousands of **refugees from the former colonies**; unemployment, inflation and acute homelessness caused very serious problems.

? DID YOU KNOW …?

■ The following overseas provinces of the former Portuguese colonial power were lost: Portuguese India (Goa) was annexed by India back in 1961; Portuguese Guinea has been independent as Guinea-Bissau since 1974; Mozambique, the Cape Verde islands (Cabo Verde), the islands of São Tomé and Príncipe, and Angola have been independent since 1975. Portuguese Timor was ceded in 1975 and occupied by Indonesia in 1976; after decades of guerrilla war, East Timor gained independence in 2002; Macau was under Portuguese administration until 1999, when it was handed back to the Chinese.

Portugal after joining the EU

The political situation stabilized after Portugal joined the European Union in 1986, and an economic upturn set in. The Liberal Conservatives ruled from 1987, followed by the Socialists and, from 2002, a Conservative coalition government was in power, made up of the PSD and CDS-PP. This government's Prime Minister was initially José Manuel Durão Barroso (PSD), who became President of the EU Commission in 2004. During **parliamentary elections called early in February 2005**, the **Social Democrat PS** achieved an overall majority, and since then **José Sócrates** has been **Prime Minister**. Sócrates is a follower of a moderate politics orientated towards a free market, and he intends to strengthen the faltering economy by promoting the technology sector. Since 2006, the **State President** has been **Anibal Cavaco Silva (PSD)**.

Portugal hosted the 2004 **European Football Championship**, through which it briefly came into the European limelight. It was hoped that the competition would revive tourism – already faltering for some time – but this failed to happen. From an **economic point of view**, recession has been spoken of since 2002, and the European Union's eastward expansion only threatens to increase the country's problems. In recent years the country has mostly been in the headlines on account of its serious **forest and wild fires**. Devastating fires rage almost every year, particularly in the Algarve. In 2003 alone, around one fifth of Portugal's total area was destroyed. In 2005, large parts of central and northern Portugal's forests stood in flames.

Portugal today

Art and Culture

The country's great cultural treasures lie in the architecture of the Pombaline Era, in which its Golden Age is immortalized. But there is much to be discovered on a smaller scale as well, in the form of tiles, mosaics, and gold-leaf sculpture. And today, Portugal's modern architecture and Lisbon's cultural scene are also of interest: the new »fadistas« are known throughout Europe.

Architecture and Art History

Until the 12th century, Portugal more or less shared the fate of neighbouring Spain. Only with the development of a national Portuguese sense of nationhood under King Afonso I (1139–1185), did the country's indigenous artistic development begin, though even then, depending on the political situation, it was often in close relationship with Spain. In addition to the ancient pre-Christian heathen heritage, artistic development reflected influences from the Asturian kingdom, which in turn was strongly influenced by France, as well as Moorish, folkloric styles. Later, similarities with the colonial culture of territories in India, Africa and South America were noticeable.

Influences in Portugal

Early Period and Antiquity

The cave paintings and rock art found in Portugal are an impressive testimony to a Stone Age culture. Paintings and engravings in the **Gruta de Escoural** near Montemor-o-Novo are over 12,000 years old. A sensational find was also made as recently as the 1990s, in northern Portugal's Côa Valley: hundreds of prehistoric **rock engravings** were discovered during the building of a reservoir. So far, it is the oldest early Stone Age site in Europe to be found **outside** rather than in caves (► Baedeker Special, p.518).

Cave paintings, rock art

The earliest large megalithic stone graves in Portugal were made from 5000 BC onwards. The most common type were dolmen, a type of burial chamber made from a vertically standing weight-bearing stone and a covering stone. A well preserved example is the Dolmen da Barrosa, north of Vial Praia de Âncora. The **dolmen in Pavia**, in the Alentejo, was rebuilt into a church. Along with gold jewellery, amber and ivory, stone cult items have also been found in these large stone burial sites. The region around Évora is especially rich in further testaments to a megalithic culture. Near **Almendres** 92 menhirs form an elliptical **stone circle**. These standing stones are roughly worked and covered in cult symbols, and are believed to date from between 4000 BC and 2800 BC.

Megalithic culture

The settlement area of the Celtiberians was already being visited by seafaring Mediterranean peoples during antiquity. The Phoenicians founded a trading post at the mouth of the Tagus which they called **Alis Ubbo**; it later became Olisipo before eventually becoming Lisboa (Lisbon). Alis Ubbo was also settled by Greeks and Carthaginians.

Phoenicians

The subjugation of the Celtiberians by the Romans lasted almost 200 years, until AD 19. The Romanization of the province of Lusitania

Romans

← *Cultural evidence of Portugal's past is sent throughout the world on postcards.*

Conímbriga – restoring the cultural traces left by the Romans can be a painstaking business.

proceeded relatively slowly. The capital of the province of Lusitania was modern-day Spanish Mérida. **Lisbon**, in those days Felicitas Iulia, was hardly of any significance and few Roman remains have survived. Most of them are in the open-air archaeological museum of Igreja do Carmo, destroyed in the 1755 earthquake, and in the Museu Arqueológico e Etnológico in Belém. The remains of a Roman theatre were found near the cathedral. In **Évora** (Liberalitas Iulia), on the other hand, which was probably a thriving town, a temple with 14 Corinthian pillars from the first century AD has survived on the settlement's highest elevation, which is traditionally ascribed to the goddess Diana; the cella, however, is no longer in existence. This temple was made into a fortification during the Middle Ages, then used as a slaughter house, and restored once more only in 1870. Many **»villae rusticae«** were built during Roman rule, grand country residences, which were predecessors of the later **Quintas**, typical for Portugal. In **Conímbriga** there was a Roman settlement from the second century BC to AD 468. Remains of walls have survived, as well as an aqueduct, and a fountain and thermal pools with magnificent mosaics. In **Coimbra** (Aeminium), which took the name of Conímbriga after its fall, Roman remains and underground passageways can be seen at the Museu Nacional de Machado de Castro. There are also Roman remains of buildings in Beja (Pax Iulia), and in the Algarve, near Milreu (Ossonoba, discovered in 1876).

Art of the Visigoths and the Moors

During the course of population migrations many Germanic tribes arrived on Portuguese territory: Vandals, Suevi and Visigoths established strongholds in the Roman provinces. After the collapse of the West Roman Empire they formed their own empires: the Visigoths in the south of the country, the Suevi in the north, with Braga as their capital and Porto as their port, which had been vanquished by the Visigoths in the sixth century. Survivors from the Visigoth era are the **Capela de São Frutuoso** near Braga, which has strong Byzantine influences, and the church of **São Pedro de Balsemão** near Lamego.

Visigoth structures

After the battle of La Janda in the year 711, Portugal fell to the Moors, though it remained more or less insignificant compared to the Spanish part of the caliphate. Under Al Oschbuna or Laschbuna, Moorish influences probably changed Lisbon's appearance very little. Today's Castelo de São Jorge – originally built by the Visigoths – was converted into the Moorish royal residence, and the Alfama quarter built: its street design probably goes back to the time of the Moors. Moorish rule seems to have left a stronger impression in the Algarve. Certain features – house designs or the design of chimneys – are often ascribed Moorish influence, though there is no proof for the theory. Unlike in southern Spain, architectural remnants from the Moorish era are extremely rare in Portugal; only the churches of Mértola and Lourosa (10th century) follow a Moorish model.

Sparse evidence of the Moors

The Romanesque

After the Reconquista Romanesque art in Portugal developed under the influence of French schools of thought, just as it did in the Auvergne and in Normandy, though the northern Spanish cathedral of Santiago de Compostela was also an inspiration. Traces of these influences can be recognized in the cathedrals of Lisbon, Coimbra, Évora, Porto and Braga, which were originally designed as fortifications. The **Cathedral of Lisbon** is the city's oldest church and was reputedly built over a mosque in 1147, by Afonso I. Through the ages, it was remodelled several times and lost its Romanesque lantern tower and the Gothic choir during the great earthquake of 1 November, in the year 1755. The Romanesque nave, the triforium, the transepts and a cast iron grille survived. The fortress-like west façade originates from 1380. The **Cathedral of Porto** was also built

Churches

? DID YOU KNOW ...?

- In Portugal, a cathedral is known as a Sé, a shortened form of the latin »sedes«, which means bishopric. This kind of abbreviation is typical in Portuguese: thus the palace, the Palácio, is habitually shortened to »Paço«, and the Lisbon suburb of Belém is actually a shortened version of Bethlehem.

Wonderful figured capitals in the former São Bento monastery in Santo Tirso

in the 12th century. On the site of a former Suevi castle, it was originally Gothic, and completely altered several times in the 17th and 18th centuries. In addition to late Romanesque remains, there is a Gothic cloister from 1385. The **old cathedral of Coimbra**, built by Afonso I in 1170, boasts a magnificently decorated west porch. The richly decorated north porch (around 1530) shows French influence, as does the stern façade from the 12th century. The **Cathedral of Braga**, begun in 1180, was substantially changed over the centuries and the Romanesque cloister from 1110 was removed in the 18th century. The **Cathedral of Évora**, with its lovely crossing tower and its festive atmosphere originates mostly from the 13th century. It was the last Romanesque church to be built and already displays a strong influence of French Gothic.

Romanesque sculpture

Very little sculpture from Romanesque times has survived and the architectural style of this epoch has also largely been lost. However, since the Reconquista originated in the north and Christianization had an influence earlier there, several Romanesque village churches can be found in **northern Portugal**, with wonderful porches and capitals.

The Knights Templar, who had been based in Portugal since 1126, began building a citadel in Tomar in 1160, a location that was on the border between Christendom and Islam in the early 12th century. Except for the imposing keep, hardly anything of note has survived of the citadel itself and it was taken over by the Knights of the Order of Christ after the dissolution of the Knights Templar. Tomar's Templar Castle and Convent of the Knights of Christ is comprised of an extensive group of buildings dating from the 12th to the 17th century, i.e. from the Romanesque to the Baroque. Inspired by the round church originally built over the **Holy Sepulchre in Jerusalem** by Emperor Constantine the Great – which was continuously destroyed and rebuilt – the Templar Knights built round churches all over Europe: so-called Holy Sepulchre Churches. The one in Tomar has a **sixteen-sided central structure in the Syrian-Byzantine style**, known as the **rotunda**. It was initially built in 1160 with a central octagonal interior that has served as a high choir (Capela-mór) since the time of Manuel I; the nave was added in Manueline style by Diogo de Arruda after 1510. The magnificent south porch is by João de Castilho (► 3D image, p.510).

Templar Castle of Tomar

Gothic

The conclusive emergence of Gothic in Portugal was marked by the abbeys of the **Cistercians** who, along with the Knights Templar, were invited into the country by Afonso I. The Gothic architectural style was **strongly influenced by France**, though in the 13th and 14th centuries different countries in Europe certainly developed their own variations. The transition in Portugal to a more austere form of Gothic can be seen in the Cathedral of Évora, founded in as early as 1204. The city of **Santarém** calls itself the **Gothic city**, and there are several successfully restored Gothic sacred buildings there. The Franciscan monastery of Santarém was completed in 1240; the cloister dating from the 13th to 15th centuries, with its arches and finely worked twin pillars, deserves special mention.

Sacred architecture

The **octagonal Dominican church of Elvas**, with its tile-decorated cupola supported on pillars, was founded in 1267 and represents the **earliest masterpiece of Gothic** in Portugal. With its broad nave and five chapels it is impressively understated and stylishly elegant in its balanced proportions. The progressive steps to a more delicate Gothic style in Portugal, initially rather severe, can be recognized in the remains of the church at **Santa Clara-a-Velha**, built in 1286 in Coimbra, which certainly achieves something of a romantic character. Today the church, with its beautiful rose window, is partly submerged in the river. The most outstanding creations of Gothic in Portugal are the two-tiered Gothic cloisters with their double ambulatories, their powerful pillars and graceful arches and one of the most beautiful **Gothic cloisters** in the land is in the cathedral at Lisbon.

Gothic sculpture Cistercian Gothic neglected the continued development of sculpture. Only headstone art flowered, and for the 14th century, the tomb of the archbishop Gonzalo Pereira in the Cathedral of Braga (from 1336) deserves special mention, as well as the **tombs for King Pedro I and Inês de Castro in Alcobaça**.

Fortified castles The mighty fortifications built by Dinis I (1279–1325) also testify to the art of Gothic building, seen for example in the tower of Braganza and the castles of Beja and Leiria. The castle of Leiria was originally built by Afonso Henriques in 1135 and extended under Dinis I. The Gothic chapel is believed to be the work of the master builder Huguet de Batalha, thought to have come from France.

Alcobaça monastery The Cistercian monastery of Alcobaça, founded by Afonso I in 1153, was a **daughter abbey to Clairvaux in Burgundy**, from which it also took its design. The monastery church was founded in 1253, but the building of the abbey dragged on into the 14th century. The earthquake of 1755, floods and destruction wrought by Napoleonic troops forced a great deal of rebuilding. The severe early Gothic church with its pointed arch vaults is home to the tombs of Dom Pedro I and his lover Inês de Castro, decorated with complex figurative sculpture on the sides and life-sized figures of the deceased on top, dating from the 14th century. The atmospheric two-tier cloister of Dom Dinis, built in 1311, is a jewel of Cistercian Gothic, though the upper tier dates from the 16th century. Pointed arch vaults with threefold window openings, separated by small twin pillars crowned by a rosette, open onto the central garden.

The Abbey of Batalha The Gothic showpiece of the 14th century is the Abbey of Batalha (1388–1402), which is considered a **symbol of Portugal's national pride** and is one of the most impressive works of Christian architecture. The master builders include Afonso Domingues (died before 1402), Huguet (documented until 1438), Martin Vásques (died before 1448), Fernão d'Évora (died 1477) and the famous João de Castilho (died before 1553). The interior of the church, displaying the finest of Gothic forms, with its in part original coloured windows (choir) and mighty pillars, is very impressive. Visitors should take a look at the tombs in the square **Founder's Chapel**. The sculpture-adorned west façade of the cathedral and the richly structured south side work particularly well because of their unimpeded location. The church is adjoined by two **cloisters**: the Claustro de Dom Afonso V, dating from the 15th century, and the Claustro Real – a truly regal cloister that leads to a garden-style inner courtyard. It is a masterpiece and a guiding example of Portuguese Gothic, containing arched vaults that demonstrate the development of Manueline ornamentation from the simplest to the most imaginatively flamboyant, as well as attractive views onto the fountain. On the east side of the church are the **Capelas Imperfeitas** (unfinished chapels): seven chapels sur-

Cloister in Batalha Abbey: Gothic architecture, Manueline ornamentation

rounding an octagonal central area whose walls rise up into the air. The Capelas Imperfeitas house, among others, the tombs of Duarte I and his wife Eleonore von Aragón (► 3D image, p.236).

Manueline Style

The country's economic and cultural flowering under Manuel I, from the Aviz dynasty, led to the establishment of the Batalha school and the development of a unique style of late Gothic. This Manueline style is characterized by elements of the early Renaissance and Moorish Mudéjar architecture, as well as exhibiting oriental and Indian influences. Typical of this specifically Portuguese style is a noticeable pleasure in decoration that – similar to the Spanish Platersesque style – often uses naturalistic details (► Baedeker Special, p.388).

Elements of Manueline style

The most imposing example of the Manueline style is the Jerónimos monastery in Lisbon. Miraculously, the Hieronymite monastery of Belém in Lisbon survived the earthquake of 1755 undamaged. It was begun in 1502, based on a design by the presumably French architect Boytaca (► Famous People). The south porch displays a wealth of sculptural decoration, an expression of the country's new power and wealth. The west porch, strongly recalling Champmol by Dijon (France), is by Nicolas Chanterène. The interior of this hall church – in the style of a Portuguese »igrejas salões« (salon church) – impresses with its spaciousness and balanced proportions as well as its finely sculpted and ornamented pillars. João de Castilho, the great mas-

Monastery of Jerónimos in Belém

ter of the Manueline style, extended the church with the magnificent cloister with its double row of arched halls (► 3D image, p.384).

More Manueline buildings

Another example of the Manueline style is the **Torre de Belém**, the tower that dominates the mouth of the Tagus at Tomar and was built between 1515 and 1521 by Francisco de Arruda, brother of the famous master builder Diogo de Arruda, who worked in Tomar. With its flat domes, fine loggias, Arabic double doors, and masonry that almost looks like embroidery, the tower creates an Arabic Moorish impression. Other outstanding examples of the Manueline style in Batalha and in Tomar have already been mentioned. Of additional note is the **famous Manueline window in the old chapter house in Tomar**, which is the work of Diogo de Arruda and shows a memorable, and for the style particularly typical, decoration – which already seems somewhat excessive. The **Palácio Nacional de Sintra** was built on the foundations of an old Moorish palace. In addition to Gothic and Renaissance building elements, it especially displays characteristics of the Manueline style.

Manueline sculpture

The Manueline architectural style attached the highest importance to sculpture. Coimbra became the centre for two schools of sculpture, of which one – influenced by Rouen – helped to establish the Renaissance. **Nicolas Chanterène** built both the west porch of the Abbey of Belém and the tombs of Afonso I and his son Sancho I in the monastic church of Santa Cruz in Coimbra. It is probable that **Jean de Rouen** created the Porta Especiosa on the old cathedral of Coimbra; and masters Loguin and Olivier of Ghent, who worked on the polychrome wooden sculptures in the chapel of the rotunda in Tomar, can also be considered part of this school. The second, more homegrown school, continued to work in the traditional style; Diogo Pires the Younger belonged to this school. Outstanding work was not only produced in the sphere of tomb and chapel sculpture, but goldsmiths – always important in Portugal – also produced some of their finest work.

Pelourinhos

From the 12th century right up to the 18th century, innumerable Pelourinhos were put up all over Portugal. These pillories were not used primarily for punishing thieves, fraudsters or counterfeiters; rather they were intended as **symbols of local justice** – »pelouro« means »civic office«, »communal authority«. This explains their frequently artistic aspect, as well as the choice of location, usually close to sites of worldly or religious power, such as town halls or churches. A great many pelourinhos are designed in the **Manueline style**, since Manuel I granted privileges to many communities. The normally richly decorated shaft of the pillar can be cylindrical, conical, prismshaped or even a spiral; occasionally it also looks like an obelisk. The tip of the pelourinho is crowned by a sculpture, which frequently features a sword as symbol of local justice.

A MECCA FOR TILE LOVERS

Portugal without azulejos? Unthinkable. Tiles are ubiquitous here. The Moors brought them to the country, and the Portuguese developed their method of manufacture further. They are still used today: not only as decoration, but also as excellent protection for façades.

Azulejos (pronounced asuléshoush) are seen everywhere in Portugal. The painted and glazed tiles are found on the walls of churches, monasteries, palaces and normal houses; they decorate park benches, wells, floors and staircases; they adorn town halls, post offices, market halls, stations. Some bear pretty painted **ornamental patterns** or exotic animals and flowers, some depict scenes from the history of Portugal; still others relate episodes from **Greek mythology**. They show the country's most beautiful sights or those of a particular town or city, serve as plaques bearing street names, house numbers or the names of companies, and are used as surfaces for city maps. Azulejos are certainly typical of Portugal – but they are by no means a Portuguese invention. The painted and glazed tile originated in Persia, and the Moors brought azulejos to the Iberian Peninsula. The name stems from this history: azulejo derives from the Arabic »az-zuley-cha«, which means mosaic stone, and not as some would have it from the Spanish or Portuguese »azul«, meaning blue.

No depicitions of human

The first tiles to come to Portugal in the 14th century bore no human figures, as this is **forbidden by Islamic law**: instead they were decorated with geometrical forms and ornamentation adapted from plants. In order to prevent the different colours flowing into each other when firing, different painted areas were kept separate with a wax or oil-based medium – the so-called Cuerda-Seca method – or separated by means of ridges – the Cuenca technique – the use of which gives azulejos a relief-like surface.

Further development in Portugal

After the end of the Moorish kingdom Granada, the Portuguese were at first supplied by the last remaining Moorish tile manufacturers in Spain. In the second half of the 16th century however less and less tiles were delivered as a consequence of the increasingly restrictive politics of the Spanish crown with regard to the Moorish population; moreover the Majolika technique developed by Italian and Flemish tile-makers was spreading, and the first azulejo manufacturers came into being in Portugal, above all in Lisbon, Porto and Coimbra.

Thanks to the **Majolika technique** it was now possible to make flat tiles without ridges: a white tin glaze was applied to the fired clay tiles on which metal oxide paints could be used without the colours running into each other. Slowly but surely the Portuguese tile painters moved away from ornamental decoration based on the Arabic model and towards figurative depictions; everyday life became a focus of decorative art. The main colours were blue and yellow, green and white. In the 17th century, »azulejos de tapete« became fashionable: large, rug-like, multi-bordered compositions in blue, white and yellow, covering every imaginable

Azulejos are an excellent protection against dampness, heat and noise, and make the walls last longer.

subject: Christian legend, historic and patriotic events, hunting motifs and love scenes. In the late 17th century, Dutch merchants brought single blue-and-white tiles of the Ming dynasty from China to Europe, and the Portuguese enthusiastically adopted the new, fashionable colours. Monumental azulejo pictures were now created in every shade of blue. Later, more colourful tiles found favour, predominantly green, brown and yellow. With the Baroque, which began in Portugal around 1700, azu-

lejo production reached a high point. Most of the azulejos admired today in the places of worship, palaces, parks and staircases come from this time. The large earthquake of 1755, which affected Lisbon in particular, heralded the end of this boom. **Mass production was necessary** for the reconstruction of the destroyed houses. For this purpose King José I founded the royal manufactory, the »Real Fábrica do Rato«. Here, however, the tiles were painted with the aid of templates and therefore unavoidably carried less interesting motifs.

When in the early 19th century the Portuguese royal court withdrew to Brazil and civil war shook the motherland, azulejo production came to an almost complete stop. It was not until the mid-19th century that there was a renewed upswing which made use of industrial manufacturing methods from Britain. The tiles were no longer painted by hand with a paintbrush; now the decoration was printed onto the surface, making tile manufacture cheaper. As in the Brazilian model, tiles were now used to cover façades and interior walls of civil, commercial and municipal buildings all over the country. Since then, inspiration for the artistic design of tiles has been drawn from changing building styles and art movements – from Art Nouveau and Art Deco to abstract art, every style has made an appearance. In the last century in particular, tile art experienced a real renaissance – the best example is the painstaking design of the Lisbon metro stations.

Not only of decorative value

The tiles that adorn the façades and interiors of hotels, banks, office buildings and underground stations are not only decorative, they also have a **structural function**: azulejos are excellent protection against damp, heat and noise, keep façades clean and ensure a long life for the walls of the building.

Those on the look-out for azulejos while walking through Portugal's towns and cities will discover the loveliest tiled façades. Often the same patterns are reproduced in different colours. At twilight azulejos give rise to the most beautiful reflections.

Mudéjar style The Mudéjar style encompasses the particular architectural and decorative style of those **Moors permitted to remain in the country**, who continued to work after the Reconquista. Some also imitated Christian masters, developing a late Gothic mixed style that often used Manueline elements. Particular characteristics of the Moorish influence include the dark boxed ceilings, and in particular the tiles (azulejos), which became a representative symbol of Portuguese art.

Renaissance

Peripheral phenomenon The political and economic collapse of Portugal began with the heavy losses during the battles of 1580 in Morocco, at which King Sebastião was killed. Since the young king did not leave an heir to the throne, Portugal fell to Spain. These events also resulted in a significant decline in the artistic development of the country. On the whole, the Renaissance was not really able to establish itself, despite intense cultural and economic links with Italy. At first, it was **delayed by the flowering of the Manueline style**; later events then prevented a decisive breakthrough. Thus the Renaissance remained a peripheral phenomenon in Portugal. The choir in the monastery church of Belém, with its marble choir and the royal tombs carried by marble elephants, betray a high Renaissance influence.

The main cloister in the monastic fortification of Tomar can be counted as late Renaissance, though its style leans heavily on the Manueline style. Though begun by João de Castilho, work was stopped after his death in 1551, and when it was restarted in 1562, the Palladian neo-classical style had already established itself. **Foreign influences** now also made themselves felt: the new architects were either trained in Italy (Diogo de Torralva) or were themselves Italian, such as **Filippo Terzi**. The Igreja de São Roque in Lisbon is by him, a beautiful example of the Jesuit style with a grandiose interior. The church also contains a masterpiece of the most exuberant Italian Baroque in the Chapel of John the Baptist. The church of São Vicente de Fora in Lisbon is also Terzi's work, but the dome collapsed during the 1755 earthquake. The influence of foreign artists continued to be strong, even after 1640, when Portugal freed itself from Spain's rule. Portugal's own artistic development, however, remained inert.

Renaissance painting The development of painting in Portugal ran along similar lines to that of Spain. The first artistic personality of note was **Nuno Gonzalves**, active between 1450 and 1480. His major work consists of the St Vincent Panels of the Altar of St Vincent, a polyptychon wing altar with many figures that clearly exhibits the influence of Flemish schooling. It can be seen in the Museu Nacional de Arte Antiga in Lisbon. With this began a flowering of late medieval painting that lasted until the middle of the 16th century and which produced its finest works in the art of portraiture. Next to Gonzales, masters of note were Jorge Afonso (died after 1540), who maintained a work-

WORKS OF ART UNDERFOOT

After the earthquake of 1755 the Lisbonites allegedly hit upon the idea of making little paving stones from the rubble and using them to make up the pavements and squares in artistic designs. Since then, pavement mosaics made of black and white stones – the black stones are volcanic basalt, the white ones lime sandstone – are seen all over Lisbon and elsewhere in Portugal and feature the most diverse range of motifs

They are to be seen on squares, pavements, and in pedestrian precincts. Sometimes the patterns are simple and geometrical, sometimes they feature animals or inscriptions, then again there are house numbers, company logos and coats of arms – above the municipal coat of arms of Lisbon itself.

The »calceteiros«

It is the so-called »calceteiros« who carry out this skilled and painstaking work. Sometimes they can be observed at their task – how they sit on the paving stone holding a mosaic stone in their hand and chisel it with a hammer until it has the desired shape and will fit into a wooden mould.

These wooden moulds are **old templates** that are carefully archived. So that the joints between the stones remain as small as possible, every mosaic stone must be precisely chiselled to the correct shape.

A dying trade

It will not be possible to see the calceteiros at work for much longer. It is a trade that will in all likelihood soon cease to exist.

The work is costly and difficult, and very badly paid, and a tarmac surface is much cheaper anyway. There were about 400 calceteiros in the first decade of the 20th century; now there are barley 30, employed primarily for repair work.

shop in Lisbon, as well as Guilherme de Belles, João Mestre (died 1528), Luís de Velasco, António Taca and Vasco Fernandes, known as Grão Vasco (died around 1542), who worked in Viseu.

Under João II the influence of Dutch and Flemish Romanesque art increased on Portuguese painters such as Gregório Lopes (died 1550), and especially on **Cristóvão de Figueiredo** (documented between 1515 and 1540), whose main work was the high altar retable at the monastery church of Santa Cruz in Coimbra, as well as on the Master of Santa Auta, the creator of the altar retable of Santa Auta which depicts the martyrdom of 11,000 virgins and can be seen at the Museu Nacional de Arte Antiga in Lisbon. The following generation of painters, such as Cristóvão Lopes (1516–1606), came under direct Italian influence, no longer transmitted by teaching from the Netherlands; but the long-held tradition of portraiture – of which Cristóvão de Morais is its most famous representative – lost its significance when A. Sanchez Coelho (1513–1590) emigrated to the Spanish Court.

Baroque and Classicism

Foreign influences on Baroque

Among Portuguese Baroque buildings, the one to mention first is the mighty **monastery palace of Mafra** which, following the Spanish example of Escorial, was designed as royal palace, church and monastery in one, and built between 1717 and 1770. With its florid forms enriched by chinoiserie, this massive construction built by the German **Johann Friedrich Ludwig** and his son **Johann Peter Ludwig**, distanced itself from the severe forms of Spanish Baroque and influenced the generation of architects of the late Baroque and Rococo, which became ever more sumptuous and ornate, with **Portuguese azulejos experiencing a Golden Age**.

Foreign masters also worked in Porto, where the Italian **Nicolo Nasoni** built the church at dos Clérigos, with its remarkable high choir and impressive tower.

Begun by the Portuguese Mateus Vicente de Oliveira (1747–1786), the Frenchman **J. B. Robillon** completed the royal palace at Queluz in 1758, as a tribute to Versailles, an idea that was further enhanced by the park, designed in the spirit of Le Nôtres. The rooms have a very splendid design, and the Throne Room and the Ambassadors' Room are especially beautiful.

Talha dourada

A form of elaborate ornamentation that appeared in Portugal during the earliest Baroque, and later found its greatest flowering here, was also taken up in other cultural spheres such as Spain. Known as Talha dourada, it is a type of **gold-leafed wood carving**, which was predominantly used in sacred art. Thus many Portuguese church altars, walls, niches, domes and ceilings were partly or even completely decorated with such wood carvings during the 18th century, with ornamental leaf and vine work with figurative sculptures flowing into each other across huge decorative areas. The gold originated in Brazil; oak, also from Brazil, was used for the wood, upon which the thin layers of gold were set.

The **art of sculpture** was hit by the cultural decline of the 17th century, as was architecture and painting, and the Baroque hardly produced any masters worth mentioning, except for **Joaquim Machado de Castro** (1736–1828), who, among other things, decorated the elaborate façade of the late Baroque Basilica da Estrela in Lisbon – built at the end of the 18th century after Roman example – with his dynamic sculptures.

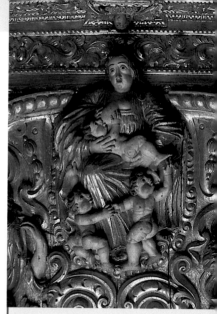

Baroque magnificence: talha dourada in the Igreja de Santo António in Lagos

Baroque painting was of little significance. It served to decorate palaces and churches. Of note are Francisco Vieira Lusitano (1699–1783), the fresco specialist Domingos António de Sequeira (1768–1837), Francisco Portuense (1765–1805) and Pedro Carvalho Alexandrino (1730–1810).

The terrible **earthquake** that laid waste to Lisbon on the **day of All Souls in the year 1755** created a unique opportunity from a town planning point of view. This was recognized by the Marquis de Pombal, who ruled for José I and who was a declared follower of progressive absolutism, and thus Lisbon became one of the most beautiful capitals in Europe. The Cidade Baixa or **Lower City** was built at that time, and is characterized by a pattern of right-angled streets and three extraordinary squares: the Praça da Figueira, the even bigger Praça de Dom Pedro IV (Rossio), and the Praça do Comércio. The latter, built in 1755 by Joaquim Machado de Castro and featuring the horse and rider statue of José I, is one of the most famous squares in the world. The unity of the square and the three surrounding coloured façades and arcades contrast appealingly with the surprising openness of the fourth side, which opens onto the Tagus.

Town planning in Lisbon

After the earthquake of 1755 there was a general reaction against the all too colourful excesses of Baroque and Rococo; a somewhat more sober Classicism established itself. In Lisbon, the Palácio da Ajuda was begun in 1802, though it remained unfinished. The Teatro Nacional de Dona Maria II was built by the Rossio in 1846.

Classicism

19th and 20th Centuries

Historicism Although Classicism remained pre-eminent in Portuguese architecture for a long time, a romantically orientated Historicism set in from the mid-19th century, just as it did in the rest of Europe. A French influence is once again recognizable, though English and German influence was also present, as for example, in the **Palácio da Pena**, built in the style of a medieval castle in 1840–1850 in Pena. It was built by Baron Eschwege for Ferdinand of Saxe-Coburg and Gotha in Sintra. Following the example of the magnificent palaces of King Ludwig II of Bavaria, an imaginative mix of Arabic, Gothic, Manueline, Renaissance and Baroque influences created a palace of almost bizarre attractiveness. The monster above the main porch is typical: an elaborately fantastic figure, half human, half fish or tree (▶ 3D image, p.500). In Lisbon, the bull ring was built in 1892 on the Campo Pequeno in **neo-Moorish style**. The Rossio railway station in Lisbon and the hotel in the magical forest of Buçaco, built as a royal summer residence in a **neo-Manueline style** at the end of the 19th century, are further examples of Historicist architecture.

Parks and gardens Portugal is particularly rich in highly impressive parks and gardens. They offer the visitor a very clear documentation of the development of garden design from the Arabic to a free English style via formal Baroque.

The Modern Age The Modern Ageestablished itself only very haltingly in Portugal. In 1877/1878 the Frenchman **Gustave Eiffel** built the famous two-tier bridge that crosses the Douro at an impressive height in Porto, the Ponte de Dom Luís I, using the metal construction technique developed by him. Mesnier de Ponsard, a Portuguese of French extraction, constructed the Elevador do Carmo (Elevador de Santa Justa); the elevator connects Lisbon's Upper City with its Lower City (▶3D image, p.366). Around 1940, the immense university city complex, Cidade Universitária, was built in Lisbon. Testament to the monumental style of an authoritarian regime is given by the mighty Monumento Cristo Rei, built on the left bank of the Tagus in Lisbon in 1959; also by the 52m/170.6ft-high Padrão dos Descobrimentos, the Monument to Discovery, which was built on the shores of the Tagus by Belém in 1960. The two Tagus bridges in Lisbon are impressive technical achievements: the Ponte 25 de Abril, a 2,227m/2,436yd-long hanging bridge inaugurated in 1966, and the 17km/10.6mi-long Ponte Vasco da Gama, opened in 1998. During the course of the Expo 98, the Expo site and a completely new urban quarter with interesting buildings was created. Today's most famous architects are **Álvaro Siza Vieira** (▶ Famous People) and Tomás Taveira, who built the Amoreiras Shopping Centre in Lisbon at the beginning of the 1980s; it was the country's largest and most elegant shopping centre at that time.

The development of **painting** ran parallel to that of Europe as a whole in the 19th century. The portrait artist Miguel Lupi (1826–1883) is worthy of note, as is Tomás de Anunciação (1818–1879). António Carvalho da Silva Porto (1850–1893) was a notable landscape painter. The **»Grupo do Leão«** art group founded in 1881 took its cue from Impressionism, while the portrait and fresco painter Columbano (1867–1929) remained true to the Romantic genre; but Fauvism, Cubism and the rather garish revolutionary Naturalism also found their supporters. Among Cubists, **Amadeo de Souza-Cardoso** (1887–1918) deserves particular mention. Between the two world wars, the **Futurist José Almada Negreiros** achieved great success with paintings, carpets and frescoes. The Salazar regime discouraged progressive artists and it was only after the Carnation Revolution of 1974 that alignment took place with the international art scene. Today, the Franco-Portuguese painter Maria-Elena Vieira da Silva (1908–1992) is greatly admired. Lourdès Castro (born 1930

The Museu de Serralves in Porto, a work by Álvaro Siza Vieira

in Funchal on Madeira) is a sculptor who often uses plexiglas to create her art. Another internationally known artist is Julião Sarmento, born in Lisbon in 1948. His large-scale paintings are put together from several canvases.

Typical Rural Architecture

Due to Portugal's location on the extreme periphery of Europe, specific building styles have survived, especially in farm architecture. As in many southern European countries, stone buildings predominate and, as a rule, farms tend to have a maximum of two storeys. In the **Minho** region a particular type of house is widespread whose ground floor is taken up by animal stalls and workshops, and whose second floor is reached by an exterior stairway leading to living quarters that reach through to a veranda. **»Espigueiros«**, small grain silos on pillars built of granite or wood, are also typical for this northern land-

Rural houses

scape. In **southern Portugal**, which was prone to Moorish influence, whitewashed façades predominate and the frames of windows and doors are often coloured to protect against insects. Single-storey farmyards are more common here, and smaller windows and door openings are favoured due to the summer heat. As winters get colder further away from the balancing influence of the Atlantic, open fireplaces are seen relatively often in the interior. In the Algarve there are two neighbouring towns, Olhão and Fuzeta, where **cubic houses with flat roofs** (açoteias) predominate; on the roofs, fruit or fishing equipment is dried in the sun. The richly and imaginatively decorated **chimneys** with lantern-style tops are especially typical for the Algarve.

Windmills　Recorded since the 13th century, the windmills are also a noticeable feature of this landscape. As a rule they are made up of a conical mill house built on a round foundation and wooden spokes are spanned with triangular sails to catch the wind. Small clay containers that make a whistling sound when moved are often tied to the sails to help gauge the force of the wind.

Rural Folklore

Romarias and festas　Church festivals hold a special place in the hearts of the Portuguese, and particularly in the rural conservative northern part of the country romarias are held to honour a saint or to commemorate a miracle or an apparition. The most important of these can last several days and involve not only religious ritual but also worldly attractions. The romaria is a type of **pilgrimage**, where masses of pilgrims in their best festive costume come together for long processions in magnificently decorated wagons. In some places, the romaria is dedicated to a particular profession, such as fishing. The highlight of this fundamentally religious ritual is the festive procession of the saint figure to the place of pilgrimage. Once they have arrived at their destination, the pilgrims circle the church several times before they position their saint inside, next to the main altar. The faithful complete all manner of rituals to seek forgiveness for their sins, or bring the saint votive gifts in thanks for help received. But the Portuguese do not always treat their saints with deference. If, in the opinion of the pilgrims, a saint is believed to have failed, fierce castigation is not uncommon, though he or she can prove themselves again the following year. Romarias are financed for the most part by **donations**, and those responsible will organize a collection several days before the actual festival, often also accompanied by musicians. Some large romarias are very well known and are ideal for getting to know Portuguese lifestyle and customs, for example the ones at Viana do Castelo, Póvoa de Varzim, Amarante and Loulé. The religious ceremonies are usually followed by so-called festas, annual markets accompanied by fun, dancing, singing, eating and drinking. The most beautiful **folk costumes** can be seen at festas and romarias and can differ substantially from region to region.

Twice a year, on 13 May and 13 October, there are important processions at the pilgrimage site of **Fátima**, though it is also a destination for smaller pilgrimages every 12th and 13th day of the month. Many places hold processions at Easter during which figures from the Passion are carried. The **Festa dos Tabuleiros**, held every two years in Tomar, is especially impressive.

Processions

Girls parade in the streets balancing presentation platters on their heads (tabuleiros), piled high with thirty loaves of bread decorated with grain, flowers and leaves. Each tabuleiro is the height of the girl carrying it (► ill. p.125). This festival is intended to recall the ceremony by which the Order of the Holy Ghost used to distribute food to the poor in the 14th century.

Unlike in Spain, the influence of Arabic Moorish **folk music** is insignificant in Portugal. Dances at religious and secular folk festivals are usually accompanied by singing and music with traditional instruments; typical instruments include guitars, violins, flutes, bagpipes, drums and the »reque-reque«, a rattle made of cane played with a wooden stick, probably originating from Africa.

Heavy load – romaria in honour of the Senhora da Aparecida

Folk dances are performed at festivals, though there are significant regional differences: in the northern coastal areas between the **Minho and Douro**, the »Vira« predominates, a lively circle dance. The Galician »Gota« is even faster; and the women wear especially beautiful costumes for the »Malhão« and » Cana Verde« dances. In the mountain regions of **Trás-os-Montes, Beira Alta and Beira Baixa**, the »Chula« is seen, as is the »Dança dos Pauliteiros«, a male folk dance with sticks, which presumably replaced the original swords of an ancient war dance. In Nazaré, on the coast of Estremadura, there is the »Vira«, a harmonious fishermen's dance, and in the **Ribatejo**, the men dance the »Escovinho« or the »Fandango« on their own. Further south, beyond the Tagus, the dances are more sedate and almost melancholic: the most famous of these folk dances in the **Alentejo** are called »Saia« and »Balha«. The »Corridinho« is a graceful dance of the **Algarve**.

Culture of the Capital City

Ignored by the rest of Europe, Lisbon has been Portugal's cultural centre for centuries. As capital city, Lisbon was always the most important meeting place for Portuguese artists, though many also orientated themselves to cultural events in the rest of Europe – mostly in France, Germany and Italy – due to their education abroad. A

Stars in Lisbon and elsewhere in Europe:
Cesária Évora of the Cape Verde Islands and the fado singer Mísia

defining role in Lisbon's cultural life, and indeed nationally, is played by the **Fundação Calouste Gulbenkian**, a wealthy charity founded by the oil millionaire Calouste Gulbenkian (► Famous People), who died in 1955. In Lisbon it has founded a museum, a centre for modern Portuguese art with event rooms, and has developed an orchestra, a choir, and a ballet.

Until the 18th century, the development of classical music in Portugal followed similar lines to other European countries. Performances of Italian works predominated in the 18th century, and this only changed in the 19th century, with the foundation of a philharmonic academy and a musical conservatory. From this point onwards, an increasingly home-grown national music developed. In the Lisbon **opera house**, re-opened in 1793, more than 60 operas by Portuguese composers were performed before 1910. The most important 20th century composers are considered to be Luís de Freitas Branco, Ruy Coelho, Frederico de Freitas and Fernando Lopes Graça. Among the younger composers, the most significant is probably **Jorge Peixinho**, who studied with Luigi Nono and Pierre Boulez, and who worked with Karlheinz Stockhausen. The most famous musician with international acclaim is the pianist **Maria João Pires** (► Famous People).

Classical music

Portuguese rock and pop music takes its cue to a certain extent from other Western groups, though elements of Portugal's folk music also make themselves felt. The singers Fausto, Sérgio Godinho, Vitorino, **José Afonso** and the bands Trovante, GNR, and Delfins have become well-known. The group **Madredeus** and the Jazz singer **Maria João** have achieved international success, along with the Fado singers Dulce Pontes, **Mísia**, **Mariza** and **Cristina Branco**. Music in the Portuguese language from Brazil plays a major role in Lisbon's musical life, as does that from the Cape Verde Islands, especially music by **Cesária Évora**, but also music from the former colonies of Angola and Mozambique. An interesting mixture is created by **João Afonso**, the nephew of José Afonso, who partly grew up in Mozambique and who combines urban African music with Portuguese music.

Rock and pop music

Diogo de Boytaca (c1470–1520)

Most important architect of the Golden Age

It is not possible to establish precise dates for the life of architect Diogo de Boytaca (also Boytac or Boitaca). It is beyond doubt only that he was active between 1490 and 1520 or thereabouts. It is also unclear what his nationality was, whether he was French, Italian, or Portuguese after all. The fact that there is a village with the similar sounding name of Boutaca near Batalha speaks for the latter possibility. The man himself is inseparably associated with the **Manueline style** and his buildings are characterized – almost without exception – by an excessive use of ornamentation. Boytaca's first significant work was the Jesus Monastery in Setúbal; after that he was instrumental in the construction of the Hieronymite monastery in Belém from 1502, and the Batalha abbey from 1509. Furthermore, he was involved in the building of the palace at Sintra, and also worked in Caldas da Rainha and in Montemor-o-Velho. He also built numerous fortifications in North Africa.

Luís Vaz de Camões (1524 ?–1580)

National poet

Lisbon and Coimbra both claim to be the birthplace of Luís Vaz de Camões, probably the most significant Portuguese poet. His date of birth is also not clearly established. He came from a respected Portuguese family and his father captained a ship for the king. After his

studies in Coimbra, Camões went to Lisbon, where he gained access to court and wrote dramas and poems to order, but he was soon banned from these esteemed circles because of an affair with a lady-in-waiting. In the hope of expediting his rehabilitation he voluntarily signed up for military service in North Africa, where he lost his right eye in a fight. No sooner had Camões returned to Lisbon than he was sent to prison because of a duel; he was pardoned but forced to leave the country. Initially he was sent to Goa, but here too he fell into disgrace and his journey continued to Macau. His position as »caretaker of the dead and missing in China« gave him plenty of time to dedicate to his poetry, and it was at this time that his great epic, *Os Lusíadas* (after Lusus, fabled progenitor of the Portuguese) was written.

Camões only returned to Lisbon in 1570, and *The Lusiads* was published there in March 1572. However, even then fate did not look favourably upon Camões, today honoured as the national poet. He spent his last years of his life in absolute poverty and died in obscurity of the plague in the Alfama quarter of Lisbon on 10 June 1580, where he was buried in a mass grave. He could not know that later, one day, June the 10th would become a national holiday.

Eusébio (born 1942)

Eusébio, known as the »Black Panther« – and not just because of the colour of his skin – has held a firm place in footballing history since 1965. During the subsequent eight years he was probably the best footballer in the world. Eusébio Ferreira da Silva was born in Loren-

Holder of the Golden Shoe

zo Marques (today Maputo), the capital of the former Portuguese colony of Mozambique, in 1942. He was discovered by the large Portuguese teams while still playing in Lorenzo Marques, and in 1961 there was a regular tug of war over him between the two large clubs in Lisbon, Sporting and Benfica. Having only just arrived in Lisbon, Eusébio was whisked off to a small port on the Algarve by the Benfica bosses to prevent him from being taken up by Sporting Lisbon. Eusébio waited half a year before he could don the colours of Benfica Lisbon, for whom he was then to play for 14 years. He broke all records: in 1965 he was voted Footballer of the Year; in 1968 and 1973 he won the Golden Shoe as Europe's top goalscorer with 43 and 40 goals respectively. His team only failed to win a national or international title twice during his time: in

1966 and 1973. He scored 43 goals during 64 international games, and 727 goals in a total of 715 games. At the 1966 World Cup in England, the only one he participated in, he ensured a furore when in just half an hour he scored four goals against the North Koreans, who were leading three–nil. With nine goals in just six games he became top goalscorer and took Portugal to third place in the World Cup. The »Black Pearl«, as Eusébio was also known, ended his career at Benfica Lisbon in 1974 after a serious knee injury. During the following six years he played for several clubs in Canada, Mexico and the USA.

Luís Figo (born 1972)

Luís Filipe Madeira Caeiro Figo was born in Almada, south of Lisbon, on 4 November 1972, and grew up in a faceless working class quarter. He played football from a young age, albeit for a pretty disastrous suburban team called the »Pastilhas«. Yet it was there that he was discovered. Aged 12 he came to the youth team of Sporting Lisbon, and he made his debut with the professional team there aged 17, in 1990. He remained with Sporting for five years before going to Barcelona, and then joining Real Madrid, from where he moved on

Portugal's football idol

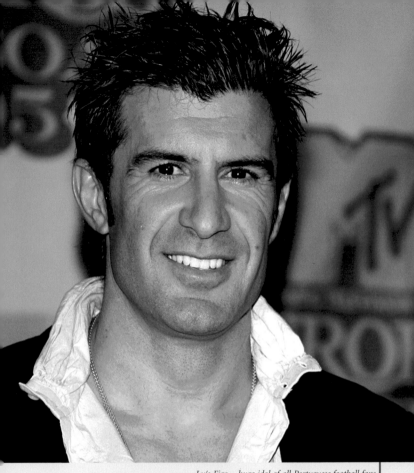

Luís Figo – huge idol of all Portuguese football fans

to Inter Milan in 2005. Europe crowned him Footballer of the Year in the year 2000, and in 2001 he was named **World Footballer of the Year**. Figo broke off a Psychology Degree for his football career. In addition to his mother tongue, he speaks fluent Spanish and English, as well as some Swedish – he is married to a Swede.

Vasco da Gama (1460?–1524)

Discoverer of the sea route to India

Contemporaries rated Vasco da Gama's discovery of the sea route to India higher than the discovery of the Americas by Columbus six years earlier. According to contemporary opinion, the Genoese had only discovered a land inhabited by savages, while Vasco da Gama, on the other hand, had discovered a highly civilized country that promised riches. The Portuguese seafarer came from the port of Sines in southern Portugal. The year of his birth is not known exactly, the dates vary between 1460 and 1469. Vasco da Gama was contracted to find the sea route to India by Manuel I, and he left the port of Restelo near Lisbon with four ships at the beginning of July 1497. The crew numbered 170, of which one third died during the journey. The ships sailed around the Cape of Good Hope on 22 November, and in May 1498 they dropped anchor off the west coast of the Indian subcontinent. Vasco da Gama began the return journey on 8 October and reached Lisbon once again on 10 July 1499. Though he returned from his journey almost empty handed, the whole world at that time felt envy and admiration for the man who had **established contact with the lands of spice**. He undertook his second voyage to India in 1502/1503, but this time at the head of an armada that was to establish trading relationships and enforce the acceptance of Portuguese hegemony. His personal qualities are less well established. In contemporary sources Vasco da Gama is described as brave, tough and proud, but also as short-tempered, confrontational and cruel: while combating Arab resistance off India's coast in 1502, he had 200 people on board an enemy ship, including women and children, locked below deck before having it then set alight. He set off for his third and final India voyage in 1524, after the king had named him Viceroy. A few months after his arrival he fell ill from an unknown disease. A contemporary source says that growths formed on the back of his neck and he died on 24 December 1524.

Calouste Sarkis Gulbenkian (1869–1955)

Almost every Lisbon visitor is confronted with the name Gulbenkian. Calouste Sarkis Gulbenkian was born near Istanbul, the son of a wealthy Armenian petroleum merchant, in 1869. He studied engineering in London and had already advanced to advisor of the Ottoman Court in matters concerning oil by 1891. In the following years he became one of the most important experts on this subject, and in 1911 he was one of the founders of the Iraq Petroleum Company, in which the largest oil companies were united at that time. Gulbenkian's percentage of five percent brought him the nickname of **»Mr. Five Percent«**, as well as a huge fortune, and he was intermittently known as the world's richest man. He was a British citizen from 1902 and invested most of his fortune in Britain. At the beginning of the Second World War Gulbenkian's »enemy property« was confiscated by the British, and his efforts to leave the country only succeeded in 1942, when he was allowed to depart for neutral Portugal. Gulbenkian settled in Lisbon, living in a suite at the Hotel Aviz – on the site of today's Sheraton – and concentrated on reviving his remaining fortune once more. Next to the oil business, Gulbenkian's interest lay in art and he said of himself that he was »irresistibly enamoured by any expression of art and beauty«. He collected choice

Oil magnate and passionate art collector

pieces of art, bought Egyptian sculptures and French furniture, Chinese porcelain and Turkish faience, as well as works by Rembrandt, Rubens, Van Dyck, Frans Hals, Degas and Monet. Over the years Gulbenkian bought around 5,000 works and thus owned one of the most important private collections in the world. He never left Lisbon until his death in 1955 and he left his entire fortune – said to be over 66 million dollars, as well as art works to the value of around 15 million dollars – to a charity: the **Fundação Calouste Gulbenkian**. The foundation built a large cultural centre with several theatres, concert halls and cinemas, as well as a library. A museum, now world-famous, opened in 1969. In 1984 the complex was extended to include a Centre for Modern Art (CAM), in which predominantly contemporary Portuguese art is exhibited.

Henry the Navigator (1394–1460)

Initiator of sea voyages and discoveries

The son of João I, Henry (Henrique in Portuguese) was born in 1394. History later dubbed him »the Navigator« (o Navegador), even though he himself never took part in any extensive sea voyage. The heir to the throne won admiration early on through the conquest of Ceuta in 1415, and the king transferred the management and defence of the city to him. By this time, at the latest, his seafaring interest had been born (► Baedeker Special, p.469). He studied maps and documents and had seafarers report to him. Apart from that, he lived in a very withdrawn manner, as described by the court biographer Zurara, characterized by an ascetic and devout way of life. His appointment as **governor of the Order of Christ** in 1418 brought him huge financial resources. Near Sagres he installed a so-called **scientific centre** in which men from all over Europe made geographical and nautical studies. At the shipyards in nearby Lagos a new type of ship was built, the light and highly manoeuvrable **caravel**, inspired by construction plans developed at Sagres. The voyages of discovery that Henry financed and organized set out from Lagos; Sagres was unsuitable as a port due to the lack of an accessible hinterland. First the Madeira island group was discovered (or rediscovered) and colonized (by 1423), then the Azores (1427), and later Henry the Navigator's ships penetrated ever further along the African west coast, reaching the Cape Verde islands, Gambia and, eventually, Guinea. By the end of his life the royal son had just about used up the enormous fortune of the Order of Christ, as expenses for the voyages of discovery far outweighed any income. But Henry's caravels had opened up the routes for further discoveries across the sea, which were used – among others – by Vasco da Gama, and they also laid the foundation for the Portuguese colonial empire, soon to assume gigantic proportions.

Manuel I (1469–1521)

Manuel I (or Emanuel I) is also known as the »Great« or the »Fortunate« because Portugal experienced its **Golden Age** under his rule. Measures taken by Manuel I, who had unexpectedly become king in 1495, after the sudden death of Afonso, heir to the throne, led to a strengthening of royal authority in the face of the nobility. Bureaucracy was centralized, the tax and customs system standardized, and with his **marriage policy** Manuel I created close **relationships with the royal house of Spain**. His first marriage in 1497 was to Isabella of Castile, the widow of the Infante Afonso. After her death, he took her sister Maria of Castile as his wife. His last and final wife was Leonor of Spain, who was supposed to be spoken for by his son. In this way the fortunate king was able to keep his country out of wars. Most of all, however, Manuel I's reign is associated with the voyages of discovery that the Portuguese monarch sponsored primarily for economic and political reasons. Vasco da Gama discovered the sea route to India in his name, and Pedro Álvares Cabral sailed to Brazil. Lisbon became Europe's leading trading port during his rule and wealth flowed into the country. Science and art flowered, and great things were achieved in architecture in particular (► Baedeker Special, p.388). To this day the buildings of Belém, Batalha and Tomar are an impressive testament to the **Manueline style** named after the king. Yet Portugal's Golden Age lasted only a short time. The glory of the country's heyday had already passed by the time of his death.

»The fortunate king«

Rosa Mota (born 1958)

All of Portugal cheered when Rosa Mota won a gold medal for the country at the Olympic Games in Seoul. The then thirty-year-old marathon runner became a national heroine. She had already attained the World Champion title in Rome in 1987. The little Portuguese sportswoman – 1.57m/5ft 15in tall and weighing 45kg/99.2lb – was born in Foz do Douro, the mouth of the Douro river near Porto. She first took part in road races at the beginning of the 1980s. In 1982 she caused an upset when she won the gold medal at the European Championships in Athens. She took fourth place at the World Championships in Helsinki, and won a bronze medal at the Olympic Games in Los Angeles. In 1986 she defended her title in the European Championships, and at the Split European Championships she won the title for the third time. Not least in her achievements is taking first place in countless urban marathons: in Rotterdam in 1983; Chicago in 1983 and 1984; Tokyo in 1986; Boston in 1987, 1988 and 1990; Osaka in 1990; and London in 1991.

The coffin of Amália Rodrigues is transferred to the National Pantheon two years after her death. In the background is a portrait of the fado singer.

quickly realized that she could earn better money with her singing than by selling fruit on the street, which is how she had been earning her living, together with her sister Celeste. At 18 she began a fairy tale career, from poor girl from the port area to woman of the world. She stood on the stage of the Retiro da Severa for the first time at 19, a very well-known Fado venue in Lisbon at that time. At 23 she gave her first debut abroad, in Madrid, and a short while later she sang at the Olympia in Paris, going on to sing in Casablanca, Rio de Janeiro, Rome, Berlin, and later in Sweden, Turkey, the USSR, Japan, Africa, and North and South America. She brought **fado to the stage all over the world**. Her greatest hits were *Uma Casa Portuguesa, Nem Às Paredes Confesso* and *Barco Negro*. In the 1940s Amália Rodriguez also featured in several of the best known Portuguese films in the role of the »fadista«, the fado singer. When she died in 1999 all Portugal mourned. Her funeral was like a state burial and she is Portugal's first woman to be honoured with her own tomb in Lisbon's National Pantheon, along with other national greats.

António de Oliveira Salazar (1889–1970)

Under the rule of the politician António de Oliveira Salazar, Portugal experienced Europe's longest dictatorship of the 20th century. The son of an agricultural worker who later became a farm manager, Salazar was born on 28 April 1889 in the village of Vimieiro in the Dão valley. He grew up in a humble environment and his childhood was characterized by his family's deep Catholicism. He received his education at the Jesuit seminary in Viseu. In 1910 Salazar began studying law and economics at the University of Coimbra, and in 1916 he became economics professor there. After already having been temporarily engaged as Finance Minister in 1926, the State President Carmona brought him to Lisbon permanently in 1928, to restore the state's ruined finances. He achieved recovery from the financial crisis – to the detriment of weaker sections of society – and increasingly established his power. In 1930 Salazar founded the fascist party **União Nacional**, and in 1932 he became Prime Minister. In 1933, he had a new constitution upheld by popular referendum, and this became the foundation for a civil authoritarian state, the so-called **Estado Novo**, designed after the fascist model. Only around 16% of the population were given the vote; illiterate people and women without a secondary education were excluded. Censorship was introduced. The **secret state police** observed and persecuted politically questionable individuals and intellectuals. The treatment of prisoners followed the methods of the German Gestapo. Independence movements in the overseas colonies were ruthlessly suppressed, which caused the **colonial wars** of the 1960s. Salazar led a very withdrawn private life and hated any kind of personality cult. He was known as a loner, and his only confidante appears to have been his housekeeper. After an accident in 1968, Salazar suffered a stroke that made him unfit to work. Marcelo Caetano was installed as Prime Minister, yet Salazar believed that he was still in power right up until his death on 27 July 1970.

Dictator

◄ ill. p.53

José Saramago (born 1922)

José Saramago is so far the only Portuguese winner of the Nobel Prize for Literature. His proper name is José Melrinho de Sousa, but since the official who was supposed to document his birth had drunk substantially, he noted the surname as Saramago, by which the farming family was traditionally known in the small village in the Ribatejo province. The mistake was only noticed years later. Saramago did an apprenticeship as a machine fitter as there was no money for his continued schooling, after which he gained skills in technical

Winner of the Nobel Prize for Literature

drawing and became a manager. His profound cultural knowledge and his literary expertise were self-taught and he patronized Lisbon's artistic and intellectual scene, earning his money as a translator and literary editor, from the 1950s onwards. He worked as a journalist at various daily newspapers between the years of 1972 and 1975, and since then he has worked as an independent translator and author. Saramago became known abroad with his novel *Levantado do Chão* (*Raised from the Ground*), published in 1980. He achieved his true breakthrough with the successful publication of *Memorial del Convento* in 1982. Saramago's books contain a critical examination of Portugal's history, often culturally pessimistic, which reflect his own political attitude: he joined the Portuguese Communist Party in 1969, whose position he more or less continues to support to this day. His book *The Gospel According to Jesus Christ*, published in 1991, caused great controversy and discussion in Portugal. The government saw it as an attack on the religious thinking of the Portu-

José Saramago – the winner of the Nobel Prize in Literature turned his back on his country.

guese, and removed the book from their suggestion list for the European Union's Literature Prize. Disappointed by this »return to the Inquisition« Saramago withdrew to the Canary Island of Lanzarote in 1993, where he continues to live with his second wife, Pilar del Río from Spain. He received the Nobel Prize for Literature in 1998.

Álvaro Siza Vieira (born 1933)

Álvaro Siza Vieira, architect of »strict poetry« and »complex simplicity« is considered one of the most important contemporary architects. He is particularly admired for his sober and fit-for-purpose style, which is nevertheless highly aesthetic. Originally this star architect, born in Matosinhos near Porto in 1933, wanted to become a sculptor, but when he saw the Sagrada Familia in Barcelona he changed his career ambition. He studied in Porto and designed his first buildings at 21. All his work seems light, delicate and airy, whether it be churches, social housing, museums or entire neighbourhoods. Among his masterpieces are the architectural faculty in Porto (1986–1996) and the **village church of Marco de Canavezes**, in which, contrary to the conventions of the Catholic liturgy, a window allows the faithful to see the wide Douro Valley during service. In the 1990s Siza Vieira's work showed a renewed tendency to monumentalism, which was particularly noticeable in the Portuguese Pavilion for the Expo 1998 in Lisbon. Numbering among Vieira's great achievements is also the reconstruction of a row of buildings in the Chiado district of Lisbon, which were destroyed by a massive fire in 1988. He had the block rebuilt without changing the original character. He also designed the new **Museu de Serralves in Porto**. The »architect of peace and quiet« has won all the major international architecture prizes. In 1992 he was presented with the Pritzker Prize, the equivalent of the Nobel Prize in the world of architecture. During its recommendation the jury pronounced that »his designs radiate a deceptive simplicity. They are honest through and through. On closer inspection, of course, his apparent simplicity reveals itself to be composed of an impressive variety.«

Architect

Practicalities

WHERE ARE PORTUGAL'S MOST
BEAUTIFUL BEACHES? WHICH ONES
ARE OVERCROWDED IN SUMMER AND
WHICH ARE DESERTED? WHERE CAN
YOU LISTEN TO GOOD FADO? WHAT'S THE FOOD
LIKE IN PORTUGAL AND WHERE ARE THE BEST
PLACES TO STAY?

Accommodation

Hotels
Hotels in Portugal are officially graded according to the star system, though there are frequently major differences in quality within one category. Luxury hotels are awarded five stars, simple hotels one. Similar categories apply to motels and aparthotels as to hotels.

Hotel price categories

- Luxury: starting at € 180/£ 120
- Mid-range: € 90 – 180/£60 – 120
- Budget: up to € 90/£ 60
  (prices for one night double occupancy)

Guesthouses (pensão, pl.: pensões), ranging from one to four stars, are also popular. Lower category guesthouses are occasionally more reasonably priced and just as well furnished and equipped as hotels that have the same number of stars. A »residencial«, similar in price and comfort, is for the most part a smaller hotel or guesthouse. »Albergarias« correspond to guesthouses of the highest category.

Pousadas
Pousadas are state-owned hotels of a higher category located in **historical buildings** in places steeped in history or of outstanding scenic beauty. The interior decoration of the building is always very tasteful and appealing. The length of the stay is usually limited to five nights. Since the number of beds is for the most part very low, reservations should be made well in advance.

Turismo de Habitação
»Turismo de Habitação« establishments are exceptionally beautiful places to stay. Owners of old townhouses or small **country residences** offer travellers the chance to stay on their beautiful estates. Visitors sleep in rooms elegantly decorated with old furniture and can even share other spacious areas of the house. The houses receive public sponsorship, are registered with the central tourism department and must have a plaque at the entrance.

Accommodation in the country
Alongside the »Turismo de Habitação« there is also the »Turismo Rural« which offers overnight stays in country homes or wineries, and the »Agroturismo«, which provides accommodation in farmhouses or outbuildings. Good lodgings are normally signposted with a tree symbol.

Private rooms
Probably the best-priced alternative is accommodation in private rooms (quartos), which is frequently offered in places frequented by tourists. The rooms are well-looked after and simply furnished. Breakfast is usually included.

Prices
The prices for hotels and guesthouses may vary considerably depending on the season. The prices for single rooms are about 30% lower than that of double rooms in both guesthouses and hotels.

A nice place to spend the night: the Casa das Torres de Oliveira in the Douro Valley

A GUEST IN PORTUGAL'S PALACES

It is hard to find more beautiful accommodation than this: old Portuguese palaces, city mansions, country houses, wine-growing estates and well-furnished farmhouses are opening their doors to guests – very special places to stay, in which visitors are extremely warmly received by their hosts.

Turismo de Habitação is the name for this form of accommodation. The owners of old mansions or country houses mostly also live on their estates and have furnished four, five or six rooms for guests. Holidaymakers are offered the possibility of living in spacious rooms that reveal a lot about high-class Portuguese home décor. There are almost always lounges tastefully furnished with old furniture, in which guests are only too happy to spend time in the evenings or during bouts of bad weather. Often the hosts will show visitors around the whole house or relate the family history associated with the house. Some land, vineyards or pretty gardens normally belong to the house – there is nearly always a swimming pool which can be used by guests. The houses receive a state grant, are registered at the central tourist office and are obliged to hang a plaque at the entrance. Furthermore, accommodation in the category Turismo Rural is offered in somewhat simple country houses or, within the framework of Agroturismo, in farmhouses or outbuildings of farms.

Casas Rústicas

Increasingly, small houses in the country – well-run Casas Rústicas – are rented complete as holiday homes, for example in the Serra de Estrela or the Peneda-Gerês National Park. These quarters can be booked through the organization (see p.100) or directly from the lessors, with whom it is often possible to negotiate favourable conditions for families with children. As a rule the hosts are very friendly to their younger guests and do all they can to ensure a they – and their parents – have a pleasant stay.

POUSADAS

► **Enatur – Empresa Nacional de Turismo**
Pousadas de Portugal
Av. Santa Joana Princesa 10
1749-090 Lisboa
Tel. 218 442 001
Fax 218 442 085
www.pousadas.pt

TURISMO DE HABITAÇÃO

► **TURIHAB – Solares de Portugal**
Praça da República
4990-062 Ponte de Lima
Tel. 258 741 672
Fax 258 931 320
www.solaresdeportugal.pt
www.center.pt

CAMPING

► **Federação de Campismo e Montanhismo de Portugal**
Avenida Coronel Eduardo Galhardo, 24 D
1199-007 Lisboa
Tel. 218 126 890/1
Fax 218 126 918
www.roteiro-campista.pt

► **Direcção-Geral do Turismo**
Avenida António Augusto de Aguiar 86

1069-021 Lisboa
Tel. 213 586 400, fax 213 586 666
dgturismo@dgturismo.pt
www.dgturismo.pt

► **Internet**
www.eurocampings.co.uk
with information on individual
camp sites in Portugal

YOUTH HOSTELS

► **Movijovem**
Rua Lúcio de Azevedo, 29
1600-146 Lisboa
Tel. 217 232 100
Fax 217 232 101
informacoes@movijovem.pt
Reservations for those travelling
alone
Tel. 00 351 707 20 30 30
Fax 217 232 102
www.pousadasjuventude.pt
reservas@movijovem.pt

► **International Youth Hostel Federation (IYHF)**
Trevelyan House
Dimple Road, Matlock
Derbyshire, DE4 3YH
Tel. 0 16 29 / 59 26 00, fax 59 27 02
www.yha.org.uk

Camping There are both public and private camp sites in Portugal, which are allocated one to four stars. A passport or a **CampingCard** must be handed in for the duration of the stay; the latter can be obtained at www.campingcard.co.uk, and means a discount on participating sites. Most camp sites are open all the year round. Spending the night on roads, motorway service stations, in parks or in cleared areas is prohibited in Portugal.

Youth hostels Youth hostels (Pousadas de Juventude) offer low-cost accommodation, especially for younger travellers. An international youth hostel

Fit for Queen Isabel: pousada in Estremoz

pass is required, which is issued by the Youth Hostels Association. There is no upper age limit. The length of the stay is usually limited to eight consecutive nights, but if there are no other reservations then the stay can be extended. Advance booking is advisable especially in July and August; this is done through Movijovem, the central booking office in Lisbon. Meanwhile there are more than 40 youth hostels in Portugal. A complete directory can be obtained from ICEP (► Information), from Movijovem or on the internet.

Arrival • Before the Journey

TAP Portugal (Transportes Aéreos Portugueses) and British Airways fly direct from London Heathrow to Lisbon; the flying time is about two and a half hours. Air France, Alitalia and Lufthansa also fly to Lisbon. TAP Portugal and Ryan Air fly direct from London to Porto, and Portugália flies non-stop from Manchester to Porto. For much of the year, TAP Portugal offers daily non-stop flights from New York to Lisbon, increasing to ten a week during peak season; flying time is 6 hours 30 minutes. Continental offers direct flights from Newark Liberty International Airport to Lisbon daily. The flight from Los Angeles takes 12 hours (plus transfer); from Toronto 9 hours 30 minutes (plus transfer); and from Sydney 22 hours 30 minutes (plus transfers). **By plane**

By car By car, depending on the point of departure, there are various possible routes from the French-Spanish border to reach different destinations in Portugal: Hendaye/Irun – Burgos – Valladolid – Zamora – Bragança – Porto (to northern Portugal); or Hendaye/Irun – Burgos – Salamanca – Vilar Formoso (Spanish-Portuguese border) – Lisbon or Hendaye/Irun – Burgos – Salamanca – Badajoz – Lisbon (to central Portugal and Lisbon); or Paris – Bordeaux – Hendaye/Irun – Burgos – Salamanca – Sevilla – Algarve (to southern Portugal). The distance between London and Lisbon is roughly 2,210km/1,380mi. Considerable tolls must be taken into account as well as the petrol costs.

By train By train from London, Portugal is best reached by taking the Eurostar from Waterloo International to Gare du Nord in Paris, negotiating urban Paris to get to Gare Montparnasse, then boarding a high-speed TGV from Paris to Irun on the Spanish border, and finally taking the Sud Express overnight to Lisbon. Alternatively, travellers can take the Eurostar and then the overnight TALGO express train from Gare d'Austerlitz to Madrid, and then board the Lisboa Express; it is also possible to spend a day in Madrid and then take the Lusitania Trainhotel overnight to Lisbon. The travel time from London to Lisbon is at least 24 hours. The price of a normal train ticket is as high as that for a moderate flight. InterRail travellers may wish to choose more circuitous routes to avoid paying extra charges for fast trains.

By bus or coach Buses leave for Portugal daily from London's Victoria Coach Station, travel by ferry across the English Channel, and arrive in Lisbon 37 hours later after stops at several places in France and Spain. There is also a service to Faro, in southern Portugal, which takes two days. Both routes are operated by Eurolines Ltd. Tickets from London to Lisbon cost £127 one-way and £187 for a return trip.

By ship Those who wish to travel to Portugal by ship should enquire at travel agencies about current connections. For a fee, Freighter World Cruises of California will supply information about freighter cruises. Brittany Ferries sails from Plymouth to Santander in Spain; crossing time is 23 to 24 hours from March to November and 30 to 33 hours between October and April. From Santander, drive west to Galicia and then head south, entering Portugal through the Minho district. In addition there is a freighter route which leaves from Rotterdam and calls in at Porto (Leixões harbour) and Lisbon.

Entry and Exit Regulations

Travel documents For stays in Portugal of up to 90 days, a valid passport is sufficient for citizens of the UK, Republic of Ireland, USA, Canada, Australia and New Zealand. A child must carry its own passport or be entered

⏵ USEFUL INFORMATION

AIRPORTS

► Lisbon
Aeroporto de Lisboa
Tel. 00 351/218 413 500
The airport is approx. 7km/4.4mi
from the city centre. The number
91 AeroBus leaves for the city
centre every 20 minutes between
7am and 9pm (travel time: approx.
25min). In addition, there is a
regular public bus service into the
centre. A taxi ride to Lisbon city
centre takes about 20 minutes.

► Porto
Aeroporto de Porto (Francisco Sá
Carneiro)
Tel. 00 351/229 432 400
13km/8mi north of Porto
An AeroBus that on request will
also stop at the major hotels drives
to the city centre (max. 40min). A
service returns to the airport from
Av. dos Aliados in the centre and
also from the hotel by prior
arrangement (tel. 225 071 054).
The bus ticket for the AeroBus is
also a same day daily ticket for the
public transport system in Porto.
A taxi ride to the centre takes
approx. 30min.

► Faro
Tel. 00 351/289 800 800
The Aeroporto de Faro is located
4km/2.5mi from Faro. The bus
service to the city is irregular; a
taxi is a good alternative (travel
time approx. 15min.)

AIRLINES

► Air Portugal (TAP)
www.flytap.com
Lisbon airport
Tel. 707 205 700

Porto, Praça Mouzinho de
Albuquerque 105
Tel. 707 205 700
Faro, Rua D. Francisco Gomes 8
Tel. 289 800 217, 707 205 700

► Portugália
Lisbon airport
Tel. 218 425 500

► British Airways
Lisbon airport
Tel. +351 (0)21 844 5353

In UK
Tel. +44 (0)870 850 9 850
Fax +44 (0)20 8759 4314
www.britishairways.com or
www.ba.com

► Ryanair
Tel. 0871 246 0000
(UK reservations)
Tel. 0818 30 30 30 (Republic of
Ireland reservations)
www.ryanair.com

► Continental
Tel. 1 800 231 0856
(US reservations)
www.continental.com

AUTOMOBILE CLUB

► Automóvel Club de Portugal
Rua Rosa Araújo 24–26
P-1250-195 Lisboa
Tel. 213 180 100
www.acp.pt

TRAIN STATIONS

► Estação de Santa Apolónia
Av. Infante D. Henrique
Arrival and departure point in
Lisbon of all trains to north and
north-east Portugal and abroad.

► **Estação Oriente**
Parque das Nações
Traffic hub east of the Lisbon city
centre with bus and metro connection to the centre and the
airport.

BUS AND COACH SERVICES

► **Eurolines Ltd.**
52 Grosvenor Gardens
London SW1W 0UA
Tel. 0870 514 3219
www.eurolines.com

FREIGHTER/FERRY SERVICES

► **Brittany Ferries**
Millbay Docks
Plymouth PL1 3EW
Tel. 0870 366 5333
www.brittany-ferries.co.uk

► **Freighter World Cruises**
180 South Lake Avenue, #340
Pasadena, CA 91101-2655
Tel. 1 800 531 7774
www.freighterworld.com

in the parent's passport. A minor under the age of 18 travelling to
Portugal without a parent or guardian must either be met at the airport or point of entry by a parent or guardian, or carry a letter of au-
thorization to travel from a parent or guardian. The letter should
name the adult responsible for the child during the stay.

It is required by law for foreign nationals to show some form of
identification if requested by the police or judicial authorities: this
normally means a passport. For those driving a car in Portugal, this
requirement is rigorously enforced; in addition, always carry the driving licence and the car's registration certificate. If the driver of the
car is not the owner then he or she must be able to present a notarized power of attorney granted by the vehicle owner. The international green insurance card, confirming third-party insurance, is required in the event of damage.

In other cases, it should be sufficient to carry a photocopy of the data
page of the passport, but visitors should be able to produce the original document if necessary.

Pets Those wishing to bring pets to Portugal will need a certificate of
health issued by an official veterinary surgeon shortly before the departure, as well as proof of anti-rabies inoculation administered at
least 30 days but no more than twelve months before the date of travel. The inoculation date and the type of vaccine must be stated.

Customs In the EU, which includes Portugal, the UK and Republic of Ireland,
regulations the movement of private goods is largely duty-free. Certain standard
maximum quantities apply (e.g. 800 cigarettes, 10l/17.5pt (21 US
pints) spirits and 90l/157.5pt (189 US pints) wine per traveller over
17 years of age).

Travellers over 17 years of age from non-EU countries such as the
USA, Canada, Australia and New Zealand can import the following
into Portugal: 200 cigarettes or 100 cigarillos or 50 cigars or 250g/

8.8oz loose tobacco; 2l/3.5pt (4.2 US pints) wine and the same quantity of sparkling wine, or 1l/1.8pt (2.1 US pints) spirits exceeding 22% alcohol by volume, or 2l/3.5pt (4.2 US pints) spirits with less than 22% alcohol by volume. Adults can bring gifts worth up to €175; for minors below 15 years the limit is €90.

Beaches

Bathing in the Atlantic Ocean should generally be approached with caution. The vehemence of the waves and currents are often underestimated and every year there are fatalities. While the beaches in the east of the Algarve are somewhat quieter, bathing on the beaches of the entire west coast is not entirely without risk.

Nudism is prohibited in Portugal. But at specially marked beaches and holiday complexes it is possible to swim or sunbathe without clothes, and as a rule it is tolerated at more remote beaches.

There are three recognized nudist beaches: Praia 19 at the Costa da Caparica near Lisbon, Praia Aldeia de Meco near Sesimbra and the Praia Barril on the Ilha de Tavira near Tavira. Topless bathing and sunbathing is widespread even at better frequented beaches, but tourists should generally show consideration for the beach habits of Portuguese families.

> ### *i* Beach signs
>
> - »area concessionada« = guarded beach
> - »praia não vigilada« = unguarded beach
> - red flag = bathing prohibited, even close to the beach
> - yellow flag = swimming further out in the water prohibited
> - green flag = all swimming allowed
> - blue and white chequered flag = beach periodically unguarded
> - »blue banner« = European seal of approval (complies with water quality, environmental protection, and safety norms)

The following overview lists the most important beaches from north to south.

▶ THE BEST BEACHES

COSTA VERDE

▶ 1. Moledo do Minho
Fine sand, dunes, restaurant; the climate on this stretch of coast is for the most part fairly harsh.

▶ 2. Vila Praia de Âncora
Fine sand with dunes; restaurant.

▶ 3. Viana do Castelo
South of the Rio Lima: shallow beaches with fine sand – probably

Beaches

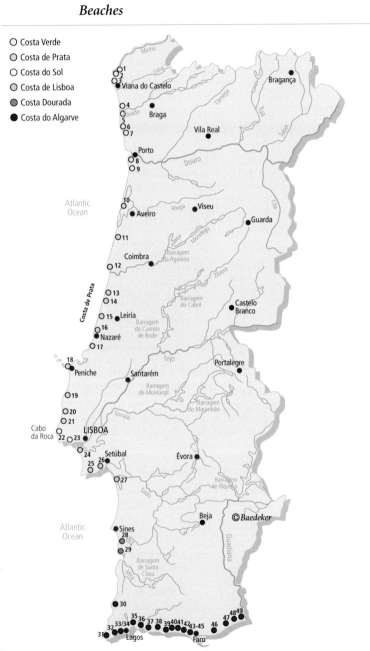

- ○ Costa Verde
- ○ Costa de Prata
- ○ Costa do Sol
- ○ Costa de Lisboa
- ● Costa Dourada
- ● Costa do Algarve

Atlantic Ocean

Minho

1
2
Viana do Castelo

Lima

Bragança

4
Cávado
5
Braga
6
7

Vila Real

Tâmega

Tua

Sabor

Porto
8
9

Douro

10
Aveiro

Vouga

Viseu

Guarda

Côa

11

Mondego

Coimbra

Barragem da Aguieira

12

Costa de Prata

13
14
15 Leiria

Barragem do Cabril

Castelo Branco

Zêzere

16
Nazaré
17

Barragem do Castelo de Bode

18
Peniche

Tejo

Santarém

Portalegre

19

Barragem de Montargil

20
21

Barragem do Maranhão

Cabo da Roca
22 23
LISBOA

Sorraia

24
25 26 Setúbal

Évora

27

Sado

Barragem de Alqueva

Beja

©*Baedeker*

Atlantic Ocean

Sines
28

29

Barragem de Santa Clara

Mira

Guadiana

30

35
32 33/34 36 37 38 39 40 41 42 43-45 46 47 48 49
31 Lagos Faro

the most beautiful on the Costa Verde. Dunes; restaurants.

► 4. Esposende
Lagoon, sandbanks; because of the frequently harsh climate the sandy beach is often better suited to walks on the beach than for bathing or basking in the sun; swimming is possible in the better protected areas at the mouth of the Rio Cávado.

► 5. Ofir
Shallow beach with fine sand, forest; restaurant, aspiring tourism centre.

► 6. Póvoa de Varzim
Sandy beach, occasionally slightly dirty; several restaurants; the scenery is not all that pretty, it rather resembles an industrial area and not a recreation area.

► 7. Vila do Conde
Sandy beach, some cliffs, altogether a little more attractive than the beach of Póvoa de Varzim; restaurants.

COSTA DE PRATA

► 8. Miramar
Shallow, sandy beach with a slight North Sea feel; several restaurants.

► 9. Espinho
Flat, sandy beach, frequently strong surf; several restaurants.

► 10. Praia de São Jacinto
Fine sand, dunes; forest behind the beach.

► 11. Palheiros de Mira
Sandy beach, slightly dirty in places.

► 12. Figueira da Foz
Urban beach on the main coastal road; flat and sandy, very crowded in the peak season; a few restaurants.

► 13. Pedrógão
Flat, sandy beach, some rocks, strong surf; small fishing port.

► 14. Praia da Vieira
Fine sand, surf; several restaurants.

► 15. São Pedro de Muel
Shallow beach with fine sand, rocks; one of the most pleasant bathing areas in this region; several restaurants.

► 16. Nazaré
Sandy beach alongside the main street; a spot should be reserved in advance during the peak season; the water is dirty at times; several restaurants.

► 17. São Martinho do Porto
Shallow, sandy beach with an almost circular bay, separated from the open sea by a rocky dune landscape; dive site; several restaurants.

► 18. Peniche
Shallow, sandy beaches in the vicinity, rocks; dive site; several restaurants; fishing port.

► 19. Praia de Santa Cruz
Fine sand, strong surf, dunes and a steep coast; restaurant.

► 20. Ericeira
Flat, sandy beaches, rocks, steep coast, pleasant area for swimming and sunbathing, very busy especially at weekends; several restaurants; fishing port.

► **21. Praia Grande**
Flat, sandy beach, cliffs; very busy at weekends; several restaurants.

COSTA DO SOL

► **22. Praia do Guincho**
Beautiful sandy bay close to town, pinewood in the background, very busy during peak season; restaurants.

► **23. Cascais/Estoril**
Several smaller bays with flat beaches with fine sand; municipal beaches of the Lisbonites; very crowded at weekends; restaurants.

COSTA DE LISBOA

► **24. Costa da Caparica**
Almost 30km/19mi of beach with sand dunes, the more remote southern stretches are especially beautiful; restaurants.

► **25. Sesimbra**
A smaller, sandy beach directly adjacent to the town, very busy at weekends; dive site; fishing boats; several restaurants.

► **26. Portinho da Arrábida**
Several protected swimming coves in beautiful surroundings, rocks; at the weekend for the most part rather busy; several restaurants; fishing port.

► **27. Tróia**
Flat headland, wide beaches with fine sand, the most beautiful ones are located some distance away from the Tróia hotel settlement; occasionally some litter in the dune areas; diving grounds; several restaurants.

COSTA DOURADA

► **28. Porto Covo**
Flat, sandy beach, rocks, strong surge; several restaurants; fishing port.

► **29. Vila Nova de Milfontes**
Long, beautiful, sandy beach, dunes; several restaurants.

► **Other beaches**
There are no further larger beach resorts along the Costa Dourada, but some pretty swimming coves are to be found (e.g. the Zambujeira do Mar and the Praia de Odeceixe); the most secluded ones are often completely deserted. In the summer there are simple beach bars in some areas.

ALGARVE

► **30. Aljezur**
Flat, sandy beach, rocks, dunes, strong surf; restaurant. Further south near Carrapateira there are two beautiful, sandy beaches good for surfing (Praia da Bordeira, Praia do Amado).

► **31. Sagres**
Flat, sandy beach, rocks; not overcrowded, but fierce winds often blow here; conveniently situated dive site; restaurants. To the north-west of Sagres lies the beautiful 500m/547yd-long Praia do Beliche; Praia do Martinhal 2km/1.3mi east of Sagres is rather nice: 750m/820yd-long white beach with dunes, protected by the harbour and thus suitable for children as well. A little further east, near Zavial, there is a 200m/219yd-long flat beach with fine

← *For many holidaymakers these are Portugal's most beautiful beaches: the small sandy bays between the cliffs of the Rocky Algarve.*

sand and no rocks where bathing is also possible. bathe.

► 32. Salema/Burgau
Near Salema there is a flat, sandy beach 750m/820yd long, often also with some fishing boats moored up; several restaurants; good surfing opportunities. A few miles to the east there is a 300m/328yd sandy beach near Burgau; fishing port; restaurants.

► 33. Praia da Luz
Broad 200m/219yd-long sandy beach, rocks; dive site and various other opportunities for water sports; several restaurants; the beach is also very suitable for children.

► 34. Lagos
Smaller sections of beach lie right next to the town, numerous other beaches in the proximity (e.g. the Praia da Dona Ana west of Lagos), rocks and good dive site south of Lagos; several restaurants; fishing port. The Meia Praia east of Lagos is one of the longest beaches on the Algarve; good windsurfing opportunities.

► 35. Alvor
Flat, sandy beach, rocks; several restaurants; various sporting opportunities here as well as in Praia dos Três Irmãos, which is not far to the east.

► 36. Praia da Rocha
A sandy municipal beach, highly populated during peak season; picturesque rocks, with the road winding above the steep cliffs; dive site; several restaurants.

► 37. Carvoeiro
Small, sandy bay, shared by sun worshippers and scattered fishing boats alike during peak season, rocks; several restaurants.

► 38. Armação de Pêra
Very long beach with fine sand – not overly crowded in comparison with other places on the Algarve, dunes; dive site; restaurants. Additional bathing opportunities further west in Senhora da Rocha, where it is also possible to explore some caves.

► 39. Albufeira
Beaches with fine sand, rocks, cliffs; dive site, several restaurants; fishing port. The beach right next to Albufeira is hopelessly crowded during peak season; there is a bit more room further east at the Praia da Oura.

► 40. Olhos de Água – Praia da Falésia
Flat beach, fine sand, rocks, cliffs; good surfing opportunities; restaurants.

► 41. Vilamoura
Sandy beach, part of the coast has cliffs; several restaurants, generously laid out tourist complex with numerous sports opportunities, excellent conditions for surfing, ideal for children.

► 42. Quarteira
Sandy beach, extensive tourist hotspot with various sports opportunities; several restaurants; an ideal place for children to play in the water.

► 43. Vale do Lobo
In part flat beach, fine sand, rocks,

cliffs; several restaurants; numerous sports opportunities, often good surfing conditions.

► **44. Quinta do Lago**
Sandy beach, dunes, lagoon; good surfing conditions.

► **45. Faro**
Long, flat beach with fine sand on a spit in the lagoon; several restaurants.

► **46. Olhão**
During peak season there are regular boat rides from Olhão to the offshore islands of Culatra and Armona with long, sandy beaches and dunes; several restaurants.

► **47. Tavira**
Tavira is a partially wooded island with sandy beaches and flat dunes. Boats leave from Tavira or Quatro Águas a little further south-east of the town; there is a footbridge near Santa Luzia (Pedras d'El Rei) to the south-west. The pace is fairly leisurely since there are no large tourist complexes nearby; restaurants.

► **48. Cabanas/Cacela**
Cross by fishing boat to an island with a flat beach with fine sand.

► **49. Monte Gordo**
Flat beach with fine sand and low dunes; several restaurants.

Children in Portugal

Those wishing to enjoy a **beach holiday** with their children have an almost unlimited choice in Portugal. Nevertheless it should be remembered that bathing in the Atlantic Ocean is not without peril; along the miles of glorious beaches of the west coast there are surf and currents which are not to be underestimated. Quieter bays are more suitable for small children. Around Lisbon the calmer beaches of the Costa do Sol lie at the **mouth of the Tagus** in the direction of Cascais, and the beach of **Portinho da Arrábida** south of the capital between Sesimbra and Setúbal is also well protected. Stormier beaches are to be found on the west coast near Sintra and on the Costa da Caparica south of Lisbon on the other side of the Tagus. The **bay of Baleal** in the north near Peniche is somewhat better protected. The coast of the Algarve is well suited for a holiday with both younger and older children. Beautiful weather can always be counted on even in autumn and spring, making life on the beach enjoyable outside

Seaside holiday

i Highlights for children

- Oceanário in Lisbon: examine the underwater world of four oceans
- A ride through the grottoes along the western coast of the Algarve
- Portugal dos Pequenitos in Coimbra: a child-scale Portugal
- Parrots, dolphins and seals demonstrate their skills in the Zoomarine park near Albufeira on the Algarve

For children the best holidays are spent in the sea and on the beach.

the peak season, too. In the east of the Algarve the Atlantic Ocean is less harsh and a little warmer than in the west. Long, sandy beaches stretch eastward, and the otherwise rough **Praia da Bordeira** and the Praia da Amoreira in the west feature some shallow lagoons. Beaches especially suited to children are located near Martinhal, Salema, Luz, Vilamoura (Praia da Falésia, Praia da Marinha), on the **Ilha de Tavira**, on Culatra and Armona, near Monte Gordo, and close to the tourist hotspots of Armação de Pêra and Quarteira. Many hotel and apartment grounds have swimming pools and shallower pools for children; some even offer a child minding service.

Many places in the Algarve offer **sailing and windsurfing classes**. The larger hotels usually have recreational and sports programmes for children and adolescents. Riding lessons are offered in the Algarve and near Lisbon, and it is also possible to have a proper **riding holiday** here.

Fun in the water and amusement parks There are several large **bathing resorts** and amusement or animal parks waiting to be enjoyed by younger and older guests alike, especially on the Algarve. The Zoomarine park hosts dolphin and parrot shows; spending the entire day here is not a problem. The Omega Parque in Serra de Monchique shows animals that are threatened with extinction.

In northern Portugal it is possible to participate in tours on the Douro, and in Lisbon regular liners cross the Tagus. On the Algarve **boat tours** and **trips through the grottoes** are offered on the western coast; there are also trips up the Rio Arade from Portimão to Silves or on the Guadiana along the Spanish border, and smaller ferries sail to the offshore lagoon islands in the east.

Boat excursions

Portugal boasts old castles and fortified villages aplenty. Some castles such as the Castelo de São Jorge in Lisbon are important sights, others are mere ruins that nevertheless spur the imagination, such as the castelo in Alcoutim in the Algarve or the one in Montemor-o-Novo in the Alentejo. Especially in the east toward the Spanish border there are many small villages which were built inside forts and are in good condition; among them are Mértola, Marvão and Monsaraz in the Alentejo. A small, pretty old town can also be found within the walls of Leiria castle.

Castles and fortresses

A drive to the south-westernmost point of Europe near Sagres on the Algarve makes for an interesting trip. North-west of Lisbon lies **Cabo da Roca**, the **westernmost point of the European continent**; visitors can even obtain a certificate to confirm that they have reached this special geographical point.

Special places

With their lively atmosphere, markets are also interesting for children. The gipsy markets that take place on fixed dates once or twice a month in many Portuguese towns are indeed something special. Animals are sometimes on sale.

Markets

Though many smaller museums are simple, they still manage to be very interesting and descriptive. It is often especially worthwhile visiting regional museums, even for children.

Museums

Certain specific suggestions are bound to get a good response from the children of those spending holidays in Lisbon. One highlight for instance is a **ride on tram 28**. The Elevador de Santa Justa, the old lift connecting Baixa and Bairro Alto, is popular with children, as are the funiculars Elevador da Bica and Elevador da Glória. Among the classic **sights**, the Castelo de São Jorge and the Torre de Belém should go down well; the Padrão dos Descobrimentos, also in Belém, is likely to be similarly well received. Of Lisbon's **museums**, the marine museum in Belém (Museu da Marinha) with both model and real ships and – also in Belém – the Museu dos Coches, the coach museum, are of interest. Also appropriate for children is the puppet museum (Museu da Marioneta); in addition there is lots to see and hear in the Casa do Fado e da Guitarra. Technically minded children will probably also enjoy the water museum and the tram museum. Finally there is Lisbon's **zoo** and, most notably, the **Ozeanário** aquarium, one of Europe's largest. The Ozeanário is located on the former Expo

In Lisbon

Slide & Splash in the Algarve: a blue maze of slides and tunnels offers fun in the water.

grounds that are otherwise less than sensational for children – though the **cable car** that passes along the bank of the Tagus can be worth a trip. A ride across the Ponte Vasco da Gama, one of Europe's largest bridges, or across the stately Ponte 25 de Abril, is also something special.

Electricity

The mains supply is 220 volts AC. An adapter is required for devices with British or other non-European plugs.

Emergency • Emergency Services

▶ BREAKDOWN SERVICES

BREAKDOWN SERVICES IN UK

▶ **RAC**
Tel. 08705 722 722 (customer services)
Tel. 0800 82 82 82 (breakdown assistance)

▶ **AA**
Tel. 0800 88 77 66 (emergency breakdown)
Tel. +44 161 495 8945 (international enquiries)

INTERNATIONAL AIR AMBULANCE SERVICES

► **Cega Air Ambulance (worldwide service)**
Tel. +44(0)1243 621097
Fax +44(0)1243 773169
www.cega-aviation.co.uk

► **US Air Ambulance**
Tel. 800/948-1214 (US; toll-free)
Tel. 001-941-926-2490 (international; collect)
www.usairambulance.net

IN PORTUGAL

► **General emergency**
Tel. 112 (toll-free)
Police, fire brigade, ambulances, medical attention, etc. The »Polícia de Trânsito«, a division of the GNR, is responsible for car accidents and car theft.

► **SOS-telephones**
Motorists can use the orange SOS-telephones on the motorways in case of emergency.

► **Breakdown service**
Tel. 707 509 510

► **Police**
P.S.P. • Polícia de Segurança Pública
Tel. 217 654 242
and tel. 800 508 810

Etiquette and Customs

The polite friendliness of the Portuguese is well known. Yet in regions where tourists invade the country in droves this aspect of the national character is severely put to the test. A hearty welcome in tourist information centres or in restaurants highly frequented by tourists cannot therefore be counted on; in contrast, the reception in more remote villages, unfrequented parts of town or old general stores is a different story. The admirable composure and courtesy of the Portuguese hosts are often an unexpected yet pleasant surprise.

Friendliness

When meeting the Portuguese personally, visitors should not be surprised to be included in the traditional welcome with two pecks on the cheek, even as a stranger – hands are shaken only during formal meetings. The same goes for farewells: after a pleasant evening there will be two pecks for goodbye.

Welcome

Many Portuguese are very patient and expect the same from foreigners. There are frequently situations where the wait lasts longer than expected and where the reason for the delay and what is actually being done about it is not clear. Flying into a rage or insisting on an explanation seldom meets with success. It is far better to accept the situation and to exercise some patience. Even the most confusing situation will be resolved in time and the lengthiest of waits will come to an end eventually.

Patience

Portugal's history
: The Portuguese still consider the decades of conquests their »golden age of discovery«. From time to time shows or articles appear in the media – for example in entertaining quiz programmes – in which the old times seem to live on, disregarding the less positive aspects of the period such as colonization, the slave trade, and so on. It is best to keep your personal views on the country's history to yourself in private conversations.

Tipping
: Service is included in the bills of **hotels and restaurants**. An additional tip of about 10% of the amount on the bill is nevertheless customary – even for that quick cup of coffee. Simply leave a small amount on the table or on the saucer after paying the bill. The chambermaids in the hotels also appreciate an extra tip; the amount depends on the length of the stay. An adequate tip should also be given to **taxi drivers, baggage porters and tour guides**.

Fado

Fado originated in Lisbon (▶Baedeker Special, p.118). In addition, a special kind of fado can be heard in Coimbra and one or two fado bars can even be found in Porto. Fado performances which are organized exclusively for tourists are not to be recommended, especially in the Algarve. As a rule, fado bars do not charge an entrance fee, though they do require a minimum consumption. Be prepared to spend sufficient time there: the best fado singers often do not perform until midnight or even later. A table reservation is to be recommended in most fado bars.

▶ FADO BARS

IN LISBON

▶ **O Senhor Vinho**
Rua do Meio à Lapa 18
Tel. 213 972 681
Very good singer and guitarist, but also more expensive than other fado bars

▶ **Adega Machado**
Rua do Norte 91
Tel. 213 224 640
Cosy room; the walls are covered with pictures

▶ **O Forcado**
Rua da Rosa 221
Tel. 213 468 579
Typical fado bar in the Bairro Alto; mostly foreign guests

▶ **Café Luso**
Travessa da Queimada 10
Tel. 213 422 281
Famous fado singers perform from time to time in the Café Luso, the classic fado bar in the Bairro Alto. Amália Rodrigues made her debut here, and Mísia took to the stage here recently.

► **Clube de Fado**
Rua S. João da Praça 92/94
Tel. 218 852 704
A good fado spot in the Alfama

► **Mal Cozinhado**
Rua do Outeirinho 11
Tel. 222 081 319
A restaurant in a medieval house where diners can listen to Portuguese folk music and fado from Coimbra

► **À Capella**
Capela Nossa Senhora da Victória
Rua Corpo de Deus
Tel. 239 833 985
The place for fado in Coimbra, in an old chapel

► **Diligência Bar**
Rua Nova 30
Tel. 239 827 667
Long-established bar, in which fado has been played and sung since the year dot – performances also given by Portuguese guests, often students

Fado being performed in an alley in Alfama, Lisbon.

PORTUGAL'S SONGS OF FATE

Fado is urban music. It is heard above all in Lisbon and Coimbra, though in very different forms in the two cities. The origins of fado are still unclear. Only one thing is certain – that it appeared in Lisbon's harbour area in the early 19th century – the rest is a matter of speculation.

Some cannot stand it, but for others it is one of Portugal's important cultural assets. Fado derives from the Latin fatum, meaning fate. And indeed many fados concern a fate that cannot be avoided – disappointed or unattainable love, farewells, social necessity, homesickness and itchy feet, grief, Lisbon's destroyed splendour, Portugal's former greatness. In short, the music exudes longing, melancholy, and, as the Portuguese put it, »saudade«, the supposed prevailing mood of the Portuguese soul, that describes something close to a reversed form of longing. But so much for the cliché that surrounds fado. From time to time the songs concern life in the city or tell saucy little stories or amusing, lively anecdotes. The singing, which for non-Portuguese listeners is mysterious and difficult to understand – even barley comprehensible – is certainly a music of the people, but does not count as folk music for the whole country. It is an urban form of music and at home primarily in Lisbon and Coimbra, though the two types are very different. Originally, Fado played no role in Porto.

Lisbon fado

Fado from Lisbon is performed by a man or a woman, the so-called »fadista«. The female singers often wear a black, fringed stole around their shoulders; the male performers are dressed entirely in black. Two men also dressed in black provide the musical accompaniment. One plays the twelve-stringed »guitarra portuguesa«, a lute that follows the melody; the other plays the six-stringed »viola«, the Spanish guitar known to all of us, which provides the rhythm. The »guitarra portuguesa«, the special

The guitarra portuguesa, the twelve-stringed fado guitar, produces a slightly metallic and vibrating sound.

fado guitar, was created from two instruments: the zither, introduced to Portugal in the 16th century from Italy and Flanders, and the English guitar, which entered the Portuguese kingdom via Porto in the 18th century.

Fado for the soul

Lisbon fado has its supporters and its detractors in Portugal. Some criticize it as sentimental and affected, as a melancholy dulling of the senses of the people. The Portuguese composer and music scientist Fernando Lopes Graça, who recorded Portuguese folk songs, disapproved strongly of fado and considered it commercial and artificial. Others however value it as an expression of Portuguese public feeling. Every Portuguese person, therefore, can find themselves in fado, because the songs are about their own destinies, their failures, their unfulfilled loves, their longings. In fado, the Portuguese find the bittersweet expression of their dreams, wishes and hopes. And they are not alone. Fado unites the lonely in a community, and invites all to take part in a kind of common ritual. As soon as a fado strikes up, every conversation comes to an end, and a loud bar becomes silent in a flash. Expressions on faces change; eyes stare into the far distance. Regardless of their social standing, the listeners feel pulled out of their loneliness into the community, and for a short time they are somehow connected to one another – in a communally enjoyed resignation. For this reason Salazar hated fado, and tried to take measures against it. It leads to a pessimistic, passive lifestyle, the dictator noticed. Salazar preferred German folk songs which inspired activity, such as *Roving is the Miller's Delight*.

Once disreputable

Even music scientists do not agree on where fado originally came from. Some claim it was inherited from the 500-year period of Moorish rule in Portugal. Portuguese troubadours are said to have taken over the melancholy love lyrics of the Moors and developed them further. This is why the from time to time plaintive

Classic fado line-up. The singer, dressed in black, is accompanied by two guitars, a »guitarra portuguesa« and a »viola«.

melodies of today's fado, in which a syllable is stretched out over several notes, are reminiscent of the Arabic singing style. Moreover, troubadour songs of the 12th century are, in terms of form and content, related to the fados of today. According to another theory fado developed from an African dance (»lundum«) which came with the slaves to Brazil and eventually became known in Portugal. Its essential musical elements are said to have been transmitted into the singing. Because of the often melancholy and wistful character of the music and text some are of the opinion that fado originated with the Portuguese sailors who sang of their homeland during their long absences. In any case, in the early 19th century fado spread throughout Lisbon's socially most impoverished quarters Alfama, Mouraria and Bairro Alto and for a long time was considered shady and disreputable. Fado was the music of the sailors, the pimps, the prostitutes, the tramps, the day labourers, poor people, criminals and, of course, unhappy lovers. That it then slowly became socially acceptable

is above all due to idle aristocrats who searched out the disreputable »casas de fado« making fado the latest fashion, and began playing it in their distinguished municipal palaces. Some of them even tried to become fado composers or singers. Others fell in love with fado singers and hit the headlines, like the young Count Vimioso, who in 1840 caused a scandal by falling for the unbelievably pretty and fiery fado singer Maria Severa. Maria Severa was the best known and most admired »fadista« of the 19th century. When she died at the age of just 26 the whole of Lisbon mourned, and many writers and poets later dedicated novels and plays to the adored »A Severa«, as she was known.

Student fado

Fado exists in Coimbra too, but it is markedly different to Lisbon fado. The younger form of fado from Coimbra came into being in the student milieu of the old university town. It is more academic and less melancholy than Lisbon fado, more amusing and humorous, predominantly lyrical, reminiscent of the ballads, and it concerns subjects from student life. It is performed exclusively by male students wearing black cloaks – and with trained voices – who are accompanied by the »guitarra de Coimbra« and often move from bar to bar.

Every now and then fado from Coimbra has a political slant. Before 1910 fado singers from Coimbra mocked the king and even encouraged the abolition of the Portuguese monarchy.

Fado today

Now, in the 21st century, fado has become known all over the world, thanks above all to a great fadista, the Lisbonite Amália Rodrigues, who in her 50-year career as a singer has brought fado to stages worldwide (▶ Famous People). In Lisbon fado is performed for tourists in not particularly cheap restaurants especially in Bairro Alto and Alfama. However, the right atmosphere is mostly lacking, as the audience – predominantly tourists – have no empathy with the music. Visitors can experience Lisbon fado in more original and significantly less expensive surroundings in hidden fado bars, not frequented by foreigners, where guests often also stand up and perform a fado themselves. However these days fado evenings in such local bars are on the wane – true fado has largely retreated behind the walls of private Lisbon homes.

Since the mid-1990s however, artistic fado has been being played more and more. The most beautiful fados, such as *Uma casa portuguesa*, *Barco negro* and *Nem às parades confesso*, are heard everywhere on newly issued CDs featuring the voice of Amália Rodrigues. But there are suddenly new fadistas on Portuguese stages, too: Dulce Pontes, Cristina Branco, Mafalda Arnauth and the male singer Camené are all oriented towards classical fado. Mísia and Mariza take to stages all over Europe with a very individual form of fado performance. Even the jazz singer Maria João devotes herself to a classical fado once in a while, and the Quinteto Amália performs fado with string quartet and voice. No doubt about it: Fado at the moment is experiencing a real renaissance!

Festivals, Holidays and Events

Saints' days Almost every town in Portugal has its own saint or saints and very special rites with which they are venerated during the »**romarias**«. In the past the romarias were mere pilgrimages, but today they have become folk festivals that last for days. People not only pray and make donations, but also sing, dance, eat and drink lavishly, and shop as well. The most impressive romarias and a selection of other events are listed on the following pages. Visitors should always inquire on location about regional festivities – even smaller village fetes are a decidedly worthwhile spectacle. Hotels and restaurants regularly offer typically Portuguese folklore performances with music, dance and local groups wearing traditional costume for the tourists. Concert series, folklore events, film and dance festivals are organized in the summer of every year.

Information on events is available at the local tourist information centres. The local press or special event calendars (agenda cultural) often on display in tourist information offices or hotels are also worth a glance.

▶ CALENDAR OF EVENTS

NATIONAL HOLIDAYS

1 January: New Year
February: Shrove Tuesday
March/April: Good Friday
25 April: Freedom Day (national holiday: anniversary of the carnation revolution on 25 April 1974)
1 May: Labour Day
May/June: Corpus Christi
10 June: national holiday (day of death of the national poet Luís de Camões on 10 June 1580)
13 June: holiday in Lisbon (Santo António day)
24 June: holiday in Porto (São João day)
15 August: Assumption Day
5 October: national holiday (proclamation of the republic on 5 October 1910)
1 November: All Hallows' Eve
1 December: national holiday (restoration of the Portugal's independence from Spain on 1 December 1640)
8 December: Immaculate Conception
25 December: Christmas
In addition to national holidays all cities in the Algarve also celebrate another local holiday (Dia do Município).

JANUARY

▶ **Vila Nova de Gaia**
Festa de São Gonçalo e São Cristovão.

▶ **Vila da Feira**
Festa de São Sebastião with processions (near Aveiro).

FEBRUARY

▶ **Ovar, Nazaré, Loulé, Portimão**
»Carnaval« is celebrated extensively in these towns. Smaller carnivalprocessions and events also take place in many other towns.

▶ Évora

Festa da Senhora das Candeias with a funfair and religious festivities in the São Brás chapel.

▶ Lisbon

Procissão do Senhor dos Passos da Graça: procession, in which a purple-garbed image of »Senhor dos Passos« from the Igreja da Graça is carried along.

▶ Loulé

Romaria da Senhora da Piedade; church consecration, procession.

▶ Braga, Póvoa de Varzim, Ovar

Festas da Semana Santa. Passion week is celebrated especially elaborately in these places, numerous processions, the streets of Bragas are decorated with flowers and lights, Ovar has a church consecration festival and fireworks.

▶ Fão and Esposende

Romaria ao Senhor Bom Jesus de Fão; church consecration in honour of Jesus of Fão with processions and fireworks.

▶ Barcelos and Guimarães

Festas das Cruzes; splendid folk festival with processions, funfair and fireworks (sometimes not until the beginning of May).

▶ Idanha-a-Nova

Romaria à Senhora do Almurtão; church consecration well worth seeing in a remote region of the Beira Baixa with folklore and religious festivities.

▶ Monsanto

Festa das Cruzes or do Castelo; religious festivities, folk festival, folklore performances – takes place in a setting of medieval character in the village whose houses are in part built directly into the rocks (sometimes not until May).

▶ Viana do Castelo

Festa da Senhora das Rosas; feast in honour of our lady of the roses with processions and fairs.

▶ Leiria

Feira de Maio: arts and crafts and other regional products are exhibited and sold during the May fair.

▶ Fátima

On 12/13 May the season for the pilgrimages to Fátima opens (in the following months until October pilgrimages take place on the 12th/13th of the month, the most important being the ones in May and October, where the greatest number of people participate).

▶ Alte

Festa da Fonte Grande or Festa do 1 de Maio; very beautiful folk festival with folklore events and many flowers (near Faro).

▶ Sesimbra

Festa do Senhor das Chagas; procession of the fishermen.

▶ Amarante

Romaria de São Gonçalo; church consecration for city's saint and the patron saint of lovers (▶Baedeker tip, p.223)

Matosinhos
Festas do Senhor de Matosinhos; folklore festival, bull run, funfair and fireworks (near Porto).

Vila Praia de Âncora
folklore festival of Vila Praia de Âncora (close to Viana do Castelo).

Amares and Vila Verde
Festas de Santo António; processions, folklore events; in Vila Verde also an exhibition of regional agricultural products and livestock (both close to Braga).

Penafiel and Monção
Festa do Corpo de Deus; Corpus Christi in Penafiel (near Porto) is celebrated with processions in old costumes and a lot of floral decorations, in Monção with folklore shows.

Lisbon
Festas de Santo António; 13 June is an official holiday in Lisbon. Celebrations in honour of the city's saint, particularly in the small streets of the Alfama – standard food: grilled sardines.

Reguengos de Monsaraz
Festas de Santo António (13 June); celebration honouring the patron saint of the city, bullfighting, male voice choirs typical of the Alentejo.

Porto, Braga, Barcelinhos, Vila do Conde
Festas de São João; this traditional celebration takes place every year from 23 to 25 June in different cities with processions, fireworks, regional folklore events and a ceramics market (in Barcelinhos).

Viseu
Cavalhadas de Vil de Moînhos; festive church service with medieval games and folklore events.

Póvoa de Varzim
Festas de São Pedro; folk celebration with dances and processions.

São Torcato
Romaria de São Torcato near Braga; church consecration festival, processions, folklore events.

Figueira da Foz
Festas de São João; midnight procession with costumes, dance in the casino, folk events.

Sintra
Feira Grande de São Pedro; large regional fair with agricultural products, antiques, arts and crafts, regional specialities.

Évora
Feira de São João; one of the most important fairs in southern Portugal, arts and crafts and folklore exhibitions.

Montijo
Festas de São Pedro in Montijo near Setúbal; folk festival, bullfights, fishermen give out sardines to the visitors.

JULY

Maia
Romaria da Senhora do Bom Despacho; church consecration festival with pilgrimage and fireworks near Porto.

Santo Tirso
Festas de São Bento in Santo Tirso near Porto; exhibition of earthenware goods, folklore festival.

The Festa dos Tabuleiros in Tomar. Women balance panels on their heads decorated with loaves of bread and flowers.

▶ Tomar

Festa dos Tabuleiros – only during even numbered years: procession with decorated panels which are carried on the head.

▶ Paredes

Festas do Divino Salvador close to Porto; procession, with animal contests and fireworks.

▶ São Torcato

Festival Internacional de Folclore de São Torcato (near Braga); the competition between the best national and international folklore groups is worth seeing.

▶ Vila do Conde

Feira de Artesanato close to Porto; arts and crafts fair, exhibition of products from different regions in Portugal.

▶ Lousada

Festas do Senhor dos Aflitos in Lousada (near Porto); processions, folkloric presentations.

▶ Gulpilhares

Festival International de Folclore de Gulpilhares (near Porto).

▶ Aveiro

Festa da Ria. The highlights of the festivities are the regatta and a boat painting competition.

▶ Vale de Maceira

Romaria da Senhora das Preces; church consecration with folk festival and market in Vale de Maceira (near Coimbra).

▶ Vila Franca de Xira

Festas do Colete Encarnado; contests, folklore performances, bullfighting.

▶ **Estoril**
Feira de Artesanato do Estoril; exhibition of handicraft items, with folklore events and specialities.

▶ **Ança**
Romaria de São Tomé e São Tiago; church consecration festival for the two patron saints in Ança (near Coimbra) with dances and folklore performances, also equestrian games.

▶ **Sintra**
Jornadas Musicais de Sintra: concerts in castles and palaces in and around Sintra (in the summer months).

▶ **Faro**
Feira da Senhora do Carmo; exhibition of regional arts and crafts, folklore shows.

AUGUST

▶ **Terras do Bouro**
Festas de São Brás in Terras do Bouro (near Braga); processions, bull run.

▶ **Mirandela**
Festas da Senhora do Amparo e Feira de Santiago; religious festivities, folk festival, cultural and sporting events.

▶ **Viana do Castelo**
Festas da Senhora da Agonia; one of the most typical pilgrimages of Portugal, processions, local costume celebration, folklore festival, folk festivals with fireworks.

▶ **Neves**
Festa da Senhora das Neves (near Viana do Castelo); religious festivities, folk festival, fireworks,

folklore event, arts and crafts exhibition. In addition, a special custom is commemorated here: in the »wedding market« the girls stroll along one side of the road, the boys along the other, and they attempt to find the right partner through eye contact.

▶ **Guimarães**
Festas Gualterianas; folk festival with regional specialities and wines, fireworks, folklore performances.

▶ **Caminha**
Festas de Santa Rita de Cássia; festival processions, with water sports contests and fireworks.

▶ **Baião and Ponte da Barca**
Festas de São Bartolomeu in Baião near Porto and Ponte da Barca; religious festivities, old dances and chants, traditional horse races, bullfighting; processions in Ponte da Barca.

▶ **Monção**
Festas da Virgem das Dores; processions, arts and crafts exhibition, folk festival, fireworks.

▶ **Porto**
Festa de São Bartolomeu e Cortejo de Papel; religious celebrations, folk festival and procession with paper figures, which are caricatures of important personages.

▶ **Viseu**
Feira de São Mateus; fair for agriculture, wine-growing, livestock breeding, arts and crafts, folklore festival, bullfighting.

▶ **Arga de São João**
Romaria de São João de Arga (near

Viana do Castelo); church consecration festival, magnificent processions, old dances and chants.

▶ **Póvoa de Varzim**
Festas da Senhora da Assunção; traditional celebration of the fishermen, procession on the sea with decorated boats, bullfighting, folklore festival, fireworks.

▶ **Esposende**
Festa da Senhora da Saúde e Soedade; traditional celebration of the fishermen, water sports competitions on the Cávado river, folklore events, processions.

▶ **Caldas de Vizela**
Festas de Vizela close to Braga; varied programme of events, festive processions, local costumes and folklore shows.

▶ **Miranda do Douro**
Festas de Santa Bárbara; folk festival with male dancers.

▶ **Peniche**
Festas da Senhora da Boa Viagem; traditional fishermen's festival honouring their patron saints with ocean processions, folklore events, fireworks and a folk festival.

▶ **Batalha**
Festas da Senhora da Vitória; folk festival, folklore performances.

▶ **Coruche**
Festas da Senhora do Castelo near Santarém; bullfighting and bull runs in the streets, folklore shows.

▶ **Alcobaça**
Feira de São Bernardo; industrial and agricultural exhibition with folklore events and arts and crafts.

▶ **Gouveia**
Festas do Senhor de Calvário near Guarda; processions, dog racing, folklore festival.

▶ **Beja**
Feira de Agosto or rather de São Lourenço e Santa Maria; good arts and crafts fair, festive programme, bullfighting.

▶ **Alcochete**
Festas do Barrete Verde e das Salinas close to Setúbal; celebration with blessing of the salt flats, bullfighting, folk festival.

SEPTEMBER

▶ **Guimarães**
Peregrinação à Senhora da Penha; pilgrimage.

▶ **Lamego**
Romaria da Senhora dos Remédios; pilgrimage followed by a folklore festival, festive processions, sports.

▶ **Vila Praia de Âncora**
Festas da Senhora da Bonança; celebrations of the fishermen honouring their patron saints, processions and blessing of the boats; folk festival with folklore shows and fireworks.

▶ **Praia da Torreira**
Romaria de São Paio da Torreira (near Aveiro); traditional »sacred bath«, processions to the sea, blessing of the boats, folk festival, fireworks.

▶ **Ponte de Lima**
Feiras Novas e Festas da Senhora das Dores; funfairs, processions, folklore festival, procession in

local costume, fireworks on the Rio Lima.

► Nazaré
Romaria da Senhora da Nazaré; church consecration festival with impressive processions; typical local costumes of Nazaré are worn; celebration with folklore performances, a funfair, large fireworks, bullfighting.

► Castelejo
Romaria de Santa Luzia e Santa Eufémia; church consecration festival with folklore performances close to Castelo Branco.

► Elvas
Festas do Senhor Jesus das Piedade e Feira de São Mateus; one of the most typical festivals of the Alentejo; processions, folk festival, bullfighting.

► Palmela
Festas das Vindimas, folk festival for the wine harvest, bullfighting, fireworks.

► Several places on the Algarve:
Festival de Folclore do Algarve; folklore festival with groups from the mainland and from the islands, processions in local costume and fireworks.

► Moita
Festas da Senhora da Boa Viagem; impressive procession with blessing of the boats in Moita near Setúbal; bullfighting and large firework display.

► Viana do Alentejo
Romaria da Senhora de Aires; church consecration festival, bullfighting.

OCTOBER

► Fátima
12/13 October: final major pilgrimage to Fátima.

► Moura
Festa da Senhora do Monte do Carmo; processions and regional folklore performances close to Beja.

► Faro
Feira de Santa Iria; there are a number of events in the centre of Faro concurrent with the industrial fair.

NOVEMBER

► Penafiel
Feira de São Martinho; fair in Penafiel near Porto with regional specialities.

► Cartaxo
Feira dos Santos; fair in Cartaxo near Santarém, during which bullfighting also takes place.

► Golegã
Feira de São Martinho – Feira Nacional do Cavalo; livestock breeding fair close to Santarém, with contests on horseback in the accompanying programme.

DECEMBER

► Freamunde
Romaria de Santa Luzia e Feira dos Capões; church consecration festival and fair close to Porto.

← *Good Friday processions enjoy great popularity throughout the country.*

Food and Drink

Going out to eat occupies quite an important place in Portuguese life. For lunch (almoço) many Portuguese go to a favourite pub close to their place of work, for supper (jantar) they like to meet friends or acquaintances in a restaurant. Family festivities and birthdays are also often celebrated outside the home. Groups of people celebrating anniversaries are a common sight in local bars.

Cuisine Portuguese fare is generally plain and light, though not particularly varied. Fish and seafood lovers get their money's worth in Portugal. Those who enjoy vegetables and salad are often out of luck – salads should be ordered on the side. Sauces are virtually absent from Portuguese cuisine; fish is occasionally served with potatoes and melted butter.

i Price categories

- Expensive: over € 25/£ 17
- Moderate: € 10 – 25/£ 7 – 17
- Inexpensive: less than € 10/£ 7
  (price for a main course)

Breakfast Breakfast (pequeno almoço) is by no means the most important meal in everyday Portugal. Many Portuguese people breakfast in simple bars on the way to work. Hotels and guesthouses normally offer a breakfast that matches central European standards. The larger hotels offer a breakfast buffet and guesthouses provide coffee or tea with rolls and jam or cheese and cold meat.

Those that wish to have breakfast at a bar can order sandwiches or rolls (sanduíche) with cheese (com queijo) or ham (com fiambre), buttered toast (torrada) or a ham and cheese toasted sandwich (tosta mista).

Lunch and evening meal Both lunch and the evening meal normally consist of an appetizer, a main course and a dessert. The appetizer (entrada) is for the most part one of the superb Portuguese soups. The main course consists of a fish or meat dish with chips, potatoes or rice and perhaps some vegetables and salad. The meal is topped off by a final course (sobremesa) consisting of one of the delicious and often homemade sweet desserts (doces), ice cream or fruit. Bread and butter are usually served beforehand, sometimes with cheese or olives.

At times, small quantities of seafood are placed on the table in advance of the main meal. Though unrequested, it is necessary to bear in mind that such trifles must be paid for, and in the case of seafood that can increase the bill considerably.

After the meal After the meal it is customary in Portugal to partake of a small black coffee (bica) and a brandy (aguardente) or schnapps (bagaço).

High-class Portuguese cuisine – but vegetables on the side are otherwise something of a rarity in Portugal.

Those looking for **good, simple dishes typical of Portugal** are best advised to eat in plain and simple local restaurants, where the food is generally light and very fresh. Good, basic meals are also often served in the even simpler »tascas«. In tourist hotspots – on the Algarve or in Lisbon – there is always an ample selection of restaurants that often serve international cuisine, or rather a mixture of Portuguese and European dishes. The menu in such restaurants is usually written in several languages, including of course English.

Restaurants

The cafés in Portugal are something special. Quite modestly furnished, traditionally they function as a **meeting place** where people gather to discuss politics and football or just to have a chat. Others read the daily paper over a cup of coffee, study work documents or just watch the street outside. Outside the city centre, there are still cafés where exclusively women meet, and those which attract only men – a mixture of a café and a pub. If you wish to indulge in cake or small sweet buns, look out for cafés – even simple ones – bearing the sign »fábrico próprio« (homemade).

Cafés

Lunch is generally served between 12.30pm and 2pm, supper between 8pm and 10pm. Small hunger pangs in between can be staved off with a **snack** in the form of toasted sandwiches, sandwich rolls or typical Portuguese titbits such as »pastéis de bacalhau« (small balls of dried cod). Many Portuguese often have a quick cup of coffee while on the move as well.

Mealtimes

Portugal's Cuisine

Soups
Light and tasty, genuine Portuguese soups are virtually a must. »Caldo verde«, a cabbage soup with a slice of sausage (chouriço), could be described as the Portuguese national soup. The vegetable soup »sopa de legumes« is invariably simple and tasty. »Cozido à portuguesa« is a delicious vegetable stew with different types of meat, and the »caldeirada«, a rich fish soup, is cooked everywhere along the coast.

Meat dishes
One of the truly noteworthy creations of Portuguese cuisine is **»carne de porco à Alentejana«**, a pork dish with scallops from the Alentejo region. Suckling pig in Portugal is also delicious: just ask for **»leitão assado«**. The **»tripas à moda do Porto«** (tripe with white beans) is not to everybody's taste but typical for Porto; »linguiças« (smoked tongue sausages) are from Porto as well. »Presunto«, smoked ham, is excellent – especially from Chaves.

Fish dishes
Portugal's fish dishes are of course especially diverse, and marine creatures such as prawns, crayfish, crab and lobster are almost always

»Queijo da serra« from the Serra da Estrela is considered to be the best cheese in Portugal.

fresh and available at moderate prices. One of the **Portuguese national dishes** is **»bacalhau« (dried cod)**. It is prepared in numerous different ways – there are said to be 365 different recipes. »Bacalhau com
todos« is dried cod with various vegetables; »bacalhau à brás« is a
very tasty version of fried pieces of dried cod with onions, potatoes
and olives; and »bacalhau dourada« is fish cooked with tomatoes,
parsley, garlic and wine. Another national dish is **sardines**. During
the lunch hour and in the evening you often see »sardinhas assadas«
(fried sardines) being prepared on grills on front doorsteps. Those
ordering »arroz de lampreia«, a speciality of Minho, can expect to
get lamprey served on a bed of rice. In the Algarve »bife de atum«
(tuna steak) and **»cataplana«** – scallops, fish or meat, steamed with
bell peppers, onions and potatoes in a large copper pot – are often
on the menu.

Portugal has savoury cheeses galore: »queijo da serra« is a sheep's   *Cheese*
milk cheese from the Serra da Estrela; also on offer in many places is
»cabreiro«, a salty goat's cheese, and, especially around Pombal,
»rabaçal«, also a goat's cheese. Produced in the Azores, but also available on the Portuguese mainland is »queijo da ilha«, a spicy, hard
cheese. The small curd cheeses known as »queijinhos« are a speciality
of the region surrounding Tomar.

The Portuguese enjoy something sweet not just for dessert but in   *Desserts and*
between meals as well, and there are many pastry shops offering deli-   *cakes*
cious small cakes. One speciality of central Portugal is **»doce de
ovos«**, a sweet egg dish. In the Algarve they make a superb »bolo de
ovos e amêndoa« (marzipan cake). Dessert lovers should try »leite
creme«, a lightly caramelized concoction of sugar, egg and milk, or
»arroz doce«, an egg and rice pudding dusted with cinnamon. Another favourite is **»pudim flan«**, a caramel pudding, and »pudim Mo-
lotov« – essentially a mass of beaten eggs that melts on the tongue in
an instant. Many desserts were created in the monasteries in the 17th
and 18th centuries with the sugar delivered from the colonies –
which is why many of them ended up with such monasterial names
as »beijos de freiras« (nun's kisses), »toucinho do céu« (bacon from
heaven) or »barriga de freiras« (nun's belly).

Beverages

Coffee is served as »café« or »bica«, a small strong coffee, or as »ga-   *Coffee*
lão«, in a glass with milk. If you order »café com leite« you will normally get a coffee with warm milk in a cup. »Meia de leite« is served
with a little less milk – also in a cup. The freshly brewed »meia de
leite à máquina« (also served with milk) is often more aromatic.

International drinks such as cola and tonic water (água tónica) are   *Refreshing*
available as well as mineral water (água mineral), either carbonated   *beverages*

(com gás) or still (sem gás). There are also good fruit juices (sumo) though they are rarely freshly squeezed.

Beer Beer (cerveja) is a very popular drink in Portugal. The most common is Sagres, brewed near Lisbon; Sagres Boémia is a brown ale. Superbock is somewhat sweeter. If you order »cerveja« you will get a bottled beer, an »imperial« is a small draught beer, a »caneca« a large one.

Medronho The high alcohol spirit »medronho« is very widespread in the Algarve. It is made from the fruit of the arbutus, which grows primarily in southern Portugal. »Bagaço«, a schnapps, and **»aguardente velha«**(old brandy) are popular spirits. »Ginjinha«, a cherry liqueur that can be ordered with (com) or without (sem) cherries, is fairly sweet (▶ Baedeker tip, p.364). Unlike at home, glasses are mostly filled to the brim.

Wine

Ancient knowledge, modern methods A table wine (vinho da mesa) or house wine (vinho da casa) usually accompanies a meal. **»Vinho tinto«** is red wine and **»vinho branco«** white wine.

Portugal is one of the traditional wine-growing countries: Portugal's wine laws are the oldest in Europe, and the country has been exporting wine since the 15th century. In the past, the UK was the most important buyer of port wine, but now France has that distinction. Mateus rosé and Gatão, a vinho verde – wines that cannot be considered representative of Portugal – have been well known in Europe for a considerable time. The quality of Portuguese wine improved after the country's admission to the EC, when modern pressing methods prevailed. These days, **both tradition and the avant-garde** define wine-growing in Portugal. Some Portuguese wines are considered outstanding and others – like the wines from Alentejo – are a real insider's tip for connoisseurs.

Wine regions Bairrada, Dão and Douro, producing predominantly full-bodied red wines and palatable sweet wines, are ancient wine-growing regions from which good wines have hailed for years. Even in Ribatejo and Estremadura some good wines are produced – especially near Óbidos, Alcobaça, Torres Vedras and Santarém. A full, dark red wine is produced near Alpiarça in the Ribatejo in Quinta da Lagoalva; excellent red wines are made west of Lisbon, in Colares, Carcavelos and Bucelas. A good **dessert wine** made of muscatel grapes is produced close to **Setúbal**. A wine-growing region previously very seldom spoken of is the **Alentejo**. Bold red wines of high quality are made in cooperatives from Borba, Redondo and Reguengos. Even the quality of the Algarve wines, for a long time considered problematic and which were drunk only as table wines, is slowly improving.

Probably the best known table wine of Portugal, vinho verde comes from the area north and north-east of Porto – for the most part from the province of Minho. The term »verde« (green) does not refer to the colour – there are even red vinho verdes – but to the type of preparation: the grapes are harvested relatively early and only fermented for a short time, resulting in a light, acidic wine, which is further fermented in the bottle and develops a fresh, often lightly sparkling style, though this does not last long after opening. About 20% of the national wine production consists of »green« wines. An especially good vinho verde is produced from the Alvarinho grape in the region of Monção.

Vinho verde

Those wine varieties from which the famous port wine is made originate on the steep slopes on the upper reaches of the Douro, the **oldest wine-growing region defined by law in the world**. Marquês de Pombal first determined its borders in the Douro region in 1756 – nowadays the growing region is about twenty times its original size. The slatey soil imparts a distinctive taste to the wine. In addition, while slate is found everywhere else in the world in horizontal layers,

Port

Port – the famous wine is produced in the Douro Valley in northern Portugal.

it dips towards the centre of earth at an angle of 60–90 degrees in the upper Douro valley. During the day the rocks do not let the sunbeams pass too far into the ground, so that bacterial life can thrive in the moist soil. At night the slate radiates heat, warming the grapes.

Port – whose name is derived from the town Porto – is **produced from partially fermented red wine** that has been fortified with brandy (approx. three quarters partially fermented wine and one quarter brandy). The high alcohol content of brandy stops fermentation, resulting in a mixture which is both strong and contains rather a lot of sugar at the same time. The wine is transported to Vila Nova de Gaia near Porto for **storage**, and kept in barrels there for between two and fifty years. Wines aged in a barrel are as a rule blended wines: wines from different locations and of various vintages and grape varieties are harmoniously blended to bring about a specific standard quality. If the conditions for the port wine were ideal in a particular year, the port will qualify to be sold as **vintage port wine**. Vintage ports are transferred into bottles after two to three years; they then still require an average of fifteen years of ageing in the bottle. Vintage port wines are as a rule sweeter than blended ports aged in a wooden barrel – the port stored in barrels ages faster and looses some of its sugar content in the process.

For some years now, **white port** has been getting more attention. It is pressed from white grapes, but the storage time is shorter than for red port. There are sweeter and drier versions but at present the trend is towards dry and extra-dry white port.

While the dry port wines are for the most part drunk as an **aperitif**, the sweeter kinds have the best reputation as **dessert wines**. The Instituto do Vinho do Porto plays an important part in securing this reputation both by ensuring that the port wine laws are adhered to and also by conducting **regular quality checks**.

Madeira
The best known product of the island Madeira is the wine of the same name, which is enjoyed as an aperitif as well as a dessert wine. Just as with port, the characteristic taste is achieved by blending. The wine is heated to 50°C for four to five months and develops that special caramel flavour. Madeira is made from four different types of grapes: Malmsey, which is in many cases considered to be the best, as well as Bual, Verdelho and Sercial.

BASIC WINE VOCABULARY

quinta	country estate, winery
adega	cellar (usually company cellar)
colheita	vintage
»Denominação de Origem Controlada«	DOC; official term for the highest category of quality wines (like the »appellation d'origine contrôlée« in France)

região demarcada	area defined by law
reserva	wine of a higher quality; »reserva« is a distinction for specially stored and aged wines; white wine must be stored at least one year, red wine two years.
garrafeira	»bottle cellar«, a legendary term for top Portuguese wine, which is first aged in barrels for many years and then in bottles in a cellar
vinho verde	»green« or young wine; area designation for the very light red and white wines of the province of Minho
vinho da casa	house wine; popular term for a table wine of simple, but for the most part reliable quality
vinho de mesa	table wine; really the lowest category of Portuguese wines, though a whole series of the best Portuguese wines are labelled as such
vinho de consumo	simple wine
vinho rosé	rosé wine
vinho regional	superior table wine
maduro	old or aged
engarrafado na origem	estate bottled
branco	white
tinto	red
rosado	rosé
clarete	light red or dark rosé
seco	dry
doce adamado	sweet
espumante	sparkling wine
vintage	vintage port, bottled early for bottle fermentation
late bottled vintage	port wine, which was stored for up to six years in a barrel prior to bottling; somewhat lighter than vintage
ruby	relatively young port wine with a deep red colour, comparatively astringent
tawny	honey coloured, yellow-brown port wine (the light colour results from a longer period of barrel storage); lighter than vintage

Health

Medical Assistance

Hospitals Telephone numbers of hospitals (hospital, pl.: hospitais) and health centres (centro de saúde) can be found in the first pages of the telephone book or under »hospitais«. Most hospitals have a 24-hour emergency service. In urgent cases, go directly to the casualty department (urgência) of the nearest hospital. Staff at the hotel reception desk will also assist in case of illness. English is spoken in most hospitals; in any case there will at least be someone available to assist communication. There are health centres in many smaller locations, which are open during the day. Many English-speaking doctors and dentists practice in Portugal, particularly on the Algarve or other resorts; the embassies and consulates will be able to furnish particulars (► Information).

i **Emergency number**

■ **Tel. 112**
for emergency doctor
ambulance
police
fire brigade

■ Tel. 118
for informations on pharmacies
on duty after hours

Health insurance

Treatment on location normally has to be paid by the patient, so comprehensive health insurance is advised. A detailed invoice will be required by the insurer before reimbursing any costs. Generally it is advisable to take out additional insurance that will cover costs should transport to the home country be necessary.

For UK residents, the European Health Insurance Card (EHIC) entitles the holder to free or reduced cost state-provided medical treatment while visiting any country in the European Economic Area (EEA). The EHIC replaced the old E111 form in January 2006. It is available from post offices.

Pharmacies

Pharmacies (farmácias) supply foreign preparations alongside the **medication** produced in Portugal, and they are sometimes cheaper than in their country of manufacture.

The normal **opening hours** of pharmacies are Mon–Fri 9am–1pm and 3pm–7pm, Sat 9am–1pm. The addresses of pharmacies offering a **night-time and Sunday service** are listed on signs outside the shops. Information on pharmacies on duty after hours (farmácias de serviço) can also be obtained in the daily papers and at the tel. 118.

Information

▶ USEFUL ADDRESSES

IN THE UK

▶ **ICEP/Portuguese Trade and Tourism Office**
Portuguese Embassy
11 Belgrave Square
London SW1X 8PP
Tel. 0845 35512112 (brochure request and information service; local call rate)
Fax 020 7201 6633
www.visitportugal.com
www.imagesofportugal.com
www.portugal.org
info@visitportugal.com

IN THE USA

▶ **ICEP**
590 Fifth Avenue, 4th Floor
New York, NY 10036
Tel. 212 723 0200 99
Fax 212 764 6137
tourism@portugal.org
info@visitportugal.com

IN CANADA

▶ **ICEP**
60 Bloor Street W, Suite 1005
Toronto
Ontario M4W 3B8
Tel. 416 921 7376
Fax 416 921 1353
icep.toronto@iceptor.ca
info@visitportugal.com

IN AUSTRALIA

▶ **ICEP**
Suite 507/147 A King Street
Sydney, NSW 2000
Tel. 2 9221 9866
Fax 2 9221 0966
info@visitportugal.com

IN PORTUGAL

▶ **»turismo«**
There are tourist information centres (turismos) in all larger cities and some of the smaller towns that will provide information on the town and the surrounding region and at times even assist with the search for accommodation. The turismos opening hours vary from office to office; normal opening times are Mon–Fri 10am–1pm and 3pm–5pm.

▶ **Information by telephone**
Tel. 800 296 296

EMBASSIES AND CONSULATES IN PORTUGAL

▶ **British Embassy**
33 Rua de So Bernardo
P-1249-082 Lisbon
Tel. 21 392 4000
Fax 21 392 4185
ppalisbon@fco.gov.uk
www.uk-embassy.pt

▶ **Embassy of the United States of America**
Avenida das Foras Armadas
Sete Ríos
P-1600-081 Lisbon
Tel. 21 727 3300
Fax 21 726 9109 or 217 271 500 (consular section)
www.american-embassy.pt

▶ **Canadian Embassy**
Avenida da Liberdade 198-200
3rd floor

P-1269-121 Lisbon
Tel: 21 316 4600
Fax: 21 316 4692
http://geo.international.gc.ca/
canada-europa/portugal/

► **Australian Embassy**
Avenida da Liberdade, 200
2nd floor
P-1250-147 Lisbon

Tel. 21 310 1500
Fax 21 310 1555
www.portugal.embassy.gov.au

► **Irish Embassy**
Rua da Imprensa a Estrela 1-4
P-1200-684 Lisbon
Tel. 21 392 9440
Fax 21 397 7363

Language

Foreign languages The foreign languages that are understood and spoken in Portugal, besides Spanish, are most likely English or French. Visitors will not usually encounter any communication problems in hotels and larger restaurants. It is advisable however – even if only as a gesture to your hosts – to pick up a few words or simple phrases in Portuguese (Language courses s. p. 163).

? DID YOU KNOW …?

■ Portuguese is the seventh most frequently spoken language in the world. Outside Portugal it is spoken in Brazil along with some former Portuguese colonies in Africa.

Portuguese is of Romance origin and has also retained some of the earlier influences of Celtic, Germanic and Arabic periods. Written Portuguese can be quickly identified as a Romance language and, with the help of Latin and other Romanic languages, perhaps even be understood in parts.

Spoken Portuguese, however, generally poses difficulties: it sounds almost like a Slavonic language. The soft pronunciation, the stringing together of individual syllables, the many sibilants and the number of differently pronounced vowels are striking. Another feature is the strong stress on individual syllables, which frequently results in the swallowing of unstressed syllables.

Pronunciation The majority of Portuguese words are stressed on the penultimate syllable. Generally: if a word ends with the letter m, or s, or with the vowel a, e, or o, then the stress will be on the penultimate syllable. If a word ends with l, r, z or with an ã, i or u, then the last syllable will be stressed. Deviating stresses are marked with accents.

Accents (´ and ` as well as ^) also further determine the pronunciation of vowels. Vowels with a tilde (~) are nasalized.

The best way to learn a language is in everyday life, →
like when shopping in the Centro Colombo in Lisbon.

PORTUGUESE PHRASE BOOK

Pronunciation

a	unstressed like a whispered e
á	long a (ah)
c	before a, o and u like a k; before e and i like an s
ç	like s
ch	like sh
e	unstressed like a whispered i, virtually swallowed in the initial sound before s (»escudo« is pronounced »shkúhdu«; »Estoril«: »shturíu«)
ê	like a closed e (eh)
é	like an open e (äh)
g	before a, o and u like a g; before e and i like the French j in »journal«
gu	like g
h	is silent
i	after u nasalized («muito pronounce »muínto«)
j	like the French j in »journal«
l	like the English double -l in »hall«, like a soft u in the final sound
lh	like lj
m	nasalizes the preceding vowel in the final sound
n	nasalizes the preceding vowel in the final sound
nh	like nj
o	unstressed and like a u in the final sound
ô	like a closed o (oh)
ó	like the open o in »ostrich«
qu	like k
r	r on the tip of the tongue, strongly rolled r at the beginning of a word
rr	strongly rolled r
s	voiceless like s before vowels; between vowels vocalized like the s in »close« before hard consonants and in the final sound like a voiceless sh; before soft consonants like j in the French »journal«
v	like w
x	like sh
z	like the vocalized s in »close«; in the final sound like sh

At a glance

Yes/No	Sim/Não
Mrs.	Senhora
Mr.	Senhor
Maybe	Talvez
Please	Se faz favor
Thank you	Obrigado/Obrigada
You're welcome/My pleasure	De nada/Não tem de quê
I beg your pardon!/Excuse me!	Desculpe!/Desculpa!

All right/Okay!	Está bem/De acordo!
When?	Quando?
Where?	Onde?
What?	Que?
Who?	Quem?
I beg your pardon?	Como?
How much?	Quanto?
Where to?	Aonde? Para onde?
Where from?	Donde?
What time is it?	Que horas são?
I do not understand.	Não compreendo.
Do you speak English?	Fala Inglês?
Can you help me please?	Pode ajudar-me, se faz favor?
I would like …	Queria …
I (do not) like that.	(Não) Gosto disto.
Do you have …?	Tem …?
How much is it?	Quanto custa?

Getting aquainted

Good morning/day!	Bom dia!/Boa tarde!
Good evening!	Boa tarde!/Boa noite!
Hallo! Hallo!	Olá!
How are you?	Como está?
Thank you. And you?	Bem, obrigado/obrigada. E o senhor/a senhora/você/tu?
Goodbye!/Cheerio!/See you! See you next time!	Adeus!/Até logo!/Até à próxima!

On the road

left	ã esquerda
right	ã direita
top	em cima
bottom	em baixo
straight ahead	em frente
nearby	pert o
far	longe
How do I get to … please?	Se faz favor, onde está …?
How far is that?	Quantos quilómetros são?

Breakdown

My car has broken down.	Tenho uma avaria.

| Could you tow me to the next shop? | Pode rebocar-me até à oficina mais próxima? |
| Is there a shop close by? | Há alguma oficina aqui perto? |

Petrol station

Where is the next petrol station please?	Se faz favor, onde ésta a bomba de gasolina mais próxima?
I would like to get … litres …	Se faz favor … litros de …
…regular petrol	…gasolina normal
…super	…súper
…diesel	…gasóleo
…unleaded	…sem chumbo
…leaded	…com chumbo
…with …octane	…com …octanas
Fill her up, please.	Cheio, se faz favor.

Accident

Help!	Socorro!
Careful!	Atenção!!
Caution!	Cuidado!
Please call … quickly	Chame depressa …
…an ambulance.	…uma ambulância.
…the police.	…a polícia..
…the fire brigade.	…os bombeiros.
It was my/your fault.	A culpa foi minha/sua.
Please give me your name and address.	Pode dizer-me o seu nome e o seu endereço, se faz favor?

Dining out

Where can I find…	Pode dizer-me, se faz favor, onde há aqui …
…a good restaurant?	…um bom restaurante?
…a restaurant that is not too expensive?	…um restaurante não muito caro?
…a typical restaurant?	…um restaurante típico?
Is there a bar/a café nearby?	Há aqui um bar/um café?
I would like to reserve a table for four for this evening.	Pode reservar-nos para hoje à noite uma mesa para quatro pessoas, se faz favor?
Can you please give me…?	Pode-me dar…, se faz favor?
knife	faca
fork	garfo

All that's missing: toothpicks (palitos)...

spoon	colher
glass	copo
plate	prato
napkin	guardanapo
toothpick	palitos
salt	sal
pepper	pimenta
Here's to you! Cheers!	À sua saúde!
The bill, please.	A conta, se faz favor.
Did you enjoy your meal?	Estava bom?
The food was excellent.	A comida estava êcelente.

Accommodation

Can you recommend … please?	Se faz favor, pode recomendarme
…a good hotel	…um bom hotel?
…a guesthouse	…uma pensão?
Do you have any vacancies?	Ainda tem quartos livres?
a single room	um quarto individual
a twin room	um quarto de casal
a room with two beds	um quarto con duas camas
with a bath	com Casa de banho
… for one night.	…para uma noite.
… for one week.	…para uma semana.

Doctor

Can you recommend a doctor?	Pode indicar-me um médico?
I have pain here.	Dói-me aqui.

Bank

Where is the nearest …	Onde há aqui …
…bank?	…um banco?

Post office

stamp	selo
How much is …	Quanto custa …
…a letter …	…uma carta …
…a postcard …	…um postal …
to England?	para a Inglaterra?
Can I send a fax to… from here?	Posso mandar aqui um fax para…?

Numbers

0	zero
1	um, uma
2	dois, duas
3	três
4	quatro
5	cinco
6	seis
7	sete
8	oito
9	nove
10	dez
11	onze
12	doze
13	treze
14	catorze
15	quinze
16	dezasseis
17	dezassete
18	dezoito
19	dezanove
20	vinte
21	vinte e um

22	vinte e dois
30	trinta
40	quarenta
50	cinquenta
60	sessenta
70	setenta
80	oitenta
90	noventa
100	cem
101	cento e um
200	duzentos
1,000	mil
2,000	dois mil
10,000	dez mil
1/2	um meio
1/3	um terço
1/4	um quarto

Ementa/menu – Sopas/soups

Açorda	bread and garlic soup
Caldo verde	Portuguese cabbage soup
Sopa de legumes	vegetable soup
Sopa de peíe	fish soup
Sopa alentejana	garlic soup with egg

Entradas/appetizers

Amêijoas	cockles
Azeitonas	olives
Caracóis	snails
Espargos frios	cold asparagus
Melão com presunto	melon with smoked ham
Pão com manteiga	bread and butter
Salada de atum	tuna salad
Salada à portuguesa	mixed salad
Sardinhas em azeite	sardines in olive oil

Peíe e mariscos/fish and seafood

Amêijoas ao natural	cockles, boiled
Atum	tuna
Bacalhau com todos	dried cod with garnish
Bacalhau à Bráz	dried cod, chips, scrambled eggs

Caldeirada	fish stew
Camarão grelhado	grilled prawns
Cataplana	scallops, fish or meat, bell peppers, onions, potatoes
Dourada	gilthead bream
Ensopado de enguias	eel stew
Espadarte	swordfish
Filetes de cherne	silver perch fillets
Gambas na grelha	grilled prawns
Lagosta cozida	cooked crayfish
Linguado	sole
Lulas à sevilhana	baked squid
Mêilhões de cebolada	mussels with onions
Pargo	sea bream
Peixe espada	silver scabbard fish
Perca	perch
Pescada à portuguesa	Portuguese style haddock
Salmão	salmon
Sardinhas assadas	fried sardines

Carne e aves/meat and poultry

Bife à portuguesa	Portuguese beef steak
Bife de cebolada	steak with onions
Bife de peru	tuna steak
Cabrito	kid
Carne de porco à Alentejana	pork with cockles
Carne na grelha/Churrasco	meat from the (charcoal) grill
Coelho	rabbit
Costelata de cordeiro	lamb cutlet
Costeleta de porco	pork chop
Escalope de vitela	veal cutlet
Espetadas de carne	skewered meat
Fígado de vitela	calf's liver
Frango assado	fried chicken
Frango na pucara	chicken in a clay pot
Iscas	braised liver
Lebre	hare
Leitão assado	suckling pig roast
Lombo de carneiro	saddle of mutton
Pato	duck
Perdiz	partridge
Peru	turkey
Pimentões recheados	filled bell peppers
Porco assado	pork roast
Rins	kidneys
Tripas	tripe

Legumes/vegetables

Batatas	potatoes
Beringelas fritas	fried eggplant
Bróculos	broccoli
Cogumelos	mushrooms
Ervilhas	peas
Espargos	asparagus
Espinafres	spinach
Feijão verde	green beans
Pepinos	cucumbers

Sobremesa/dessert

Arroz doce	rice pudding
Compota de maçã	stewed apples
Gelado misto	mixed ice cream
Leite creme	butterscotch pudding
Maçã assada	baked appel
Pêra Helena	pear belle-hélène
Pudim flan	pudding with caramel sauce
Sorvete	sorbet
Tarte de amêndoa	almond tart

Lista de bebidas – list of beverages

Aguardente	schnapps
Aguardente de figos	fig brandy
Aguardente velho	aged brandy
Bagaço	pomace brandy
Ginjinha	cherry liqueur
Madeira	madeira wine
Medronho	brandy made with the fruit from the strawberry tree
Porto	port wine

Cerveja e vinho/beer and wine

Cerveja/Imperial	draught beer
Caneca	large draught beer
Vinho branco	white wine
Vinho tinto	red wine
Vinho Verde	light wine with natural acid

»A Bola«, Portugal's most popular newspaper for both active and passive sport lovers

Antonio Tabucchi: *Requiem: A Hallucination*, W W Norton & Co Ltd 2005 – Lisbon from the viewpoint of an Italian who has adopted Portugal as his home country.
The Missing Head of Damasceno Monteiro, dtv 1999 – A mystery, in which the GNR (Guarda Nacional Republicana) plays the lead.

Portuguese society

Mariana Isabel Barreno, Maria Teresa Horta, Maria Velho da Costa: *New Portuguese Letters*, Readers International 1994 – Essays, poems and letters exchanged by the »three Marias«, in which they discuss the importance of women in a society stamped by male values. Abortion, oppression and humiliation are among the subjects dealt with, and another Maria also plays a central role: the now famous Maria (Mariana) Alcoforado from Beja. Censored by the dictatorship, the book was nevertheless published abroad in various languages.

Illustrated book / Azulejos

Falcato J. Sabor: *Portuguese Decorative Tiles: Azulejos*, Abbeville Press Inc., US 1998 – This hardcover book provides beautiful illustrative material for those interested in Portugal's azulejos.

Media

Newspapers, magazines

English **daily newspapers and glossy magazines** are generally available in larger cities and holiday centres one or two days after publication. There are several Portuguese publications printed in English, such as the *Anglo-Portuguese News* and T*he Portugal News* newspapers, and the magazines *Essential Algarve* and *Portugal Magazine*. The **daily newspapers of Portugal** are the *Público* and the *Diário de Nóti-*

cias, which along with the day's news stories contain what's-on listings and useful addresses as well as telephone numbers of doctors, hospitals and pharmacies. The largest weekly paper is the *Expresso*, *A Bola* (the ball) is the most important Portuguese sports magazine and lists all current sporting events.

What's-on guides (agenda or agenda cultural) for the town or region can be found in tourist information centres and hotels.

The **BBC World Service** can be received on short wave or cable FM. *Radio*
Offering regular news bulletins as well as cultural and entertainment programmes, it broadcasts on 9410 kHz on the 31m waveband and on 6195 kHz on the 49m waveband. Full details can be found at www.bbc.co.uk/worldservice. Voice of America is also available on short wave.

Portuguese Television at present has four channels, the two effective- *Television*
ly state-owned stations RTP 1 and 2, and the private stations TVI and SIC. Foreign films are generally shown in the original language with subtitles.
Hotels and many guesthouses and cafés have satellite reception, and can therefore offer such channels as BBC World, CNBC Europe, CNN International, Euro News, MTV and Sky News.

Money

Portugal's official currency is the euro. At the time of going to press €1 is worth £0.68 or US$1.36. Current exchange rates are given at www.oanda.com. Any bank will exchange foreign currency. Cash can be obtained at **cash dispensers** which are found in all the larger towns. The machines are equipped with multilingual operating instructions. Money can be withdrawn from dispensers using all common credit cards, naturally using the corresponding PIN number.

Banks, major hotels, higher class restaurants, car rental companies as well as some retail shops will accept most international **credit cards**. Visa and Eurocard are widely used, American Express and Diners Club are used somewhat less frequently.

i Lost or stolen card?

- There is a number on the back of every credit card which should be called in the case of the card being lost or stolen – it is a good idea to make a note of this number as well as those given by the bank. Some emergency contact numbers are listed below:
- HSBC: tel. +44 (0) 1442 422 929
- Lloyds TSB Bank: tel. +44 (0) 1702 278 270
- Barclays Bank: tel. +44 (0)1904 544 666
- NatWest Bank: tel. +44 (0) 142 370 0545
- Citibank: tel. +44 (0) 207 500 5500
- MasterCard: tel. 0800 96 4767
- American Express: tel. +44 (0)1273 696 933

Museums

The most important museums are mentioned in »Sights from A to Z« under the respective location. In addition there are also numerous smaller museums of regional importance, often lovingly established with more modest means. They offer interesting insights into the nature, culture and way of life in a region and are therefore definitely worth a visit.

Opening hours
Most museums are open Tue–Sun from 10am–5pm, though many of them close at midday for one or two hours. All state-owned museums, and quite a few others, are closed on Mondays. However there are always exceptions to the rule: it is best to enquire at the local tourist information offices.

Free admission to museums
Some museums do not charge an entrance fee on Sunday mornings – mostly until 2pm, but sometimes even the whole of Sunday. This applies to the larger museums in particular.

Post and Communications

Telephone
Telephone calls within Portugal and abroad can be made from public call boxes, post offices and private telephone companies. In both the **post office** and with the **private telephone companies**, register the call at the counter first and pay afterwards. Either coins or a telephone card (cartão para telefonar) can be used in **public call boxes**; the

▶ INFORMATION AND DIALLING CODES

DIRECTORY ENQUIRIES
▶ **Tel. 118**
www.118.pt

DIALLING CODES
▶ **Dialling code to Portugal**
from the UK and Republic of Ireland:
Tel. 00 35 1
from the USA, Canada and Australia:
Tel. 00 11 35 1
The countrywide nine-digit telephone number follows the country code.

▶ **Dialling code from Portugal**
to the UK: tel. 00 44
to the Republic of Ireland: tel. 00 353
to the USA and Canada: tel. 00 1
to Australia: tel. 00 61
The 0 that precedes the subsequent local area code is omitted.

▶ **Phoning within Portugal (mobile)**
For telephone calls to numbers in Portugal, use the country code: tel. 00 35 1

card can be purchased at post offices or from telephone companies. Using a **mobile phone** that is not registered in Portugal requires dialling the country code of Portugal (+351 or 00 35 1) before entering the number of a participant in Portugal. Reception for mobiles is fine throughout the country.

Letters and postcards from southern Portugal to central Europe and the UK generally take three to four days by regular mail. Letters sent by the considerably more expensive express service »correio azul« will usually get to the UK within two days. **Stamps** (selos) can be purchased at the post office (correios) or in shops with the »CTT Selos« sign. The **postage** for letters up to 20g/0.7oz (cartas) and cards (postais) is €0.57 within Europe; for »correio azul« it is €1.75. **Letter boxes** for regular mail are red freestanding columns or red boxes on the walls of houses. The letter boxes for »correio azul« are blue. **Post offices** are generally open from Mon–Fri 9am–1.30pm and 2.30pm–6pm.

Post

Prices and Discounts

The days of exceptionally low-priced trips to Portugal are over. It is still possible in many parts of the country to find moderately priced accommodation and restaurants, but in the tourist hotspots and in Lisbon the prices are comparable to those in the UK. However there are still ways to plan for a fairly moderately priced holiday. Reasonable guesthouses are available that are neat and clean but do not

▶ WHAT DOES IT COST?

Double room
from 45 €

Simple meal
from 6 €

Train ticket from Lisbon to Porto
approx. 24 €

Beer on draught
approx. 1.50 €

1l petrol
approx. 1.38 €

A »bica«
approx. 0.55 €

offer any extras. It is a very good idea to be on the lookout for inexpensive restaurants – many simple bars provide good food at low prices. While the major museums and sights have strongly increased their entrance fees, the smaller museums are still moderately priced.

Public transport Public transport is not overly expensive, and the same applies to taxis. In Lisbon, a 1-day or 5-day ticket is very reasonably priced and can be used on almost all means of public transport (buses, trams, metro, lifts). Such tickets can be easily obtained at machines. Porto offers tickets for one or three days. Train travel is also very good value. There are special tourist tickets for 7, 14 or 21 days.

Tourist cards Those staying a little longer in Lisbon or Porto with a full itinerary are well advised to purchase a **Lisboa Card** for Lisbon or a **Passe Porto** for Porto. The cards allow use of almost all means of public transport (bus, tram, metro, lifts) as well as free or sharply reduced entry to various museums. Card holders also get a reduced rate for sightseeing tours and boat rides. In addition, holders of the **Lisboa Restaurant Card** – valid for three days for one or two persons or families (two adults and two children up to 14 years of age) – and the **Lisboa Shopping Card** receive a discount of up to 20% in number of restaurants and shops. The cards are sold in tourist information services, among other places.

Golden Age tariffs Old age pensioners (reformados) often receive a considerable discount in museums and for train tickets (50%) upon presentation of identification. Pousadas also grant special tariffs.

Shopping

Ceramics In Portugal many folk art products are used in everyday life – especially ceramics in various shapes and styles, depending on the region. The diversity of items ranges from darkish tableware to decorative pieces painted in vibrant colours. The gaily coloured Barcelos rooster, made of clay, is widely known and has become a symbol for the entire country (► Sights from A to Z, Barcelos).

Azulejos One special type of ceramics are the azulejos, colourfully painted glazed tiles whose origin dates back to the time of the Moors. Nowadays tourists are offered mostly off-the-shelf articles, though there are occasionally some very pretty pieces among them. Azulejos that bear old patterns can however be found in antique shops or junk shops (► Baedeker Special p.69).

Arraiolos rugs These colourful woollen rugs are woven using a cross-stitch like technique in Arraiolos in the Alentejo. They are on display in a shopping exhibition (in the Arraiolos town hall), but can also be purchased in other Alentejo towns, in particular Évora.

Beautiful lace is produced along the coast; in the heart of the country there are hand-woven fabrics and covers. Wood carvings, basketwork and wrought iron items can also be found.

Other arts and crafts

Chouriço, the spicy Portuguese sausage, makes a good souvenir as do the famous Pastéis de Belém – also called Bolo de Nata – which are packaged in small cardboard boxes on request. A bottle of vinho verde, red or white wine, a bottle of Ginjinha (a cherry liqueur that is typical for Lisbon and Obidos) or a bottle of Medronho (a brandy made of the fruit of the strawberry tree that is high in alcohol content) are also popular souvenirs which can be bought in the Algarve.

Culinary souvenirs

Port is another typical gift to bring back from Portugal. Although the best known brands are not particularly better priced in Portugal than elsewhere, the selection of different types and qualities of port is considerably better. A wine tasting is usually part of a guided tour

Port

One of the nicest markets in Portugal: the Mercado do Bolhão in Porto

● MARKETS

LISBON

▶ **Feira da Lada**
Campo de Santa Clara
Curios, antiques, junk and assorted odds and ends change hands at the famous »thieves' market«, highly frequented by tourists and Lisbonites alike; Tue, Sat 9am–6pm

▶ **Rua de São Pedro**
(in the Alfama)
Bustling open-air fish market in a narrow lane in the Alfama district. Mon–Sat before noon.

PORTO

▶ **Mercado do Bolhão**
Entrances: Rua de Fernandes Tomas and Rua Formosa
A beautiful, colourful market in an old open market hall with gallery walkways.
Mon–Fri 8am–5pm,
Sat 8am–1pm

through the port lodges of Vila Nova de Gaia (▶ Sights from A to Z, Porto). Afterwards there is generally a chance to purchase bottles directly from the port lodge. In the Douro Valley it is even possible to buy port directly from the grower.

Music Fado recordings on CD or cassette, offered at low prices at the weekly markets, are a musical reminder of a holiday in Portugal. Really good fadois really only to be had in specialist shops though. The historical recordings of Alfredo Marceneiro or Carlos Ramos with the famous Portuguese »fadista« Amália Rodrigues are now available and are highly recommended. The purely instrumental fado of Rão Kyāo (flute and saxophone), Carlos Paredesand Pedro Caldeira Cabral is also interesting. The group Madredeus incorporates elements of Portuguese folk music and is known all over the world. The music of the legendary José Afonso is also very popular. Dulce Pontes interprets traditional fado and Portuguese folk music. Newer fado recording artists include Mísia, Mariza, Mafalda Arnauth, Cristina Branco and Camané. The internationally famous Portuguese jazz singer Maria João was also inspired by fado at times.

Markets

Covered markets The larger cities in Portugal usually have a covered market (mercado) that is open from Monday to Saturday in the mornings. Here, fruit, vegetables, fish and meat are available; there are often simple textile goods and sometimes household items, too.

Weekly markets There is one weekly market in almost every smaller town; some stalls sell fruit and vegetables on other days of the week.

Country markets, held regularly on specific weekdays once or twice a month mostly on the edge of town, are also well worth a visit. Food, clothes and other textiles on a large scale, household items, music cassettes, plants and sometimes even live animals – chicks, chicken, sheep and cattle – are sold here. Finally there are the special markets that are held once a week in the larger cities such as coin markets, plant markets or bird markets. Local tourist information services will be able to provide details on when markets take place.

Country markets

Sport, Outdoors and Language Courses

Sports

Anglers have various opportunities to fish in Portugal. The fishing grounds are rich near the coast as well as in rivers and lakes further inland. The region around Sagres (Algarve) is a good **sea angling area**. Licences and fees do not apply to sea angling, unless the sport is carried out professionally. It is possible to charter boats for angling trips, especially in Vilamoura, Portimão and Lagos. Anglers can even fish from the coast with long rods. Fishing in creeks and lakes requires a permit (the tourist information centres will furnish particulars).

Angling, sea angling

▶Beaches

Swimming

Golf has been played in Portugal since 1890, when the Oporto Golf Club was founded – the **second course in Europe**. In the Algarve, the stronghold of golf, Penina was the first larger course built in the sixties, designed by the British golf legend Sir Henry Cotton. In the meantime Portugal boasts more than 60 golf courses with varying levels of difficulty, and the number is still rising. There are approximately 20 courses in the broad vicinity of Lisbon, while golfers in the Algarve can choose from 33 courses.

Golf

The Algarve and the region surrounding Lisbon are especially good for horse riding. Most riding stables give riding courses but you can also just take a few lessons.

Riding holidays

In many coastal towns the sailing clubs rent out boats and offer beginner's and advanced sailing courses. Alongside Vilamoura (Algarve), probably the most beautiful marina with the best amenities, there are many smaller harbours and anchoring berths along the Portuguese coast. The **Algarve** is recommended for sailors, in particular Albufeira, Armação de Pêra, Alvor, Lagos, Monte Gordo, Porti-

Sailing

◉ ADDRESSES FOR SPORTING HOLIDAYMAKERS

GOLF

▶ **www.portugalgolf.net**
Everything concerning golfing
holidays incl. hotels, etc.

▶ **www.portugalgolf.pt**
Lists almost all golf courses in
Portugal with detailed informa-
tion.

HORSE RIDING

▶ **Albufeira region**
Centro Hípico Vale Navio
Estrada da Branqueira
Tel. 289 542 870

▶ **Aljezur region**
Estância Equestre Herdade do
Beiçudo
Vilarinha – Carrapateira
Tel. 967 095 937(mobile)

▶ **Lagoa region**
Casa Agrícola Solear
Areias das Almas
Tel. 282 381 444
Fax 282 381 440

▶ **Lagos region**
Happy Horse
Sítio da Carrasqueira – Barão de
São João
Tel. 282 688 245

▶ **Loulé region**
Centro Hípico Pinetrees
Almancil
(between Quinta do Lago and Vale
do Lobo)
Tel. 289 394 369

▶ **Portimão region**
Centro Hípico do Meridien Golf
Penina
Montes de Alvor
Tel. 282 415 415

▶ **Tavira region**
Quinta do Caracol
Tel. 281 323 175

SAILING

▶ **Quima Yachting**
Castelo da Nave
8550-244 Monchique
Tel. 282 912 993
www.quima-yachting.com

SURFING

▶ **Escola Windsurf**
Estrada da Meia Praia Bairro 1º de
Maio 4
8600 Lagos
Tel. 282 792 315
www.windsurfpoint.com

▶ **Centro de Desportos Aquáticos**
Quinta do Lago
8100 Loulé
Tel. 289 394 929

DIVING

▶ **In Extremis**
Faro, Av. Almeida Carrapato
bloco b – r/c esq.
Tel./fax 289 807 197
www.netonet.net/inextremis

▶ **Lagos – Sub**
Lagos, Estrada de Sopro Mar
Estaleiro Naval 1
Tel./fax 282 782 718
lagos-sub@hotmail.com

▶ **Portitours –
Emoção e aventura**
Portimão, Alto do Quintão
Tel. 282 470 063
www.portitours.pt

▶ **Centro de Mergulho do
Sudoeste Algarvio**
Edifício Tempomar – Burgau –

Budens, Vila do Bispo
Tel. 282 697 290, fax 282 697 281
tempomar@mail.telepac.pt

TENNIS

► **Carcavelos Ténis**
Parede (near Lisbon) Quinta do
Junqueiro
Tel. 214 563 668

► **Club Internacional de Ténis**
Lisbon, R. Prof. S. Câmara 95
Tel. 213 882 084

► **Clube de Ténis do Estoril**
Estoril, Av. Amaral
Tel. 214 681 675

HIKING

► **Hiking in the eastern Algarve**
Odiana
Information on developed hiking
trails:

Castro Marim Rua 25 de Abril 1
Tel. 281 531 171
odiana@mail.telepac.pt

► **Turinfo**
Town centre in Sagres
Tel. 282 620 000

► **Overview of hiking in Portugal**
Pili Pala Press
www.pilipalapress.com

SURFING

► **Surfing school**
Praia do Amado Carrapateira,
Algarve

YACHT HARBOURS AND MARINAS

► **Marina Viana do Castelo**
www.ipnorte.pt

mão, Praia da Falésia, Praia da Oura, Praia da Rocha, Quinta do Lago, Olhão, Tavira, Vale do Lobo and Vilamoura. Cascais and Estoril near **Lisbon** also offer good sailing possibilities, as does Sesimbra or, further north, Póvoa de Varzim and Viana do Castelo.

Experienced surfers meet on the beach of Costa da Caparica south of   Surfing
Lisbon. The beaches of the Costa Vicentina in the western **Algarve** with their strong surf are also suited for windsurfing or surfing. There is a school in Praia do Amado near Carrapateira.

Divers bringing their own equipment will find beautiful beaches and   Diving
almost untouched diving grounds in the south-west region of the Algarve around Sagres, on the Costa Verde and on the Costa de Prata. Those wishing to take lessons or rent out equipment must stick to the **Algarve**. Its diving centres include Albufeira, Alvor, Lagos, Monte Gordo, Praia da Falésia and Vilamoura. The most interesting diving grounds are at depths of between 5 and 30m (16 and 98ft), also giving **snorkellers** a chance to experience the wonderful underwater world.

Most major hotels and many pousadas offer tennis courts, many of   Tennis
which are equipped with floodlights. Besides this, there are also pub-

lic tennis facilities or tennis centres managed by coaches: one of the best is the Roger Taylor Tennis Centre in Vale do Lobo (Algarve). In addition to the Algarve, primarily the area around Cascais and Estoril is excellently equipped with tennis courts, where the players play mostly on sand.

Hiking

Hiking in Portugal is getting more and more popular. Some travel agents offer **hiking holidays** in the Algarve – especially in the ▸ Serra de Monchique. For **tourists who want to escape the masses** the trails of the ▸ Peneda Gerês National Park are also ideal for walking trips. In the eastern Algarve the organization »Odiana« has developed 19 circular hiking trails, and offers special information on flora, fauna, irrigation systems, traditional architecture and so on. Information brochures on the individual routes are available at the Odiana office in Castro Marim.

Water skiing

It is possible to hire water skiing equipment and take lessons in Cascais and Estoril, Sesimbra, the major tourist hotspots of the Algarve and on the Costa Verde in Ofir, Vila do Conde and Póvoa de Varzim.

Wind surfing

The protected bays on the Algarve offer ideal conditions for wind surfing beginners. Wind surfing classes and rental boards are available on numerous beaches of the Algarve. Good conditions for the

Kite surfing – possible on many Portuguese beaches at low tide

sport can be found on the middle and western Algarve coast roughly between Quinta do Lago and Sagres, but wind surfing is also gaining popularity on the beaches along Estoril's coast. The beach of Carcavelos is ideal for beginners, while the beach of Guincho – like the beaches further south and north on the open coast – is a challenge for experts.

Language Courses

Various institutes in Lisbon, Porto, Coimbra and the Algarve offer Portuguese language courses. There are beginner's as well advanced classes which usually last two to four weeks. University courses last

▶ LANGUAGE SCHOOLS

ALGARVE

▶ **Faro**
CIAL
Rua Almeida Garrett 44
Tel. 289 807 611; fax 289 803 154

▶ **Lagos**
Centro de Línguas de Lagos
Rua Dr. Joaquim Tello 32-1 Esq.
Tel. 282 761 070

▶ **Portimão**
CLCC – Centro de Língua,
Cultura e Comunicação
Rua D. Maria Luísa 122
Tel. 282 430 250

COIMBRA

▶ **Universidade de Coimbra**
Faculdade de Letras
3004-530 Coimbra
Tel. 239 859 991/43
Fax 239 825 991
www.fl.uc.pt

▶ **Cambridge School**
Pr. Da República, 15
3000-343 Coimbra
Tel: 239 834 969, 239 829 285
Fax: 239 833 916
info@cambridge.pt

LISBON

▶ **Universidade de Lisboa**
Faculdade de Letras
Alameda da Universidade
1600-214 Lisboa
Tel. 217 920 001; fax 217 960 063
www.fl.ul.pt

▶ **Cambridge School**
Avenida da Liberdade 173
1250-141 Lisboa
Tel. 213 124 600; fax 213 534 729
www.cambridge.pt

▶ **CIAL – Centro de Línguas**
Avenida da República 41-8°
1050-187 Lisboa; tel. 217 940 448

PORTO

▶ **Universidade do Porto**
Faculdade de Letras
Via panorâmica
4150-564 Porto
Tel. 226 077 100; fax 226 077 153
www.letras.up.pt

▶ **Cambridge School**
Rua Duque da Terceira 381
4000-537 Porto
Tel. 225 360 380; fax 225 102 652
www.cambridge.pt

one term. Some courses include a supporting programme; others are targeted specifically at business people. Travel agencies also offer special language-learning holidays. The following is a selection of language schools.

Time

Western European Time applies in Portugal, which is the same as Greenwich Mean Time. From the end of March to the end of October, Western European Summer Time applies, the same as British Summer Time.

Transport

By Car

The Portuguese **road network** is well developed. Besides country roads there are many expressways (IC) which have two or three lanes and are at times not unlike motorways. The motorway network (A or IP) is well constructed and still being expanded.

While drivers can make swift progress even on the **national roads** in the sparsely populated south of the country, it is unwise to plan for average speeds higher than 25mph/40kmh in the mountainous regions of the north. The roads here are extremely winding and opportunities to overtake few and far between.

i Beware: »via verde«

- On no account use a »via verde«, a lane at the toll gate labelled with a green »V« (»reservado a aderentes«), located for the most part on the far left. These lanes are for long-term users only and their use can result in considerable fines for other drivers.

Tolls are usually charged on **motorways**, but as a rule they are free of traffic and very pleasant to use. Drivers collect a ticket (»retire o título«) at the so-called **»porta-gem«**, the entry point to the motorway. A charge must be paid at the exit according to the distance travelled.

Those wishing to explore the country on minor roads should bring along a good **road map** as the signage in smaller places is at times inadequate: the road map of the Portuguese automobile club (ACP) is re-edited every two years. Apart from that, use maps for the individual regions.

Generally speaking, driving a car in Portugal can be nerve-racking. Many Portuguese drive at high speeds and often with little consideration for other road users. **Excessive speeding** and **risky overtaking manoeuvres** are par for the course. Portugal consistently records the highest number of fatal road accidents per head of population in the EU; the UK has one of the lowest.

There is a fairly dense network of petrol stations in Portugal – at least near the main roads –though it may be a little difficult to get petrol away from tourist hotspots at night.

Petrol station network

In **Lisbon** and **Porto** visitors are best advised to abandon the car, apart from at weekends. The cities are hopelessly congested during the week and finding a place to park can be a real problem. Even driving in smaller towns in the country is not particularly enjoyable during the rush hour, and parking is often difficult.

City traffic

The traffic regulations generally do not differ much from those in central Europe. The keep right rule applies and traffic signs comply with international standards. As a rule, drivers who have been in possession of their licence for less than a year are not allowed to drive faster than 56mph/90kmh on roads outside towns and cities; they must affix the corresponding sticker of the Portuguese Automobile Club (ACP) to their car. The international green insurance card must be presented in the event of damage. If the driver of the car is not also the owner then he or she may need a notarized power of attorney from the owner of the vehicle. A warning vest must be in the car. Vehicle inspections and speed checks are generally fairly frequent in Portugal. The **speed limit** for passenger cars and motorcycles is 31mph/50kmh within built-up areas and 56mph/90kmh outside towns. The speed limit on expressways is 63mph/100kmh, on motorways 75mph/120kmh. For vehicles with trailers, the speed limit is around 44mph/70kmh outside towns, and around 50mph/80kmh on motorways. The minimum speed on motorways is 25mph/40kmh. Traffic on the right has

Traffic regulations

> ### ℹ️ Good to know
>
> - Mobile phones may only be used with a hands-free kit while driving.
> - The drink-drive limit is 0.5mg/ml. Drivers who get caught with higher levels can expect stiff penalties.
> - There is a general requirement to wear a seat belt.
> - A warning vest must be in the car, which is to be worn when leaving the vehicle in the case of a breakdown.

right of way on smaller roads which are not specially marked. Main roads with priority are marked by a yellow diamond. Smaller priority roads are for the most part not signposted as such, but the roads merging in will have a stop sign. Motorized road users always have the right of way over non-motorized users.

Car rental

Persons under 21 years of age are not permitted to rent a car in Portugal. Those wishing to rent a car must have been in possession of a driving licence for at least one year. The international car rental companies are spread all over Portugal and have branch offices in many towns. A rental car of the lowest category will cost at least €150/£100 per week; at times, Portuguese car rental firms undercut the price of the international companies considerably.

By Taxi

Taking a taxi in Portugal is fairly reasonably priced. Most taxis are ivory coloured but the old black taxis with a green roof are still sometimes in service. The vehicles are equipped with a taximeter, and outside cities there are fixed tariffs that passengers can enquire about beforehand. Up to 50% higher fees often apply for journeys at night or for carrying baggage. There will frequently be an extra charge for an empty run in the case of longer drives overland. Passengers should negotiate a special tariff beforehand for pleasure trips. A taxi ride from Faro to Albufeira (approx. 36km/23mi) costs about €40/£27. It is customary to give a tip of 10%.

By Bus or Coach

Since the rail network is not particularly dense, buses are the means of travel of choice for journeys inside Portugal. Long distance buses, the so-called **expressos**, go further afield; they are relatively speedy, comfortable and very reasonably priced. Various companies offer bus rides in often very comfortable vehicles. Tickets should be purchased in advance, especially if travelling at weekends. Unlike many train stations, the **bus stations** (Estação Rodoviária) are normally centrally located. Larger cities have several bus stations that operate with different bus companies. In some regions, special **tourist passes** (passe turístico) are available; tourist information services or bus stations can provide details.

By Rail

In Portugal the railways are operated by the half state-owned company Companhia dos Caminhos de Ferro Portugueses (CP). Services consist of **Regionais** (regional trains), **Interregionais** (inter-regional trains), **Intercidades** (inter-city trains) and the fast **Alfa Pendular**, which takes about three hours to get from Lisbon to Porto.

The rail network is not very dense outside Lisbon and Porto and many routes have been shut down. The railway lines often go through beautiful remote areas, and this is a major reason for the charm of travelling by train in Portugal.

Prices for train tickets are comparatively modest in Portugal. Children under four years of age do not need a ticket, children between four and twelve years of age pay half-fare, as do senior citizens of 65 and older on presentation of identification. A tourist card allows the

Elevador da Bica – one of three cable railways in Lisbon

use of the entire Portuguese railway network and is valid for one, two or three weeks. The tourist information offices (► Information) or the information desk at the train station will provide further details; additional information at www.cp.pt, tel. 808 208 208)

By Air

There are international airports in Lisbon, Porto and Faro. TAP (Air Portugal) and Portugália operate scheduled flights within Portugal: propeller-driven aircraft regularly head for Lisbon, Porto, Chaves, Bragança, Vila Real, Viseu, Covilhã, Coimbra, Faro and Portimão. Air fares are generally fairly reasonable, provided the tickets are purchased in Portugal.

Public Transport in the Cities

The cities mainly rely on bus services. In Lisbon and Porto there is also an underground and a tram system, though Porto's tram service is limited. Lisbon's underground train system (metro) has four lines; it is still under construction. The public transport system in Lisbon also includes funiculars or »elevadores«, as well as a large lift (closed at present), which help bridge the differences in altitude in the city. Tickets for buses and trams are available directly from the drivers or from machines; sometimes there are ticket machines in the vehicle itself. For the underground a ticket must be purchased at the window or from a ticket machine in the station.

● USEFUL ADDRESSES

AUTOMOBILE CLUB

► **ACP (Automóvel Club de Portugal)**
Rua Rosa Araújo 24
P-1250-195 Lisboa
Tel. 213 138 110
www.acp.pt

There are additional branch offices are in Aveiro, Braga, Bragança, Castelo Branco, Coimbra, Estoril, Évora, Faro, Figueira da Foz, Guarda, Leiria, Porto, Setúbal, Vila Real and Viseu.

► **ACP breakdown service**
Tel. 707 509 510
Help can be summoned from the orange SOS telephone on the motorways. There may be reciprocal arrangements with garages and institutions in Portugal for members of the AA or RAC in the UK. Check with the association before departure.

► **Additional emergency telephone numbers**
►Emergency services

CAR RENTAL

► **Avis**
Reservations in UK:
Tel. 0844 581 0147
www.avis.com

► **Europcar**
Reservations in UK:
Tel. 0845 758 5375
Reservations in Portugal:
Tel. 21 940 77 90
www.europcar.com

► **Hertz**
Reservations in UK:
Tel. 08708 44 88 44
www.hertz.com

► **Auto Jardim**
Tel. 800 200 613
dep.reservas@auto-jardim.com
www.auto-jardim.com

► **Other national providers**
Local tourist information services will be able to provide details on smaller national providers.

BY RAIL

► **Caminhos de Ferro Portugueses**
Tel. 808 208 208
www.cp.pt

BY BUS OR COACH

► **Rede Nacional de Expressos**
www.rede-expressos.pt

BY AIR

► **Faro airport**
Tel. 289 800 800

► **Lisbon airport**
Tel. 218 413 500

► **Porto airport**
Tel. 229 432 400

► **Internet**
www.ana-aeroportos.pt

Travellers with Disabilities

Travelling in Portugal is not always easy for tourists with physical disabilities. Airports, larger train stations, modern hotels and the most important museums and sights are for the most part equipped to allow the disabled visitor access in relative comfort. ICEP offices (► Information) or local tourism offices will be able to provide general information.

USEFULL ADRESSES

► **RADAR (UK)**
12 City Forum
250 City Road
London EC1V 8AF
Tel. 020 7250 3222
Fax: 020 7250 0212
www.radar.org.uk

► **Mobility International USA**
132 E. Broadway, Suite 343
Eugene, Oregon USA 97401
Tel. Tel: (541) 343-1284
Fax: (541) 343-6812
www.miusa.org

► **MossRehab ResourceNet**
MossRehab Hospital
1200 West Tabor Road
Philadelphia, PA USA
Tel. 215 456 9900
www.mossresourcenet.org

► **Accessible Travel (UK)**
Avionics House
Naas Lane
Quedgeley
Gloucester GL2 2SN
Tel. 01452 729 739
Fax 01452 729853
www.accessibletravel.co.uk

Wellness • Spas

Toward the end of the 19th century Portugal boasted the most elegant European spas with high-class bathing facilities, casinos, exclusive hotels and restaurants. The tradition persists to this day and there are more than 40 Portuguese spas. Especially during the summer, more than 150,000 people visit the spas to take one to two week cures. Though many baths are by now somewhat less elegant than at the end of the 19th century, a good number have been able to maintain some of their turn of the century charm. Exclusive hotels are also to be found in some spas. Many have tried to keep up with the times and also offer more modern wellness packages.

Tradition

● A SELECTION OF SPAS

► **Caldas da Rainha**
Indications: rheumatism, respiratory problems, gynaecological disorders

► **Caldas de Chaves**
Indications: gastro-intestinal, liver, rheumatism and metabolism

► **Caldas de Manteigas**
Indications: rheumatism

► **Caldas de Monchique**
www.monchiquetermas.com
Indications: gastro-intestinal, liver, rheumatism and respiratory problems

► **Caldas de Vizela**
Indications: rheumatism, skin, respiratory problems and gynaecological disorders

► **Caldas do Gerês**
Indications: liver, diabetes

► **Curia**
Indications: kidneys and urinary passages, rheumatism

► **Luso**
Indications: kidneys, urinary passages, rheumatism, skin, cardiovascular system

► **Melgaço**
Indications: diabetes

► **Monção**
Indications: rheumatism, respiratory problems

► **Pedras Salgadas**
Indications: gastro-intestinal, liver

► **Termas de Monte Real**
Indications: gastro-intestinal, liver

► **Termas de São Pedro do Sul**
Indications: rheumatism, skin, airways, gynaecological disorders

► **Vidago**
Indications: gastro-intestinal, liver, metabolism

► **Vimeiro**
Indications: gastro-intestinal, liver, skin

When to go

2,500 to 3,000 hours of sunshine per year, warm summers and mild winters – those are the basic statistics for Portugal's climate. Thanks to the Atlantic Ocean, the country enjoys maritime temperate climatic conditions with ample rainfall in the north and in the mountains. All parts of the country have the Mediterranean dry summers in common; they last two months in northern Portugal and five to six months on the coast of the Algarve. The radiant weather is due to the Azores High, a semi-permanent anticyclonic region with consistent high pressure which moves according to the position of the sun.

In its northern summer position it keeps the Atlantic lows away from Portugal, and as it moves south as of September weather fronts carry rain first to the north, and then in October down to the Algarve as well. Rainfall and cloud cover generally decrease moving from the north-west to the south-east, while temperatures and hours of sunshine increase.

The best seasons to undertake a round trip through Portugal, to stay on the southern coast or to visit places of cultural interest in Lisbon are **spring and autumn**. At the height of summer, round trips should be restricted to the interior of the north of the country. The south is best explored in May and September: June, July and August are too hot for drives through the Alentejo.

Round trips, cultural visits

Those planning a holiday by the sea should go in the **height of summer** – even if the beaches around Lisbon and the smaller bays of the Algarve can get crowded in August, which is the main tourist season of the Portuguese.

Seaside holidays

3,000 hours of sunshine in the Algarve – in the summer, fine weather is guaranteed.

Portugal *Typical Regional Weather Stations*

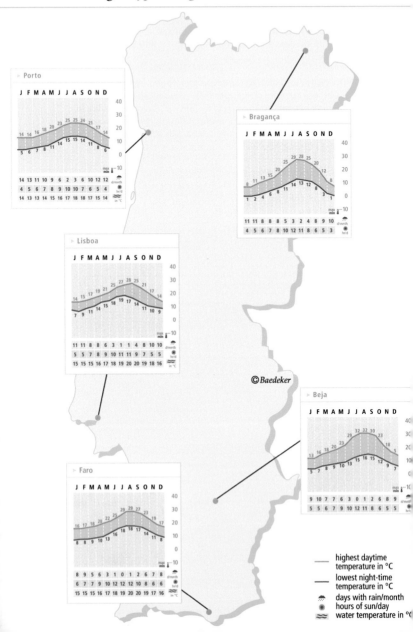

©Baedeker

Legend:

— highest daytime temperature in °C
— lowest night-time temperature in °C
☂ days with rain/month
☀ hours of sun/day
≈ water temperature in °C

July and August are definitely the best months to visit the **northern Atlantic coast**. Constant strong winds ensure that it never gets too hot. North of Lisbon the enjoyment of the beach may be dampened slightly by the low water temperature (max. 18°C/64°F) and the frequent haze on the coast.

A stay on the **Algarve** at the height of summer can actually be tolerable, as the maximum temperature seldom exceeds 30°C/86°F even here. It often rains in May and June and then gets very dry. The water temperature on the eastern Algarve (Tavira) is roughly 1°C higher than on the western Algarve (Sagres). In spring and autumn the weather on the Algarve is usually pleasantly warm and quite consistent, though rain is possible. An autumn holiday should be scheduled to end by the middle of October even in southern Portugal; good weather after this is a matter of luck.

Tours

FOUR TOURS THROUGH
PORTUGAL WITH SOMETHING FOR EVERYONE:
THROUGH THE SUNNY SOUTH, IN THE MOUN-
TAINOUS NORTH OR AROUND THE CULTURAL SITES
OF CENTRAL PORTUGAL. THOSE WITH PLENTY OF
TIME CAN GET TO KNOW THE ENTIRE COUNTRY IN
THE GREAT PORTUGAL ROUND TRIP.

TOURS THROUGH PORTUGAL

The beauty of Portugal can be discovered little by little on one of these four tours. Three tours take you to very different regions: the sunny and warm south, the green and mountainous north, and central Portugal with its cultural riches. The fourth route will take those with lots of time and wishing to discover all of Portugal through the entire country.

▬▬▬ TOUR 1 **Recreation and sightseeing in southern Portugal**
The touristy Algarve with its marvellous beaches, the sparsely populated wide open spaces of the Alentejo with a few scattered snow-white villages, and as a contrast the beautiful metropolis of Lisbon with its unique atmosphere and numerous sights. ► **page 180**

▬▬▬ TOUR 2 **Arts and culture: through central Portugal**
Time-honoured monasteries and castles, remarkable villages in the middle of nowhere and two beautiful cities: the provincial capital Lisbon and Évora, the rural centre of the Alentejo. ► **page 183**

▬▬▬ TOUR 3 **Northern Portugal – unspoilt countryside and two cities steeped in history**
A journey through regions reminiscent of central Europe, with vineyards and low, wooded mountain ranges, and remote villages in the far north-east that foreigners hardly ever come across. Both the port city of Porto and the old university city of Coimbra are interesting and lively destinations. ► **page 185**

▬▬▬ TOUR 4 **The great Portugal round trip in four weeks**
For those wishing to discover more: this peaceful journey through Portugal is an easy way to discover the entire scenic and cultural spectrum of the country. ► **page 188**

Lisbon
»White city«
on the Tagus

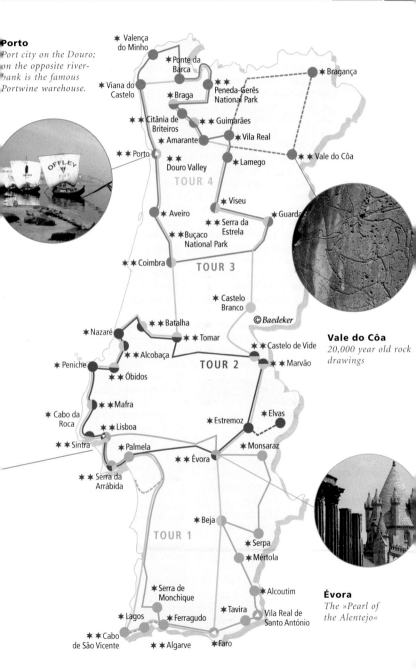

Porto
*Port city on the Douro;
on the opposite river-
bank is the famous
Portwine warehouse.*

★ Valença
do Minho

★ Ponte da
Barca

★ ★ Bragança

★ Viana do
Castelo

★ Braga

★ ★
Peneda-Gerês
National Park

★ ★ Citânia de
Briteiros

★ ★ Guimarães

★ ★ Porto

★ Amarante

★ Vila Real

★ ★
Douro Valley

TOUR 4

★ Lamego

★ ★ Vale do Côa

★ Viseu

★ Aveiro

★ ★ Serra da
Estrela

★ Guarda

★ ★ Buçaco
National Park

★ ★ Coimbra

TOUR 3

★ Castelo
Branco

© *Baedeker*

Vale do Côa
*20,000 year old rock
drawings*

★ ★ Batalha

★ Nazaré

★ ★ Tomar

★ ★ Castelo de Vide

★ ★ Alcobaça

★ Marvão

★ Peniche

TOUR 2

★ ★ Óbidos

★ ★ Mafra

★ Elvas

★ Cabo da
Roca

★ ★ Lisboa

★ Estremoz

★ ★ Sintra

★ Palmela

★ Monsaraz

★ ★ Évora

★ ★ Serra da
Arrábida

★ Beja

TOUR 1

★ Serpa

★ Mértola

★ Serra de
Monchique

★ Alcoutim

★ Lagos

★ Ferragudo

★ Tavira

Vila Real de
Santo António

★ ★ Cabo
de São Vicente

★ ★ Algarve

★ Faro

Évora
*The »Pearl of
the Alentejo«*

Getting In the Mood to Travel

Swimming, sun-bathing, relaxing

Most holidaymakers travel to Portugal to swim and relax – and they have indeed come to the best place for that. When deciding **when to go**, travellers should bear in mind that there could still be rain in southern Portugal as late as May or as early as October. In the summer months, fine weather is just about guaranteed – remember to pack high-protection factor suntan lotion for Portugal's beaches. The **most beautiful beaches** are on the Algarve – in part scenic and enchanting coves between rocks, but also long, sandy beaches in the east that are almost Mediterranean in character as the Atlantic Ocean is no longer quite as powerful here. The west of the Algarve and the entire remaining Portuguese coast is rougher: the waves are stronger and the water is always fairly cold. Actually, only some sections of the beach near Lisbon are overrun with holidaymakers, otherwise the beaches are often empty. The western coast of the Algarve, the Alentejo coast and the areas in the south and west of the Serra da Arrábida peninsula near Lisbon feature magnificent, sparsely populated beaches. Further up north, sandy beaches devoid of people can be found for miles along the coast. Before midday it can get cloudy on the coast of northern Portugal, even in the summer months.

Culture: cities, monasteries, palaces

Those planning a trip with a purely cultural focus will also get their money's worth in Portugal and discover the works of the Manueline period, decorative azulejos and the typical talha dourada of the Baroque. Several **large monastery sites** such as Alcobaça, Batalha or Tomar are on the cultural agenda, and the convent palace in Mafra as well as the **castles** of Sintra and Queluz are tourist highlights. Wonderful cultural relics from the era of Portugal's great voyages of discovery, that is from the 15th and 16th centuries, have been preserved in Lisbon. Indeed, **Lisbon** is a good place to spend several days; and visitors to the capital don't even have to miss out on relaxation, thanks to the numerous good beaches nearby which offer a welcome break from treading the pavement. But **Porto** is worth the trip, too: also with beaches right on the doorstep and numerous good museums, this interesting city is in addition saturated with the history of port wine. Finally there is **Coimbra**, the third largest city in Portugal, an old and lively university city on the shores of the Mond-

! *Baedeker* TIP

Organized trips and thematic tours
Primarily, organized trips go to cities or destinations of cultural interest such as monasteries and castles. The Portuguese Turihab offers different thematic tours including overnight stays in beautiful quintas and mansions, for example trips to wine-growing regions or gardens, holidays where the focus is on wellness, golf, or cooking, and trips to see the most beautiful »azulejos« (information and booking: Center, tel. 00 351/ 258 931 750, info@center.pt www.center.pt).

Douro Valley: vineyards and old wine-growing estates. This is where the grapes ripen for the famous port.

ego. Moreover, there are the numerous relatively unknown **intact Portuguese villages**, whose medieval face has been preserved almost unchanged: of particular note are the white Alentejan villages of Marvão and Monsaraz, as well as – a little less charming – Piódão with its archaic granite houses and Monsanto featuring houses built directly into the rocks. A cultural pearl from a completely different era can be found in the far east of the country: the **petroglyphs in the valley of the river Côa**, which were created about 20,000 years ago and were discovered purely by chance at the end of the 20th century.

Journeys through the country in south-western Europe traverse the most diverse landscapes. The **mountains in the north** may be magnificent, but the **Douro Valley**, where the world famous port wine comes from, is impressive as well. The centre of Portugal is rather more charming; almost an insider's tip is the countryside of the **Alentejo**, which can match up to Tuscany but is less well known and less frequented. As for lovers of the **ocean**, Portugal boasts a shoreline of 850km/528mi from which visitors can select the most beautiful spot.

Landscapes

Camp sites can be found all over the country, especially near the coasts. But it is also possible to pitch a tent on the premises of some

Accommodation

farms. The range of holiday homes and flats, hotels and guesthouses is broad and the standard of accommodation usually good. A very special overnight stay is offered by the **pousadas**, state-controlled hotels of high quality that can be found in historical buildings or near special scenic sites. At least as beautiful, rather more private and more moderately priced is accommodation in the so-called **solares**, old country residences, wineries or mansions, in which four to six rooms are furnished for guests, often with old furniture of the house. **Accommodation in the country** can be found in country houses or at small farms.

Car, bus or train

Travelling extensively or to remote and isolated regions requires a car. But there is also something to be said for using public transport. **Train rides**, generally through countryside far removed from cities and villages, are beautiful – but sometimes the train stations themselves are located outside the towns. Taking the **bus** is convenient. There are quite a few bus services even in the country, and express intercity coaches drive between the cities – a relaxing alternative to driving a car.

Tour 1 Recreation and Sightseeing in Southern Portugal

Distance: approx. 820km/513mi   **Tour duration:** 3–7 days

A round trip through Southern Portugal lends itself especially well to those wishing to combine a relaxing holiday on the Algarve with a sightseeing tour. The trip can be managed in three days but also extended to last longer than a week.

The border town of ❶ **Vila Real de Santo António** in the country's extreme south-east in the ✳ ✳ **Algarve** is for many the point of entry to Portugal. From here the coastal road (N 125) leads to the west up to Portimão. In the eastern section, in the so-called sand Algarve with its flat dune beaches, ❷ ✳ **Tavira** and ❸ ✳ **Faro**, the main city in the Algarve, are worth a stopover. West of Faro the scenery slowly changes, on the part of the coast called the rocky Algarve; especially bizarre rock formations can be admired near **Carvoeiro**. ❹ ✳ **Ferragudo** is a relatively unspoilt fishing town in a region which is otherwise characterized by tourism; **Portimão** lies nearby. An excursion (approx. 100 km/63mi there and back) leads from Portimão to ❺ ✳ **Lagos**, ✳ **Sagres** and further on to ❻ ✳ ✳ **Cabo de São Vicente**, the south-westernmost point of Europe. The clearly harsher climate in this part of the Algarve ensures that tourism does not dominate the scenery.

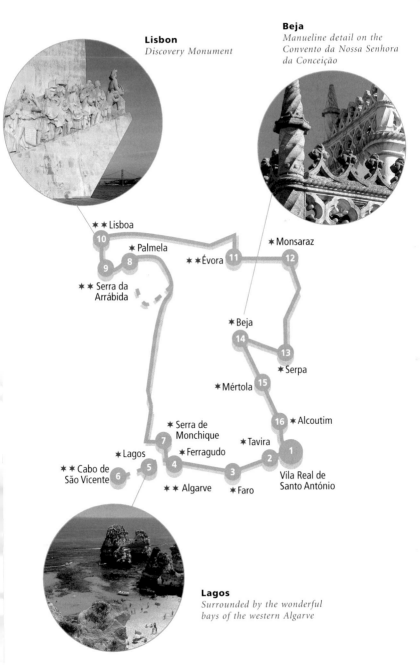

Beja
Manueline detail on the Convento da Nossa Senhora da Conceição

Lisbon
Discovery Monument

★★Lisboa
10
★Palmela
9 **8**
★★Serra da Arrábida
★★Évora
11
★Monsaraz
12

★Beja
14
13
★Serpa

★Mértola
15

16 ★Alcoutim

★Serra de Monchique
7
★Tavira
2 **1**
★Lagos
5
★★Cabo de São Vicente
6
4
★Ferragudo
3
Vila Real de Santo António
★★Algarve
★Faro

Lagos
Surrounded by the wonderful bays of the western Algarve

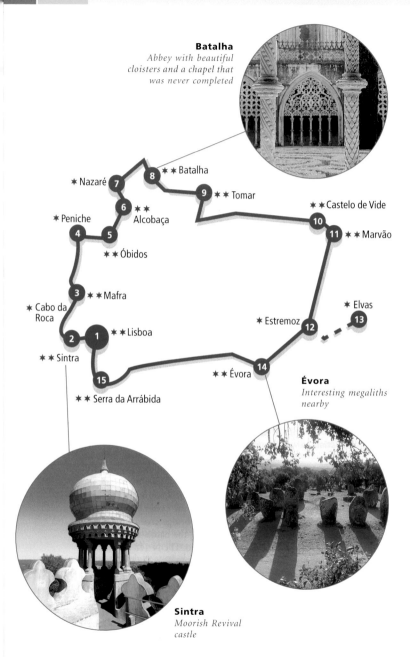

Batalha
Abbey with beautiful cloisters and a chapel that was never completed

✶ ✶ Batalha 8

✶ Nazaré 7

9 ✶ ✶ Tomar

✶ ✶ Castelo de Vide

6 ✶ ✶ Alcobaça

10

✶ Peniche

11 ✶ ✶ Marvão

4 5

✶ ✶ Óbidos

3 ✶ ✶ Mafra

✶ Elvas

✶ Cabo da Roca

✶ Estremoz 12 13

2 1 ✶ ✶ Lisboa

✶ ✶ Sintra

14

15 ✶ ✶ Évora

Évora
Interesting megaliths nearby

✶ ✶ Serra da Arrábida

Sintra
Moorish Revival castle

A side trip via Borba 11km/6.8mi distant leads to ✳ **Vila Viçosa**, a former royal residence with the vast Bragança palace. Proceed east to ⑬ ✳ **Elvas**, a once heavily fortified border town where it is still possible to see a number of well-preserved fortifications and a gigantic aqueduct.

On the drive from Estremoz to Évora it is worth making a short stop in ✳ **Évoramonte** to visit its old town centre surrounded by battlements. From here it is still a good 40km/25mi to ⑭ ✳ ✳ **Évora** with its numerous sights. The return journey to Lisbon is via Montemoro-Novo and **Setúbal** and from there on through the ⑮ ✳ ✳ **Serra da Arrábida** (detailed description in tour 1).

Tour 3 Northern Portugal – Unspoilt Countryside and Two Cities Steeped in History

Distance: approx. 850km/531mi   **Tour duration:** at least 7 days

Unique, in part still largely unspoilt countryside, two interesting, completely different national parks and two impressive cities – Porto and Coimbra – are part of the round trip through northern Portugal. Since the roads are often winding and only allow slow travelling, at least one week is necessary to enjoy this tour.

The starting point is ① ✳ ✳ **Porto**, the metropolis of northern Portugal; a day or two is needed to see the sights here, and a visit to one of the port lodges in Vila Nova de Gaia should definitely be part of the programme. From Porto the tour heads north to Vila do Conde. The Costa Verde in the region surrounding Porto is strongly shaped by industry, and it is only further north in Esposende that things start to quieten down. The town of ② ✳ **Viana do Castelo**, with a lovely old town centre, is another 20km/12.5mi north, situated on the broad mouth of the Rio Lima. Further north lies **Caminha** at the mouth of the Minho. The route then follows the river upstream and finally reaches ③ ✳ **Valença do Minho**, which is surrounded by battlements, and the sleepy little Kurbad Monção to the east. The winding N 101 leads south to ④ ✳ **Ponte da Barca** and ✳ **Ponte de Lima** – both on the shores of the Lima, good places to stop for a while. Only a few miles east of Ponte da Barca lies the ⑤ ✳ ✳ **Peneda-Gerês National Park**, an extensive, unspoilt area that is definitely worth a trip. South-west of this national park lies ⑥ ✳ **Braga** – a town with numerous churches including the pilgrimage church Bom Jesus do Monte on the edge of town – and the Celtiberian settlement

7 ✳✳ **Citânia de Briteiros**. The next point of interest is **8** ✳✳ **Guimarães**, the town reverentially called the »cradle of the nation«, which is protected by UNESCO as a World Cultural Heritage Site. In **9** ✳ **Amarante**, a little further south east, the tour crosses the Rio Tâmega. The fully developed IP 4 connects Amarante with **10** ✳ **Vila Real** 36km/22.5mi further east, which merits a visit especially because of the nearby Solar de Mateus.

If there is enough time for a side trip on in part very winding roads, consider the following addition to the tour which passes through the most remote area of Portugal. The route goes through the austere mountainous province of Trás-os-Montes, a largely unspoilt and very impoverished area even today. Passing through **Chaves**, move on to **11** ✳ **Bragança** in the far north-east of the country on the Spanish border. Head south from Bragança and continue on the IP 4 and then the IP 2 to **12** ✳✳ **Vale do Côa**, which has been declared a UNESCO World Cultural Heritage Site because of its sensational prehistoric petroglyphs. The drawings can be viewed on one of the guided jeep tours (reservations one week in advance!). The winding N 222 leads on to the ✳✳ **Douro Valley** and rejoins the main route in Peso da Régua.

The next destination is **13** ✳ **Lamego** with the pilgrimage church located above the town. Continue south via Castro Daire to **14** ✳ **Viseu** with its pretty burgher houses of the 16th to 18th centuries, and from there go east to **15** ✳ **Guarda**, the city with the highest elevation in Portugal (1057m/3,468ft). The tour then continues to ✳ **Belmonte** and Covilha, two very different small towns at the foot of the ✳✳ **Serra da Estrela**. The N 230 and the IC 6 now head west, and a trip on winding roads leads to the tradition-steeped university town of **16** ✳✳ **Coimbra**.

Leave Coimbra on the N 110 heading north to Penacova, passing through uniquely beautiful countryside above the Rio Mondego. Eventually the road arrives at ✳✳ **Buçaco National Park**, a wonderful place to take long walks. The Luso spa on the northern edge of the park is also worth a visit.

The motorway now leads north to **17** ✳ **Aveiro**, a pretty little town on the edge of a spit with numerous canals in its centre. From Aveiro, it is a short drive back to Porto on the motorway.

Coimbra
*»Academic« Fado can
be heard here*

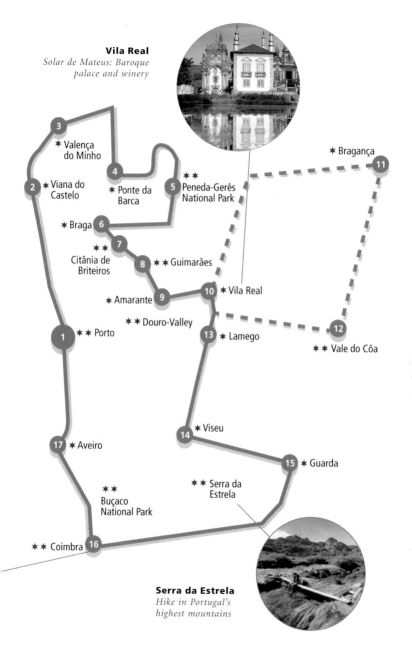

Vila Real
Solar de Mateus: Baroque palace and winery

3
★ Valença do Minho

2 ★ Viana do Castelo

4
★ Ponte da Barca

5 ★★ Peneda-Gerês National Park

★★ Bragança 11

★ Braga 6

7
★★ Citânia de Briteiros

8 ★★ Guimarães

★ Amarante 9

10 ★ Vila Real

1 ★★ Porto

★★ Douro-Valley

13 ★ Lamego

12
★★ Vale do Côa

17 ★ Aveiro

14 ★ Viseu

15 ★ Guarda

★★ Buçaco National Park

★★ Serra da Estrela

★★ Coimbra 16

Serra da Estrela
Hike in Portugal's highest mountains

Tour 4 The Great Portugal Round Trip in Four Weeks

Distance: a good 2,000km/1,250mi **Tour duration:** 4 weeks

The three Portugal tours described above can also be combined in a big round trip. If you want to visit the most important cities, see all the sights and have time to enjoy the scenic beauty, you will need at least four weeks.

The route begins by heading west from ① * **Faro** along the coast of the * * **Algarve** to Portimão and then inland through the delightful * * **Serra de Monchique**. Vila Nova de Milfontes presents a perfect spot for those wanting to enjoy a restful day. A side trip from Setúbal through the beautiful ② * * **Serra da Arrábida** is highly recommended. From here, the Portuguese metropolis ③ * * **Lisbon** is easy to reach. ④ * * **Sintra** and ⑤ * * **Mafra** are a must for any round trip through Portugal. After that continue north via * **Peniche** and ⑥ * * **Óbidos** to ⑦ * * **Alcobaça** and the seaside resort of Nazaré. One of the highlights of Portuguese architecture can be seen in ⑧ * * **Batalha**. From here, drive inland to Fátima and ⑨ * * **Tomar** and then continue to ⑩ * * **Coimbra**. The route via Penacova to the * * **Buçaco National Park** passes through areas of outstanding scenic beauty.

The next destinations are * **Aveiro** and then ⑪ * * **Porto**. The route continues north along the Costa Verde to * **Viana do Castelo**, then upriver along the Rio Lima and via * **Ponte da Barca** to the * * **Peneda-Gerês National Park**. Next on the itinerary is the city of churches, ⑫ * **Braga**. A side trip to the Celtiberian settlement * * **Citânia de Briteiros** is another must. The following destinations are ⑬ * * **Guimarães** and * **Amarante**. From here, follow the Rio Tâmega a little way downriver on the N 312, then cross it and continue in the direction of the Douro near Marco de Canaveses, finally taking the N 108 above the Douro to Peso da Régua. Next on the route are the rewarding destinations ⑭ * **Viseu** and ⑮ * **Guarda**, the city with the highest elevation in the country, and finally * **Belmonte**. A drive from here into the * * **Serra da Estrela** should not be passed up. Continue via Fundão to ⑯ * **Castelo Branco** with its pretty gardens. The well-preserved little old towns of ⑰ * * **Castelo de Vide** and ⑱ * * **Marvão**are highlights of any round trip through Portugal, and * **Estremoz** and * **Évoramonte** are also beautiful destinations. Eventually the route reaches one of the most important cities in the country, ⑲ * * **Évora**. Drive on across the plateaus of the Alentejo to ⑳ * **Beja**, returning to Faro via Castro Verde and through the Serra do Malhão.

Douro Valley
The best time is late summer during the grape harvest.

✶✶ Peneda-Gerês
National Park

12 ✶ Braga

13 ✶✶ Guimarães

✶✶ Porto 11 ✶✶ Douro
Valley

✶ Viseu

14   ✶ Guarda

15

✶✶ Serra da
Estrela

✶✶ Buçaco
National Park

✶✶ Coimbra 10

✶ Castelo
Branco 16

✶✶ Batalha

8

✶✶ Alcobaça 7   9

✶✶ Tomar

✶✶ Castelo
de Vide

6   ✶✶ Óbidos   17

18

✶✶ Marvão

✶
Cabo da
Roca 5   ✶✶ Mafra

4 3 ✶✶ Lisboa

✶✶ Sintra   19 ✶✶ Évora

2

✶✶ Serra da
Arrábida

Algarve coast
Ponta da Piedade with bizarre rock formations

20 ✶ Beja

✶ Serra de
Monchique

✶✶ Cabo
de São Vicente   ✶✶ Algarve   1 ✶ Faro

Sights from A to Z

IT MAY BE TEMPTING TO STAY IN PRETTY ÓBIDOS FOR A WHILE, BUT TRY NOT TO LINGER TOO LONG. THERE ARE MANY BEAUTIFUL VIL AND CITIES TO VISIT IN PORTUGAL, AND A VARIETY OF CHARMING AND MAGNIFICENT LANDSCAPES TO SEE!

✳ Abrantes

J 20

Historical province: Ribatejo	**Elevation:** 190m/617ft
District: Santarém	**Population:** 20,000

High above the north bank of the Tagus lies the quaint little town of Abrantes, whose pretty historic centre with white houses and flower-bedecked lanes have retained an originality all their own.

Its exposed location has always made Abrantes a key position for the defence of the Beira provinces to the south. A tasty **local speciality** is the so-called »Palhas de Abrantes«, a dessert made of egg flower.

What To See in Abrantes

Castelo
The ruins of the once mighty castle built in 1303 under King Dinis stand above the city. The castle was damaged by an earthquake in 1533 and finally destroyed in 1807 by the troops of Marshal Junot, who was appointed Duke of Abrantes by Napoleon.
The 13th-century Santa Maria do Castelo church is preserved within the castle grounds. Today it hosts the Museu Dom Lopo de Almeida. Along with the late Gothic tombs of the Almeida family (15th/16th centuries), precious tiles dating from the 16th century, Gothic sculptures and a Roman statue from the first century AD can be seen. A visit to the castle is worthwhile primarily because of the magnificent view onto the little town of Abrantes, the Tagus valley and the surrounding mountain range.

Old town
Below the castle grounds lies the old town of Abrantes, parts of which feature narrow, picturesque lanes. Take a look at the **Igreja São João Baptista** with its beautiful Renaissance coffered ceiling and abundant wood carvings, as well as the 16th-century Misericórdia church with paintings of the Portuguese school of the 16th century. The **Convento de São Domingos** in the south of the old town close to the Misericórdia church was built in 1472, though it was remodelled several times in the following centuries; don't miss its beautiful two-storied cloister. The Igreja São Vicente with beautiful marble Renaissance altars is in the north of the old town; it was renovated in the second half of the 16th century.

Around Abrantes

Constância
Constância is 12km/7.5mi west of Abrantes. The town named Pugna Tagi by the Romans is located at the mouth of the Rio Zêzere. The Misericórdia church, decorated with tiles, and the parish church of 1636 are of local relevance. The latter was restored in the second half of the 19th century; the ceiling fresco also dates from this time.

About 5km/3mi further south-west on a small rocky island in the Tagus stands the castle of Almourol, a Knights Templar stronghold
with eleven towers. The master of the order, Gualdim Pais, had it
built in 1171 on Roman and Moorish foundations as protection
against the Moors. In the 19th century the buildings were restored in
the spirit of the Romantic period – for this reason the castle now
possesses a rather enchanted atmosphere.

★
Castelo de
Almourol

If the view from the river bank does not suffice, visitors can always
cross over to the castle by boat (only during peak season). The
mighty keep offers a beautiful view across the delightful river scenery
of the Tagus.

The town of Castelo de Bode, 10km/6.2mi north of Constância, is a
favourite amongst the Portuguese because of its water sports and recreational opportunities. A retaining wall of approx. 115m/374ft – the
lowest of several dams – means that the Rio Zêzere is dammed to become an immense lake (Barragem do Castelo de Bode) with numerous coves. Altogether the chain of lakes spans more than 50km/
31mi. Boat trips on the reservoir can be organized in Castelo de
Bode.

Castelo de Bode

*Castelo de Almourol: before the Portuguese, the Romans and Arabs had already
built a castle in an exposed position on an island in the Tagus.*

▶ VISITING ABRANTES

INFORMATION
Esplanada 1° de Maio
2200-320 Abrantes
Tel. 241 362 555
www.rtribatejo.org

WHERE TO STAY •
WHERE TO EAT

▶ **Mid-range**
Pousada de São Pedro
2300-196 Castelo de Bode
Tel. 249 381 159/75
Fax 249 381 176
The Pousada de São Pedro is situated
above the river Zêzere, at the dam of
Castelo do Bode. Angling and water
sports opportunities on one of the
largest artificial lakes in Portugal.

Hotel De Turismo Abrantes
Largo de Santo António
2200-349 Abrantes
Tel. 241 361 261
Fax 241 365 218
Well renovated hotel with almost 40
rooms, situated in a beautiful park
above the city. Magnificent view across
Tagus valley. The hotel has a restaurant
that serves traditional dishes.

Belver   The townscape of Belver, located on the right bank of the Tagus
30km/19mi east of Abrantes, is dominated by a castle built around
1200 during the reign of Sancho I. In the castle chapel there is a
beautifully carved 13th-century reredos. There is a splendid view into the Tagus valley from the so-called »Sancho I's balcony«.

Albufeira

J 34

Historical province: Algarve	**Elevation:** 0–35m/115ft
District: Faro	**Population:** 18,000

**Albufeira is one of the most important tourist centres of the Al-
garve. The town is situated in an exceptionally delightful setting in
a bay protected by bizarre rocky cliffs on the southern coast of
Portugal.**

**From insider's tip
to top tourist
destination**   The small, beautifully situated fishing village was at first a well-kept
secret. In the 1960s and 1970s Albufeira was a dream destination for
travellers from many different corners of Europe who cultivated a
bohemian lifestyle and lived a night-owl existence. The dream came
to an end in the seventies, when major tourism companies developed
an interest in Albufeira. Today the little town has a distinct tourist
infrastructure. All types of water sports are available here, and tennis,
golf and horse-riding are possible anywhere in the surrounding area.
In the west of Albufeira a large marina has developed.

In the meantime the **densely built-up area** extends along the entire Albufeira Bay; but although tourism dominates the scenery, it does so in a fairly tolerable manner. The whitewashed houses lend an appealing atmosphere to the town centre, a pedestrian zone. The typically Portuguese mosaics with which the streets are paved are very pretty. There are souvenir shops, jewellery shops and boutiques everywhere. In the evening and night-time hours Albufeira is a **haven for night-owls**. Those who like to stroll from pub to pub have come to the right place – the selection is enormous. The same goes for restaurants and cafés. In Rua Cândido dos Reis in particular the bars are lined up one after the other.

> **! Baedeker TIP**
>
> **View of the sea of white houses**
> To the east, above Praia dos Pescadores, there is a small look-out point, accessed via steep stairs. The magnificent setting of the city is best revealed from up here: there is a spectacular view of the houses of Albufeira, the sandy beach and the coast.

What to See in and around Albufeira

The Igreja Matriz was rebuilt after the earthquake in 1755 on the orders of Francisco Gomes de Avelar, the then bishop of the Algarve. The whole building was renovated in 1993.

Igreja Matriz

The Igreja Sant' Ana on the Largo Jacinto d' Ayete, on the corner of Rua 1° de Dezembro, is decidedly pretty. This typical whitewashed 18th-century Algarve church adds a decidedly rural element to the urban surroundings. The crossing cupola and the Baroque curved gables framing it on all four sides are striking.

Igreja Sant' Ana

The newly designed Largo Engenheiro Duarte Pacheco is the main square of Albufeiras and the lively centre of activity where locals and tourists meet. Rows of cafés, restaurants and snack bars are interspersed with postcard stands and costume jewellery shops. The churches of the town are depicted on the well; one azulejo image shows a view of the old Albufeira.

Largo Engenheiro Duarte Pacheco

Archaeological finds from the Algarve are on display in the Museu Municipal, including 6,000–7,000 year old menhirs and a Roman mosaic.

Museu Municipal

The municipal beaches are the **Praia do Peneco** and the **Praia dos Pescadores**, which are for the most part hopelessly crowded in the summer. West of Albufeira there are several small beaches in pretty bays as well as the long **Praia da Galé** that stretches all the way to Armação de Pêra. The beaches of Oura, Balaia and Maria Luisa to the east of Albufeira are part of the touristic periphery of Montechoro

Beaches

▶ VISITING ALBUFEIRA

INFORMATION
Rua 5 de Outubro
Tel. 289 585 279
www.turismodoalgarve.pt

SHOPPING
The town centre of Albufeira is simply one big shopping area, especially in the Rua 5 de Outubro with row upon row of souvenir shops and boutiques. The largest shopping centre of the Algarve, Algarve Shopping, with more than 130 shops, is located on the N 125 shortly before reaching Guia (coming from the east).

ENTERTAINMENT
Probably the best-known club for night-time entertainment in the Algarve is the Kadoc, situated on the road between Albufeira and Vilamoura.
Those preferring a shorter trip home after a somewhat less spectacular night of partying will find enough bars and discotheques in Albufeira itself – most in the Rua Cândido dos Reis and on the Largo Eng. Duarte Pacheco. Another area featuring extensive nightlife is the »Strip«, located east of the centre between Praia da Oura and Montechoro.

WHERE TO EAT
▶ Expensive
① *Vila Joya*
Road to Praia da Galé
Tel. 289 591 795
This restaurant is considered to be one of the best in Portugal.

▶ Moderate
② *Três Palmeiras*
Areias de São João
Tel. 289 515 423
A well-known restaurant approx.

2.5km/1.5mi east of the centre, popular with both locals and tourists.

▶ Moderate/Inexpensive
③ *A Ruina*
Cais Herculano
Tel. 289 512 094
Freshly caught seafood and a splendid view of the »beach of the fishermen«. It is especially pleasant on the roof terrace.

④ *Bravo Diebels*
Largo Eng. Duarte Pacheco 50
Tel. 289 589 240
As almost everywhere in the centre of Albufeira, the menu here is very tourist oriented; in addition there is good (German) beer. The service is exceedingly friendly and fast.

⑤ *O Penedo*
Rua Latino Coelho 15
Situated directly above the cliffs with a beautiful view across the city and the water. The fish dishes are good.

WHERE TO STAY
▶ Luxury
Sheraton Algarve e Pine Cliffs Resort
Praia da Falésia
Tel. 289 500 100; fax 289 500 122
www.sheraton-algarve.com
The hotel east of Albufeira in the direction of Quarteira is considered to be one of the most beautiful hotels on the Algarve: 215 rooms and suites in a generous two-storied facility.

▶ Mid-range
① *Hotel Sol e Mar*
Rua José Bernardino de Sousa
Tel. 289 580 080; fax 289 587 036
This 74-room hotel, located between the cliffs on the main beach, heralded

the beginnings of the tourist industry in Albufeira in the early 1960s.

② *Hotel Boavista*
Rua Samora Barros 20
Tel. 289 589 175; fax 289 589 180
www.portugalvirtual.pt/belver
Beautiful hotel with a view of the ocean, though the water is not right on the doorstep. Charming and elegant interior decoration, no organized recreational programmes.

Alfa Mar holiday complex
Praia da Falésia
Tel. 289 501 351; fax 289 501 404
Large holiday complex with hotel, apartments and guesthouses, situated between Albufeira and Quarteira on the Falésia beach. Large range of sports offered (not included in the price).

► **Mid-range/Budget**
Aparthotel Auramar
Areias de São João
Tel. 289 587 607; fax 289 513 327
Located east of Albufeira; friendly atmosphere, all the necessities without many extras.

③ *Residencial Vila Recife*
Rua Miguel Bombarda 6
Tel. 289 583 740
Centrally located, though somewhat removed from the hustle and bustle, in a beautiful house with a marvellous garden. 92 modern, simply furnished rooms.

Sheraton Algarve: buffet on the cliffs above the beach

Albufeira Plan

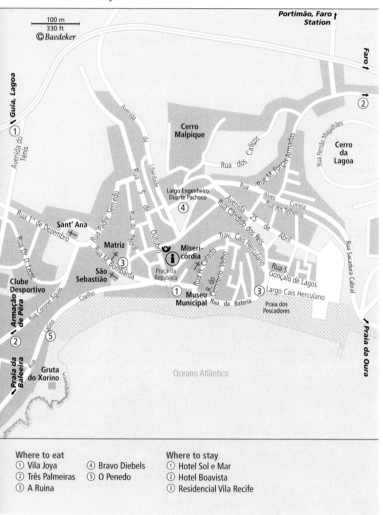

100 m
330 ft
© Baedeker

Portimão, Faro
Station

Guia, Lagoa

Faro

Avenida do Ténis

Cerro
Malpique

Rua dos Caliços

Rua Fernão Magalhães

Cerro
da
Lagoa

Avenida da Liberdade

Rua Padre Semedo

Rua 5 de Outubro

Rua do Toural

Largo Engenheiro
Duarte Pacheco

④

Rua M. Fortas Armadas

Rua Alves Correia

Avenida 25 de Abril

Rua Cândido dos Reis

Rua dos Telheiros

Rua 1° de Dezembro

Sant' Ana

Rua Dr. D. Leira

Matriz

Rua M. Bombarda

③

São
Sebastião

Misericórdia

ℹ

Praça da
República

Rua H. Calado

Trav. Cais Herculano

Rua S. Gonçalo de Lagos

Rua Sakadura Cabral

Clube
Desportivo

Armação de Pêra

Rua Coronel Aguas

Coelho

①

Museu
Municipal

Rua do Cemitério Velho

Rua da Bateria

③ Largo Cais Herculano

Praia dos
Pescadores

Praia da Oura

Praia da
Baleeira

Latino

②

⑤

Gruta
do Xorino

Oceano Atlântico

Where to eat
① Vila Joya
② Três Palmeiras
③ A Ruina
④ Bravo Diebels
⑤ O Penedo

Where to stay
① Hotel Sol e Mar
② Hotel Boavista
③ Residencial Vila Recife

and Areias de São João. The **Praia da Falésia**, whose scenic beauty makes it one of the most well known beaches of the Algarve, is located even further east, just outside Vilamoura. There are good water sports opportunities and restaurants everywhere.

Zoomarine park The well known Zoomarine park is located near Guia, 6km/3.8mi north-west of Albufeira, and is visited by roughly 400,000 holiday-

Breathtakingly beautiful: the cliffs at the Praia da Falésia

makers a year. In the nicely set out site with its small lakes, gardens and restaurants, visitors can observe the animals: parrots perform whimsical tricks; dolphins and seals perform; various types of fish swim in different pools and aquariums. Both children and adults can splash about in a large swimming pool. Visitors should schedule at least four hours for the main attractions and the animal shows alone ⏱ (open: daily 10am–5pm, April–Oct until 6pm, in midsummer until 7.30pm).

►Algarve

Other sights

Alcácer do Sal

Historical province: Baixo Alentejo
District: Setúbal

Elevation: 30m/98ft
Population: 16,000

The quaint town of Alcácer do Sal, meaning »salt fortress«, lies on the right bank of the Rio Sado, whose lowlands have been framed by salt marshes from time immemorial.

Alcácer do Sal was already in existence in Roman times, when it was called Salacia. To this day several buildings bear witness to a prosperous past. The trade with salt and crops as well as the cultivation of

VISITING ALCÁCER DO SAL

INFORMATION
Rua da República 66
Tel. 265 610 040
www.costa-azul.pt

WHERE TO EAT
► **Inexpensive/Moderate**
A Descoberta
Av. João Soares Branco 15-16
Tel. 265 623 877
A pleasant and modestly designed

restaurant offering refined regional
cuisine.

WHERE TO STAY
► **Mid-range**
Pousada D. Afonso II
7580-123 Alcácer do Sal
Tel. 265 613 070, www.pousadas.pt
This beautiful pousada has been es-
tablished in the Castelo of Alcácer do
Sal.

rice in the marshy, hot river basins brought affluence and esteem for
the town from the Middle Ages on. Several salt works were abandoned during the last centuries, while the cultivation of rice gained
increasing importance.

What to See in Alcácer do Sal and Surroundings

Castelo   Above Alcácer do Sal stands the fort: today, a pousada has been established here. If offers a beautiful view of the city and the river
landscape. Take a look at the 12th/13th-century Romanesque church
of Santa Maria, with a nave and two aisles and a beautiful Renaissance entrance to the sacrament chapel.

Santo António   The former monastery of Santo António north of the town centre
was built in the 16th century. The monastery church boasts the
»Chapel of the 11,000 Virgins« with its rich marble decorations also
dating back to the 16th century.

Museu Municipal   The former Espírito Santo church near the town hall today houses
the city museum. On display are Stone Age and Roman finds and remains from the time of the Moors, as well as coins.

Santuário do Senhor dos Mártires   On the western edge of town stands the Roman Gothic church of Senhor dos Mártires from the 13th/14th centuries. The interior con-
tains the stone coffin of Diogo de Pereira (1427); the grandmaster of
the São-Tiago order of knights made a major contribution to the recapturing of the town which was seized by the Moors in 1217.

Grândola   The small town Grândola gained fame across the border with the
song *Grândola, vila morena* (Brown City of Grandola), which initiated the Carnation Revolution in April 1974 (► Baedeker Special,

p.55). The rural town 23km/14.3mi south of Alcácer do Sal, with a population of approximately 5,500, is the centre of the Portuguese cork industry.

✶ ✶ Alcobaça

E 19

Historical province: Estremadura
District: Leiria

Elevation: 42m/138ft
Population: 7,000

Alcobaça's primary attraction is its fabulous Cistercian abbey. The little town is the cultural and economic centre of a fertile, agriculturally important region, whose early heyday was initiated by the monks of St Bernhard as far back as the 14th century.

Alcobaça is situated approximately 20km/12.5mi south of Batalha in a delightful setting between the two small rivers Alcoa and Baça. The Romans named the little town Eburóbriga.

✶ ✶ Real Abadia de Santa Maria de Alcobaça

The Cistercian abbey of Alcobaça – once one of the wealthiest and most influential abbeys in Portugal – today numbers among the most important architectural monuments in the country. It was declared a World Cultural Heritage Site by UNESCO in 1985 (open: daily 10am to 5pm, in the summer until 7pm).

In 1154 Afonso Henriques, Portugal's first king, presented his fellow believer and comrade in arms **Bernhard of Clairvaux** with the land on which the abbey was later to be built, which had been seized from the Moors in the course of the liberation of Santarém (15 March 1147). Bernhard of Clairvaux, who stood by the king during the lengthy negotiations concerning the papal recognition of the newly created Kingdom of Portugal, received the terrain as a feudal tenure for the foundation of a Cistercian abbey. The king laid the foundation for the first church in 1148, and the con-

▶ ALCOBAÇA

INFORMATION

Praça 25 de Abril
2460-018 Alcobaça
Tel. 262 582 377
www.rt-leiriafatima.pt

WHERE TO STAY

► **Budget/Mid-range**
Hotel Termas da Piedade
Fervença
2460-743 Alcobaça
Tel. 262 596 979
Fax 262 596 971
www.hoteltermaspiedade.com
Very well suited for relaxation after a day of sightseeing; situated a little outside of Alcobaça with a swimming pool and tennis courts.

struction of the first monastic buildings was begun in 1154. As a consequence of the influx of friars from Burgundy the quarters soon required enlargement: the construction of a new abbey commenced in 1178 and was essentially completed in 1222, though the building was altered considerably in the following centuries while maintaining a remarkably harmonious overall appearance.

In accordance with the regulations of the order of the Cistercians the abbey always accommodated »one less than a thousand«, that is **999 friars**, who laid out orchards and vineyards in the river valley of Alcoa and Baça and thus created the basis for what is to this day Portugal's most important horticultural area. The monks established the kingdom's **first state school** in the 13th century, an act which later generated the essential momentum for the foundation of Portugal's oldest university in Coimbra. The abbot, who also called himself the »council of his majesty and keeper of the crown's alms«, commanded thirteen villages, three seaports and two castles. One of the most notable intellectual centres of the country therefore existed in Alcobaça from the 13th to the 18th century. Alcobaça was both refuge and place of meditation for Portuguese kings.

The earthquake of 1755 ravaged Alcobaça, amongst other places, and heavily damaged the abbey. Napoleonic troops conquered it in 1811 under the reign of Junot and destroyed a large proportion of the art treasures. Secularization followed in 1834 and the buildings were consequently subject to alteration, often for highly profane purposes such as barracks, stables and the like. It was not until 1930 that the art historical significance of the abbey was recognized and a preservation order put on it.

Site layout

The layout of the Real Abadia de Santa Maria de Alcobaça abbey is a mirror image of the Cistercian abbey of Cluny; its good state of preservation has made it the best example of Cistercian architecture in Europe today. The basically Gothic building has a nearly square floor plan and includes, along with the mighty church and the usual utility rooms, five cloisters, seven dormitories, accommodation for guests, a library and a huge kitchen. Not all of the premises are open to the public; some parts of the building accommodate government authorities as well as a school.

Abbey church

Dating from 1725, the **Baroque façade** of the abbey church with its two lower steeples dominates the 221m/725ft main front of the abbey. Of the originally Gothic gable end only the doorway decorated with Baroque sculptures as well as the great rose window have been preserved.

The **interior** of the early Gothic hall church exhibits Cistercian clarity, austerity and plainness. The **largest church interior in Portu-**

← *The Cistercian abbey church of Alcobaça. The doorway and the rose window have been preserved from the originally gothic façade.*

Real Abadia de Santa Maria *Plan*

1 Tomb of Pedro I.
2 Tomb of Inês de Castro
3 Choir
4 »Death of St Bernhard«
   (terracotta)
5 Funerary chapel
6 Chapel of the Sacrament
7 Manueline doorways
8 Sacristy
9 Chapter house
10 Dorter (dormitory/
    upper floor)
    Pantry
    (lower floor)
11 Kitchen
12 Refectory
13 Fountain house

Cloisters Dom Dinis

King's Hall

Abbey Church

© Baedeker

gal with a length of 106m/348ft, a width of 21.5m/70ft and a height of 20m/66ft is divided into a nave and two aisles all of the same height, the aisles being conspicuously narrow. 24 mighty pillars carry twelve Gothic vaults. The choir is encircled by a corona of nine chapels, and eight circular columns surround the main altar. In the transept on both sides of the crossing are the ostentatious tombs of King **Pedro I** (on the right) and his mistress **Inês de Castro** (on the left), who was murdered at the behest of Pedro's father, King Afonso IV, and exhumed by Pedro upon his accession to be formally crowned queen post mortem in Coimbra. The tragic love story of the heir to the throne and the beautiful lady-in-waitingas well as the bitter vengeance wielded by Pedro after his accession on the murderers of his mistress – which earned him the nickname »the cruel one« – is sung of by Camões in the third canto of his *The Lusiads* (►Baedeker Special, p.284). On the request of Pedro the tombs were placed facing each other so that the two lovers would see each other at once upon their resurrection on judgement day. The sarcophaguses, sumptuously adorned with figures – carved from the soft limestone of Ançâ – were created in the second half of the 14th century in the Flamboyant style. They suffered severe damage in 1811 at the hands of Junot's troops.

The **sarcophagus of Inês**, carried by crouching figures, bears the prone figure of the dead queen which is surrounded by six praying angels. The long sides of the tomb are decorated with pictures of the life of Christ; at the foot there are scenes of the Last Judgement, with

Christ on Calvary at the head end. The **stone coffin of Pedro** is carried by six lions. It also bears the prone figure of the dead king, similarly surrounded by angels. The side panels show scenes of the life of St Bartholomew, at the head end there is an unfortunately heavily damaged **wheel of fortune** with 18 episodes from the lives of the two lovers and a depiction of the murder of Inês underneath.

The painted terracotta sculptures in the side chapels of the transept were created by unknown monks in the 17th century; amongst them, the depiction of the death of St Bernard is especially notable. Added to the west of the right transept is the Sala dos Túmulos (funerary chapel) with other tombs.

On the north side of the abbey church stand the medieval monastic buildings. From the left aisle, visitors first enter the **King's Hall** (Sala dos Reis) whose walls are covered with azulejos showing scenes from the abbey's history. The clay sculptures, which were probably made by the monks, depict Portuguese kings up to José I. From the King's Hall there is an entrance to the two-storied **Claustro do Silêncio** or Claustro de Dom Dinis. The ground floor, the work of Domingo and Diogo Domingues, was created between 1308 and 1311; the upper gallery was added by the Castilho brothers in the 16th century by order of King Manuel. The Gothic fountain house is located on the north side of the cloister. The entrance to the **refectory**, one of the oldest parts of the abbey and with a notable pulpit, is here. The 18m/59ft-high **kitchen** with its imposing open fireplace is decidedly impressive. Since the consumption of meat was prohibited the fish pond, fed by water from the Alcoa, was of utmost importance to the Cistercians. Next to the kitchen there are stairs leading to the **dormitory**; from here visitors can look down on the second cloister. On the south-eastern side of the Claustro de Dom Dinis is the 14th-century **chapter house** (Sala do Capítulo).

Monastic buildings

Around Alcobaça

Located on the road to Batalha on the eastern edge of Alcobaça, the Museu Nacional do Vinho provides information on the traditions and processing methods of the wine growers of this region.

Museu Nacional do Vinho

The same road continues on to Aljubarrota, known for the battle of the same name in which the Portuguese army, fighting under its commander **Nuno Álvares Pereira**, achieved a decisive victory over the Spaniards on 15 August 1385. As a reward King João I founded the abbey at ► Batalha. Aljubarrota features pretty 17th and 18th-century houses; of the originally Roman main church Nossa Senhora dos Prazeres, only the 13th-century doorway remains.

Aljubarrota

Termas da Piedade 2km/1.3mi north of Alcobaça is a small spa whose thermal springs promise alleviation of gastro-intestinal problems.

Termas da Piedade

Coz   A former monastery can be visited in Coz, another 5km/3.1mi further north. The Manueline doorway of the church dates back to the 17th century.

★ Alentejo

E–R 19–32

Historical province: Alto Alentejo, Baixo Alentejo	**Area:** 28,747 sq km/11,099 sq mi
Districts: Portalegre, Évora, Beja, Setúbal	**Population:** 370,000
Principal city: Évora	

The Alentejo spans the seemingly endless plateau south of the Tagus up to the Algarve and reaches from the Spanish-Portuguese border to the Atlantic Ocean. It is one of the most unspoilt regions of the entire Iberian peninsula. Few tourists ever find their way here.

Alem do Tejo: beyond the Tejo   This does not do the region justice, because the Alentejo (»Alem do Tejo« = »beyond the Tejo«), which includes the northern Alto Alentejo (upper Alentejo) and the southern Baixo Alentejo (lower Alentejo), is an area of impressive scenic beauty. There are also quite a few little towns here to enchant the visitor, in part thanks to their medieval appearance, such as ► Beja, ► Elvas, ► Estremoz, ► Castelo de Vide and ► Marvão. ► Évora, the capital of the Alentejo, should be part of the itinerary on any Portugal round trip.

The **landscape** here is completely different from the mountainous and lush provinces further north. Geographically speaking, the Alentejo is an extension of the Castilian Meseta. The middle elevations are between 150m/492ft and 350m/1,148ft, and the highest peaks in the south-west reach almost 400m/1,312ft. The only »true« mountain range, the Serra de São Mamede, reaches elevations of up to 1,025m/3,363ft.

Climate ►   The climate is Mediterranean, though with some continental traits: cold winters clear of snow, a short spring with low precipitation, very hot and arid summers and rainstorms in the autumn. The rainfall used to average 600–700mm/24–28in per year some years ago, but now it stands at around 400mm/16in – with a downward trend.

Vegetation   In keeping with the climatic conditions the natural vegetation is limited to evergreen heather and oaks as well as hard-leaved ever-

Single cork trees amidst the fertile red soil of the Alentejo

green plants. The tree population is sparse; cork oaks are widespread, representing an important economic factor (► Baedeker Special, p.208).

The Alentejo is thinly populated with only 370,000 inhabitants – which is around 4% of the population of Portugal – in one fifth of the total area of the country (21 inh./sq km or 54 inh./sq mi). The population is concentrated in a few smaller towns and larger villages featuring typical whitewashed houses. Outside the towns the Alentejans are scattered across the country, mostly in isolated **manors (montes)** which often stand on small knolls, consisting of the manor house, the servant quarters and utility buildings and often surrounded by vast estates. These estates represent the **classic type of Portuguese large-scale land-holding** that has always given rise to social tensions. The expropriations carried out in 1974 after the Carnation Revolution have since been for the most part revoked, and the farmhands and day labourers have fallen by the wayside. They hardly find sufficient means of earning a living in the Alentejo – the unemployment rate of 11% here is distinctly higher than in the rest of the country.

Alentejans

CORK – MORE THAN JUST A BOTTLE TOP

In the 17th century there was a revolution in European drinking culture. First came chocolate from Central America, then coffee from Arabia, finally tea from China. After that spirits made their entrance, after the Dutch had developed the art of distilling. Beer kept longer with hops, and in the cities there was finally clean water – from pipes, like the Romans once had. It only remained to find a way to keep wine longer…

Since Roman times wine had been stored in barrels, which had two distinct disadvantages: the long period of storage in wood made the bouquet disappear, and after opening the barrel the wine soon lost its character. From the beginning of the 17th century glass bottles were in use, but merely to bring the wine up from the cellar. Until it was discovered that in neutral, airtight glass, sealed with a cork, wine could be carefully allowed to mature and kept longer…

However the bottles in those days were very bulbous and could only be stored **standing up**, so that the cork dried out and air could enter the bottle.

In the late 18th century slimmer wine bottles were developed which could be stored lying down – in this way the cork was permanently kept damp by the wine, did not dry out and sealed the bottle so that it was airtight. Port bottles were still bulbous carafes at the beginning of the 18th century; bottles in their modern form were first created in 1812.

Every nine years

Portugal is the **largest cork producer** in the world, making 55% of the world's corks. It has been an exporter of cork for over 200 years; about 30 million corks are manufactured in Portugal every day, and 500 million champagne corks are made every year. Portugal's 70 million cork oaks grow predominantly in the Ribatejo, the Alentejo and the Algarve. The trees reach 6–10m/20–33ft in height and have an average lifespan of 150 years. The first stripping is only allowed to take place when the cork oak, the »sobreiro«, is at least twenty years old. The cork, the bark of the tree, is harvested in the hot summer months when the metabolism of the tree is at its most intensive and the bark can be removed easily. When doing so the

virgin layer, from which the cork continues to grow, must not be damaged. It is at least nine years until the trunk has generated new cork and can be stripped once again. A number is written on the trunk after harvesting: a »5« means for example that the tree was stripped in 2005 and the next stripping should take place in 2014.

Versatile uses

After harvesting, the cork bark is stacked, dried for three months and then transported to cork factories for further processing. In order to remove pests from the cork, and to remove mineral salts and tanning agents, it is first boiled. During boiling the cork cells expand, making the cork elastic and flexible. After this the bark is pressed, dried, sliced and sorted according to use. Because cork is very long-lasting, light and elastic, gas and watertight, not flammable and does not conduct electricity, it is made into many useful items: coasters, seals, life jackets, isolating materials, insoles, wall tiles, buoys for fishing nets and so on. The most important product, however, remains **wine corks**. Because of the little suckers on the walls of the cork and the excellent ability of the natural material to expand, bottles are best sealed with cork. Putrefiers cannot enter. As cork is neutral in terms of taste and odour, contains no poisons and does not change its essential character, it is the best material for the storage of wine. Worldwide, vintners agree that there is no better material for their purposes – even though cork producers are increasingly busy making synthetically manufactured cork.

Cork is in short supply

Cork is a renewable resource. Nevertheless, old corks do not belong in the dustbin – and for a variety of reasons. In Europe, millions of corks are **thrown away** each year. When the rubbish is burned, the cork releases poisonous gases due to its resin content. Added to this, the natural renewal of cork in Portugal and other countries is no longer to be taken for granted. The large number of eucalyptus plantations for the paper industry remove water from the soil, and cork oak groves in the vicinity of eucalyptus plants are often completely dried out, even deep under the ground: The water necessary for growth is lacking, and the ecological balance is disturbed. The versatile raw material could become even more precious in the future, which has already led to the development of alternatives in the wine industry.

▶ VISITING THE ALENTEJO

INFORMATION
▶ Évora, ▶ Beja

WHERE TO EAT
▶ Moderate
Herdade do Esporão
Apartado 31
7200-999 Reguengos de Monsaraz
Tel. 266 509 280
Fax 266 519 753
Well known winery near Reguengos de Monsaraz (signposted in the town as »Turismo Rural« or »Enoturismo«). The restaurant offers refined Alentejan cuisine (only open at lunchtime).

WHERE TO STAY
▶ Mid-range/Luxury
Pousada de Castelo de Alvito
7920-999 Alvito
Tel. 284 485 343
Fax 284 485 383
Beautiful pousada, established in a 15th-century fortress. 20 rooms, swimming pool, good restaurant.

▶ Mid-range
Pousada de Vale do Gaio
7595-034 Torrão
Tel. 265 669 610
Fax 265 669 545
Above the dam of the Vale do Gaio, in a magnificent natural setting. Angling, water sports and hunting opportunities, 14 rooms, swimming pool.

Pousada de São Gens
7830 Serpa
Tel. 284 544 724
Fax 284 544 337
This comfortable pousada with 18 rooms and a swimming pool lies outside the old town of Serpa.

Pousada de Santa Clara
7665-879 Santa Clara-a-Velha
Tel. 283 882 250
Fax 283 882 402
In an old engineering building on the dam of Santa Clara-a-Velha. Not luxurious, but quiet and comfortable, 19 rooms, swimming pool.

Baedeker recommendation

▶ Budget/Mid-range
Corte Ligeira
Monte da Corte Ligeira
Cabeça Gorda
Tel. 284 947 216
Fax 284 947 391
www.corteligeira.com
Beautiful accommodation in a typically Alentejan estate located in the countryside 15km/9.4mi south of Beja.

Arts and culture The Alentejo is an ancient cultural area. A great deal of evidence of stone-age settlements has been preserved: **dolmens** (antas), **menhirs** and **stone circles** (cromeleques) can be found here, especially in northern Alto Alentejo. The remains from Roman and Moorish times are also numerous.

The strongly agricultural character of the region is reflected in the architecture: the decor of the Manueline epoch, whose ornamental symbolism was essentially borrowed from seafaring, is in the Alentejo often replaced with agricultural motifs such as ears of corn, plants or agricultural devices.

Even though one fifth of the Portuguese coast is in the Alentejo, the region is still mostly oriented to the interior. Tourism on the west coast is developing only haltingly. Many of the endlessly long, sandy beaches are to this day almost deserted. Even fishing only plays a minor part: just 1% of Portugal's entire catch of fish is from here. The inhabitants of the Alentejo continue to make a living almost exclusively from **agriculture**. In the west one-crop agriculture (grain cultivation) prevails on low fertility soil; in addition, agricultural activity consists of year-round management of pastures – one third of the Portuguese cattle livestock comes from the Alentejo – as well as cork oak cultivation, accompanied by pig breeding and charcoal burning. The wet and fertile coastal zones as well as the part of the Serras in the north-east facing the rainy side are considered the breadbasket of Portugal. Alongside fields of grain with wheat, rye and maize there are luscious orchards and olive groves. Overdue rainfall in the southern regions has caused a drastic decrease in yields in recent years. The river courses crossing the area are nearly dry in the summer and hardly suited for irrigation purposes. Economic benefits are expected from the recently created **Barragem de Alqueva**, a reservoir which collects the water of the Guadiana. Construction of the dam started as early as 1977, but the project was shelved for decades because of serious ecological and economic disputes.

Economy

The Alentejo is home to the breed of horse known as the »Alter Real«, which has been bred since the middle of the 18th century in this region and is held in especially high esteem for dressage.

»Alter Real« horse

★ ★ Algarve

E–O 31–35

Historical province: Algarve
District: Faro
Principal city: Faro

Area: 4,960 sq km/1,915 sq mi
Population: 350,000

Spring in the Algarve must be one of the best things imaginable for northern and central Europeans who are tired of winter, and the Algarve is indeed one of the most popular destinations in Europe, but not only in the springtime. 3,000 hours of sunshine per annum, beautiful beaches and scenic cliffs are inviting at any time of the year.

Broad slopes with cork oak groves, fig and carob trees, yellow blooming mimosa bushes, lush almond and pear plantations, red poppy fields – and above all the chirping of the cicadas and the sweet

Portugal's southernmost province

aromatic scent of the orange blossoms. The southern Portuguese Algarve region in the southernmost part of Europe stretches along the southern Atlantic coast of Portugal with a length of about 155km/ 97mi and a width of at most 50km/31.3mi between the Cabo de São Vicente and the mouth of the Guadiana on the Portuguese-Spanish border. The Algarve is very different from the rest of Portugal not only in agricultural and climatic terms, but also with regard to culture: there are far fewer art-historical sights here than in other parts of the country.

Name

The name Algarve is derived from the Arabic term »Al-Gharb« meaning »the west«, referring to the location of southern Portugal within the then Arabic territory (►History).

★ ★
Scenic beauty

Two large mountain ranges shield the region in the north: the Serra de Monchique in the north-west and the Serra do Caldeirão in the north and north-east. The Algarve can be roughly divided into a narrow and in part very tourism oriented coastal strip (Litoral), the foothills (Barrocal), and the thinly populated mountain regions (Serra) that are barely developed for tourism at all. The landscape of the Algarve is decidedly diverse; the coast alone shows the most varied types of landscapes. The western part of the southern Algarve coast, from Cabo de São Vicente to Vale do Lobo just outside Faro, is called the **Rocky Algarve** or Barlavento (windward side). Here, visitors find steep, rocky coasts with small, sandy bays as well as longer beaches that are interspersed with picturesque rock formations. Numerous grottoes and caves, offshore rocks standing alone in the water and on occasion highly bizarre cliff formations account for the allure of this region. The eastern **Sand Algarve** stretches roughly from Vale do Lobo to the mouth of the Guadiana. This coastal region, also known as Sotavento (leeward side) is far more exposed to the influence of the Atlantic than the coast further west. Here there are miles of long, broad, sandy beaches on the one hand and an extended lagoon system on the other. This mudflat-like lagoon area located west and east of Faro is protected by flat, elongated dune islands along the coast.

> **! Baedeker TIP**
>
> **Hiking in the Algarve**
>
> The remote mountain and coastal regions of the Algarve make beautiful areas for hiking. Walking trips are organized in the Serra de Monchique. The Odiana organization in Castro Marim draws up hiking trails in the eastern Algarve (see ► Sport and Outdoors).

Climate

3,000 hours of sunshine per year make the Algarve one of the most reliable areas on earth with regard to the weather. The climate of the Algarve coast is comparable to that of North Africa. Protected against cool climatic conditions by mountain chains in the north and north-

▶ VISITING THE ALGARVE

INFORMATION
Associação Turismo do Algarve
Avenida 5 de Outubro 18
8000-076 Faro
Tel. 289 800 403
www.visitalgarve.pt

ENTERTAINMENT
Entertainment hotspots in the Algarve are ►Albufeira, ►Praia da Rocha and ►Lagos.

WHERE TO EAT
► Moderate/Expensive
►Hotel Quinta do Lago, ►Estalagem Monte do Casal

► Moderate
►Pousada de São Brás

WHERE TO STAY
► Luxury
Hotel Quinta do Lago
Quinta do Lago
8135-024 Almansil
Tel. 289 350 350
Fax 289 396 393
www.quintadolagohotel.com
This golf hotel, integrated into the landscape, is a beautiful holiday spot with all possible conveniences for non-golfers as well. The house cuisine is especially recommended.

► Mid-range
Pousada de São Brás
Tel. 289 842 305; fax 289 841 726
www.pousadas.pt
This pousada is beautifully situated on a hill above the little town of São Brás de Alportel with a magnificent view across the hilly landscape. It offers accommodation of a high standard in a quiet location; 30 rooms, swimming pool, tennis court and a good restaurant.

Estalagem da Cegonha
Tel. 289 302 577; fax 289 322 675
Unique accommodation with nine rooms for those demanding particularly high standards. An exceptionally idyllic location in the vast natural landscape east of Vilamoura.

Hotel Alte
Estrada de Santa Margarida
Montinho
Tel. 289 478 523, fax 289 478 646
A well-kept hotel with 25 rooms, a swimming pool and tennis courts; located a little outside Alte – a place to enjoy some peace and quiet.

Baedeker recommendation

► Mid-range/Luxury
Estalagem Monte do Casal
Cerro do Lobo
Tel. 289 991 503; fax 289 991 341
www.montedocasal.pt
A beautifully-kept country house between Estói and Moncarapacho with beautiful rooms and suites. The restaurant enjoys a good reputation.

► Budget
Pensão das Dunas
Carrapateira, Rua da Padaria 9
Tel. 282 973 118
Lovely guesthouse on the edge of Carrapateira near the west coast; reservations are necessary.

Casa d'Alvada
Quinta do Freixo – Benafim
Tel. 289 472 153; fax 289 472 148
10 quiet rooms for rent on a farm between Alte and Salir north of Rocha da Pena, within the scope of »Agro-turismo«.

west and tempered by the water of the Atlantic Ocean, the Algarve does not experience extreme weather conditions.

Even in the winter the temperature seldom drops below 10°C/50°F. The summers are dry and hot, but a light breeze from the ocean provides a constant pleasant cooling effect. In the evenings it can get chilly, even in the summer. The average yearly rainfall of 350–600mm/14–24in is very low.

The wind conditions should be taken into consideration when choosing a holiday destination on the Algarve: the seaside resorts in the western quarter of the Algarve are better suited for those who enjoy harsh bathing conditions or for divers and anglers. A stiff breeze always blows in from the Atlantic Ocean here; the climate is relatively harsh and the surf is very strong.

Vegetation Olive, fig, carob and almond trees thrive in the Algarve, the latter blooming as early as January or February. In the irrigated valleys

Orange grove in the Algarve: in the spring there is a stunning perfume across the land.

there are orange groves, cotton plantations, and rice and sugarcane fields. Many gardens and fruit tree groves are surrounded by agave hedges. Camelia and oleander bushes give the landscape a southern flair.

History

The geographical shield towards the north brought about an isolated development of the Algarve. The unusual fertility of this coastal strip as well as the pleasant climate has attracted people for millennia. Although only scant evidence remains, it is certain that the Phoenicians and later the Greeks had colonies here. In the 6th and 5th centuries BC the Celts settled in the region, and some time later the Carthagians followed. Portimão is said to have been founded by Hannibal. Named Cyneticum in Roman times, the Algarve was the centre of an area of higher cultural development; numerous finds bear witness to the busy trade of that time.

The Roman reign was succeeded by the almost three-hundred-year reign of the Visigoths. They in turn were replaced by the Moors, who stayed for 500 years and deeply influenced the region's inhabitants and culture. Architecture and traditional costume exhibit Moorish features and names and language still have numerous Arabic features, not least the name Algarve itself (► p.212). In 1249 Afonso III of Portugal ordered that Faro be conquered – this put an end to Arabic rule in southern Portugal as well. In 1250 the Algarve was placed under the control of the Portuguese crown in personal union.

In the 15th/16th centuries the Algarve played a part in world affairs: Henry the Navigator founded a scientific centre in Sagres and, employing systematic research methods, created the technical basis for the great ocean sailing expeditions and voyages of discovery that initially cast off from the harbours of the Algarve.

Economy

The most important economic factor of the Algarve today is tourism. 50% of all those holidaying in Portugal spend their break in the Algarve. Mass tourism as it has developed in the Algarve in the last decades does not exist to the same extent in the rest of Portugal. Every year about 2 million holidaymakers come to the region. Whole sections of the coast are disfigured by sprawling colonies of hotels and guesthouses. In the meantime attempts are being made to preserve the specific character of the landscape and to adjust the hotel conglomerations to the environment. Prices in the Algarve are higher than in the rest of Portugal; many Portuguese cannot afford a stay on the southern coast.

The economic importance of agriculture and fishing is declining rapidly – until the end of the 1960s they were the main sources of income for the Algarvians. Industry in the Algarve has never been of much significance in Portugal; though there is a minor presence of the fish and cork processing industries, the most important industrial zones are located further north. The building materials industry, one of those to profit from the busy building activity on the Algarve coast, is located in the centre and north of Portugal.

A Drive Along the Algarve Coast

* *
From Cabo de São Vicente to Lagos

The western tip of the Algarve coast forms the Cabo de São Vicente, a rocky headland towering 60m/197ft above the ocean, which is at the same time the south-westernmost point of the European mainland (▶ Sagres). From Cabo de São Vicente the coastal road leads through austere heath towards the north-east. About 1km/0.6mi from the headland directly on the cliffs stands the **Fortaleza de Beliche**, built in 1632 in its present shape and currently in peril of collapse due to strong coastal erosion: it may therefore not be entered. From here ▶**Sagres**, with the Fortaleza de Sagres, is only 5km/3.1mi away.

Vila do Bispo

In Vila do Bispo, the »city of the bishop« 10km/6.3mi north of Sagres, stands a pretty 17th-century parish church; the interior is richly decorated with blue azulejos and gilded wooden carvings. A side-trip on well-made tracks leads from Vila do Bispo to the **Torre de Aspa**, an obelisk marking the highest point (156m/512ft) of the south-western Algarve coast 3.5km/2.2mi to the west.

*
Ermida de Nossa Senhora de Guadalupe ▶

East of Vila do Bispo on the N 125 at the eastern exit of Raposeira stands the chapel in which Henry the Navigator is said to have retreated for prayer. The oldest little church in the Algarve was built in the 13th century a features an early Gothic doorway.

! Baedeker TIP

Via do Infante

The N 125 runs all the way from west to east along the Algarve coast. Driving on this road is not necessarily fun – it is considered to be Portugal's most accident prone road. Those wishing for a speedy trip without hitting each and every coastal town can instead use the »Via do Infante« motorway, named after Henry the Navigator, in the east of the Algarve; as yet no fee applies and the road is usually empty.

Roads branch off from the N 125 and head to the coastal towns **Salema, Burgau and Luz**, all of them with beautiful sandy beaches. A few larger hotels and apartment buildings were erected in recent years around Salema with its picturesque centre. Burgau has been able to preserve its originality even more than Salema. In Luz a larger tourist hotspot has developed along the beautiful Praia da Luz. Behind Luz, an increasingly fertile landscape stretches to ▶Lagos. The solitude is no more: new hotel and holiday apartment complexes have sprouted up everywhere. In spite of that, Lagos has been able to retain some of its charm.

Once an idyllic fishing village, today a popular →
holiday destination: Carvoeiro

From Lagos to Portimão

Barely 20km/12.5mi east of Lagoslies the pretty town of **Alvor**. Named »Portus Hannibalis« by the Romans and »Albur« by the Moors, the town is situated on the estuary of the Rio Alvor. Up until the 1970s the residents here lived mainly from fishing; today tourism shapes the scenery – in a rather pleasant way. The town centre which is crossed by small lanes consists of low, white fishing houses. There are some restaurants, cafés and souvenir shops, but, all in all, the place is fairly rural. The entire waterfront at the harbour has been re-designed. East of Alvor near Torralta and on Praia dos Três Irmãos there are even larger hotel complexes.

Near the coast there is a small road from Alvor to ► **Praia da Rocha**, a high-rise haven owing its fame to the picturesque rocks fringing the beach. The harbour town ►**Portimão** borders on Praia da Rocha in the north. Neither a pretty townscape nor interesting sights are to be found here, but Portimão offers good shops and some rather original pubs. One of the most scenic places on the Algarve is considered to be **Ferragudo**, Portimão's neighbour on the eastern side. From Portimão a road leads up to the ►Serra de Monchique.

Ponta da Piedade – a tourist magnet in summer

The rural town of **Lagoa** 8km/5mi east of Portimão is the centre of one of the four wine areas of the Algarve. The well known bathing resort »Slide & Splash«, offering fun in the water to children in particular, is close by. In Lagoa a road branches off towards to ► Silves; to the south lies **Carvoeiro**. The centre above the small bay is still made up of pretty, narrow streets and lanes winding up the rocks. Care was taken to develop an appropriate design for the building work which took place around the former village, and many of the holiday settlements were created in the style of Moorish architecture. This careful planning is precisely what gives Carvoeiro its good reputation. The area covered by new buildings has however spread out, so that meanwhile almost the entire coastal section around Carvoeiro has become built up. The infrastructure is more than sufficient, and cafés and restaurants abound. Fishermen offer rides along the coast. There are fantastic views of the rocks from the water, and, over millennia, the Atlantic Ocean has created bizarre shapes in the soft limestone.Especially fantastic formations can be admired near Algar Seco, 2km/1.3mi east of Carvoeiro. Over the course of time, wind, weather and water have created a peculiar landscape. A small café is placed invitingly amidst the limestone world – protected by crags but with a view onto the sea. **Porches** is the centre of ceramics manufacture, with numerous large sales centres. Another widely popular water amusement park bearing the name »The Big One« is also located here. In both Porches and Alcantarilha roads branch off to **Armação de Pêra**, a dismal coastal town with austere, uniform high-rises, but with a truly splendid, endlessly long beach to make up for it. On a high, rocky outcrop a good 1km/0.6mi west of Armação de Pêra there is a real gem in the form of the 13th-century **Nossa Senhora da Rocha chapel**. The small, brilliant white church contrasts sharply with the blue water.
Approximately 5km/3.1mi east of Alcantarilha a road leads to ► **Albufeira**, the Algarve's largest and best known tourist hotspot.

Vilamoura, 10km/6.3mi east of Albufeira, is an urban centre designed on the drawing board and offering every conceivable recreational opportunity: golf courses and tennis courts, casino, open air theatre, etc. The yacht harbour, known for its international clientele, should most likely be considered the centre of town. Almost 1,000 moorings are available for both luxurious yachts and simple jolly boats. Cafés and restaurants line the harbour promenade. During construction work in Vilamoura the remains of the originally Roman settlement **Cerro da Vila** were found close to the marina. Along with other building foundations, the mosaic house from the third century AD is especially worth taking a look at. Finds from the excavations are displayed in the small site museum. **Quarteira**, situated 3km/1.9mi to the south-east, is far less appealing than Vilamoura, with unattractive rows of hotels and apartment buildings. By comparison, **Vale do Lobo** and **Quinta do Lago** a few miles south-east of Quar-

From Portimão to Albufeira

✷ ✷
◄ Algar Seco

From Albufeira to Faro

teira are exclusive holiday complexes. The luxurious bungalows and hotels are spread out across the parkland. There are several golf and tennis courts, and the beach offers various opportunities for water sports.

! *Baedeker* TIP

Sampling Cataplana

Originally »Cataplana« referred not to the food, but to the copper container in which the delicacies were cooked: scallops, fish or meat, bell peppers, onions and potatoes. Classic Cataplana is offered fairly frequently in the Algarve, so there is ample opportunity to try it.

Just outside the sprawling town of Almansil a road branches off to ► **Loulé**, a lively little place in the Algarve hinterland.

Directly outside **Almansil** in the direction of Faro, to the left of the road on a small hill, stands São Lourenço church. The interior of this Baroque building is covered with azulejos from 1730 depicting scenes from the life of St Lawrence. From São Lourenço it is only 10km/6.3mi to ►**Faro**.

From Faro to the Spanish border The roads east of Faro pass through fertile, rolling countryside. Magnificent wide, sandy beaches stretch from Faro up to the Spanish border, partly on narrow islands lying just offshore from the lagoon system on this section of the coast. The region is not as highly frequented by tourists as the Rocky Algarve. Visitors to the region come across larger hotel complexes and holiday home settlements every now and again and a fairly secluded spot can be found on most beaches – at least outside the peak season.

Olhão The next larger town after Faro is ► Olhão, a fishing town whose outskirts have meanwhile been built up with high-rises. Its quite distinct character can only really be appreciated during a stroll through the town centre. Cross the small pedestrian zone and proceed to the covered market directly beside the water.

Tavira A visit to ►Tavira, 22km/13.8mi east of Olhão, is exceedingly worthwhile. The river Gilão, flowing through its centre, is the primary reason for the light and friendly character of the town. Tavira's houses have the hipped roofs typical of the area.

East of Tavira lie the sprawling fishing towns **Cabanas** and **Cacela**. So far, tourist accommodation exists only in Cabanas – and even here only on a moderate scale.

Monte Gordo Not quite 20km/12.5mi beyond Tavira a road branches off to the sober seaside resort of Monte Gordo, frequented mostly by English and Dutch holidaymakers and the only town in this part of the Algarve with high-rises. A promenade with areas of greenery stretches along the wide beach; a casino does its best to provide international flair. Only 3km/1.9mi north-east of Monte Gordo is ► **Vila Real de Santo António**, the border town on the Guadiana river.

✳ Amarante

Historical province: Douro Litoral
District: Porto

Elevation: 125m/410ft
Population: 11,000

Well known for its wine, the small town of Amarante enjoys a very picturesque location on both sides of the Rio Tâmega roughly 70km/43.8mi east of Porto on the north-western slopes of the Serra do Marão.

With its pretty domestic architecture of the 16th–18th centuries, Amarante is really romantic; many houses in the town are clad with wooden shingles and surrounded by long wooden balconies. The best views of the historic district and the old bridge across the Rio Tâmega, the Ponte de São Gonçalo, are from the new river bridge or from one of the cafés on the southern river bank – most of them have terraces with views of the river.

What to See in Amarante

In the middle of the old town centre the massive Ponte de São Gonçalo, a three-arched granite bridge, spans the Rio Tâmega. It replaced an old river crossing in 1790.

Ponte de São Gonçalo

View onto the old town and the old bridge over the Rio Tâmega. On the right the dome of the São Gonçalo monastery church is visible.

▶ VISITING AMARANTE

INFORMATION

Alameda Teixeira de Pascoaes
4600-011 Amarante
Tel. 255 420 246
www.rtsmarao.pt

WHERE TO EAT

▶ Inexpensive
Confeitaria da Ponte
Rua 31 de Janeiro
Beautiful café on the end of the bridge
with a view of the monastery church.
Inside is a nicely furnished room,
outside on the terrace visitors sit high
above the river.

▶ Inexpensive/Moderate
Casa do Zé da Calçada
Rua 31 de Janeiro 79
Tel. 255 426 814
Well-run restaurant with a beautiful
terrace facing the river. The turkey
cutlets in cream sauce are decidedly
tasty; half portions are available, too.

WHERE TO STAY

▶ Mid-range
Pousada de São Gonçalo
Curva do Lancete
4600-520 Amarante
Tel. 255 461 113
With 15 rooms, the Pousada de São
Gonçalo enjoys a very peaceful loca-
tion amidst the hills of the Serra de
Marão. It was one of the first pousadas
in Portugal and thanks to its sur-
roundings is the best known.

▶ Budget
Albergaria Dona Margarita
Rua Cândido dos Reis 53
4600-055 Amarante
Tel. 255 432 110
Fax 255 437 977
One of the most beautiful hotels in
town, at least in terms of location. The
rooms facing the river offer a pretty
view; those on the street side are rather
loud.

Convento de São Gonçalo The 16th-century Convento de São Gonçalo directly at the end of
the Ponte de São Gonçalo stands beside its towering monastery
church which has a mighty crossing cupola. The São Gonçalo monastery was first founded by João III and his wife Catharine of Castile
and was extended during the reign of Philip II in the Renaissance
style associated with him. The granite façade, featuring arcades decorated with sculpture, is reminiscent of Italian Renaissance façades.

In the interior of the monastery church to the left of the high altar is
the funerary chapel of St Gonçalo (died about 1260). Paintings depicting scenes from the life of the saint are kept in the sacristy.

The monastery complex has two cloisters. Today, one of them is
home to part of the town council as well as to the **Museu Municipal
Amadeo de Souza-Cardoso**, a museum displaying modern Portuguese art from 1900 onwards. It is named after the cubist Amadeo
de Souza-Cardoso (1887–1918) who originated from the area around
Amarante. Archaeological finds are on display in a separate section.

! *Baedeker* TIP

Love-stricken

São Gonçalo is Amarante's patron saint, and a large celebration is organized in his honour every year at the beginning of June. Since São Gonçalo is also the patron saint of married couples and lovers, gifts in the form of phallic-shaped pastries of every size are made during the feast – the celebration is probably a relic of a pre-Christian fertility cult.

Above the monastery stands the 17th-century São Pedro church with a façade from 1724. The interior is richly decorated with talha dourada and azulejo adornments, and the sacristy has a beautiful coffered ceiling. **São Pedro**

Around Amarante

In Travanca, situated 25km/15.6mi north-west of Amarante in a valley bottom, the three-aisled fortified church of the former Benedictine abbey São Salvador is an inviting place to visit. The Roman church, which was founded in 970, has been essentially preserved, though the apse was added in the 16th century and the magnificent sculpture decoration also dates from that time. The main doorway is particularly opulently decorated with animals and mythical figures. **Travanca**

A drive through the attractive countryside of the well wooded Serra do Marão east of Amarante is appealing. The highest elevation here is the Sejarão at 1,415m/4,643ft. Situated below the summit of the Alto do Espinho (1020m/3,347ft), the Pousada de São Gonçalo (885m/2,904ft) offers an excellent view, although forest fires and the construction of a major road have tarnished the scenery somewhat. **★**
Serra do Marão

Arraiolos

K/L 24

Historical province: Alto Alentejo
District: Évora

Elevation: 275m/902ft
Population: 6,000

The old Alentejo town situated on soft slopes above broad lowlands is known all over the country for the colourful woollen rugs that are produced here using a cross-stitch like technique.

The town Ptolemy called »Arandia« is situated approximately 20km/12.5mi north of Évora in a beautiful setting. The special method of

► ARRAIOLOS

INFORMATION

Praça Lima e Brito
7040-040 Arraiolos
Tel. 266 490 240, www.rtevora.pt

WHERE TO STAY •
WHERE TO EAT

► **Mid-range/Luxury**
Pousada de N. Senhora da Assunção
Vale das Flores - Apartado 61
7041-909 Arraiolos
Tel. 266 419 340; fax 266 419 280
The pousada has been established
within a 16th-century monastery. It is
situated in the countryside outside
Arraiolos.

rug manufacture, probably adopted from the Moors, has been practised here since the 17th century. At first predominantly oriental patterns were used, imitating Persian rugs; later, traditional regional patterns and geometrical shapes were introduced. The town hall of Arraiolos hosts a permanent sales exhibition. Arraiolos rugs, for the most part featuring strong colours, are sold not only in Arraiolos itself but also in other cities of the Alentejo.

What to See in Arraiolos

The mighty ruins of a 14th-century **castle tower** above the white houses of the town. Two gates and six square towers as well as the outer walls have been preserved. The church inside the castle walls dates back to the 16th century. From this high vantage point there are extensive views of the town and across the fertile Alentejo plains.

Igreja da Misericórdia The 16th-century Misericórdia church was decorated with beautiful azulejos in the 18th century; take a look at the remarkable paintings in the interior.

Quinta dos Lóios It is worth having a look at the 16th-century former monastery, Quinta dos Lóios, a little outside the town to the north, which today functions as a well-appointed pousada. A Manueline doorway leads into the monastery church; the interior is completely covered with azulejos (c1700) and illusionistic paintings give the impression that it is larger than it really is. The marble basin in the two-storey cloister dates from 1575.

Around Arraiolos

Santana do Campo The church in the village of Santana do Campo 6km/3.8mi north-west of Arraiolos was built on top of the ruins of a Roman temple.

Montemor-o-Novo Montemor-o-Novo is a bustling little town about 23km/14.4mi south-west of Arraiolos. The remains of the medieval castle stand above the city. Another highlight is the archaeological museum in the former Convento de São Domingos (16th–18th century). Paintings and finds from the Gruta de Escoural are among the exhibits.

Rock paintings and engravings over 12,000 years old have been dis- **Gruta de**
covered in the Gruta de Escoural, located 12km/7.5mi south-east of **Escoural**
Montemor-o-Novo above the little town of Santiago do Escoural.
The cave was discovered by chance in 1963 during some blasting op-
erations. It has since been declared a Monumento Nacional (open: ⊙
Tue 1.30pm–5.30pm, Wed–Fri 9am till noon and 1.30pm–5.30pm,
Sat, Sun 9am–noon and 1.30pm–5pm).

✳ Aveiro

G 13

Historical province: Beira Litoral **Elevation:** sea level
District: Aveiro   **Population:** 38,000

**Aveiro is often called »the Venice of Portugal«, though with a
grand total of three canals the comparison could be seen as rather
daring. But the pretty town on the Ria de Aveiro, an extensively
branching lagoon, is nevertheless a worthwhile destination. Canal
rides on the »barcos moliceiros« are a nice attraction.**

Aveiro is about halfway between Porto and Coimbra on the eastern **City on the**
edge of the 47km/29.8mi-long and up to 7km/4.8mi-wide lagoon, **lagoon**
the Ria de Aveiro. The locals gave the widely branching and flat lake
the name »pólipo aquático« (octo-
pus). Aveiro is the district's principal city, episcopal see and one of
the most important ports on the
west coast of Portugal. Many beautiful Art Nouveau buildings and
façades decorated with azulejos are
still to be found here. The population lives mostly on sea salt harvesting in the salt flats of the Ria
de Aveiro, on the lagoon's kelp
which is a popular fertilizer, and on the porcelain and ceramics industry which settled here in the early 19th century. Alongside Aveiro
itself there are several other worthwhile destinations in the surrounding area: the magnificent, broad Atlantic beaches located directly west of Aveiro near Barra and Costa Nova or further north
near Torreira; and the scenically beautiful inland lagoon Ria de
Aveiro.

> ! **Baedeker TIP**
>
> **Passeios na Ria**
> Tours through the Ria de Aveiro start at the bank
> of the canal close to the tourist information
> office. The boat trips through the lagoon last
> either one or two hours.

The town, called Talábriga by the Romans, was located directly be- **History**
side the ocean in ancient times. Over the years the sediment washed
ashore by the Rio Vouga formed a dune spit, which only left the narrow connection of Barra open to the ocean, making the town one of
the **best protected harbours** on the Iberian west coast. In the 15th

VISITING AVEIRO

INFORMATION
Rua João Mendonça 8
3800-200 Aveiro
Tel. 234 423 680
Fax 234 428 326

WHERE TO EAT
► Inexpensive/Moderate
① *Mercado do Peixe*
Largo da Praça do Peixe
Tel. 234 383 511
Well-run restaurant under the roof of a covered fish market. Diners can look down onto the marketplace or over one of the canals. There is of course good, fresh fish on the menu.

② *Bombordo*
Largo da Praça do Peixe 10
Tel. 234 428 638
Typical Portuguese restaurant of the cosy variety. Large selection of fish and seafood, including cockles.

③ *O Rodel*
Rua Barbosa Magalhães
Tel. 234 383 065
A simple, good restaurant typical of the area.

WHERE TO STAY
► Mid-range
① *Hotel Moliceiro*
Rua Barbosa Magalhães 15/17
Tel. 234 377 400
Fax 234 377 401
www.hotelmoliceiro.com
Pleasant and modern hotel, tastefully but unobtrusively furnished rooms.

► Budget/Mid-range
② *Mercure Aveiro*
Rua Luís Gomes de Carvalho 23
Tel. 234 404 400
Fax 234 404 401
www.mercure.com
Beautiful old building with a well-kept hotel in whose 49 rooms guests can feel at home.

③ *Hotel Arcada*
Rua Viana do Castelo 4
Tel. 234 423 001
Fax 234 421 886
www.hotelarcada.com
Old Art Nouveau house directly on the canal. The 52 rooms are beautifully furnished and have large bathrooms.

and 16th centuries Aveiro experienced its heyday as the port used by the ships starting out on great voyages of discovery. Many of the historical buildings that still shape the appearance of the town date from this time. A heavy storm in 1575 sealed off access to the ocean, and thereafter the disconnected harbour soon lost its significance. All attempts to clear the blocked passage artificially failed. The fishermen, now impoverished, were resettled in the new harbour town of ►Vila Real de Santo António located at the mouth of the Guadiana and founded by Pombal in the 18th century. In 1808, the surge caused by another storm flushed out the old passage; it is now protected by dykes and weirs against silting up again. Thus, over the last two centuries, Aveiro has been able to regain its importance as one of the best harbours in Portugal.

Aveiro Plan

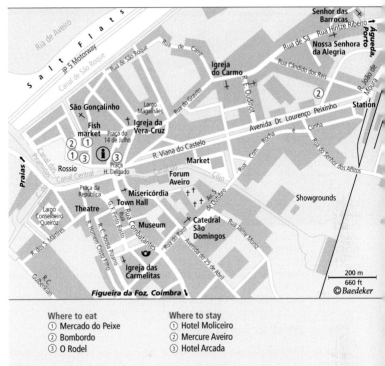

Where to eat
① Mercado do Peixe
② Bombordo
③ O Rodel

Where to stay
① Hotel Moliceiro
② Mercure Aveiro
③ Hotel Arcada

The kelp fishermen of Aveiro who go out with their characteristic boats, the »**barcos moliceiros**«, to »harvest kelp« in the Ria de Aveiro are called »moliceiros«. »Moliceiro« is derived from »moliço«, the Portuguese term for algae or kelp – or rather the natural agricultural fertilizer obtained from it. Aboard their wooden sailing boats decorated with naive paintings, moliceiros collect the kelp from the waters of the wide lagoon with a large rake. With strong enough winds they will set trapezoid sails on the up to 15m/49ft-long and 2–2.5m/6.5–8ft-wide boats; the rest of the time they move the boats with long punts or tow them with long ropes in the narrow canals. In the last decades the number of boats in Aveiro has decreased from more than a thousand to a mere handful of registered vessels. Due to the development of artificial fertilizers, the formerly lucrative profession of kelp fishing is almost extinct. Owing to increasing difficulties in the market, seaweed is now collected as well: it is then dried and used as bedding for livestock. The working conditions are hard, the income is low and the profession of the moliceiros has become unattractive. On the occasion of the **Festa da Ria** that takes place every

Kelp fishermen

»Barcos moliceiros« in Canal Central in Aveiro

year in the second half of July, the last kelp fishermen of Aveiro meet in the Ria for a regatta, combined with tests of skill and a competition for the most beautiful boat painting.

What to See in Aveiro

Igreja da Misericórdia The Misericórdia church, built at the end of the 16th century, stands on the Praça da República across from the town hall. Its doorway was clad with blue azulejo decoration in the 19th century.

Catedral São Domingos The Catedral São Domingos is situated further south-east. It was a gift for the Dominicans from the Infante Dom Pedro. It was consecrated in 1464. In the 18th century the Baroque doorway was placed in front of the granite façade. Inside the cathedral, take a look at the tomb of Caterina de Attayde (died 1551), who Luís de Camões – under the name of »Natercia« – sung about in his sonnets. The **Gothic Cruzeiro de São Domingos** in front of the cathedral is one of the most beautiful wayside crosses in Portugal.

✱ Museu de Aveiro The rooms of the former Dominican convent opposite the cathedral are now home to the Museu de Aveiro. In 1472 the **Infanta Joanna**, daughter of Afonso V, entered this convent against the wishes of her father in order to live the simple life of a nun. She died here in 1490 at the young age of 38 and was buried in the convent church. She earned much admiration because of her willingness to suffer privation and her complete renunciation of privileges; even today St Joanna is revered by the people as the **patron saint of the city**. A monument was erected in front of the convent in 1990 in her honour. The Museu de Aveiro was established in 1911 in the church, cloisters and other convent rooms. It provides a good and almost complete overview of Portuguese art in the Baroque era; in addition it shows paintings from the 15th to the 18th centuries, sculptures and archaeological finds. One of the most significant exhibits is the portrait of St Joanna attributed to Nuno Gonçalves (15th century). The convent church is richly decorated with gold talha dourada and azulejos. The Baroque tomb of St Joanna in one of the antechambers of the church was created between 1699 and 1711 by João Antunes (open: Tue–Sun 10am–5.30pm).

The Ecomuseu in the area of the salt flats directly north of the town provides information on the salt flats and the Ria de Aveiro.

Ecomuseu

Around Aveiro

To the west of Aveiro are the broad, sandy beaches of the ►Costa de Prata: The most beautiful beaches are in Barra as well as in Costa Nova. Costa Nova is surely one of the prettiest coastal towns of this region.**Fishermen's houses with colourful vertical stripes** add to the special charm of the place. Though in recent years many hotels and apartment buildings have been constructed around Costa Nova and the other seaside resorts of this region, the beach itself is never overcrowded even in the peak season.

✱ **Costa Nova**

A boat ride through the Ria de Aveiro is exceedingly worthwhile. The houses on stilts that are adapted to the ever-changing water level, and the racks for drying cod brought in from the high seas seem peculiar. With a little luck visitors might catch sight of the last boats of the kelp fishermen sailing in or out of Bico harbour near Murtosa.

✱ **Ria de Aveiro**

In Avanca, 25km/15.6mi north-east of Aveiro, a small museum commemorates the doctor António Egas Moniz, who was awarded the Nobel prize for his contributions to medicine in 1949.

Avanca

At the north end of the Ria de Aveiro is the little town of Ovar, known for its carnival with beautiful street processions. Its Way of the Cross with six chapels has been declared a Monumento Nacional. The local museum has modern art, folk art and ethnographic exhibits on display.

Ovar

It is worthwhile continuing on from Vila da Feira to Arouca approximately 40km/25mi to the east. Small, narrow streets pass through a solitary mountain landscape. The monastery of Arouca was founded in the 10th century, though today's buildings mostly date back to the 17th and 18th centuries. Inside the monastery church, the choir stalls

Arouca

from 1725 and the Baroque organ from 1739 are especially notable. The museum on the first floor of the former monastery keeps a valuable selection of Portuguese sacred art (open: Tue–Sun 9am–noon and 2pm–5pm).

Ílhavo The former fishing port of Ílhavo about 7km/4.4mi south of Aveiro is completely silted up today. Numerous exhibits in the regional and maritime museum bear witness to the past. In addition, porcelain from Vista Alegre is also on display here.

Vista Alegre The porcelain known all over the country has been manufactured in Vista Alegre since 1824. A museum affiliated with the factory and a sales exhibition provide insight into the history of porcelain manufacture (open: Tue – Sun 9am–12.30pm and 2pm–4.30pm).

★ Barcelos

G 7

Historical province: Minho	**Elevation:** 40m/131ft
District: Braga	**Population:** 8,000

Barcelos is the home of the colourful ceramic rooster, the Portuguese mascot seen all over the country. A visit to Barcelos is especially worthwhile on Thursdays when the Portugal's largest weekly market is held here.

Barcelos rooster Located 20km/12.5mi west of Braga, Barcelos was once the capital of the country's first earldom founded in 1298. Legend has it that a citizen of Barcelos, who had allegedly stolen from a fellow pilgrim on his pilgrimage to Santiago de Compostela and had been sentenced to death, sent a hurried prayer to St Jacob. He was presented to the judge who was just about to eat a roast rooster. The condemned man declared in his despair that the rooster would come back to life if he was innocent. With that, the rooster is said to have risen from the plate and to have crowed audibly. In thanks for his salvation the citizen donated a clay rooster.

What to See in Barcelos

Campo da República The focal point of urban life in Barcelos is the spacious Campo da República, one of the largest squares in Portugal. Every Thursday thousands of visitors gather at the market here to buy the fruit, vegetables, meat and wine, as well as arts and crafts and homemade furniture on offer; naturally, the Barcelos rooster is found here, too. On other days of the week the market is considerably smaller. Adjacent to the square is the Passeio dos Assentos, a park with glorious herbaceous borders.

On the north side of the Campo da República is the Nossa Senhora do Terço church, part of a Benedictine convent founded in 1705. The interior is decorated with a coffered ceiling with numerous painted panels as well as 18th-century azulejo-clad walls.

Nossa Senhora do Terço

The Baroque church Bom Jesus da Cruz (16th/17th centuries) in the south-west of the square clearly shows Italian influence. The free-standing central building is spanned by a stately granite cupola.

Bom Jesus da Cruz

Near the church stands the Torre de Menagem or Porta Nova, a re-minder of the town's 16th-century fortifications. Today this is home to the tourism office and to a permanent exhibition of the arts and crafts produced in Barcelos and the surrounding areas.

Torre de Menagem

A little further downhill past the Torre de Menagem is the old town where the ruins of the Paço dos Duques de Bragança, the former comital ducal palace, stand. The remains of the 15th/16th-century building together with the broad terrace of the palace are the setting for an archaeological museum. The open-air lapidarium shows ex-

✶ Paço dos Duques de Bragança

The Barcelos rooster – popular souvenir with history

▶ VISITING BARCELOS

INFORMATION
Largo da Porta Nova
(Torre de Menagem)
4750-329 Barcelos
Tel. 253 811 882
www.rtam.pt

WHERE TO EAT
▶ **Moderate**
Bagoeira
Av. Dr. Sidónio Pais 495
Tel. 253 811 236

Good regional dishes are served in this large hotel restaurant.

WHERE TO STAY
▶ **Budget/Mid-range**
Casa dos Assentos
4750-640 Barcelos, Quintiães
Tel. 258 942 729
www.solaresdeportugal.pt
Beautiful 17th-century hotel with rooms and apartments, located between Barcelos and Ponte de Lima.

hibits from the Roman period to the Middle Ages. The Cruzeiro do Senhor do Galo, a 14th-century wayside cross, is particularly notable; it relates to the legend of the crowing rooster.

Igreja Matriz Beside the palace stands the parish church (Igreja Matriz). Originally built in the 13th and 14th centuries, it was remodelled in the 18th century. The late Romanesque doorway features an impressive rose window decoration. Once again, fine azulejos adorn the interior.

Solar dos Pinairos Opposite the Paço dos Duques de Bragança is the Gothic palace of Solar dos Pinairos, a granite building from 1448 with two towers and an arcaded courtyard. In the middle of a small area of greenery between the former duke's palace and the Solar dos Pinairos stands a Gothic **pelourinho**, a 15th-century pillory column, symbolizing the jurisdiction of the municipal authorities.

Capuchin monastery The former Capuchin monastery and the Misericórdia hospital today house the **town hall** of Barcelos.

Stone bridge Below the former duke's palace a five-arched stone bridge crosses the Rio Cávado. The bridge, originally built in the 14th century, was fully restored in the 19th century. The other side of the river offers a beautiful view of the old town.

Around Barcelos

Esposende The somewhat sober little town of Esposende lies about 15km/9.4mi west of Barcelos, where the broad mouth of the Cávado meets the Atlantic Ocean. The town owes its moderate tourism industry to the fine sandy beach. There are a few larger hotels (▶Costa Verde), but

Esposende remains a seaside resort geared more towards offering rest and relaxation than a broad recreational programme. The mouth of the river, with the São João Baptista fort that has been converted into a lighthouse, is really quite impressive.

South of the mouth of the Cávado is Ofir – a fishing village up until a few years ago that has now developed into a small holiday town.

Ofir

On the peak of the Monte Franqueira (298m/978ft) about 5km/3.1mi south-west of Barcelos stands the pilgrimage church Nossa Senhora da Franqueira. It was built in the 1100s and remodelled several times in subsequent centuries. There is a beautiful view of the surrounding region from here. The remains of the Castelo da Faria from 1373 as well as signs of a pre-Roman settlement are nearby (Citânia de Franqueira).

Monte Franqueira

✶ ✶ Batalha

F 19

Historical province: Beira Litoral
District: Leiria

Elevation: 70m/230ft
Population: 5,000

Batalha, situated between Lisbon and Coimbra in a fertile basin of the Lena, is a simple rural town known throughout the world for its Dominican abbey. One of the largest and most significant monastery complexes in Portugal, the abbey has been under UNESCO protection as a World Cultural Heritage Site since 1983.

Besides the famous abbey, the small town features a number of houses from the 17th and 18th centuries as well as the Santa Cruz parish church (1512) with its splendid doorway.

✶ ✶ Mosteiro de Santa Maria da Vitória

The Mosteiro de Santa Maria da Vitória was founded in 1388 by João I to fulfil a vow he had made on 14 August 1385 at the onset of the battle of Aljubarrota. Though outnumbered by the troops of the Castilian King Juan I, João's followers under commander Nuno Álvares Pereira won the battle, which took place near Aljubarrota (► Around Alcobaça), and thus ensured **independence of Portugal from Spain**. To commemorate the victory the abbey is mostly referred to as Batalha Abbey or Mosteiro da Batalha (batalha = battle).

Origins

Afonso Domingues was commissioned as the abbey's first architect and provided the plans for the entire monastery complex. By the time of his death in 1402, the choir and nave of the church, the Claustro Dom João and some of the other monastic buildings had

History

been completed. His successor was David Houet (also known as Huguet or Huet), and under his control the church was finished and the Capela do Fundador added by 1438. In addition, Houet started building the funerary chapels which later came to be known as the Capelas Imperfeitas. Martim Vásquez (died before 1448) and Fernão de Évora (died 1477) continued work on them, as well as on the second cloister. Construction work largely ceased in the subsequent decades. It was not until the beginning of the 16th century – in the reign of Manuel I – that Mateus Fernandes the Elder (died 1515) and Mateus Fernandes the Younger (died 1528) completed the vestibule between the choir and the Capelas Imperfeitas. It was during this period that the splendid decoration adorning the abbey buildings was created, primarily by sculptor Diogo Boytaca (died around 1525). The last significant master builder to contribute to the construction of Batalha Abbey was **João de Castilho**, the builder of the Hieronymite monastery of Belém (▶ Lisbon). The final work on the abbey was carried out in 1533. The earthquake of 1755 damaged Batalha Abbey, but French troops did far more damage in 1810. The Dominican monastery was abolished in 1834, and in 1840 the abbey was declared a national monument; since then it has been carefully restored, and today appears to be in excellent condition.

Abbey church The abbey church, built during the reign of King João I, is an especially well conceived example of the finest in Gothic style. Both the western façade, richly adorned with sculptures, and the vividly structured southern side are delightful.

Interior The 80m/88yd-long and 32.5m/106ft-high **interior** of the abbey church is extraordinarily impressive. It is given structure by mighty pillars and is lit by tall stained glass windows, some of which are original. Directly behind the main doorway the flat tombstone of the master builder Mateus Fernandes the Elder is inserted in the floor. The southern aisle provides access via a marvellous doorway to the funerary chapel of the abbey's founder, the **Capela do Fundador**. It was built to a square floor plan with a side length of nearly 20m/66ft. In its centre stands the sarcophagus of João I (died 1433) and his English spouse Philippa of Lancaster (died 1416) which is supported by eight lions. In the alcoves on the southern side of the chapel are the graves of four of the royal couple's children: on the left is the tomb of the Infante Dom Fernando, the »Príncipe Constante« (»steadfast prince«) of Calderon's tragedy of the same name, who died in Moroccan captivity in 1443; next to that is the double grave of the Infante João (died 1442) and his wife Isabella; the grave of the Infante Dom Henrique (1394–1460; ▶ Famous People), who went down in history as »Henry the Navigator« is also here, as is that of the Infante Dom Pedro (1392–1449). On the western wall are the graves of King Afonso V (died 1481) and his spouse, as well as those of King João II (died 1495) and his son Afonso.

▶ VISITING BATALHA

INFORMATION

Pr. Mouzinho de Albuquerque
2440-121 Batalha
Tel. 244 765 180
www.rt-leiriafatima.pt

WHERE TO STAY · WHERE TO EAT

▶ Mid-range/Luxury
Pousada do Mestre Afonso Domingues
2440-102 Batalha

Tel. 244 765 260; fax 244 765 247
Beautiful luxury hotel with 21 rooms and every convenience. Highly recommended restaurant.

▶ Mid-range
Pensão Batalha
Largo da Igreja
2440-901 Batalha
Tel. 244 767 500 fax 244 767 467
Pleasant hotel with 22 rooms in the centre of Batalha.

The northern aisle of the church leads into the Claustro Dom João I (1386–1515), a masterpiece of Portuguese Gothic, which displays its entire development here – from the simplest shapes to fantastic exaggerated ornamentation. The tracery galleries are for the most part modern. From here, the view of the rich northern church façade is magnificent.

Claustro Dom João I

On the east side of the cloister is the **chapter house** (Sala do Capítulo) with a mighty entrance gate. The sufferings of Christ are depicted on the colourful stained glass window. A guard of honour constantly watches over the tomb of the two unknown soldiers of the First World War. The northern stretch of the cloister is taken up by the chapel-like **pump room** (Pavilhão) that also offers views from delightful perspectives.

The Museum of the Unknown Soldier has been established in the former refectory, and in the former dorter various architectural fragments are exhibited.

The north-west side of the Claustro Dom João I leads to the Claustro Dom Afonso V, a cloister with simple double windows and a simple upper porticoed gallery (15th century). The Claustro João III, which was destroyed by fire in 1811, once bordered it on the east side.

Claustro Dom Afonso V

Adjoining the abbey church at the eastern end are the Capelas Imperfeitas, decorated in the richest Manueline style (entrance on the northern façade, no direct access from the abbey church itself). The octagonal central space is surrounded by seven large chapels, which house the tombs of King Duarte, the son of João I, and Duarte's wife Leonor of Aragón. The overall impression of the space is a strange one, as the ceiling is completely missing, making it possible to look directly up into the sky. The massive buttresses on the interior of the

Capelas Imperfeitas

mausoleum would have been necessary to support the originally planned cupola. A large vestibule with a magnificent doorway almost 15m/50ft high was added on the west side of the chapel.

Equestrian statue The equestrian statue that was erected 1961 in front of the southern façade of the abbey church shows Nuno Álvares Pereira, King João's commander in the battle of Aljubarrota.

Around Batalha

São Jorge The chapel of São Jorge was built about 5km/3mi south-west of Batalha on the edge of the former battlefield of Aljubarrota, on the spot from which Nuno Álvares Pereira led the battle; to this day there is always a jar of fresh water next to the chapel entrance that once stood there for the thirsty fighters.

Porto de Mós 9km/5.6mi south of Batalha Abbey, on the bank of the Rio Lena, lies Porto de Mós. A widely visible castle, whose origins date back to the 9th century, stands on a hill above the town. The earthquake of 1755 destroyed large parts of the castle which has been restored several times in recent years. Today its design is modelled on the Moorish style with two pretty green pointed roofs, similar to those that can be seen in Morocco. It offers a panoramic view of the area surrounding Porto de Mós.

Around Batalha several impressive dripstone caves can be viewed, such as the Grutas de Alvados here.

The **Grutas de Alvados** are about 10km/6mi south-east of Porto de
Mós (open: daily 9.30am–6pm, in summer until 8.30pm). The cave
landscape, featuring dripstone forms and underground lakes, was
discovered in 1964. Approximately 1km/0.6mi from here, the **Grutas
de Santo António** make a similar impression (open: daily 9am–6pm,
in summer until 8.30pm). This cave system covers a space of 6,000
sq m/64,560 sq ft, and the largest single cave measures 80 x 50m (260
x 164ft) and has a height of 43m/141ft. Steps lead down to another
cave system near the town of Mira de Aire, the **Grutas de Mira de
Aire**; the return journey is made in a lift. The **Grutas da Moeda** are
located near São Mamede, 15km/9.4mi south-east of Batalha. In
these caves (open: daily 9am–6pm, in summer until 7pm), discovered by two hunters in 1971, visitors can descend 350m/1,150ft.

★
Dripstone caves

Beira

E–S 10–19

Historical provinces: Beira Alta, Beira
Baixa, Beira Litoral
Population: 1,923,000

Districts: Viseu, Guarda, Castelo Branco,
Aveiro, Coimbra
Principal cities: Guarda, Castelo
Branco, Coimbra

**The Beira region lies in northern Portugal and stretches across the
jagged mountain region and the harsh plateaus between the
Douro in the north and the Tagus in the south.**

Beira means »edge« or »shore« – in the Middle Ages the region was a
heavily contested frontier to the Moors and its cities were fortified
for this reason. The Beira is divided into three historical provinces of
rather differing nature.

The Beira Alta (high Beira) occupies the forested highlands that
stretch from the highest peaks of the Portuguese mainland, the ►Ser-
ra da Estrela (highest elevation: 1,991m/6,532ft), to the valleys of the
Douro (►Douro Valley) and the Mondego. From a geological viewpoint, it is the continuation of the central Spanish Cordilleras. The
climate is dry and hot in the summer; in the winter it is cold, and
there is snow at higher elevations. Extensive arable farming and
management of pasture with sheep prevails. The wines have a good
reputation, especially those from the Dão valley and the Mondego
valley. Settlement is sparse, in keeping with the moderate fertility
and limited area of the cultivable land. The capital of Beira Alta is
►Guarda, the largest city of the Viseu region.

Beira Alta

The Beira Baixa (lower Beira), whose capital is ►Castelo Branco, extends across an arid plain between the southern foothills of the Serra
da Estrela and the Tagus. The economic conditions of this province

Beira Baixa

▶ VISITING THE BEIRA

INFORMATION

Beira Alta
▶Guarda,▶Viseu

Beira Baixa
▶Castelo Branco

Beira Litoral
▶Coimbra

WHERE TO STAY • WHERE TO EAT

▶ Mid-range/Luxury
Pousada Convento do Desagravo
3400-758 Vila Pouca da Beira
Tel. 238 670 080; fax 238 670 081
21 rooms in an old convent. Sophisticated restaurant.

▶ Budget/Mid-range
Quinta da Geia
Largo do Terreiro do Fundo do Lugar
3400-214 Aldeia das Dez

Tel. 238 670 010
fax 238 670 019
www.quintadageia.com
Located in the midst of the mountains of the Beira, this is a 17th-century building with beautiful rooms and a restaurant serving typical regional dishes.

WHERE TO STAY

▶ Budget
Casa da Padaria
6285-018 Piódão
Tel. 235 732 773
Rural, simple, friendly accommodation with 4 rooms in Piódão.

Estalagem do Piódão
6285-018 Piódão
Tel. 210 403 900; fax 210 403 951
Reliable and well-run mountain hotel a short distance outside the actual village.

Piódão – completely isolated granite village in the Serra de Açor

are similar to those of the Alentejo: one-crop agriculture – mostly grains – on latifundia, along with Mediterranean-style mixed arable farming with grains, vegetables, fruit, citrus fruits and olives in the river valleys.

Beira Litoral (coastal Beira) covers the narrow coastal strip, broadening out around the level of the capital ►Coimbra between Ovar and Monte Real. It is confined by the hills of the Serra do Caramulo, the Serra da Estrela and the Serra da Lousã in the east. Dune landscapes with pine forests, swampy estuaries on the Vouga and the Mondego and the saltpans of the Ria de Aveiro define the appearance of this region. Grains and vegetables are cultivated only in the parts of the province that are far from the coast.

Beira Litoral

★ Beja

L 28

Historical province: Baixo Alentejo
District: Beja

Elevation: 282m/925ft
Population: 20,000

Beja is visible from far and wide, situated on a hill in the midst of the fertile plain of the Baixo Alentejo. It is the largest city of the Alentejo next to Évora and a worthwhile destination because of its pretty old town. And then there is the story of Sister Mariana Alcoforado...

Beja is the district's capital and the main trading centre for agricultural products. As Pax Iulia, Beja was an important town for the Romans, and some remains of the town wall on the northern side and an archway on the southern side have been preserved. Even if the town centre can essentially be explored in a two hour stroll, Beja still lends itself to an overnight stay; the pousada, one of the most beautiful in Portugal, provides the most stylish accommodation.

At first glance, Beja's sea of houses seems rather unattractive, but once in the old town there are narrow lanes and an appealing pedestrian zone to be explored. Many of the brilliant white little houses are endowed with remarkable details, including iron bars, windows, gates, and arcades. The prettily designed municipal park or the small park with its simple café at the Praça Diogo Fernandes are good places to rest after a sightseeing tour.

★ Appealing old town

What to See in Beja

A good starting point for a walking tour through the historic district of Beja is the Largo da Conceição, adorned with a **statue of queen Leonor** (1458–1525) from 1958. The small former Poor Clares con-

★ Convento N. S. da Conceição

▶ VISITING BEJA

INFORMATION
Rua Capitão F. de Sousa 25
7800-451 Beja
Tel. 284 311 913
www.rt-planiciedourada.pt

PARKING
Parking spaces can be found in the town centre at the Largo dos Duques de Beja under some tall trees near the monastery.

WHERE TO EAT
▶ Moderate/Expensive
① *Pousada de São Francisco*
Largo D. Nuno Álvares Pereira
Tel. 284 313 580
The most beautiful pousada also hosts the best restaurant in town. Diners enjoy the very special ambience along with their meal.

▶ Moderate
② *Adega 25 de Abril*
Rua da Moeda 23
Good bar with typical Alentejo dishes. Locally produced wines.

③ *Pipa*
Rua da Moeda
Very popular with the people of Beja. A lot of good meat dishes.

WHERE TO STAY
▶ Mid-range
① *Hotel Melius*
Avenida Fialho de Almeida
Tel. 284 321 822
Fax 284 321 825
Besides the pousada this is the best hotel in town with pleasant, comfortable rooms.

▶ Budget/Mid-range
② *Corte Ligeira*
▶ Alentejo

▶ Budget
③ *Pensão Residencial Bejense*
Rua Capitão Francisco de Sousa 57
Tel. 284 311 570
Fax 284 311 579
www.hotelarcada.com
Beautiful guesthouse right in the centre of Beja – simple, inexpensive and quite comfortable.

vent, Nossa Senhora da Conceição, which today houses the Museu Regional, is also here. The convent, whose church and cloister have been preserved, was built between 1459 and 1506 at the behest of the Infante Dom Fernando and his spouse Dona Brites and shows noticeable elements of Manueline style. The nun **Mariana Alcoforado** (▶Famous People) lived in the convent. In 1665, from her window on the first floor, she set eyes on Chevalier de Chamilly, to whom she was later introduced by her brother. A short love affair developed that ended suddenly on Chamilly's return to France in 1667. Allegedly Mariana Alcoforado sent her lover five sentimental letters that were first published as early as 1669. The love letters, which were to enter into world literature as the *Lettres Portugaises*, were in actual fact probably not penned by the nun, but by the Frenchman Gabriel-Joseph Guillerague (1636–1715).

Both the former convent church, richly adorned with talha dourada, and the cloister with its terrific 16th-century azulejos are part of the **Museu Regional de Beja**. It is well worth seeing the archaeological exhibits, paintings, azulejos, coins, folk art, costumes and furniture in the museum's collection (open: Tue–Sun 9.30am–12.30pm and 2pm–5.15pm).

Obliquely opposite and somewhat below the convent is the 13th-century Santa Maria church. Four small towers connected with Gothic arches decorate the main façade. The Baroque and Rococo altars inside are also worth taking a look at.

Igreja de Santa Maria

The lanes of the old town that exit opposite the convent entrance lead to the Praça da República, the centre of Beja. The Manueline pillory and a Manueline arcade here are attractive.

Praça da República

At the western end of the square stands the Misericórdia church, built in 1550 by the Infante Dom Luís as a covered market hall. A chapel was later added and the building was converted into a place of worship with a very spacious portico. The building's original function as a market is clearly noticeable even today.

Igreja da Misericórdia

Further west stands the castle which was erected above the ruins of a Roman fortification in around 1300 during the reign of Dinis I. The crenellated tower, partly made of marble, is visible from far and

Castelo

Beja *Plan*

Where to eat
① Pousada de São Francisco
② Adega 25 de Abril
③ Pipa

Where to stay
① Hotel Melius
② Corte Ligeira
③ Pensão Residencial Bejense

Station • Serpa, Moura

Rua Tenente Valadim • R. da Muralha
Rua General Teófilo da Trindade
Terreirinho das Peças
Rua dos Prazes
Rua da Casa Pia
Rua André
Rua do Esquivel
Igreja do Salvador • Largo do Salvador
Rua D. Alfonso Henriques
Rua D. Nuno Álvares Pereira
Municipal park
Rua Afonso Lopes Vieira
Sé
Castelo • Largo do Lidador
Rua Dr. Aresta Branco
Largo de Sta. Maria
Igreja de Santa Maria • Largo dos Duques de Beja
Pousada
Lg. D. Nuno Álvares Pereira ②
Igreja da Misericórdia • Praça da República
R. dos Infantes
R. da Moeda
Rua do Touro
Largo da Conceição
Convento N.S. da Conceição ③
Post Office
Rua do Canal
Rua D. Manuel I
Largo de S. João
Rua do Sembrano
Terreiro dos Valentes
Rua Capitão João Francisco de Sousa
Rua Luís de Camões
Av. Miguel Fernandes
Praça Diogo Fernandes
Aljustrel ↓ • Mértola, Castro Verde ↘ ①
Lisboa, Évora
Ermida de Santo André

100 m
330 ft
© Baedeker

Manueline decoration on the Convento Nossa Senhora da Conceição

wide. Its height of 40m/130ft makes it the highest keep tower in Portugal. Visitors have to climb almost 200 steps before enjoying the magnificent view of the town. There is a small chapel as well as a hall with a magnificent stellar vault in the lower storeys.

Capela de Santo Amaro   Near the castle walls, beyond the Roman Évora gate, stands the early Romanesque Capela de Santo Amaro that dates back to the 9th/10th centuries. This, the oldest church of the town, is one of only four churches in Portugal that have been preserved from that time. Today it is home to a **museum** exhibiting **Visigothic sculptures**.

Sé   The former cathedral situated east of the castle is a Renaissance building from 1590. Substantial restoration work was carried out in 1940.

Ermida de Santo André   South-west of the town centre is the Ermida de Santo André, constructed in 1162 in gratitude for the recapture of the destroyed town from the hands of the Moors. The towers and the crenellated vestibule give the church a fortress-like character.

Around Beja

The Roman excavation sites of Pisões about 8km/5mi south-west of **Pisões**
Beja are reached by turning off the N 18 near Penedo Gordo and
heading north to Aljustrel.

In Ferreira do Alentejo approximately 25km/16mi west of Beja there **Ferreira do**
is a pretty 16th-century parish church. The 16th-century retable in **Alentejo**
the Misericórdia church also deserves attention.

Located about 30km/19mi south-east of Beja, the little town of Serpa ✳
is worth seeing because of its peculiar appearance. The town has had **Serpa**
this name since ancient times. The ruins of a 13th-century fort tower
above the city, offering a good view of the town and the surrounding
region. White houses, some of them decorated with azulejos, can be
found in the narrow lanes of the old town.
The 13th-century Gothic church Santa Maria with 17th-century
polychrome tile decorations in the interior, the former monasteries
São Paulo and São António from the 15th/16th centuries and the remains of an ancient water pipe near the Porta de Beja are particularly
worth taking a look at.

Belmonte

O 14

Historical province: Beira Baixa
District: Castelo Branco

Elevation: 610m/2,000ft
Population: 2,000

**Belmonte was the seat of the Cabrals and birthplace of the sea-
farer Pedro Álvares Cabral, who discovered Brazil in 1500. A monument on the main street, which was erected to celebrate the 500th
birthday of Cabral, is one of the ways the town remembers its
great son.**

In the centre of Belmonte, situated on a hill at the foot of the ►Serra
da Estrela between Covilhã and Guarda, skilfully restored houses
around a square bear witness to the prosperity and renown of times
past.

What to See in Belmonte

A little above the centre of town are the ruins of a mighty castle, **Castelo**
which was built in the early 13th century under King Dinis, given to
Fernão Cabral in 1466 by king Afonso V, and restored in 1940.
There is an extensive view from up here of the mountainous country
of the Beira provinces. The castle's gate still shows the Cabral coat of
arms with a goat (= cabra).

▶ VISITING BELMONTE

INFORMATION

Largo do Brasil
Castelo de Belmonte
6250 Belmonte
Tel. 275 911 488
www.rt-serradaestrela.pt

WHERE TO STAY •
WHERE TO EAT

▶ Mid-range/Luxury

Pousada do Convento de Belmonte
6250 Belmonte
Tel. 275 910 300
One of the oldest Portuguese pousadas, with 24 rooms. On the highest hill above the Vouga valley. The pousada restaurant offers a magnificent view of the surrounding scenery.

▶ Budget

Hotel Belsol
6250-176 Belmonte
Tel. 275 912 206
www.hotelbelsol.com
Pleasant, reliable hotel with 53 rooms, a beautiful garden and a view of the Serra da Estrela. The restaurant, which serves good dishes typical of the region, also provides a panoramic view.

Capela de Santiago
Next to the castle gate is the Romanesque and Gothic Capela de Santiago. The very modest interior contains the Gothic sculpture *A Imagem da Nossa Senhora da Esperança* (Image of Our Lady of Hope). Pedro Álvares Cabral (1467–1520) took the sculpture along on this journey of discovery to Brazil and afterwards donated it to a Franciscan monastery near Belmonte, which he had founded. After the closing of the monastery the Madonna was brought to her present location. In the choir inside the chapel there are some remains of old fresco decorations; in addition the tomb of Cabral's mother as well as the 17th-century graves of Fernão Cabral and Enrico Francisco Cabral are found in an adjoining courtyard.

Around Belmonte

Centum Cellas
★
To get to the Centum Cellas, the remains of a Roman tower, follow the main road from Belmonte in the direction of Guarda. About 1.5km/1mi north of the town centre a small road branches off towards the right and leads to the tower remains in the midst of some fields about 200m/220yd away. The Centum Cellas was erected to a square floor plan with two storeys and a crenellated trim. It is said to have been the exile of the Roman bishop Cornelius in the 2nd century BC. Apart from that it was probably used as a watchtower.

Sabugal
The town of Sabugal approximately 30km/19mi north-east of Belmonte is increasingly dominated by modern buildings. The castle, with its five towers from the 13th/14th centuries and its 28m/92ft-high keep, is well preserved.

✴ Braga

Historical province: Minho
District: Braga

Elevation: 185m/607ft
Population: 164,000

Braga is one of the largest cities in the country and the see of the Archbishop of Portugal. The city has been a significant religious centre from time immemorial – because of its many churches it is flatteringly called the »Portuguese Rome«. As common parlance has it: »In Porto we work, in Lisbon we live and in Braga we pray.«

There was probably a settlement where Braga is now located as far **History** back as prehistoric times. The Romans turned the place into the capital of the Callaeci Bracarii under the name of Bracara Augusta. During the mass migration, Braga was the **capital of the Suevian kingdom** and was occupied in 716 by the Moors. In 1040 the town was reconquered for Castilia and Christianity, and early in the 12th century it became the **residence of the Portuguese kings**. This heralded Braga's heyday, which is attested by numerous buildings even today. When the attention shifted more and more to the harbour towns during the time of the great voyages of discovery, the power and wealth of the city started to dwindle.

Next to the outstanding number of churches the buildings of the bourgeoisie and the aristocracy, with their typical granite architecture, shape the centre of Braga. The Praça da República would be a good place to start a sightseeing tour – the tourism office is also located here. Passing the Torre de Menagem, Rua do Souto leads into Braga's historic centre, which is designed as a pedestrian zone. Around the Praça da República there are two cafés with a special atmosphere: the »Brasileira« and the »Vianna«.

What to See in Braga

The **Torre de Menagem**, a massive tower built in 1378, still remains from the medieval town fortifications.

Shop window in Braga, Portugal's religious centre

► VISITING BRAGA

INFORMATION
Avenida da Liberdade 1
4710-251 Braga
Tel. 253 262 550
www.rtvm.pt

CAFÉS
Vianna
Praça da República
Time-honoured and popular café.

A Brasileira
Rua do Souto
Not particularly cosy, but an interesting and originally furnished spot for a cup of coffee nevertheless.

The A Brasileira has a charm all its own.

WHERE TO EAT
► Inexpensive/Moderate
① **O Alexandre**
Campo das Hortas 10
Tel. 253 614 003
Recommended restaurant serving typical dishes from the Minho.

② **Bem-me-quer**
Campo das Hortas 5/6
Tel. 253 262 095
Nice little bar. The sea bass (cherne) is especially tasty here.

③ **Tapas do Bosque**
Rua D. Gonçalo Pereira
Pleasantly furnished; an alternative to Portuguese cuisine.

WHERE TO STAY
► Budget/Mid-range
① **Hotel do Elevador**
Bom Jesus do Monte
4710-455 Braga
Tel. 253 603 400, Fax 253 603 409
www.hotiesbomjesus.web.pt
This hotel outside Braga beside the famous pilgrimage church was built for pilgrims at the end of the 1960s. The spacious rooms offer a magnificent panoramic view.

► Budget
② **Quinta de Infias**
Largo de Infias
4700 Braga
Tel. 253 209 500
quintainfias@mail.telepac.pt
Quinta on the edge of Braga with a very beautiful hotel inside.

③ **Albergaria da Sé**
Rua D. Gonçalo Pereira 39/45
4700 Braga, Tel. 253 214 502
Very centrally located; simple and well-kept accommodation.

150m/165yd down Rua do Souto in a westerly direction stands the former archiepiscopal palace, whose buildings surround a small square with a pretty fountain from 1723. The palace was created by connecting three wings dating from the 14th to the 17th centuries; today it houses one of the finest old libraries in Portugal together with the district archives: 550,000 volumes and more than 10,000 valuable manuscripts – the earliest dating from the 9th century – are kept here. The oldest book dates back to the year 1476. The stock of books increases by about 7,000 volumes each year.

★
Antigo Paço Episcopal

The western façade of the archbishop's palace faces the Praça do Município, adorned with an 18th-century pelican fountain. The city hall is on the western end of the square. The staircase inside the Baroque building is decorated with azulejos depicting buildings of the city that are no longer in existence.

Câmara Municipal

The Palácio dos Biscainhos lies to the west of the town hall. Originally built in the 16th century, the palace underwent considerable constructional changes in the following centuries. The interior houses an ethnographic museum.

Palácio dos Biscainhos

From here it is only a few steps to the south to reach the Arco da Porta Nova. For centuries the 18th-century gateway served as Braga's main point of entry.

Arco da Porta Nova

Braga *Plan*

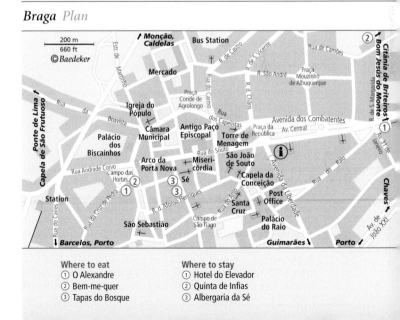

★ ★
Sé

It is only a short distance from the Arco da Porta Nova to the cathedral, across the pedestrian zone to the east. Braga's main sight was built in the 11th century in place of an early church built in Romanesque style, and was later enlarged several times and remodelled in Manueline style, especially in the early 16th century. Its most striking external features are the **west porch** with three bays of groined vaulting and a beautiful iron grille. A charming figure of the Virgin Mary, **»Nossa Senhora do Leite«** (Our Lady of Milk), probably by the French sculptor Nicolas Chanteren, is on the rear wall of the choir. In the **interior of the cathedral**, a richly ornamented Manueline baptismal font as well as a magnificently carved organ on both sides of the nave catch the eye. The chancel is decorated with a 14th-century Madonna, and the choir stalls in the high choir date back to the 15th century. Among the many monuments the sarcophagus of the Infante Dom Afonso (15th century), the son of João I, to the right of the entrance is of particular interest.

The left aisle provides access to the **cloister**, erected in the 18th century in place of its Gothic predecessor. Situated here is the entrance to a small **museum of religious art** whose exhibits include beautiful talha dourada and azulejo decorations from the 17th and 18th centuries. Affiliated with the museum is the **treasure chamber**, positively overflowing with precious objects.

Other sights

There is a total of about 30 churches in Braga. The 18th-century church of São João de Souto south of the city centre with the Capela da Conceição (Capela dos Coimbras), donated in 1525 by João Coimbra, and the church of Santa Cruz, with its beautiful Rococo façade, are definitely worth seeing. West of the church of Santa Cruz, on the Campo de São Tiago, is the **Arco de São Tiago**; a nearby building houses the Museu Pio XII with displays of archaeology and religious art. The **Palácio do Raio** (or Casa do Mexicano; 18th century) in the south-eastern part of the historic district has a tiled Rococo façade. Nearby is the Fonte do Idolo; this sculpture-bedecked fountain ranks as a national monument.

Around Braga

★
Capela de São Frutuoso

In the suburb of Sao Jerónimo Real, 3km/1.9mi north-west of the centre of town, is the peculiar Capela de São Frutuoso, **one of the oldest Christian religious buildings in Portugal**. It was founded by and named after the bishop of Braga, Frutuoso de Dume, in the second half of the 7th century. The central part and the east wing date from the late 7th century and show a strong Byzantine influence – an unusual feature in Portugal. Other parts of the chapel were rebuilt or added after its destruction by the Moors in the 11th century. The simple interior decor of this place of worship exhibits a variety of styles, with Visigothic, Romanesque and Lombard elements. Against the rear wall of the chapel is the sarcophagus of St Frutuoso. His

The pilgrimage church Bom Jesus do Monte near Braga

mortal remains rest in the Baroque church of São Francisco that was added in the 18th century. Church and chapel were affiliated with a Franciscan monastery in the 18th century.

The Bom Jesus do Monte pilgrimage church (400m/1,312ft) in the town of the same name 6km/3.8mi east of Braga is definitely worth seeing. It is situated in the midst of a park on the western slopes of the Monte Espinho, whose beautiful gardens, small lake and pretty footpaths make it a favourite spot for excursions and picnics. There is a road up to the church, but Bom Jesus do Monte can also be reached by means of a water-driven funicular or on foot up a Way of the Cross. It leads to a terrace from which a magnificent Baroque staircase exits, by which visitors ascend to the pilgrimage church passing allegorical figures and fountains. Originally from the 15th century, the church was rebuilt in the 18th/19th centuries. The effort of the climb is rewarded by a panoramic view.

★
Bom Jesus do Monte

About 3km/2mi south of Bom Jesús do Monte, on the Monte Sameiro (582m/1,910ft) another pilgrimage church was added rather thoughtlessly to the landscape in the 20th century. This is Portugal's second most visited pilgrimage site after ▶Fátima. It is accessed via an enormous modern flight of steps, at the foot of which stands a monument to Pope Pius IX that was placed there in 1954.

Monte Sameiro

Citânia de Briteiros A visit to the pilgrimage churches can be combined well with a tour of the Iron Age settlement Citânia de Briteiros (▶Guimarães) just a few miles further east.

✴ Bragança

S 6

Historical province: Trás-os-Montes	**Elevation:** 670m/2,198ft
District: Bragança	**Population:** 15,000

Situated in the extreme north-east corner of Portugal, Bragança is the cultural and economic heart of a region which is mainly given over to agriculture. Many villages around Bragança seem strangely from another time. They are characterized by a harsh day-to-day life with few comforts.

Seat of the House of Bragança Bragança, the Roman Iulióbriga, lies in a pleasantly cool setting on a hill above the valley of the Rio Sabor. The town is the original seat of the House of Bragança, which ruled in Portugal from 1640 to 1910 –

A Portuguese rarity: Domus Municipalis, the old Romanesque town hall of Bragança

for the last part of the period in the female line of Saxe-Coburg-Bragança – and also as Emperors in Brazil from 1822 to 1889. Bragança is also the capital of the district of the same name with 6,608 sq km/ 2,551 sq mi and a population of about 185,000. The **medieval city centre**, the upper city, is surrounded by a fortified wall about 2m/ 6.5ft thick. In the lower city, which started to develop in the 15th century, Renaissance façades on burgher houses and aristocratic mansions predominate.

What to See in Bragança

In the middle of the lower city on the long Largo da Sé stands the cathedral (Sé de Sao João Baptista), originally a Jesuit church. The Sé is a sturdy and plain Renaissance building with an almost secular air. The aisle-less interior is partly clad with azulejos. Above the choir, reticulated vaulting with bosses bearing coats of arms catches the eye. A coffered ceiling and wall panels with scenes from the life of St Ignatius Loyola decorate the sacristy.

Sé de São João Baptista

Outside the main entrance to the cathedral is the pelourinho of 1689, the symbol of municipal authority.

Pelourinho

From the cathedral, Rua do Conselheiro Abilio Beça leads to the former bishop's palace, now occupied by the Museu do Abade de Baçal. It shows exhibits from the fields of archaeology, fine art, folk traditions and arts and crafts.

Museu do Abade de Baçal

Above the town stands the massive Fortaleza, a fortification long regarded as impregnable, which was built by King Sancho I in 1187 and later reinforced by João I. Originally the castle enclosed the whole of Bragança within its double circuit of walls. However historic depictions document that by the 15th century the town had already expanded beyond the castle walls.

★
Fortaleza

In front of the castle gate is a modern **statue of Dom Fernando**, the Duke of Bragança and governor of Ceuta, erected to commemorate the 500th anniversary of the ceremonial granting of a charter to the town in 1464.

Within the walls are the **remains of the ducal palace** from the 12th century, ancestral home of the dukes of Bragança. The **Torre de Menagem**, the 34m/112ft-high keep with two fine Gothic twin windows on the south and east side, was added to the palace in the 15th century. It now houses a small military museum.

The 6m/20ft-high **pelourinho**, whose Gothic shaft rests on the back of a wild boar carved from granite, probably dating from the late Iron Age, is surely unique in Portugal.

The **church of Santa Maria do Castelo** with a magnificent Renaissance doorway was built in the 16th century within the castle walls.

In art historical terms, the most important building of the old

▶ VISITING BRAGANÇA

INFORMATION
Avenida Cidade de Zamora
5300-111 Bragança
Tel. 273 381 273
www.rt-nordeste.pt

WHERE TO EAT
▶ **Moderate**
Restaurante la em Casa
Rua Marquês do Pombal
Tel. 273 322 111
Fine Portuguese cuisine prepared in
unusual ways.

WHERE TO STAY
▶ **Mid-range**
Moinho do Caniço
Av. Abade de Baçal 663

5300-068 Bragança
Tel. 273 323 577
www.bragancanet.pt/moinho
Beautiful »turismo rural« accommodation: a cosy and rustic little granite
house in the midst of the landscape
about 12km/7.5mi from Bragança on
the bank of the Rio Baceiro.

Pousada de São Bartolomeu
Estrada do Turismo
5300-271 Bragança
Tel. 273 331 493
Fax 273 323 453
Modern pousada on Bartolomeus
mountain with a magnificent view of
Bragança.

stronghold and one of the few Romanesque secular buildings in Portugal is the town hall – known as **Domus Municipalis** – next to the
church. The severe granite building with the pretty dwarf gallery was
built above a Roman well in the 12th century with a floor plan in the
form of an irregular pentagon.

Around Bragança

Panoramic view The Capela de Sao Bartolomeu, 5km/3.1mi south of Bragança, offers
an exceptional panoramic view over the castle grounds.

Parque Natural de Montezinho The Parque Natural de Montezinho (Montezinho National Park) extends north of Bragança to the Spanish border across a still relatively
unspoilt area well away from major roads. There are 91 villages on
an area of approximately 75,000ha/187,000ac; many of them are now
deserted except for the new houses. The younger people have moved
away to the cities – the province of ▶Trás-os-Montes with the Montezinho National Park ranks as one Portugal's poorest regions. The
national park derives its name from the village of Montezinho, which
lies a good 20km/12.5mi north of Bragança. Its population today to-
tals 50 individuals.
Hills with rocky plateaus, forests of oak, fir and chestnut, areas of
boulders and gentle slopes covered in heath and gorse shape the
scenery. The farmers use the narrow valleys to grow grains, potatoes,

vegetables and wine grapes. Almost all of them also own sheep and goats, and overgrazing is one of the main problems faced by the park administrators. Fires are constantly being deliberately lit to create new pastures. The pine tree monocultures burn like tinder, largely destroying plant life, with the result that the roots of bushes can no longer prevent erosion of the soil. The park administrators own three simple shelters (Casas Abrigos) in the region, and these can be hired on a weekly basis by hikers by prior arrangement (details can be obtained from the tourist information office in Bragança).

Castro de Avelās

In the village of Castro de Avelas about 5km/3mi west of Bragança are the remains of a 12th-century Benedictine abbey; parts of the abbey church, the only brick-built church in Portugal, have been incorporated into the present village church.

✱ ✱ Buçaco National Park

H 14

Historical province: Beira Litoral
District: Aveiro

Elevation: 220–541m/720–1,775ft
Area: 105ha/260ac

It is best to explore this »fairy tale forest« using the network of footpaths leading to enchanted squares, picturesque fountains, and magnificent vantage points. A good starting point for walks is the Palace Hotel do Buçaco.

The Buçaco National Park is virtually unrivalled in its scenic beauty and the richness of its flora. The forest (Parque Nacional do Buçaco or Mata Nacional do Buçaco – formerly spelled Bussaco) lies 25km/15.5mi north-east of Coimbra on the northern slopes of the Serra do Buçaco. Although it is possible to drive through the Buçaco Forest's 105ha/260ac, enclosed by a wall of 5,700m/3mi, it is well worth taking the time to hike through it on foot. There is a car park at the Palace Hotel do Buçaco, which is accessed through the Porta das Ameias, the Porta da Serra or the Porta da Rainha. There is a fee to enter the national park.

History

In the 6th century the Benedictine monks of Lorvão (►Coimbra) established a hermitage in the middle of the forest on the eastern slopes of the Cruz Alta hill. In the 11th century it passed into the hands of the canons of Coimbra, who always strenuously upheld their claim to the area and maintained it with great care. In 1622 women were forbidden to enter the area. In 1628 a Carmelite convent was established in the forest of Buçaco, enclosed by the wall with ten gates which still exists today, and the monks planted an **arboretum** which quickly became famous and was continuously enriched by exotic species brought back by the Portuguese explorers re-

Parque Nacional do Buçaco Map

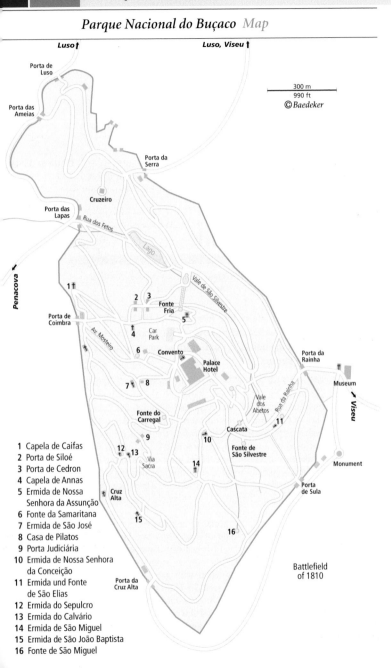

1 Capela de Caifas
2 Porta de Siloé
3 Porta de Cedron
4 Capela de Annas
5 Ermida de Nossa
   Senhora da Assunção
6 Fonte da Samaritana
7 Ermida de São José
8 Casa de Pilatos
9 Porta Judiciária
10 Ermida de Nossa Senhora
   da Conceição
11 Ermida und Fonte
   de São Elias
12 Ermida do Sepulcro
13 Ermida do Calvário
14 Ermida de São Miguel
15 Ermida de São João Baptista
16 Fonte de São Miguel

turning from their journeys overseas. A papal decree in 1643 prohibited the damaging or felling of any of the trees. The British-Portuguese army beat the invading French troops in 1810 near Buçaco under the supreme command of Wellington – and thus defeated Napoleon's third attempt to conquer Portugal. After the secularization of convents and monasteries in Portugal in 1834 the forest of Buçaco passed to the crown.

What to See in Buçaco National Park

The pride of Buçaco today, among some 400 native and **300 exotic plant species**, are the enormous cedars from the Lebanon, Mexico, India and Africa; other specimens include mighty cypresses, ancient ginkgo trees, sequoias, araucarias, giant ferns and palms. Besides its trees the park is also an experience for its numerous grottoes, ponds, springs, chapels, hermitages, oratories and well-planned footpaths. The springs, once carefully constructed by the monks, are particularly worth seeing: north of the Palace Hotel the Fonte Fria (cold spring), with a cascade of 144 steps descending to a basin surrounded by beautiful flowering shrubs and conifers; and the Fonte do Carregal, flowing out of a grotto, to the south of the hotel.

✱ ✱
Unique flora

Colourful herbaceous borders surround the Palace Hotel do Buçaco in the centre of the national park. Carlos I had a palace added to the dilapidated remains of the former monastery between 1888 and 1907. The Italian architect Luigi Manini created a building in the sumptuous neo-Manueline style featuring a great deal of sculpture and azulejo decoration that today has a certain nostalgic charm. Since 1909 it has served as the luxurious Palace Hotel do Buçaco.

✱
Palace Hotel do Buçaco

All that remains of the monastery buildings is the little church decorated with sculptures and paintings as well as the cloister and a few monk's cells.

Convento

From the hotel a Way of the Cross leads up the hill to the Cruz Alta (high cross: 541m/1,775ft); a road goes there via the Porta da Cruz Alta. A look-out point provides a superb panoramic view extending to the ► Serra da Estrela and the Atlantic Ocean.

✱
Cruz Alta

An obelisk (Monumento à Batalha do Buçaco) just outside the park walls near the Porta da Rainha and a small military museum both commemorate the glorious battle of Buçaco.

Obelisk and museum

Around the Buçaco National Park

On the north-western edge of the park lies the spa resort Luso (380m/1,247ft) in a picturesque setting at the foot of the Cruz Alta. The springs of Luso are said to assist in the treatment of rheuma-

Luso

◉ VISITING BUÇACO NATIONAL PARK

INFORMATION
Rua Emídio Navarro
3050-224 Luso
Tel. 231 939 133
Fax 231 939 007
jtluso-bussaco@mail.telepac.pt

WHERE TO EAT
▸ Expensive
Hotel Palace do Buçaco
In the Buçaco National Park
Tel. 231 937 970
Very spacious, dignified restaurant in
the luxury hotel in the national park.

▸ Moderate
Grande Hotel de Luso
Luso, Rua Dr. Cid de Oliveira 86

The hotel restaurant serves good
international cuisine.

Alegre
Rua Emidio Navarro 2
3050-224 Luso
Tel. 231 930 256
The menu features traditional dishes
of the region.

WHERE TO STAY
▸ Luxury
Hotel Palace do Buçaco
In the Buçaco National Park
3050-261 Mealhada
Tel. 231 937 970
Fax 231 930 509
www.almeidahotels.com
Luxury hotel with 62 rooms in the middle
of the national park housed in a famous
palace that was built toward the end of the
19th century in the neo-Manueline style.

▸ Budget/Mid-range
Alegre
Rua Emidio Navarro 2
3050-224 Luso
Tel. 231 930 256
Fax 231 930 556
www.alegrehotels.com
Established in a traditional building
that still harbours the charm of days
gone by, Luso has become an attractive
health spa.

*Palace Hotel in Buçaco's
National Park*

Baedeker recommendation

Vila Duparchy
3050-235 Luso
Tel. 231 930 790
Fax 231 930 307
Beautiful old villa with personal flair situated
in park-like forest grounds on the edge of
Luso. Friendly and rather lively atmosphere.
Six rooms for rent.

tism, joint diseases and disorders of the upper airways. Spa facilities and hotels are surrounded by beautiful parks. The mineral water bottled in Luso, still and mineral-rich, is Portugal's most popular brand.

Curia, about 10km/6mi north-west of the Buçaco National Park, is a well known spa. Its hot springs containing calcium sulphate are favoured for ailments of the joints and the metabolism. Curia has modern treatment facilities, a variety of sport and recreational amenities and well maintained spa gardens.

Curia

Caldas da Rainha

D 20

Historical province: Estremadura
District: Leiria

Elevation: 50m/164ft
Population: 20,000

Caldas da Rainha, the »Queen's hot baths«, is one of Portugal's leading health spas. The hot sulphurous springs (34.5°C/94.1°F) are particularly recommended for the treatment of rheumatism.

Legend has it that Queen Leonor, wife of João II, discovered the springs while driving by: she observed simple peasants bathing in the water to cure pains in their joints. Allegedly Leonor then sold her jewels and founded a spa hospital in 1484, to which she herself often came to take the cure. Caldas da Rainha, located about 100km/62mi north of Lisbon and about 10km/6mi from the Atlantic, today owes its name to this story.

The Monday market in the central square is a weekly attraction. There are always some stalls selling the characteristic Caldas da Rainha ceramics. The bright and often rather crudely coloured pottery, which is also obtainable throughout the town, is very different from that found in the north.

Ceramics

What to See in Caldas da Rainha

This bath house (Hospital Termal) in the town centre was founded by Queen Leonor and rebuilt in the mid-18th century under King Joao IV, who also frequented Caldas da Rainha.

Hospital Termal

Adjoining the bath house to the east is the Igreja Nossa Senhora do Pópulo. This too was founded by Queen Leonor around 1500 and built by the famous architect Boytaca. It has a separate belfry, the lower part of which is square and the upper part octagonal. Notable features of the interior are the triptych as well as a Manueline chancel arch. The little baptistry and the baptismal font are richly decorated with azulejos.

Igreja de Nossa Senhora do Pópulo

▶ CALDAS DA RAINHA

INFORMATION
Rua E. Duarte Pacheco
2500-198 Caldas da Rainha
Tel. 262 839 700

The origins of the spa park, the Parque Dom Carlos I **Parque Dom Carlos I**, also go back to Queen Leonor. It has beautiful gardens with old trees and a small lake in the centre.

The pavilion in the park houses the **Museu de José Malhôa**. The collection contains modern Portuguese paintings and sculptures, including works by Malhôa who was born in Caldas da Rainha in 1855.

Museu de Cerâmica
The ceramics museum is housed in a villa on the edge of the park. Exhibits include works by Rafael Bordalo Pinheiro (1847–1905), who ran a pottery workshop in Caldas da Rainha.

Other museums
Diagonally across from the Museu de Cerâmica is the studio museum of the portrait and decorative sculptor António Duarte, born in Caldas da Rainha in 1912.

Around Caldas da Rainha
From Caldas da Rainha it is 7km/4.8mi to ▶Óbidos. A side-trip to the coast (▶Costa da Prata, ▶Peniche) is also worthwhile.

Caminha

E/F 5

Historical province: Minho	**Elevation:** 30m/98ft
District: Viana do Castelo	**Population:** 2,000

The border town of Caminha is charmingly situated on a spit between the Coura and Minho rivers just a few miles from the point where the Minho flows into the Atlantic Ocean.

What to See in Caminha

Praça do Conselheiro Silva Torres
Caminha's main square is the Praça do Conselheiro Silva Torres with its impressive ensemble of 15th-century buildings: the town hall, with a coffered ceiling in the council assembly hall; next to it the clock tower, remains of the former fortifications; and the Gothic Palácio des Pitas at the south end of the square.

★ **Igreja Matriz**
Caminha's most notable building is located about 150m/164yd beyond the arch of the clock tower. The church was built by order of the township between 1488 and 1565 and thus combines elements of late Gothic with early Renaissance style. Two buttresses with pinnacles structure the Renaissance façade; the crenellated tower is also

▶ VISITING CAMINHA

INFORMATION
Rua Ricardo Joaquim de Sousa
4910-155 Caminha
Tel. 258 921 952
www.rtam.pt

WHERE TO STAY
▶ **Budget**
Quinta da Cantareira
Caminho do Ranhada (Marinhas)

4910-585 Vilar de Mouros
Tel. 258 724 167
Fax 258 724 168
www.quintadacantareira.com
Small, tastefully furnished accommodation with only five rooms. The old granite house from the late 18th century is approx. 5km/3mi outside Caminha in an easterly direction. Garden and swimming pool.

a Renaissance construction. The Mudéjar-style ornately carved wooden ceiling in the interior is the work of a Spanish master.Its chapel is the oldest example of plateresque style in Portugal.

Around Caminha

To the south-west of Caminha stretch several beaches: near Moledo do Minho, a small seaside resort, Praia de Moledo; to the south this adjoins Praia do Pirata as well as the beach of Vila Praia de Âncora. All of them have fine, clean sand and numerous dunes and are lined with beautiful pine forests.   **Beaches**

Approximately 2km/1.3mi inland of Vila Praia de Âncora is one of Portugal's best preserved megalithic monuments: the Dólmen da Barrosa, a large stone tomb from the Neolithic Age.   **Dólmen da Barrosa**

Cascais

B 24

Historical province: Estremadura   **Elevation:** 0–20m/66ft
District: Lisboa   **Population:** 30,000

The former quiet fishing port of Cascais expanded in the early 20th century to become an elegant, almost cosmopolitan, coastal resort. Little of this elegance remains today, however: in the summer months the beaches of Cascais throng with an endless stream of sun seekers from Lisbon.

Situated 25km/15.5mi west of the centre of Lisbon on the Costa do Sol, Cascais has a wide range of sporting and recreational facilities. Due to its proximity to Lisbon, and not least because of the advanta-   **Seaside resort** geous climate – the Serra de Sintra affords shelter from north winds – the town has undergone rapid development.

As the summer residence of the kings of Portugal from 1870 and the President of the Republic, the end of the 19th century saw Cascais becoming a meeting place for high society. In recent decades Cascais has merged with ► Estoril to become an unbroken built-up area. Around the outskirts of the town high rise apartments predominate, and there are also some extended exclusive residential areas inhabited by rich Portuguese and many British, French and Germans. Luckily the beautiful old centre of town has been preserved. A few outlying quiet alleys still show traces of the former fishing village. The smart centre of the town is now a mass of restaurants, cafés and stalls catering to the tourist trade.

Cascais Plan

What to See in Cascais

On the south-west side of the bay stands the 16th-century **citadel** with an open air artillery museum. From the citadel, Avenida de Dom Carlos I runs to the north-east; a surfaced path directly at the water's edge leads to ►Estoril.

North of the citadel is the Manueline church **Nossa Senhora da Assunção**. The walls of the aisle-less church were clad with blue-white azulejos in 1745.

To the west of the citadel stretches the **Parque Municipal da Gandarinha**. The Conde de Castro Guimarães had a country residence built here in the early 20th century, in which the town council of Cascais established a library and a small museum in the 1920s. The collection of paintings contains several portraits of the founder's

▶ VISITING CASCAIS

INFORMATION
Rua Visconde da Luz
2750-415 Cascais
Tel. 214 868 204
www.estorilcoast.com

WHERE TO EAT
▶ Inexpensive/Moderate
① *Porto de Santa Maria*
Estrada do Guincho (Guincho)
Tel. 218 870 240
This is the place for seafood lovers. A glance at the guest book confirms it: the likes of Mick Jagger, Plácido Domingo and Dustin Hoffman have enjoyed the food here.

③ *Reijos*
Rua Frederico Arouca 35
Tel. 214 830 311
Good, simple dishes at moderate prices.

Baedeker recommendation

② *Mar do Inferno*
Avenida Rei Humberto II de Itália
Tel. 214 832 218
Located in the immediate vicinity of the Boca do Inferno, this restaurant serves marvellous fish dishes and seafood, and offers a good selection of wines. Especially recommended: the fish platter for 2 persons.

WHERE TO STAY
▶ Luxury
① *Hotel Albatroz*
Rua Frederico Arouca 100
Tel. 214 847 380
Fax 214 844 827
www.albatrozhotels.com
Stylish palace on a cliff directly at the beach. Sea view.

A lovely location in a bay: the small Hotel Albatroz

family, as well as local prehistoric findings, porcelain, and wrought gold and silver objects.

Museu do Mar

The Museu do Mar north of the park provides information on the sea and seafaring – subjects fundamental to the history of Cascais.

✳
Boca do Inferno

At the western exit of Cascais the Boca do Inferno, the »Mouth of Hell«, shows the spectacle of the primordial force of the sea. Integrated into a bizarre rocky coast, a viewing platform close to a 15–20m/50–65ft-high chain of cliffs, partly hollowed out by the force of the sea, provides a vantage point from which to observe the powerful waves surge and pound against the rocks, sending spray and surf into the air.

Beaches

The little sandy beaches of Praia da Rainha, framed by bays, are rather picturesque, and further in the direction of Estoril is the beach of Praia da Duquesa with good facilities for bathers. In the summer months all these beaches are rather crowded.

Around Cascais

On the coast north-west of Cascais there are some larger beaches and pretty, smaller bathing resorts. Visiting the westernmost point of the European mainland, the Cabo da Roca (►Costa do Sol), is a special experience.

✳ Castelo Branco

O 18

Historical province: Beira Baixa
District: Castelo Branco

Elevation: 375m/1,230ft
Population: 28,000

Lying close to the Spanish border, the central Portuguese town of Castelo Branco has always had great military importance. Of the medieval Templar castle Castelo Branco, probably built in the reign of King Dinis I, only scant remains have survived. The main sight here is the bishop's garden, the Jardim Episcopal.

White castle

Castelo Branco (white castle) is the capital of the district which bears its name. In spite of its defensive city walls, the town suffered throughout its history from repeated enemy assaults and raids – most recently in 1807, when Napoleon's troops did considerable damage.

»Colchas«

The famous »Colchas« have been produced in Castelo Branco since the 17th century; these brightly coloured embroidered woven blankets are usually used as bedspreads. They were traditionally made by the bride for her trousseau and decorated with figures, which symbolized good wishes for the new family's future.

▶ VISITING CASTELO BRANCO

INFORMATION

Praça do Município
6000-458 Castelo Branco
Tel. 272 330 339
www.cm-castelobranco.pt

WHERE TO EAT

▶ **Inexpensive/Moderate**

① *Praça Velha*
Praça Luís de Camões 17
Tel. 272 328 640
Very beautifully and cosily furnished

restaurant with typically Portuguese
cuisine and very good waiting staff.

WHERE TO STAY

▶ **Budget**

① *Pensão Arraiana*
Avenida 1 de Maio
Tel. 272 341 634, fax 272 331 884
Well-managed guesthouse with 31
large rooms equipped with old furniture. Pensão Arraiana has its own
restaurant.

What to See in Castelo Branco

★ Jardim Episcopal

The park, considered Portugal's most beautiful Baroque garden, was laid out in the early 18th century for Dom Joao de Mendoça. It is a true collection of curios marked by Baroque playfulness: carefully clipped trees and shrubs and elaborately patterned flower beds are interspersed with ponds and water features. There is a real curio among the Baroque sculptures: flanking the flight of steps are the Portuguese kings – but the Habsburg kings from the days of the loathed Spanish interregnum from 1580 to 1640 are pointedly represented by much smaller figures.

Museu Francisco Tavares Proença Júnior

On the north-west side of the park stands the old bishop's palace (Antigo Paço Episcopal). The originally Gothic building, remodelled in Baroque style in 1726, today houses the Museu Francisco Tavares Proença Júnior, exhibiting prehistoric and Roman finds from the Castelo Branco area, pictures from Portuguese masters of the 16th, 18th and 19th centuries, tapestries, coins, furniture and armour. The museum's chief treasures are the skilfully made »Colchas«.

Other sights

Today's Castelo Branco is centred around the broad Alameda da Liberdade and the adjacent long square with stretches of green. West of this newer part of town, grouped around the Praça Luís de Camões, stand the old 16th-century town hall and some aristocratic houses (16th–18th centuries). The Manueline doorway at the Convento da Graça diagonally across from the bishop's palace catches the eye. Above the town stand the ruins of the little church of Santa Maria do Castelo that was part of a 12th century Templar castle, of which only some remains have survived. A flight of steps leads down to the vantage point Miradouro de São Gens.

Around Castelo Branco

Nossa Senhora de Mércoles
About 5km/3mi east of the town is the Gothic pilgrimage church Nossa Senhora de Mércoles, which dates back to the 15th century.

✳ Idanha-a-Velha
The little village of Idanha-a-Velha some 50km/31mi north-east of Castelo Branco boasts an illustrious past: founded by the Romans, it became the **episcopal see under the Visigoths** in the 6th century, before sinking back into obscurity following the Moorish invasion in the 8th century. An archaeological walking tour leads to the other sights of town: parts of a street, bridge and gateway are left over from Roman times, and there are the remains of a basilica and an episcopal palace from the Visigothic era.

✳ Monsanto
10km/6mi north-east of Idanha-a-Velha is the peculiar town of Monsanto (alt. 758m/2,487ft), whose granite houses are grouped around the peak of a rocky hill. Many houses were built between two granite cliffs and sometimes hewn directly out of the rock. Only 250 people are left in Monsanto, a town that emerged from a competition in 1940 **under Salazar as «the most Portuguese village».** Steep and bumpy lanes lead up to the ruins of a castle offering a fine view.

About 30km/19mi south-west of Castelo Branco the Tagus has carved out the **Portas de Ródão**, a rocky gorge 45m/150ft wide; the best view is from the Tagus bridge near Vila Velha de Ródão.

It is worthwhile taking a trip to the **Serra da Gardunha**, a range of hills north of Castelo Branco which in places take on an Alpine character, with bizarrely shaped rock formations bearing such names as »Cabeça de Frade« (monk's head) and »Pedra Sobreposta« (rockpile). Alpedrinha (alt. 555m/1,855ft) lies 30km/19mi along the Castelo Branco road to ▶Covilhã. The hill town is a good starting point for walks: there is a lovely route to the Penha da Senhora da Serra (hermitage), with beautiful panoramic

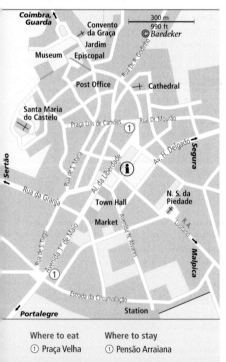

Castelo Branco *Plan*

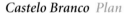

Coimbra, Guarda

Convento da Graça

Jardim Episcopal

Museum

Post Office

Cathedral

Santa Maria do Castelo

Praça Luís de Camões

Rua Dr. Mourão

Rua Dr. R. Godinho

300 m
990 ft
© Baedeker

Sertão

Rua da Granja

Rua de S. Maria

Al. da Liberdade

Avi. H. Delgado

Segura

N. S. da Piedade

Town Hall

Market

Rua de S. Tiago

Avenida 1º de Maio

Avenida N. Álvares

R. A. Lusitano

Malpica

Estrada da Circunvalação

Portalegre

Station

Where to eat
① Praça Velha

Where to stay
① Pensão Arraiana

Some of Monsanto's houses are hewn directly into the rocks.

views, and then on to the Pirâmide (alt. 1,223m/4,013ft), the highest point in the Serra da Gardunha. The climb to the Pirâmide is also possible from Castelo Novo (700m/2,300ft), a scenic mountain village below the hermitage. Worthwhile sights in the town include the 18th-century town hall and a Manueline pillory.

The principal town in the Serra da Gardunha is Fundao, located **Fundão** 45km/28mi north of Castelo Branco on the northern slopes of the mountain range (alt. 496m/1,627ft) and with a population of 6,000. The fertile surrounding region allows intensive fruit-growing, and local people also make a living in the textile industry. The small town has two attractive churches, the 18th-century Misericórdia church and the Sao Francisco chapel.

✶ ✶ Castelo de Vide

O 20

Historical province: Alto Alentejo   **Elevation:** 460–628m/1,509–2,060ft
District: Portalegre   **Population:** 4,000

Although Castelo de Vide is considered to be one of Portugal's most picturesque places, tourism is still kept within limits. The townsfolk continue to earn their living mostly from agriculture and handicrafts. The spas also bring in a little income: the cold mineral springs containing Glauber's salt are visited for the treatment of diabetes and skin ailments.

VISITING CASTELO DE VIDE

INFORMATION
Praça D. Pedro V
7320 Castelo de Vide
Tel. 245 901 361
www.rtsm.pt

WHERE TO EAT
▶ Moderate
Marino's
Praça D. Pedro V- 6
Tel. 245 901 408
Good traditional specialities.

A Palmeira
Estrada de São Vicente
Tel. 245 900 000
Rustic hunting atmosphere. The menu features dishes of the region.

WHERE TO STAY
▶ Budget/Mid-range
Residencial Casa do Parque
Avenida da Aramenha 37

7320-101 Castelo de Vide
Tel. 245 901 250
Fax 245 901 288
Recommended guesthouse with 26 rooms located at the town's entrance right behind the park. Large rooms, in-house restaurant.

Baedeker recommendation

▶ Budget
Quinta da Bela Vista
Póvoa e Meadas
7320-014 Castelo de Vide
Tel. 245 968 125
Fax 245 968 132
Old manor house in the middle of the country on the edge of the village Póvoa e Meadas with five rooms for rent. Those looking for relaxation in beautiful surroundings will find it here.

The pretty town of Castelo de Vide is on the north-west side of the bleak Serra de São Mamede, 20km/12.5mi north of Portalegre in the immediate vicinity of the Spanish border. The old centre of town extends up to a hilltop with a castle. The fortified town of ▶ Marvão 12km/7.5mi to the south-east and the small town of ▶ Portalegre about 20km/12.5mi to the south are also definitely worth visiting.

★ ★
Medieval and picturesque

Castelo de Vide has managed to preserve its medieval townscape virtually intact: picturesque lanes and trim whitewashed houses, many a charming little square and various nooks and crannies add to the beauty of the place. The rising lanes are decorated with flowerpots and there is hardly a house in the old centre of town that is not resplendent with climbing blossoms.

What to See in Castelo de Vide

Praça de Dom Pedro V

A suitable starting point for a sightseeing walk is the Praça de Dom Pedro V. The square, framed by the Baroque palace, churches and the town hall, gives a harmonious and unified impression. In the centre of the square stands the statue of Dom Pedro V, created in 1873. The Baroque church of Santa Maria with its twin towered façade and a squat pyramidal crossing tower stands at the edge of the square.

Castelo

From the Praça de Dom Pedro V, picturesque lanes point the way up to the castle, built in the early 14th century on the remains of a Moorish fortification; the ingenious ventilation system of the Moorish predecessor still survives. There is a wonderful view of the town and the surrounding region from the massive keep. Within the castle's perimeter stands the church of Nossa Senhora da Alegria, completely covered with 17th-century azulejos.

Judiaria

Just left of the exit from the castle is the old Jewish quarter, the Judiaria. Here, time seems to have stood still – there are no cars in the narrow alleyways. Many houses have fine Gothic and Manueline windows and doors. Look out for the 14th-century synagogue on the main street; it is barely distinguishable from the other houses.

Fonte de Vila

The main street ends in a square with a covered Renaissance fountain, the Fonte da Vile.

Convento de São Francisco

Heading south from the Praça de Dom Pedro past the gardens and the Fonte do Montorinho fountain, the street leads to the former Franciscan monastery at the other end of the town.

Flower-bedecked alleys and whitewashed houses in the historic centre of the hill town Castelo de Vide

Castro Verde

K 30

Historical province: Baixo Alentejo
District: Beja

Elevation: 245m/804ft
Population: 6,000

Located 60km/37mi south-west of Beja in the midst of the deserted plains of the Baixo Alentejo, surrounded by pastureland for sheep and forests of cork oak, lies the small town of Castro Verde – »green castle«.

What to See in Castro Verde

Igreja da Conceição
The aisle-less church of Nossa Senhora da Conceição has an interior completely clad with early 18th-century azulejos depicting scenes from the battle of Ourique (see below).

Igreja das Chagas do Salvador
Also of interest is the church of the Chagas do Salvador, decorated with Azulejos in a style typical of the region, which was built by Philip II of Spain in the 16th century on the remains of an earlier place of worship.

Around Castro Verde

Ourique
Legend has it that the battle of Ourique, in which Afonso Henriques won a **decisive victory over the Moors** in 1139, took place about 15km/9mi south-west of Castro Verde near the modest little village of Ourique. The actual site of the battle is said to be Campo de Ourique, between Castro Verde and the Castro Verde. Historians however cast doubt on whether the battle in fact happened that far south in the country.

▶ CASTRO VERDE

INFORMATION
Praça da Liberdade
7780 Castro Verde
Tel. 286 328 148

About 15km/9.8mi south of Ourique a little road branches off to the ruins of the early historical settlement **Castro da Cola**, known in Roman times as Ossonoba. The settlement is roughly rectangular in shape and surrounded by a rampart 5m/16ft high.

Almodôvar
Almodôvar, some 20km/13mi south of Castro Verde, has a 17th-century Franciscan monastery with a beautiful cloister as well as a well-preserved Gothic and Manueline parish church.

Aljustrel
Some 20km/13mi north of Castro Verde lies the small town of Aljustrel; its copper mines have been worked since ancient times.

Chaves

Historical province: Trás-os-Montes
District: Vila Real

Elevation: 324m/1,063ft
Population: 14,000

The antiquated little town of Chaves on the Rio Tâmega lies in the far north of Portugal near the Spanish border. The town still presents a sturdy defensive face to the world, its powerful fortifications rearing above the white houses with their balconies and arbours.

Chaves lies on a plateau in an area through which the Rio Tâmega flows and which has been intensively cultivated since ancient times. As far back as the Romans there has been recourse to the town's hot springs (73°C/163°F) for the treatment of rheumatism and bilious complaints. The modern thermal baths are below the castle.

The town has a history dating back to pre-Roman times. With a substantial stone bridge over the Rio Tâmega built in the reign of Trajan (98–117), the former »Aquae Flaviae« became an important staging post on the road between Asturica Augusta (Astorga) and Bracara Augusta (Braga). During the Middle Ages Chaves was a stronghold against Spain in the north. **History**

What to See in Chaves

Chaves is known for the well-preserved 140m/155yd-long Roman bridge spanning the Rio Tâmega with 12 arches from the second century AD. The two milestones in the middle of the bridge have Roman inscriptions. **Ponte Romana**

▶ VISITING CHAVES

INFORMATION
Terreiro da Cavalaria
5400-193 Chaves
Tel. 276 340 661
www.rt-atb.pt

WHERE TO EAT
▶ Moderate
Carvalho
Alameda do Tabolado
5400-523 Chaves
Tel. 276 321 727
Popular restaurant in a classical,
modern design. Traditional cuisine is
on the menu.

WHERE TO STAY
▶ Mid-range
Hotel Forte S. Francisco
Alto da Pedisqueira
5400-435 Chaves
Tel. 276 333 700
www.forte-s-francisco-hoteis.pt
4-star top hotel with 58 rooms inside
the castelo.

São João de Deus

On the left river bank near the bridge stands the Baroque church of São João de Deus. The octagonal structure is made particularly impressive by its fine granite facade.

Igreja Matriz

Life in the old town centre revolves around the Praça da República Praça da República which boasts a Manueline pelourinho. The original Romanesque parish church stands at the square. It was heavily remodelled in the 16th century, and only the tower and part of the portal have survived from the earlier building.

Igreja da Misericórdia

Behind the parish church is the 17th-century Baroque Igreja da Misericórdia. The inside of the church is entirely covered with azulejo pictures depicting scenes from the Bible. The 18th-century ceiling frescoes are also notable.

Museu da Região Flaviense

The regional museum was established in the palace of the Dukes of Bragança, dating from the 17th century. It contains archaeological material found locally, as well as coins, tiles and exhibits of folk art.

Monastery church of the Convento de Santa Cruz with Manueline doorway

The castle was built on the site of a Roman fort that was strengthened after the Moorish conquest of the town, badly damaged during the Reconquista and rebuilt by King Dinis in the 13th/14th centuries. In the 17th century, Vauban-style ramparts were added to the castle, but were later destroyed. In the 15th century the fort served as the sometime residence of the first Duke of Bragança, a son of King Joao I. The massive keep now houses a small military museum.

Castelo

Around Chaves

In Outeiro Seco, about 4km/2.5mi north of Chaves, stands the beautiful church of **Nossa Senhora da Azinheira**, an aisle-less Romanesque building. Take a look at the figural decoration on the outer façade, among them animal figures raising their rear ends in the direction of Spain. The medieval frescoes in the interior have been much altered in the course of the centuries.

★
Outeiro Seco

Vidago (alt. 350m/1,148ft) located about 15km/9mi south-west of Chaves, has hot springs used to treat internal ailments. Some unused sanatoria and hotels are evidence that the spa has seen better days, but the splendid palace hotel from around 1900 is still worth a visit.

Vidago

The name of Pedras Salgados 12km/7.5mi south of Vidago is on everybody's lips in Portugal. A popular mineral water is bottled here which is sold all over the country in litre bottles.

Pedras Salgadas

★ ★ Coimbra

H 15

Historical province: Beira Litoral	**Elevation:** 75–100m/246–328ft
District: Coimbra	**Population:** 148,000

In Coimbra, everything evolves around the university: there are after all 18,000 students in a city with a total population of 100,000. Rich in tradition, Coimbra is Portugal's most important city next to Lisbon and Porto – it has shaped the intellectual life of the country for centuries. Its considerable artistic and cultural treasures make it a tourist destination of the first rank.

The students of Coimbra's tradition-steeped university still wear the **black garb** consisting of a robe (batina) with a black cape (capa) to festive events. There are **ribbons** of different colours for the various faculties. On the occasion of the Queima das Fitas, the examination celebrations held in the middle of May, these ribbons are ceremonially burned in a giant spectacle. The celebrations last for a week and also include a procession of the university's faculties and live concerts.

Queima das Fitas

Highlights Coimbra

Convento de Santa Cruz
Monastery tour followed by a visit to a café in the formerly holy site
▸ page 276

Sé Velha
The fortress-like old cathedral
▸ page 277

Museu Nacional Machado de Castro
Extensive art collection and museum café with a magnificent view!
▸ page 280

Universidade Velha
Coimbra's tradition-steeped university. Don't miss the superb library
▸ page 280

Quinta das Lágrimas
The site of Portugal's most tragic love story.
▸ page 283

Conímbriga
Important Roman excavation site
▸ page 283

History The origins of Coimbra stretch back to prehistoric times. The town was known to the Romans as Aeminium, but later, having become the see of a bishop, it took the name of the nearby Roman town Conímbriga which was destroyed by the Suevi in 468 (see below). In the 12th century Coimbra became the capital of the new Portuguese kingdom. After it lost this status to Lisbon, it was compensated by the foundation in 1307/08 of a university which until 1911 remained the only one in Portugal.

✶ ✶
On the bank of the Mondego Coimbra lies in a particularly picturesque setting amidst a lovely hilly landscape on the right bank of the Rio Mondego. From the more modern lower city on the river, steep lanes climb to the upper city where the extensive university buildings are located.

Sightseeing tour A good starting point for a tour of the town is the Largo da Portagem, which is also where the tourist information centre is located. Pretty green stretches with cafés line the broad Avenida Emídio Navarro. There is a beautiful view of the town from the Ponte de Santa Clara. Those less keen on walking can take a »Linha Azul« bus through the alleys of the old town.

What to See in Coimbra

✶
Praça do Comércio Below Rua Visconde da Luz to the west of the Praça do Comércio lies the old marketplace of the town. Tradesmen and craftsmen have always lived in the quarter around the square.

Monastery church of the Convento de Santa Cruz →
with Manueline doorway

São Tiago

The Romanesque church of São Tiago stands at the north end of the square. It was built in the 11th century after the town had been recaptured from the Moors.

★ ★
Convento de Santa Cruz

The Convento de Santa Cruz on the Praça 8 de Maio was founded in 1131, but in later periods was much enlarged and altered. Fundamental extension work was carried out in the 15th and 16th centuries in the reign of Manuel I by his celebrated architect Boytaca, and continued by Nicolas de Chantarène after Boytaca's death. The north wing of the former Augustinian monastery today houses the **town hall** of Coimbra. The south wing contains the aisle-less **monastery church** from 1131/1132. The façade consists of several layers: the Manueline doorway dates back to the first half of the 16th century, but the archway was added a little distance in front of it in the 18th century. The nave, spanned by a reticulated vault, is framed by side chapels.

On the north wall is a magnificent pulpit from 1522, a relic of the rich furnishings of the church interior referred to in historical documents. The stalls in the gallery date back to the early 16th century; the fine carvings on the backrests show representations of Vasco da Gama's voyages as well as scenes from *The Lusiads* by Camões.

The right aisle provides access to the **sacristy**, a Renaissance building from 1622 with a coffered barrel-vault ceiling and clad with colourful azulejos. A number of notable pictures by Portuguese artists are kept here (*Pentecost* by Cristóvao de Figueiredo; *Calvary* by Sao Bento).

In the **choir** there are the late Gothic **tombs of the first Portuguese kings**, created by Nicolas de Chanterène at the behest of Manuel I. On the left lies the recumbent figure of Afonso Henriques (1139–1185), on the right is Sancho I (1185–1211); each is surrounded by saints.

In the picturesque **Claustro do Silêncio** (cloister of silence), a two-storied 16th-century Manueline cloister, there are three magnificent reliefs with scenes from the Passion (in the south-west and north-east corners as well as on the south side).

> **! Baedeker TIP**
>
> **Café Santa Cruz**
>
> Directly adjacent to the church, an unusual café has been established in some former monastery rooms with beautiful vaulted ceilings (Praça 8 de Maio).

Jardim da Manga

Adjoining the monastery complex to the east is the Jardim da Manga (garden of the sleeve) , all that is left of a second, later cloister. It was built by Joao III according to a design drawn on his sleeve – hence the name. The domed building in the centre is surrounded by moats and four small, round chapels. Access to the round chapels used to be by drawbridge only. Once these were raised, nothing could disturb the monks' meditation.

The upper city is reached on foot by turning south down the Rua Visconde da Luz and going up through the Arco de Almedina. The arch is a relic of the Moorish town walls, and a Gothic two-storey tower was built over it in the 15th century. It was occupied by a municipal court in the 16th century and now houses the city archives.

Arco de Almedina

From the Arco de Almedina it is a short way up a flight of steps to Rua de Sub Ripas, where the 16th-century palace of the same name stands with its fine Manueline doorway.

Palácio de Sub Ripas

Steps and narrow alleys lead up to the old cathedral (Sé Velha), a fortress-like structure. On the square in front of it Dom João I was proclaimed King of Portugal in 1385. The fortified church was built in the reign of Afonso Henriques in the 12th century with a plain exterior, crenellation and a massive Romanesque west portal. The Porta Especiosa, a delicately decorated doorway on the north side, dates back to the early Renaissance.

★ Sé Velha

The Romanesque **interior** of the old cathedral, with a nave and two aisles, is strikingly impressive. The most notable features are a number of tombs, including that of Bishop Almeida from the 16th century, the large late Gothic high altar with scenes of the Assumption of the Virgin Mary created by the Flemish masters Oliver of Ghent and John of Ypres, as well as the Renaissance baptismal font. From

View of Coimbra's old town and university from the opposite side of the Mondego

The well-fortified old cathedral. In the background stands the tower of the university.

the south aisle, a flight of steps leads up to the early Gothic cloister which exudes a reflective calm.

Sé Nova   From the north side of the old cathedral the steep Rua do Cabido leads up to the broad Largo da Feira, whose south side is the site of several newer university buildings. The new cathedral (Sé Nova) on the north side was originally constructed for the Jesuits. The construction of the church was started in the late 16th century, but work continued well into the 17th century.

With the banishment of the Jesuits in the second half of the 18th century, the place of worship was raised to cathedral status. It has a handsome early Baroque facade and, inside, coffered barrel vaulting, Baroque altarpieces and a 17th-century organ.

! **Baedeker TIP**

Fado »a cappella«

The special form of fado found in Coimbra can be heard every evening in very special surroundings: the Capela Nossa Senhora da Victória, an old chapel in Rua Corpo de Deus.

► VISITING COIMBRA

INFORMATION
Largo da Portagem
3000-337 Coimbra
Tel. 239 488 120
Fax 239 825 576
www.turismo-centro.pt

Largo D. Dinis
3000-143 Coimbra
Tel. 239 832 591
www.turismo-centro.pt

DIRECTIONS/PARKING
The signs "Turismo – Largo da Portagem» are a useful means of orientation for those entering Coimbra by car. They lead to the area down by the river, and a little to the southeast directly on the river bank is a good-sized car park from which it is easy to access the city centre area on foot. On weekdays a trip by car to the centre should be avoided if possible – the roads are solid with traffic and parking spaces scarce.

SHOPPING
The most important shopping streets of Coimbra are Rua Ferreira Borges – a pedestrian zone – and Rua Visconde da Luz.

WHERE TO EAT
► Inexpensive
② *Italia*
Parque Dr. Manuel Braga
Tel. 239 838 863
Good Italian restaurant situated in the greenery above the Mondego.

③ *Viela*
Rua das Azeiteiras 33
Tel. 239 832 625
Small and simple restaurant; it is nice to sit outside in a courtyard. Bacalhau is a speciality of the house.

④ *Praça Velha*
Praça do Comércio 69-71
Tel. 239 836 704
Pleasant restaurant on Coimbra's most beautiful square. Typical dishes of the region.

Baedeker recommendation

► Inexpensive/Moderate
① *A Taberna do Parque*
Parque Verde do Mondego
Av. da Lousã
Tel. 239 842 140
Directly down by the Mondego. Seating is either outside on the water or inside amid very aesthetic ambience. Excellent appetizers. Those wishing to smoke may order a Cohiba.

WHERE TO STAY
► Mid-range/Luxury
① *Quinta das Lágrimas*
Santa Clara
3041-901 Coimbra
Tel. 239 802 380
Fax 239 441 695
www.quintadaslagrimas.pt
High-class hotel in a quinta steeped in history.

► Budget/Mid-range
② *Hotel Astória*
Avenida Emídio Navarro 21
3000-150 Coimbra
Tel. 239 853 020
Fax 239 822 057
www.almeidahotels.com
Wonderful hotel with the charm of its time of origin (19th century). Centrally located on a noisy street; in some rooms there is a view of the Mondego. Beautiful furnishings; the lounge area is nothing less than

extraordinary. The former ballroom now hosts a restaurant.

► **Budget**

③ *Hotel Bragança*
Largo das Ameias 10
3000-024 Coimbra
Tel. 239 822 171
Fax 239 836 135
A multi-storey building near the train station; 83 rooms with modern furnishings.

④ *Residência Coimbra*
Rua das Azeiteiras 55
3000 Coimbra
Tel. 239 837 996
Fax 239 838 124
Small and simple guesthouse right in the city centre.

★
Museu Nacional Machado de Castro

Below the Sé Nova, housed in the former bishop's palace and the adjoining São João church, is the Museu Nacional Machado de Castro. It is named after the Coimbra-born sculptor Machado de Castro (1731–1822). The exhibits include medieval sarcophaguses, Roman and Gothic sculptures in stone and wood, gold works, furniture, tapestries, and faience works, as well as paintings of the 16th–18th centuries, among them some notable Flemish pictures and a separate section devoted to the works of modern Portuguese painters and religious art. In Roman times the Forum of Aeminium could be found here. The underground corridors and an aqueduct that were discovered can be viewed during a visit to the museum. The two-storey pillared gallery on the west side of the interior courtyard offers a fine view across the town, with the Sé Velha and the university, all the way down to the Mondego. The same view can be enjoyed from the small museum café on the north side of the interior courtyard (open: ☉ Tue 2pm–6pm, Wed–Sun 10am to 6pm).

★
Universidade Velha

At the highest point of the upper city, on the site once occupied by the royal palace of which only a Manueline doorway remains, is the **old university**, which was partly rebuilt in the 17th/18th centuries (open: 1.10.–4.4.: 9.30am–12.30 and 2pm–5.30pm; 5.4. to 30.9.: 9.30am–7.30pm).

The Porta Férrea (iron gate) from 1634 leads into the spacious **interior courtyard**. Enclosed on three sides by buildings, it has a terrace on the south side from which there is a magnificent view.

On the north side stands the actual old **university building** with the rectorate and the law faculty. Up flights of steps is the Via Latina colonnade – where the students were once allowed to speak only Latin. On the west of the courtyard is the

---

𝑖 Repúblicas

■ How do students live in Portugal? Many live with their parents or have a room at a relative's house. In Coimbra – and only here – there are the so-called Repúblicas, a type of flat-sharing community, each with a different name and all with a rather left-wing political orientation. The number of Repúblicas is on the wane due to the general lack of accommodation. A few are left in the lanes north of the Museu Machado de Castro.

university church, the **Capela de São Miguel**. It was built from 1517–1552 as the palace chapel, and its 33m/110ft-high tower dates back to the year 1733. Affiliated with the church is a small museum of sacred art.

Adjoining the church is the sumptuous old library, one of the most magnificent in the world. It was built from 1716 to 1723 and based on the court library in Vienna – João V's queen, Ana Maria, was from Austria. Besides the 300,000 books and 3,000 medieval manuscripts from all parts of Portugal, the ceiling and wall frescoes by António Simões Ribeiro are notable, as is the precious inlaid furniture. The library was in use until 1910; since that time it can only be viewed with a special permit (registering for a viewing highly recommended, tel. 239 859 800).

✹ ✹
◄ Library

The Jardim Botânico (botanical garden) was commissioned by the Marquês de Pombal (►Famous People) and laid out in terraces on the slopes of a side valley of the Mondego. The park is lavishly endowed with subtropical plants; unfortunately only a part of it is open to the public, the rest being affiliated with university institutes.

✹
Jardim Botânico

Students in Coimbra – tidily dressed, from time to time even in the traditional »capa«, a long, black cloak

Coimbra Plan

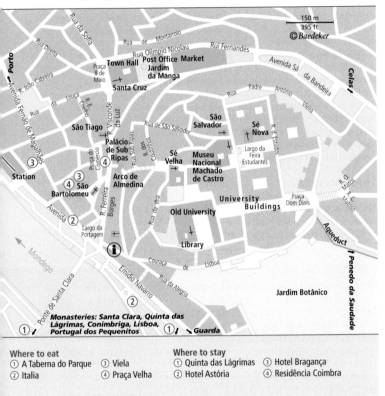

150 m
395 ft
© *Baedeker*

Where to eat
① A Taberna do Parque   ③ Viela
② Italia   ④ Praça Velha

Where to stay
① Quinta das Lágrimas   ③ Hotel Bragança
② Hotel Astória   ④ Residência Coimbra

On the Left Bank of the Mondego

Monasterio de Santa Clara-a-Velha

A little to the left behind the bridge over the Mondego are the ruins of the Gothic monastery of Santa Clara-a-Velha, which have meanwhile sunk almost 5m/16ft into the alluvial land. The location of the monastery founded in 1286 was poorly chosen – the almost annual flooding of the Mondego has gradually destroyed the building and caused it to sink. Comprehensive restoration work started in the 1990s to counteract the disintegration.

The **saintly Queen Isabel** (1271–1336) spent the last ten years of her life in the Convento de Santa Clara-a-Velha and was buried here; as was the murdered **Inês de Castro** (►Baedeker Special, p.284 and ► Alcobaça), the secret lover and later wife of Pedro I. Their mortal remains were moved elsewhere after the monastery started to sink. The monastery was abandoned in 1677.

Opposite the old monastery of Santa Clara-a-Velha, a miniature village was established in 1940, the »Portugal dos Pequenitos Parque« (open: March–June 10am–7pm, July–Sept 9am–8pm, otherwise 10am–5pm). It shows reproductions of the country's most important buildings as well typical homes and buildings from the former colonies. The miniature buildings are in a beautiful garden setting which makes a visit enjoyable for both adults and children.

Portugal dos Pequenitos Parque
🕐

About 1km/0.6mi south stands the Quinta das Lágrimas, which today houses a luxury hotel. Allegedly, **Inês de Castro was murdered in 1355** in the »villa of tears«. To this day, the Fonte dos Amores (lovers' fountain) and the Fonte das Lágrimas (fountain of tears) in the openly accessible park recall her tragic love story.

✷ Quinta das Lágrimas

Since the old Convent of Santa Clara was almost completely destroyed in the 17th century, a new convent, the Convento de Santa-Clara-a-Nova, was built between 1649–1696 to the right on the Monte da Esperança. It is possible to visit the Renaissance style **convent church**, which is dedicated to St Isabel, the patron saint of Coimbra and wife of King Dinis I. Her silver shrine (1614) which was originally in the old convent was transferred to the choir of the new convent church by Pedro II in the late 17th century. St Isabel's stone sarcophagus, now empty, is from the first half of the 14th century. It is borne on six crouching lions. The recumbent figure of the queen is dressed in the simple habit of the Poor Clares, but wears a crown to show her rank.

Convento de Santa Clara-a-Nova

Around Coimbra

Located 15km/9mi south-west of Coimbra, Condeixa boasts some fine palaces, including the 17th-century Palácio dos Lemos.

Condeixa

Conímbriga lies 2km/1.3mi south-east of Condeixa. Although still being excavated, it is already clear that this settlement constitutes the largest Roman site in Portugal. The name of the Roman town, which existed here from the second century BC until its destruction by the Suevi in AD 468, was eventually taken over by the at first less significant Coimbra.

The town was secured by a wall about 2km/1.3mi long, and some of it, dating from the third century AD, still remains. Numerous ruins of houses, thermal baths and fountains – not least because of the mosaics adorning them, some of which are quite well preserved – bear testimony to the town's wealth and good taste. The third century »House of Fountains« is especially well worth seeing; the mosaics depict hunting scenes, dolphins and Perseus with the decapitated head of Medusa.

At the entrance of the **Museu Monográfico** material recovered by the excavators is displayed – mosaics, ceramics, marble busts, a colossal

✷✷ Conímbriga

LOVE BEYOND DEATH

Pedro and Inês – Portugal's most famous lovers. Their love ended tragically; their affection was not tolerated in the royal court. When Pedro was crowned king, his revenge for the violent death of his lover knew no bounds.

Lisbon, July 1340. King Afonso IV is satisfied: his son, the 20-year-old Infante Dom Pedro, and Constanza, the somewhat older but ideal marriage partner according to the monarch, say »I do«. The king was nevertheless uneasy – and rightly so, as became clear a few years later.

Love against the father's wishes

In the entourage of the married couple was a Galician member of the nobility, **Inês de Castro**, a woman of exceptional beauty with whom the heir to the throne immediately fell **passionately in love**. While Pedro bowed to the will of his father and married Constanza, his amorous feelings were solely for the lady-in-waiting from Galicia. It was at this time a hidden love; only in secret could the two young people meet and show their affection for one another.

The king, however, had known all about it for a long time. In order to avoid a scandal he requested Inês to leave the country, which she did. But when Constanza died giving birth to Prince Fernando a short time later, Pedro – against the express wishes of his father – had Inês brought back to Portugal. The couple had **four happy years** in Coimbra, in which Inês bore the same number of Pedro's children. King Afonso IV watched the relationship between Pedro and Inês with growing concern; he was afraid that the Galician could allow his son to come under Castilian influence. The disapproval of his father however only pushed Pedro more firmly to the beautiful Inês's side. Not only did he openly show his love for her in public, he also, for all to see, spent a great deal of time with her brothers and other members of the Castilian nobility. On the other hand he had little

Today a azulejo plaque in the garden of the Quinta das Lágrimas on the Fonte das Lágrimas, the Spring of Tears, commemorates the murder of Inês de Castro.

concern for his duties as the heir to the throne, and paid no attention to his legitimate son, whom Constanza had borne for him.

Afonso became increasingly afraid that his son's love for Inês would result in the hard won Portuguese independence being gambled away to Portugal's powerful neighbour Castile. At the beginning of January 1355 he summoned his crown council in order to find a way to remove the beautiful Inês from the picture. The solution was a **death sentence**.

On a dull winter day on 7 January 1355, three hired assassins forced their way into the same estate that throughout the years had served as a love-nest and in which Inês was now staying – later this fateful place was named »Quinta das Lágrimas«, house of tears. The henchmen had chosen their moment well: Pedro was out hunting. But on his return he made a gruesome discovery: they had beheaded Inês. Pedro almost lost his mind, and only one thought filled his head: **revenge!** With his power base he unleashed a bloody civil war

The king called his council into session to find a way to get the beautiful Inês out of the way…

against his father, but Pedro's troops could not overcome the forces of the king. After his mother mediated between the two sides, Pedro eventually submitted and swore he would no longer seek retaliation for what had happened. The men however who were responsible for Inês's death were not convinced by the oath; they quickly fled to Castile.

Gruesome revenge

In the year 1357 Afonso IV died. In the kingdom something dreadful was expected to occur. But the new king, Pedro I, appeared to be holding to his oath and was apparently not planning revenge. Perhaps, it was conjectured,

The tomb of Pedro I in Alcobaça. True to his wishes he was placed directly opposite the sarcophagus of Inês, which was already standing in the left aisle.

his **new lover**, who had borne him another son, João – who would later become Grand Master of Avis and founder of the second Portuguese royal dynasty – had helped Pedro to get over the disgraceful crime against Inês. Appearances, however, were deceptive.

Pedro struck up a close relationship with the neighbouring Castile and in this way achieved the extradition of two of the three advisers of his father who had planned Inês's murder; the third had made a timely exit and fled to England. Pedro's revenge was terrible. First the prisoners were **tortured in the most gruesome way**; then their hearts were torn out before his eyes. According to legend he then gave the order to bring the body of his lover from the Santa Clara convent, in which she had been laid to rest, to the cathedral of Coimbra, in order to solemnly crown her queen.

Here an extremely **bizarre scene** took place: the story goes that two thrones were placed at the front of the cathedral; on one of them sat Pedro, on the other the skeleton. The dead body was clothed in coronation garments, covered with jewels, and wore a crown on its head. Then it is said that the whole court had to file past her, pay homage and kiss her dead hand. In order to underline the legitimacy of this macabre coronation, no less a figure than the Bishop of Braga is said to have made it known that he had once officiated at the secret marriage of Pedro and Inês. Afterwards, in the darkness of the night, the corpse was taken over land in an eerie procession lit by torches to the abbey church at Alcobaça and laid to rest.

So that their eyes meet

This story is not historically documented, but Pedro claimed in no uncertain terms that he had married Inês in secret and that his one-time love should be buried in the abbey church of Alcobaça. He did indeed have **two magnificent sarcophagi** made, each adorned with the figure of the dead person. The coffins stand opposite one another, »so that on the day of the Last Judgement they will each see their beloved«, as the king wished.

Conímbriga Plan

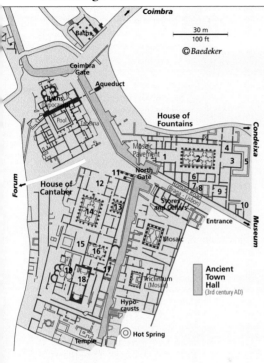

HOUSE OF FOUNTAINS (3rd century)

1 Atrium (entrance hall)
2 Peristyl (colonnade hall) with mosaic pavement at the south-west corner (Perseus with Medusa's head)
3 Triclinium (living and dining room)
4 Room with mosaic pavement (hunting scenes, chariot scenes, the seasons)
5 Pool
6 Room with mosaic pavement (dolphins, sea monsters, wading birds, fish)
7 Cubiculum (bedroom) with mosaic pavement
8 Impluvium (pool for collecting rainwater)
9 Side-room with mosaic (stag hunt)
10 Kitchen and domestic offices

HOUSE OF CANTABER (5th century)

11 Porticus
12 Atrium (entrance hall)
13 Impluvium (pool for collecting rainwater)
14 Peristyl (colonnade hall)
15 Triclinium (living and dining room)
16 Colonnade hall with pool
17 Ornamental basin
18 Frigidarium (cold bath)
19 Tepidarium (warm bath) and caldarium (hot bath); hypocausts (underfloor hot air heating system)

head of Augustus, different articles of daily use and jewellery (open: March–Sept daily 9am–8pm, in winter: daily 9am–6pm; museum closed on Mondays).

Convento de São Marcos

Only the convent church is left of the Convento de São Marcos about 15km/9mi west of Coimbra. The other convent buildings were destroyed by fire in 1860. The interior of the church, built around 1510, contains 15th and 16th-century sculptures.

Lorvão

In this case the journey is far better than the destination: the road going from Coimbra towards Penacova passes above the Mondego through the beautiful, virtually unspoilt river landscape – and turns at the village of Rebodosa towards Lorvão, 25km/15mi away in all. The last part of the route is through woods with some fine walking routes; then the first houses in this remote little village suddenly appear, together with Lorvão convent, of which records exist from as early as 878. The buildings that originally date from the 10th century were remodelled in Renaissance times. Only the convent church, built towards the end of the 16th century, and the simple cloister are open to the public, the rest of the complex today housing a psychiatric hospital. Inside the church, take a look at the elaborately inlaid 18th-century silver shrines with the remains of Sancho I's daughters, Sancha and Teresa (13th century), as well as the choir stalls. The cloister is enclosed by intricately wrought latticework.

North of here is ►Buçaco National Park.

> ## ! *Baedeker* TIP
>
> ### Kayaking on the Mondego
>
> Rental kayaks are available for trips on the Mondego from Penacova to Coimbra – it is about a four-hour journey through the exceptionally beautiful river landscape to the university city. The tourist information office in Coimbra or Penacova (tel. 239 470 300) or »O Pioneiro do Mondego« (tel. 239 478 385) will give details.

It is worth planning a somewhat longer stopover in **Penacova**, a village on a hill above the Mondego. From the village square there is a magnificent view into the river valley, and the same view can be enjoyed from the café directly on the square, a meeting place primarily for the men of the town.

Penela

About 15km/9mi south-east of Condeixa is Penela with a fort from the 11th/12th centuries; it is picturesquely situated on a mountain spur.

Serra da Lousã

South-east of Coimbra lies the Serra da Lousã, which extends south to the Rio Zêzere valley. The main crop here is maize, which is grown on terraces in the often narrow river valleys. The little town of **Lousã**, with its beautiful 18th-century burgher houses, lies at the northern foot of the range. The Igreja da Misericórdia, built around 1550 and with a beautiful Renaissance doorway, is worth taking a look at. High above the town – 3km/2mi south on the road to Castanheira de Pêra – the Miradouro de Nossa Senhora da Piedade provides panoramic views. There is a castle nearby with a massive 14th-century keep. A rewarding walk from Lousã passes through the narrow valley of the Rio Aronce, framed by many small white chapels, to Penhasco dos Eremitas.

Serra de Açor

★

Piódão ►

The Serra de Açor stretches further east. A stay in this area should definitely include a drive to Piódão – a somewhat lengthy undertaking as progress along the winding roads is slow. The drive at first leads through deciduous forests; then the landscape becomes more austere, with gorse shrubs and French lavender lining the road. A walk through Piódão must rank among the most impressive experiences of any tour of Portugal. The village is nestled in the hills of the Serra de Açor in total seclusion. A row of simple cabins made of dark stone wind up the hill, and the same dark stone is used for the steps and small lanes. Elder trees and figs grow in the small gardens framing the village. Since being declared one of the aldeias históricas (historical villages of Portugal), Piódão has become an increasingly popular tourist destination. In the meantime, it is even possible to stay overnight here. One of the few little shops in town offers products of the Serra de Açor, for example a delicious honey: the »mel da Serra de Açor«.

◄ Accommodation in Piódão see p.240

About 40km/25mi east of Coimbra lies the little village of Lourosa. There is a pre-Romanesque church here which probably dates back to the early 10th century. The belfry has been relocated: it was removed when a very old burial site was discovered in its location.

Lourosa

Costa de Lisboa

C – F 25/26

Historical province: Estremadura   **District:** Setúbal

The Costa de Lisboa south of the capital has been left largely untouched by international tourism, but it is popular with the people of Lisbon throughout the summer. The coast is especially attractive thanks to its charming scenery and fine beaches.

This section of coast surrounds the peninsula which is formed by the Serra da Arrábida and its northern foothills between the mouths of the Tagus and Sado. The southern section of the Costa de Lisboa in particular has appealing and still fairly unspoilt towns and relatively empty beaches. The main access to Lisbon via the Ponte 25 de Abril is for the most part hopelessly congested at weekends and in the summer.

Summer beaches of the Lisbonites

What to See on the Costa de Lisboa

Costa da Caparica, once a small fishing village south-west of Lisbon, has developed in recent years into a none too attractive resort, complete with concrete apartment blocks and fast-food outlets. The local beach is a favoured weekend destination of the Portuguese, especially the surfers.
The **Convento dos Capuchos** above the town was fully restored in 1960; concerts are now staged in the former Capuchin convent in the summer.

Costa da Caparica

The Praia do Sol runs south from Costa da Caparica for some 22km/14mi. The broad dune beach is fringed by wooded hills and surely numbers among the most beautiful beaches of Portugal. Access to the more remote beaches is via a narrow-gauge beach railway that runs as far as Fonte da Telha. There are simple beach stalls offering food along this entire stretch.

★
Praia do Sol

VISITING THE COSTA DE LISBOA

INFORMATION

Costa da Caparica
Avenida da República 18
Tel. 212 900 071

WHERE TO STAY

► **Mid-range**
Costa da Caparica
Av. Gen. Humb. Delgado 47

2829-506 Costa da Caparica
Tel. 212 918 900
Fax 212 910 687
www.hotelcostacaparica.pt
Large hotel with 340 rooms in the
centre of town. The surroundings are
fairly urban. The location of the hotel
directly on the beach of Caparica is its
main attraction.

Cabo de Espichel The rough Cabo de Espichel is the western tip of the peninsula, formed by a foothill of the Serra da Arrábida. It affords impressive views of the coastal scenery, the cliffs falling sheer into the sea. Just north of the lighthouse is the Baroque pilgrimage church of Nossa Senhora do Cabo. It is flanked by long two-storey buildings to accommodate the pilgrims.

Sesimbra, Setúbal Some 13km/8mi east of the cape is the fishing town ►Sesimbra, and another 25km/15.6mi east lies the industrial and harbour town of ► Setúbal.

Portinho da Arrábida Portinho da Arrábida is a tiny fishing village that is increasingly popular with tourists. Its idyllic setting in a sandy bay lies about halfway between Sesimbra and Setúbal at the base of the steeply soaring southern slope of the Serra da Arrábida. Several small rocky coves are strung along the coast near the town, and they provide ideal conditions for scuba diving (e.g. Praia de Galápos and Praia da Figueirinha). The Museu Oceanográfico exhibits an important collection of rare sponges and other ocean creatures. The museum is housed in the Fortaleza de Santa Maria da Arrábida built 1670 on the western edge of town.

Approximately 500m/550yd west of Portinho da Arrábida, traces of early man have been discovered in the Lapa de Santa Margarida, a small cave (access via steps by the ocean).

★ ★
Serra da Arrábida It is worthwhile taking a trip to the secluded mountains of the Serra da Arrábida, which have been declared a nature reserve. The variety of plant life is unusual here; along with wild olive trees there are strawberry trees, mastric trees, holm oaks, as well as heather, cistaceas, woodbine and myrtle. A small lane leads up from Portinho da Arrábida to the **Convento Novo da Arrábida**, founded by Franciscan monks in 1542. The walled complex is in private hands. The road winds up further to the highest peak of the Serra da Arrábida – the

Alto do Formosinho (501m/1,643ft). Time and again there are spectacular views of the coast near Tróia, and with good visibility even of Lisbon.

The dune-rich and in part wooded Tróia peninsula south-west of Setúbal is hardly developed with regard to a road network and constitutes an ideal hiking area. A 30km/19mi sandy beach stretches along the ocean side – the longest in Portugal. There is a ferry service from Setúbal to Tróia. The **Tróia holiday colony**, widely visible because of its high rises, is situated on the northern tip of Península de Tróia, a narrow spit offshore from the estuarine lagoon of the Rio Sado. The remains of the Roman town of **Cetóbriga**, destroyed by a storm tide in the 5th century, lie about 6km/4mi south-east of Tróia.

Tróia

Costa de Prata

B–F 13–24

Historical provinces: Beira Litoral, Estremadura

Districts: Aveiro, Coimbra, Leiria, Lisboa

The endless sandy beaches of the Costa de Prata between the Cabo da Roca and the mouth of the Douro north of Lisbon are a popular summer holiday destination of the Portuguese.

Azenhas do Mar is a popular subject matter for landscape painters.

▶ VISITING THE COSTA DE PRATA

Silver coast The combination of broad beaches, in part with towering cliffs and partially lined with dunes, pine forests, olive groves and scattered windmills makes for beautiful scenery. The cold water temperatures and mostly rather harsh climate make the Costa de Prata a less than ideal location for holidays spent solely on the beach.

Seaside Resorts and Beaches on the Costa de Prata

Praia das Maçãs The Praia The Maçãs about 30km/19mi north-west of Lisbon is a popular beach frequented mostly by the inhabitants of Sintra and the surrounding area, but even some Lisbonites would not shun the long drive.

Azenhas do Mar A little further north isAzenhas do Mar, a small village whose beautiful hillside location on the cliffs and idyllic charm make it one of the most appealing seaside resorts of this region. Many painters were drawn to the beautiful village in the early 20th century.

Ericeira Further north is Ericeirawith a population of 4,500, located on a steep and rocky coast full of chasms and grottoes. It has a long history as a trading and fishing village, but the harbour lost its importance in the early 20th century. The fishing nowadays is mainly for crayfish. Most money is meanwhile made from the tourism generated by the beautiful nearby beaches.

From Ericeira to Espinho There are vast beaches with fine sand around Santa Cruz and Porto Novo, framed by rocks and green hills. About 4km/2.5mi inland is the health spa of **Vimeiro**, which is frequented by those with ailments of the liver, stomach or skin; further north lies ▶ Peniche and the

On the beach of Miramar. Once a year a beach procession in honour of the Senhora da Agonia marches to the chapel right next to the sea.

well known seaside resort of ►Nazaré. **São Pedro de Muel**, a pretty beach resort surrounded by pine woods, lies some 20km/12mi north of Nazaré. The seaside resort of ►Figueira da Foz is well-visited, and ►Aveiro remains relatively unspoilt. The seaside resort of **Espinho**, about 15km/9mi south of Porto, has been developed in a plain, rational manner and is dominated by tourism. A bustling seafront promenade borders on the broad beach with coarse sand. A golf course, a landing field for light aircraft and a casino are part of the wide range of recreational facilities. A little further north is **Miramar** with a beach chapel built directly by the water.

Costa do Sol

Historical province: Estremadura   **District:** Lisboa

The Costa do Sol west of Lisbon is also known as the »Portuguese Riviera«. It is in part strongly influenced by its close proximity to the metropolis, but further north this section of coast turns into one of the loveliest on the western coast of Portugal.

Thanks to the appealing landscape and good beaches as well as the pleasant climate and the lush vegetation, the towns and seaside resorts of the Costa do Sol are highly frequented especially by the Portuguese. Crowded beaches and a congested coastal road can be counted on at all times during the peak season.

Sun coast

Where to Go on the Costa do Sol

Caxias Caxias lies some 10km/6mi west of Lisbon. During Salazar's dictatorship, the fort in the small town was one of Portugal's most notorious jails for political prisoners; another fort is today a youth hostel.

There is a country seat of the Marquês de Pombal (► Famous People) in **Oeiras**, 4km/2.5mi west of Caxias. The 18th-century villa is set in handsome gardens and surrounded by statues and water features.

About 2km/1.3mi beyond Oeiras left of the road looms the **Forte São Julião da Barra**. The fortification, complete with tower and ramparts, dates back to the 17th century.

Estoril, Cascais The well made four-lane expressway ends in the large built-up area where the two seaside resorts ► Estoril and ► Cascais have merged. At the exit from Cascais is the viewing platform above the Boca do Inferno (►Cascais).

Cabo Raso Behind the Boca do Inferno, rows of stalls for the tourists line the left and the right of the road in the summer. The lighthouse of Cabo Raso, some 5km/3mi away, offers a magnificent view towards the Cabo da Roca.

! **Baedeker** TIP

The westernmost point of Europe

A certificate can be obtained at the Cabo da Roca, stating that the holder has indeed reached the westernmost point of the continent. And if that is not enough, hit a golf ball down the cliffs into the Atlantic – as some Japanese are prone to do – or invent your own personal ceremony for this place with its unique geography.

▶ VISITING THE COSTA DO SOL

INFORMATION
►Estoril, ►Cascais

WHERE TO STAY •
WHERE TO EAT

► Mid-range/Luxury
Fortaleza do Guincho
2750-642 Cascais
Tel. 214 870 491
Fax 214 870 431
www.guinchotel.pt
Small hotel in a former fort directly on the sea. Glorious location – wonderful

rooms. The restaurant, with a sea view, offers international gourmet cuisine.

► Mid-range
Quinta do Rio Touro
Caminho do Rio Touro
2705-001 Sintra
Tel. 219 292 862
www.quinta-riotouro.com
Small house near the Cabo da Roca with seven rooms and suites.

The Praia do Guincho is a truly beautiful beach 3km/2mi from Cabo Raso, though it is hopelessly crowded during the peak season. The beach is considered to be an eldorado for experienced surfers.

Praia do Guincho

A small road branches off from the main road 7km/4.3mi beyond Praia do Guincho and leads down to Cabo da Roca. The western-most point of the European mainland, which is marked by a stone column close to the light house, towers 144m/472ft above the ocean. Named Promontorium Magnum by the Romans, the Cabo da Roca is a granite foothill of the Serra de Sintra (►Sintra).

★
Cabo da Roca

Back on the main road from Cabo da Roca, the town of Colares (► Sintra) lies further north. Known for its wine, this small place at the foot of the Serra de Sintra is distinctly filled with atmosphere.

Colares

Costa Dourada

E/F 27–32

Historical province: Baixo Alentejo   **Districts:** Setúbal, Beja

Between the mouths of the Rio Sado and the Ponta da Arrifana, which are part of the Algarve, stretches the »golden coast«, still only partially developed in terms of tourism.

Although the Costa Dourada with its cliffs and seemingly endless beaches is very scenic, the climate is relatively harsh, and there is a constant stiff breeze coming from the Atlantic. Only a few coves surrounded by rock walls are sheltered enough for swimming.

Towns and Beaches on the Costa Dourada

The Algarve town of Aljezur is a short distance inland about 40km/25mi north of Sagres. The ruins of a Moorish castle tower over the town.
The entire coastal region south and north of Aljezur, **Costa Vicentina**, is protected, meaning that for the most part the wonderfully scenic beaches have remained unspoilt. The remote and vast Praia de Carriagem and Praia de Arrifana are beautiful.

Aljezur

About 50km/31mi north of Aljezur at the mouth of the Rio Mira lies Vila Nova de Milfontes with a population of 2,000. Tourism is gradually taking possession of the small fishing village. A few newer holiday domiciles – guesthouses and apartment buildings but no larger hotels – have sprung up around the centre of town, but Milfontes still remains quiet for ten months of the year.
The situation changes in July and August: the town is then filled with mostly younger holidaymakers who appreciate the magnificent

Vila Nova de Milfontes

VISITING THE COSTA DOURADA

INFORMATION

Vila Nova de Milfontes
Rua António Mantas
7645-221 Vila Nova de Milfontes
Tel. 283 996 599
www.cm-odemira.pt

Aljezur
Largo do Mercado
8670-054 Aljezur
Tel. 282 998 229
www.turismodoalgarve.pt

WHERE TO EAT

▶ **Inexpensive**
Tasca do Celso
Rua dos Aviadores 34-A

7645 Vila Nova de Milfontes
Tel. 283 996 753
Simple yet lovingly decorated restaurant which serves good food. The menu features down to earth regional dishes which are always prepared fresh.

WHERE TO STAY

▶ **Budget**
Casa dos Arcos
Rua do Carris
7645-235 Vila Nova de Milfontes
Tel. 283 996 264
Fax 283 997 156
Small hotel with 18 rooms. Modern, simple and reliable.

---

beaches south of the estuary. In the summer, a shuttle ferry service operates across the river from the centre of town.

Porto Covo   Porto Covo, 20km/12mi further north, is also surrounded by dream beaches to the south and north, though the surf is really strong. The former fishing village is slowly developing into a tourist destination. A beach promenade has been created, and apartment buildings and terraced houses have been built; more construction work is planned.

Costa Verde

E/F 5–12

Historical provinces: Douro Litoral, Minho

Districts: Porto, Braga, Viana do Castelo

The beaches of the Costa Verde in the far north between the mouths of Douro and Minho are a popular summer destination of the Portuguese. The spacious beaches with plentiful dunes and fine sand are protected in many places by rocky cliffs.

Green coast   As on the Costa de Prata, water temperatures are fairly low and there is often a stiff sea breeze – which is why the Costa Verde is not the best of locations for a holiday spent solely on the beach. But the hin-

▶ VISITING THE COSTA VERDE

INFORMATION

Esposende
Av. Eng. Eduardo Arantes de Oliveira
4740-204 Esposende
Tel. 253 961 354
www.rtam.pt

WHERE TO STAY

▶ **Budget/Mid-range**
Suave Mar
Av. Eng. Eduardo Arantes e Oliveira

4740-204 Esposende
Tel. 253 969 400
Fax 253 969 401
info@suavemar.com
Very pleasant and well-kept hotel with
approx. 85 rooms, some of which
have a view of the water. In the hotel
restaurant – also with a beautiful view
– good international cuisine is on the
menu.

terland also offers some worthwhile destinations: ► Braga, ► Guimarães and the ►Peneda-Gerês National Park.

Several seaside resorts are strung along the coast moving northwards   **Seaside resorts**
from ► Porto: first come ► Vila do Conde and Póvoa de Varzim,
which are dominated by industry; they are followed by the more
tranquil towns of Ofir and Esposende (►Barcelos) and ► Viana do
Castelo with its pretty townscape. Further endless beaches stretch all
the way to the Spanish border. The small tourist towns of Vila Praia
de Âncora and Moledo do Minho (► Caminha) are the holiday destinations here.

✶ ✶ Douro Valley

G – V 7 – 10

Historical province: Douro Litoral,   **Districts:** Porto, Vila Real, Viseu, Guarda,
Beira Alt, Trás-os-Montes   Bragança

**The steep Douro Valley and some of its neighbouring valleys have
been wine-growing areas for some 2,000 years now; the oldest
wine-growing region defined by law in the world can be found
here. Boat excursions on the Douro or a ride along the banks of
the river are most worthwhile.**

The Douro(pronounced »Doru«) – called Duero in Spain – is one of   **Course of the**
the most important water courses of the Iberian peninsula. It origi-   **river**
nates at the Pico de Urbión (2,252m/7,388ft above sea level) in the
Spanish province of Soria. Its 925km/578mi course first crosses the
plateau of Old Castile and León, then forms the Spanish-Portuguese
border for 122km/76mi with canyons up to 400m/1,300ft deep, and

after flowing through a picturesque valley between Trás-os-Montes and the Beira provinces, finally joins the Atlantic near Porto – or to be more precise, at Foz do Douro (Foz = mouth).

Impoundments

Impoundments on the river are used to produce electricity in the vicinity of the Spanish-Portuguese border within the framework of a bilateral agreement. The Portuguese also use the further course of the river to produce energy. In this way the dam walls turn the Douro into a broad, languid river beyond Pinhão.

★ ★
Wine-growing region

The **oldest wine-growing region defined by law in the world** is situated about 70km/44mi east of Porto in the region of Peso da Régua and Pinhão. Port wine may only be produced in this region. The slatey slopes of the Douro Valley have been skilfully reshaped into narrow terraces which are in many places no more than 2m/3.3ft wide. The use of machines to work the small areas is limited. It is much to be hoped that the cultivated land, which has been developed over centuries, will not be destroyed to create better conditions for production. The wine region was placed under the protection of UNESCO in 2001.

> ! **Baedeker TIP**
>
> ### By train through the Douro Valley
> You don't have to be a train-lover to enjoy this ride along the Douro. The stretch of railway line Porto – Régua – Pocinho directly follows a longer section of the river, roughly between Pala and Tua. For those with less time it is possible to board the train at Régua, for instance, and travel on to Tua; this short yet impressive journey takes about 40 minutes. It also passes the train station of Pinhão, widely known for its azulejo pictures (information: www.cp.pt)

Shipping

The highly differing waterlines have impeded regular shipping on the Douro in centuries past. For a long time, only flat riverboats, the so-called **rabelos**, traversed above Porto, transporting the port from the **wine-growing region near Peso da Régua** to the cellars at the estuary; today the precious liquid cargo is transported to Porto in tanker lorries. It was not until the late 1980s that the last 210km/131mi to the mouth of the Douro became navigable for deeper hulled vessels.

← *Every year in September: grape harvest in the Douro Valley*

Pleasure trips on the Douro
Pleasure trips on the Douro are a delight. Smaller boat tours are offered very near to Porto, which allow a panoramic view of the city and the imposing bridges of the urban area. There are also one or two day tours through the Douro Valley up to Peso da Régua and Pinhão or starting from Peso da Régua. Drives along the river banks are also enjoyable (▶Lamego).

 ## VISITING THE DOURO VALLEY

INFORMATION

Peso da Régua
Rua da Ferreirinha
5050 Peso da Régua
Tel. 254 312 846
Fax 254 322 271

Pinhão
Largo da Estação
5085 Pinhão
Tel. 254 731 932
www.rtsmarao.pt

WHERE TO EAT
▶ **Inexpensive/Moderate**
Régua Douro
Largo da Estação da CP
Tel. 254 320 700
Traditional cuisine. Outside seating with a view across the Douro and the vineyards.

WHERE TO STAY
▶ **Mid-range/Luxury**
Vintage House
Lugar da Ponte

Casa das Torres de Oliveira with view to the Douro Valley vineyards

5085-034 Pinhão
Tel. 254 730 230, fax 254 730 238
www.hotelvintagehouse.com
Luxurious and widely known hotel
with 43 rooms in a sensational
location directly on the bank of the
Douro.

Pousada do Solar da Rede
5040-336 Mesão Frio
Tel. 254 890 130
Fax 254 890 139
This pousada is located in the midst
of a vineyard: the old manor house
contains a total of 31 nicely furnished
rooms.

► Budget/Mid-range
Casa das Torres de Oliveira
Oliveira
5040-225 Mesão Frio
Tel. 254 336 743
Fax 254 336 195
Wonderful old winery about 8km/5mi

from Péso da Régua. It is situated in
the middle of the vineyards with a
view down into the Douro Valley and
onto a tiny part of the river. Six rooms
are available, with a swimming pool
and a small garden surrounded by the
vineyard. Supper is available in the
house by prior arrangement.

► Budget
Casarão
Igreja
4640-465 Santa Marinha do Zêzere
Tel. 254 882 177
Fax 254 888 151
The »Casarão« in Igreja near Santa
Marinha do Zêzere west of Mesão
Frio also offers a spectacular view
across the Douro Valley. The rooms
are simple but well-kept, with beautiful old wooden floors. The recreation room which features a chimney
is open to all, and the old stone
kitchen is lovely.

✴ Elvas

Historical province: Alto Alentejo
District: Portalegre

Elevation: 300m/984ft
Population: 15,000

As a staging post against the nearby Spanish Badajoz, Elvas was ever more strongly fortified from the late Middle Ages onwards and remained reinforced in the 17th/18th centuries by powerful forts, which are today among the best preserved of their period in Portugal.

Elvas has retained its former Moorish character in many aspects. The town lies on approximately the same elevation as Lisbon in the vicin-ity of the Spanish border in the midst of rich olive groves and fruit-growing regions. It is today the marketing and trans-shipment point for the agricultural produce of the fertile surrounding area, though it is popular with tourists as well. There are several larger hotels around the town centre some of which are surrounded by rather fine parks. While in Elvas it is worth sampling the delicacy of the town: candied plums.

Fortified border to Spain

 VISITING ELVAS

INFORMATION
Praça da República
7350-126 Elvas
Tel. 268 622 236
www.rtsm.pt

WHERE TO EAT
► **Moderate**
A Coluna
Rua de Cabrito 11
Tel. 268 623 728
Down to earth and very tasty dishes
from the Alentejo.

WHERE TO STAY
► **Mid-range**
Pousada de Santa Luzia
Av. de Badajoz

7350-097 Elvas
Tel. 268 637 470
Fax 268 622 127
The oldest pousada in Portugal – it
opened in April 1942 – is tastefully
furnished with antiques. The most
exclusive hotel in Elvas; 25 rooms,
swimming pool and tennis court.

► **Budget**
Hotel D. Luís
Av. de Badajoz
7350-096 Elvas
Tel. 268 622 756
Fax 268 620 733
Simple, reliable and well-kept hotel
with 90 rooms in all.

✳ Labyrinthine old town
The convoluted alleys of the old town still feature some houses with
ornate grilles, pretty archways and many picturesque squares. The
Praça da República, paved with a black and white mosaic, is the
centre of town. The 16th-century town hall, which also houses the
tourism office, is found at the southern end of the square.

What to See in Elvas

Igreja de Nossa Senhora da Assunção
The Igreja de Nossa Senhora da Assunção on the north side of the
central Praça da República served as a cathedral from 1570 to 1882 –
when Elvas was the episcopal see. In the 16th century the originally
late Gothic building was remodelled in the Manueline style. The
main façade with its classical entrance dates back to the 17th/18th
centuries. The interior with a nave and two aisles is decorated with
beautiful tiles.

Igreja de Nossa Senhora da Consolação
Heading upward past the former cathedral leads to the Igreja de
Nossa Senhora da Consolação. The peculiar octagonal central building belonged to the Dominican monastery founded around the mid-
16th century. However the church underwent considerable structural
changes in the mid-17th century. If at all possible, take a look at the
interior: the cupola, supported by columns, is entirely clad with
beautiful azulejos.

The picturesque Largo Santa Clara opens out at the Dominican church. The square is surrounded by handsome houses with fine iron grilles and in its centre stands a beautiful 16th-century pelourinho.

Largo Santa Clara

The castle with the massive keep stands to the north-east of the Largo Santa Clara. It was built by the Moors in the 13th century on the site of some Roman fortifications and expanded in the 15th century. There is a fine view from the castle ramparts.

Castelo

South of the Praça da República, the former 17th-century Jesuit monastery houses an archaeological and ethnological museum as well as the town library. The exhibits include coins, paintings and sculptures of the 13th–16th centuries, Roman mosaics and folk art. Among the 55,000 volumes in the library are some very rare editions, including a 16th-century Bible.

Convento dos Jesuitas

East of the Jesuit monastery stands the former Dominican monastery. It was founded in 1267, and the buildings were remodelled several times in the 15th, 16th and 17th centuries. The monastery church, with an impressive stellar vault in the choir, is open to the public.

Convento de São Domingos

The fortress Nossa Senhora da Graça (18th century) north of the town centre is also known as Forte de Lippe, named after **Count Wilhelm von Schaumburg-Lippe**, who lead the Portuguese army from 1762–1764.

Forte de Nossa Senhora da Graça

The Santa Luzia fort stands in the south of the town; it is an excellent and well-preserved example of Portuguese fortification architecture of the 17th century.

Forte de Santa Luzia

The road from Estremoz and Lisbon to Elvas passes the impressive Aqueduto da Amoreira, which is more than 7km/4.8mi long, at the entrance to the town. The water conduit was built from 1498–1622 on the foundation walls of a Roman aqueduct and to this day carries water to the 17th-century Misericórdia well on the western edge of the town centre.
The **843 arches** of the aqueduct – about half of them are original – are in part **positioned one above the other in four rows**; the highest elevation is 31m/102ft.

★
Aqueduto da Amoreira

Around Elvas

About 20km/12.5mi north-east of Elvas lies Campo Maior, with a closed circular wall (17th/18th centuries), a fort built by King Dinis in the 14th century, and a Gothic parish church with a small ossuary. The shady city park is a good place to linger a while.

Campo Maior

Estoril

B 24

Historical province: Estremadura   **Altitude:** sea level
District: Lisboa (Lisbon)   **Population:** 25,000

Estoril, with its extremely mild climate and subtropical parks, has been frequented by a distinguished international set since the end of the 19th century as an elegant seaside resort and winter spa. Even today it is the domicile of many an illustrious personality.

Once an exclusive seaside resort

However, there is not much left of Estoril's exclusiveness of bygone days. The former fishing village – pronounced »Shturiu« – has virtually merged with the neighbouring ► Cascais and is meanwhile almost a suburb of Lisbon. It is a short trip to Estoril on the suburban train, starting from Cais do Sodré station in Lisbon and heading towards Cascais, part of the route running right along the banks of the Tagus. The beaches are very popular with the city dwellers.

International flair

Tourists are also primarily drawn to Estoril because of the beaches. But the international flair, the elegant and well-tended villas, the palm-lined avenues, the casino and the beautiful spa park with its tropical and exotic plants are also appealing. An annual world class tennis tournament and an auto racetrack add to the atmosphere. Newer elegant and exclusive residential areas have developed, especially around Monte Estoril about 1.5km/0.9mi west of the spa park.

Estoril Plan

Where to eat
① La Villa

Where to stay
① Hotel Palácio do Estoril
② Hotel Vila Galé

▶ VISITING ESTORIL

INFORMATION
Arcadas do Parque
2769-503 Estoril
Tel. 214 664 414
Fax 214 672 280
www.estorilcoast-tourism.com

ENTERTAINMENT
This evening's entertainment in Estoril is provided by the casino or the bars and discotheques directly at the beach near the station.

WHERE TO EAT
▶ **Moderate/Expensive**
① *La Villa*
Praia do Estoril
Tel. 214 680 033
A view onto the sea and modern international cuisine.

WHERE TO STAY
▶ **Luxury**
① *Hotel Palácio do Estoril*
Rua do Parque do Estoril

Tel. 214 648 000
Fax 214 684 867
www.hotel-estoril-palacio.pt
An old, large, traditional hotel with about 200 rooms. The exclusive flair of times gone by is still preserved here. There is a swimming pool in the garden which is fed by a mineral spring. The hotel's own restaurant is first-class.

▶ **Mid-range**
② *Hotel Vila Galé*
Avenida Marginal
Tel. 214 648 000
Fax 214 648 432
A large, pleasant hotel with 126 rooms, between the beach and the casino. Suitable even for visitors to Lisbon: the station for the suburban train is in the immediate vicinity.

Estremadura

A–H 17–26

Historical province: Estremadura
Districts: Leiria, Lisboa, Setúbal
Capital city: Lisbon

Area: 11,430 sq km/4,413 sq mi
Population: 3,000,000

Together with the landscape of Ribatejo adjoining on the east, Estremadura has been the centre of Lusitanian and later Portuguese culture since Roman times due to its fertility and its scenic variety in a comparatively small area.

Estremadura encompasses the estuarial area of the Tagus and stretches across the Serra de Sintra from far up in the north down to the area south of Coimbra. To the south it spans the area from the other side of the Setúbal peninsula with the ►Serra da Arrábida up to the mouth of the Rio Sado. Estremadura contains Portugal's intel-

Former frontier against the Moors

lectual centre, ▶Lisbon, and the main spiritual focal points ▶Alcobaça and ▶Batalha, as well as the former royal residences of ▶Queluz, ▶Mafra and ▶Sintra. The biggest wine-growing region of the country lies in Estremadura and neighbouring ▶Ribatejo.

Landscape and economy

In almost no other province of Portugal is there such **economic and cultural variety** as in Estremadura, as befitting its rich geological and scenic makeup. In the northern **hilly landscape** where sparse macchia prevails, sheep and goat farming are the predominant ways to make a living. To the west is a chain of hills of fertile clay and sandstone – the agricultural focal point of the province. Here – around Alcobaça – wheat, maize, citrus fruits, vegetables, olives and winegrowing dominate the Mediterranean-style mixed farming. To the south, the Serra de Sintra is covered by splendid parkland thanks to the fertile soil and the damp and mild oceanic climate; the region has become a recreation area of the first order not least because of its numerous thermal springs (▶u. a. Caldas da Rainha). The **coast** of the Estremadura consists of long sections of sandy beach. A comparatively high number of rivers flow into the Atlantic Ocean in the Estremadura area, including the Tagus, Sado, Mondego and Vouga, with their often very wide and partly marshy estuaries. The traditional ports from which deep-sea fishing boats depart – particularly to Newfoundland – are situated here, with their fish canning factories and drying plants, as well as extensive salt marshes. Rice is cultivated on the marshy fluvial plains.

? DID YOU KNOW …?

■ Estremadura: the outermost frontier. This name dates back to the time of the Reconquista when Portugal was reconquered Arab reign ended; the province of Estremadura formed the border to the Arabian south.

★ Estremoz

Historical province: Alto Alentejo
District: Évora

Altitude: 430m/1,411ft
Population: 10,000

Estremoz lies in the midst of the lightly hilly landscape of the Alto Alenjo. The town is divided into an older, elevated upper city with a castle and picturesque narrow lanes, and a busy lower part of town which developed from the 16th century onward.

The centre of the lower city is the Praça Do Marquês de Pombals, also called »Rossio«. The market is held on this vast square on Saturdays, though on other days of the week some stalls can usually be found selling the characteristic Estremoz red earthenware. The large quantity of white marble, mined in the surrounding area and prized

● VISITING ESTREMOZ

INFORMATION

Praça da República
7100-505 Estremoz
Tel. 268 339 200
www.rtevora.pt

WHERE TO EAT

► Moderate

Zona Verde
Largo Dragões de Olivença 86
Tel. 268 324 701
Attractive premises and well-prepared
Alentejan specialities.

WHERE TO STAY

► Mid-range

Pousada da Rainha Santa Isabel
7100-509 Estremoz Codex

Tel. 268 332 075
Fax 268 332 079
The castle of Estremoz contains 33
rooms. There is valuable furniture in
this especially stylish and widely
known pousada.

Pousada de São Miguel
7470-999 Sousel
Tel. 268 550 050
Fax 268 551 155
Those looking for peace and quiet will
find it in this modern and attractively
furnished pousada. The 32-room
house is completely secluded, situated
on a hill surrounded by olive tree
plantations.

since medieval times, is striking. Beside it, Estremoz is significant as
a centre of pottery, wood carving and leather processing. However,
agriculture remains the most important economic factor here.

What to See in Estremoz

The town hall stands at the southern end of the Rossio. The building, **Lower city**
built in 1698, was originally a monastery; the interior shows scenes
from the life of St Philip on beautiful azulejos. The Largo do Geral
Graça with the 17th-century Tocha palace, containing azulejo depictions of scenes from the war of independence against Spain, borders
on the Rossio to the north. Pedro I died in the former Franciscan
monastery on the same square in 1367.

The upper city lies within the 17th-century Vauban style fortifica- **✱**
tions with several mighty gates. The white paint and the narrow win- **Upper city**
dow openings of the houses are supposed to offer protection against
the intense heat of the summer months.

The highest elevation in the town is occupied by the **fort**, built in
the first half of the 13th century. The massive 27m/89ft keep is the
only part of the original building remaining; it is crowned by closed
battlements. The **royal palace** was added to the keep at the beginning of the 14th century. The palace and fort served at times as the

▶ VISITING ÉVORA

INFORMATION
Praça do Giraldo
7000-508 Évora
Tel. 266 730 030
www.rtevora.pt

DIRECTIONS/PARKING
The town centre is surrounded by a ring road onto which drivers are automatically guided. Those that have booked a hotel room in advance are strongly advised to follow the hotel signposts, as there is a risk of getting hopelessly lost otherwise in the tangle of narrow lanes and one-way streets. Those wishing to pay a visit to the tourist information centre first should follow the »Giraldo« signs. However, it is best to park the car at one of the big car parks by the city wall; from here it is only a few minutes on foot to the Praça do Giraldo right in the middle of the town centre.

WHERE TO EAT
▶ Moderate
① *Fialho*
Travessa dos Mascarenhas 16
Tel. 266 703 079
Classy cuisine, very good game specialities.

▶ Inexpensive
② *A Muralha*
Rua 5 de Outubro 21
Tel. 266 702 284
Try the Alentejan food, e.g. »Migas à Alentejana«, a dish with pork.

WHERE TO STAY
▶ Budget
① *Solar de Monfalim*
Largo da Misericórdia 1
Tel. 266 750 000
Fax 266 742 367
www.monfalimtur.pt
Stylish Albergaria in the historic centre with a beautiful loggia where visitors can sit outside and enjoy the view of the square.

② *Hotel Santa Clara*
Travessa da Milheira 19
Tel. 266 704 141
Fax 266 706 544
Simple hotel with 43 rooms in an old manor house in the centre of Évora.

③ *Residencial Policarpo*
Rua Freira de Baixo 16
Tel. 266 702 424
Fax 266 703 474
www.pensaopolicarpo.com
Very pleasant guesthouse in a beautiful old building.

Solar de Monfalim:
sit outside in the loggia

Évora *Plan*

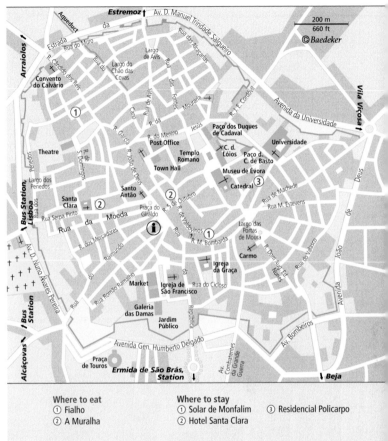

Where to eat
① Fialho
② A Muralha

Where to stay
① Solar de Monfalim
② Hotel Santa Clara
③ Residencial Policarpo

What to See in Évora

Today the long Praça do Giraldo is rather picturesque, even though it was a place of execution during the inquisition and the site of many a sorrowful scene. Stop at one of the street cafés to take in the scenery: pretty houses and arcades surround the square. A marble Renaissance fountain now stands on the site of a Roman triumphal arch demolished in 1570. The church of Santo Antao was built in 1557 on the north side of the square by the then archbishop who later became King Henrique I. Rua 5 de Outubro, brimming with souvenir shops and the favourite street for promenading, leads to the cathedral.

★
Praça do Giraldo

★★
Catedral

The cathedral (Catedral or Sé) is a severe and fortress-like early Gothic style structure, whose construction was begun in 1186 and completed in the 13th and 14th centuries. The façade is dominated by the two asymmetrical towers flanking the massive portal. Above the crossing is an octagonal belfry with a helm roof of scale-like tiles. The figures of the twelve apostles on the doorway are considered to be masterpieces of Portuguese Gothic sculpture. The **interior** made of white granite ashlars exhibits impressive simplicity and harmony. Only the choir is Baroque in character; it was remodelled in the 18th century by Johann Friedrich Ludwig, architect of the convent of ▶Mafra, in the style of the time and lavishly decorated with marble.

The right (southern) aisle of the cathedral provides access to the **cloister**, the high choir and a small museum of religious art. From the Gothic cloister, with statues of the evangelists in the corners, several dark, narrow corridors lead up to the roof terrace. From here visitors can have a closer look at the unusual scaled helm roof of the

Several eras at a single glance: the unusual dome of the Gothic cathedral and the columns of the Roman temple

crossing tower, as well as enjoying a nice wide view over the rather compact looking town and its surroundings. Via the high choir with fine carved choir stalls from 1562 there is access to the **Museu de Arte Sacra**. The precious exhibits include a triptych in the form of a Madonna with child (13th century) made of ivory; the three finely carved altar wings show scenes from the life of Mary. Moreover, there are some excellent gold and enamel works from the 16th and 17th centuries on display.

The former archbishop's palace with the Museu de Évora borders on the cathedral to the north. The exhibits include Roman archaeological findings, Romanesque and Gothic architectural fragments, Portuguese and Flemish paintings of the 16th to the 18th centuries, gold works, and two cenotaphs, created in the 16th century by Nicolas Chanterène for Dom Álvares de Costa and Dom Afonso de Portugal (open: Tue 2pm–6pm, Wed–Sun 10am–6pm).

Museu de Évora

Opposite the entrance of the Museu de Évora is what has become the landmark of Évora, the Templo Romano. Dating probably from the first century, it is one of the best preserved Roman buildings in Portugal. Popularly known as the **Temple of Diana**, it is nevertheless not entirely clear to which deity the temple was dedicated. On the 3m/10ft-high base, which is almost completely preserved, 14 of the originally 18 Corinthian columns still stand, connected to one another by the remains of the architrave. In the Middle Ages, the temple was fortified and later served as a slaughterhouse for a long period, a fate which ultimately saved it from demolition. The structural alterations were not removed until 1870. Archaeological excavations and investigations have been carried out since 1986, focusing among other things on the position of the temple within the Roman town centre. It has been discovered that the open square in front of the temple was covered with large slabs of marble (they lie about three feet below the present ground level) and in 1992 the southern border as well as the western gate of what was probably the forum were brought to light. The gardens behind the temple open onto a terrace which offers a good view of the northern part of town.

★
Templo Romano

> **!** *Baedeker* TIP
>
> **Relaxing under the columns of Diana**
> The Quiosque right next to the Temple of Diana is a wonderful place to take the weight off your feet in a light, airy atmosphere after a visit to the cathedral and the museums.

Opposite and to the east of the Roman temple is the church of the Convento dos Lóios, which was built between 1485 and 1491 but was repeatedly reconstructed in the following centuries. The Manueline vestibule with the coat of arms of the de Melos family dates from the first construction phase; the family founded the church and se-

Convento dos Lóios

lected it as a burial site. The premises of the former Lóios monastery have in part been converted into a **pousada**. The beautiful cloister now serves as a garden for the hotel guests, and the hotel restaurant has been set up in the galleries. The cloister leads to the former chapter house with a Manueline stellar vault. The **Biblioteca Pública** (public library) is in another part of the building; about 2,000 incunabula and manuscripts are kept there.

Paço dos Duques de Cadaval

There used to be direct access from the north front of the convent church to the Paço dos Duques de Cadaval. Joao I gave this palace to the de Melos, ancestors of the Cadavals, at the end of the 14th century. Because of its pentagonal north tower – originally built as part of the medieval town fortifications – it is also called the »Palácio das Cinco Quinas« (palace of the five corners).

Paço dos Condes de Basto

The Paço dos Condes de Basto is just a few hundred yards to the right beyond the Paço dos Duques de Cadaval. Part of the Romanesque or rather Visigothic town walls were integrated into this Gothic Manueline palace of the count of Basto, which was intermittently the residence of various kings.

University

On the other side of the street is the extensive university complex. The Jesuit college first built in 1551 in the style of the Italian Renaissance was raised to the status of a university in 1558 but closed in 1759 after the Jesuit order was dissolved in Portugal. After Évora acquired another university in 1979, auditoriums were reinstated around the cloister. It is well worth having a look inside: many of the rooms are embellished **with azulejos and marble decorations**.

The university church (Nossa Senhora da Conceiçao) was consecrated in 1574. The interior of the aisle-less church is also lavishly decorated with marble and talha.

✶ Largo das Portas de Moura

The Largo das Portas de Moura is an unusual square, its quaint character stemming above all from the **Renaissance fountain** in its centre. A globe rests over the basin with marble borders as the symbol of the dawning of a new age.

The south side of the square is bordered by the Casa Cordovil, a dainty palace in the Moorish-Manueline style of the 16th century. The loggia and the four graceful pillars catch the eye.

Igreja da Graça

The Igreja da Graça, west of the Largo das Portas de Moura, was founded by Joao I in the 16th century. Its façade is reminiscent of those of the Italian Renaissance. The interior is extremely plain and likewise designed in the Renaissance style.

Igreja de São Francisco

It is only a few steps to the Igreja de São Francisco. The former convent church dating from the second half of the 15th century was built in the Manueline style.

The Casa dos Ossos was added to the right transept of the church in the 17th century. Parts of human skeletons and bones, carefully piled up on top of each other, form the walls of the Casa dos Ossos. One skeleton is hung on the bone wall and the inscription above the entrance of the bone chapel says: »Our bones that lie within are waiting for yours« (entrance next to the church; open: daily 9am–1pm and 2.30pm–5.30pm, Sun from 10am).

★
◄ Casa dos Ossos

The Jardim Público stretches south of the Franciscan church. Shady paths and pretty herbaceous borders make it an inviting place to linger. The Galeria das Damas within the park grounds is a relic of the 15th/16th-century palace of Manuel I. The building, decorated with jagged Moorish arches, today serves as exhibition hall. The palace was once the setting for a glamorous court life and it was also here that **Manuel I received Vasco da Gama.**

Jardim Público

South of the centre – outside the city wall – stands the Ermida de São Brás. The fortress-like sacred building was erected in 1485 to commemorate the survival of the plague. Its architecture is of historic interest in that it represents one of the few instances in Portugal in which **Islamic and Christian building styles have been combined.** Six conical pinnacles rise above the two lateral sides of the late Gothic place of worship with a clear Moorish influence; the flat roof is surrounded by battlements. The interior is unusually plain.

Ermida de São Brás

Other sights are also worth taking a look at for those staying in Évora for a longer time. The Termas Romanas have been excavated in the town hall; they can be seen on the ground floor. The former convent of Santa Clara, west of the Praça do Giraldo, was founded in 1452 and substantially altered in the 16th century; the church with its elegant belfry is worth seeing. Further north, the church and cloister of the Convento do Calvário is open to the public. Not far from the Calvário monastery to the north-east the remains of an aqueduct can be seen. It was probably built in the 16th century to replace a water pipe from Roman times.

Other sights

Around Évora

The area surrounding Évora is full of evidence of megalithic culture. The stone ring of Almendres (Cromeleque dos Almendres) is particularly impressive. It can be reached from Évora via the N 114; near São Matias about 8km/5mi west of Évora there is a turning in the direction of Guadalupe; signposts point the rest of the way. The Cromeleque dos Almendres consists of 92 standing stones that form an ellipse 60m/66yd in length and 30m/33yd wide. The stone blocks are roughly worked and decorated with symbolic signs. The grounds, which were presumably used for ritualistic purposes, date from between 4000 and 2800 BC.

★
Cromeleque dos Almendres

The ritual stone circle of Almendres is the most significant testament to megalithic culture in Portugal. It consists of a total of 92 menhirs.

Anta do Zambujeiro

A few miles south of the Cromeleque dos Almendres, near the town of Valverde, stands the Anta do Zambujeiro, a 6m/20ft-high megalithic tomb. The dolmen has been covered with earth for a long time. The burial objects found in these tombs are now on display in the Museu de Évora.

Convento de São Bento de Castris

The Convento de Sao Bento de Castris is situated 4km/2.5mi north-west of Évora on the road to Arraiolos (N 114-4), at the base of the hill with the same name. The monastery was founded in 1274, and the church dates back to the 14th/15th century. The interior is clad with 18th-century azulejos. The cloister, from the 16th-century, is also lovely.

★ **Évoramonte**

Évoramonte, about 35km/22mi north-east of Évora, is worth a visit. Prominently situated above the newer town on a hill, the old town centre, with its winding alleys and little white houses, is still surrounded by walls. On its highest peak stands a castle that was built in the 14th century on the remains of a Moorish fortress. It was rebuilt after an earthquake in 1531, and today the restored fort building has been painted yellow and is open to the public. A memorial plaque on the wall of a simple house (after passing the fortification walls on the left side of the main road) commemorates the treaty of Évoramonte, which was signed here on May 26 1834. It ended the so-called Miguelite Wars of the 19th century.

★
Monsaraz

Monsaraz, situated 50km/31mi east of Évora, is definitely worth seeing. The sleepy little village near the Spanish border still appears quite medieval. Its fortified walls date from the 16th century. Strolling through Monsaraz, visitors will be drawn to the Gothic parish church, the 17th-century pelourinho, the Gothic former palace of justice and above all the castle, erected during the reign of King Dinis in the 14th century.

Cromeleque do Xerez

A few miles along the narrow road leading south from Monsaraz to Mouraoafter stands the Cromeleque do Xerez. The impressive collection of menhirs here is, however, not quite as spectacular as the stone circle at Almendres.

Mourão

A little further east on the N 256 lies the town of Mourão, which is also guarded by a medieval castle. The cylindrical chimneys with a hemispherical cover are characteristic of this border town.

Portel

The small country town of Portel lies about 40km/24mi south-east of Évora. Its 13th-century Bragança castle was largely rebuilt at the behest of Manuel I; there is a charming view from here. Inside the little chapel of Santo António are beautiful polychrome azulejos.

Viana do Alentejo

From Portel a road runs west past the Alvito reservoir to Viana Do Alentejo 30km/18.8mi away. The town includes a 15th-century castle and a 16th-century parish church with a pretty Manueline doorway.

Alvito

In Alvito, 10km/6mi south of Viana de Alentejo, stands a 15th-century fortified castle – once the seat of the Marquêses de Alvito and today a pousada (Where to stay ► Alentejo) – and a church with 17th-century beautiful azulejo decoration, one of the few churches in Portugal exibiting Moorish influence.

From Alvito, a narrow road leads north-east to the town of **Água de Peixes**, where the Cadavals, who owned a magnificent city palace in Évora, erected a country residence in the Moorish-Spanish style (16th century).

! **Baedeker** TIP

Nossa Senhora d'Aires

The pilgrimage church Nossa Senhora is located slightly north-east of Viana Do Alentejo in the middle of the countryside. A pilgrimage to the portrait of the Virgin Mary in the church takes places every year in September. Among other things there are quite a few photographs to be seen in the church with which the Senhora is thanked for her help in emergencies.

Alcáçovas

It is worth making the short side trip to Alcáçovas, located 18km/11mi north-west of Viana do Alentejo at the base of the Serra de Sao Joao. The palace of the Counts of Alcáçovas dates from the 15th century and the parish church from the 16th century.

Other sights in the surrounding area

North of Évora lies ► Arraiolos, noted for its pretty townscape and the rugs that are manufactured there; 25km/15.6mi west of this is Montemor-o-Novo (► Arraiolos) and the Grutas de Escoural. ► Estremoz, located approx. 45km/28mi east of Évora, is beautiful, and in Redondo (► Estremoz) there is a castle to see.

★ Faro

L 34

Historical province: Algarve	**Altitude:** sea level
District: Faro	**Population:** 52,000

The Algarve's international airport is located near Faro. Most holidaymakers will arrive and leave from here, but spend their holiday elsewhere in the Algarve; they will only make a trip into town should the need arise. Faro, then, is not a real tourist attraction, but it has a very pretty centre and is a small shopping paradise.

The city lies north of an extended lagoon system – the coastline here being characterized by several offshore islands and sandbanks. The airport is located almost 10km/6.3mi west of the centre, with year-round daily charter and scheduled flights from different countries in Europe landing here and bringing holidaymakers to southern Portugal. Faro is the capital of the historical province of the Algarve and at the same time capital of the district and the county of Faro, making the town the administrative and economic centre of the ► Algarve. It is a port, some industry is based here, and there has been a university in Faro for some years now.

★ Pleasant Algarve town

Portuguese everyday life essentially runs its course in Faro. It is prepared for tourism, but the town is not dominated by the holiday industry, unlike so many other places in the Algarve. Faro does not seem particularly attractive at first glance. On the town's outskirts there are extensive and somewhat dismal commercial districts and, closer to the centre, some high rises. In contrast however, the city centre is really inviting. Most houses date from the 18th and 19th centuries. A major part of the centre has been designed around Rua S. António as a pedestrian and shopping zone. Numerous street cafés and restaurants provide light relief from the hustle and bustle. Every-

*Arco da Vila – one of the city gates of the historic →
centre of Faro. Storks nest here in Spring.*

where, visitors come across smaller or larger squares with pretty trees or parks. The **historical town centre** in particular is full of atmosphere, located around the old cathedral somewhat apart from the pedestrian zones – and surrounded by a city wall.

What to See in Faro

Praça de Dom Francisco Gomes The central Praça de Dom Francisco Gomes at the harbour is a good starting point for a tour of Faro. An obelisk erected in 1910 commemorates the diplomat Ferreira d'Almeida, who was born in Faro in 1847, founded a naval college, and played a substantial role in promoting the fishing industry during his time in office as minister of maritime affairs.

Jardim Manuel Bivar The Jardim Manuel Bivar to the south of the square is a lot quieter. With its attractive flower beds, tall palms and jacaranda trees, the

 VISITING FARO

INFORMATION
Rua da Misericórdia 8–12
8000-269 Faro
Tel. 289 803 604
www.turismodoalgarve.pt

PARKING
There is free parking on the large Largo de São Francisco in the south of the town near the Centro Histórico.

SHOPPING
There are a lot of small shops around Rua de Santo António in the pedestrian precinct. In the Forum Algarve – with its award-winning architecture – located on the outskirts of town on the road to the airport, everything is found under one roof; and the shops are open well into the evening.

EXCURSIONS
Riosul
Rua Infante D. Henrique, 63
800-363 Faro
Tel. 289 899 180
Fax 289 899 189

www.riosul-tours.com
Excursions on the Guadiana and in the east of the Algarve.

Ilha Deserta
Located on the dock of the Ilha Deserta
Tel. 917 811 856
www.ilha-deserta.com
Boat trips to the Ilha Deserta and into Ria Formosa.

WHERE TO EAT
► **Moderate**
① *A Taska*
Rua do Alportel 38
Tel. 289 824 739
Good selection of fish dishes. The speciality is »xarém«, a maize paste, prepared for instance with zebra mussels.

② *Club Naval*
Doca de Faro
Tel. 289 823 869
Restaurant on the yacht harbour with a marvellous view of the lagoon. A lot

garden is a favourite spot mostly for the elder citizens of Faro who sit here and watch the world go by. On the east side of the park stands the Igreja da Misericórdia, a 14th-century church that was restored after the earthquake in 1755.

At the southern end of the park is the **Arco da Vila**, built by the Italian architect Francisco Xavier Fabris, with a bell tower and a statue of Faro's patron saint, St Thomas Aquinus. The gateway provides access to the very attractive historical centre of Faro, which is in part still surrounded by a 13th-century city wall.

★
Centro Histórico

The historical centre's main sight is the cathedral. Part of its history is visible from the outside: large parts of the originally Gothic church were destroyed in the earthquake of 1755 and rebuilt later. Only the tower and a window on the south side remain of the original building. The cathedral displays elements of the Gothic, Renaissance and Baroque styles. The church's interior is notable for its almost hall-like, airy character. Laid out as a nave and two aisles, the three parts

Sé

of fish and a large selection of seafood.

③ *Tasca Rasca*
Rua do Forno 21
Tel. 289 825.996
Large menu and a selection of unusual specialities.

► **Inexpensive**
④ *Marisqueira da Baixa*
Rua Conselheiro Bivar
Very popular with the Portuguese; plenty of fish and seafood.

⑤ *Dois Irmãos*
Largo Terreiro do Bispo 20
Tel. 289 823 337
Faro's oldest restaurant – in existence since 1925. Large rooms; also seating in an interior courtyard. Tasty, typically Portuguese dishes.

WHERE TO STAY
► **Mid-range**
① *Hotel Eva*
Avenida da República 1

Tel. 289 001 000, Fax 289 001 002
eva@tdhotels.pt
Reliable, modern hotel in central location directly on the yacht harbour. It doesn't look especially inviting from the outside, but its 140 rooms are conveniently and pleasantly furnished. There is also a pool with sun loungers on the roof.

► **Budget**
② *Residencial Algarve*
Rua Infante D. Henrique 52
Tel. 289 895 700, Fax 289 895 703
www.residencialalgarve.com
Recommendable, relatively new guesthouse in a quiet street in the centre – the rooms are small, simple and well-kept.

③ *Pensão Madalena*
Rua Conselheiro Bivar 109
Tel. 289 805 806, Fax 289 805 807
Informal, friendly and typically Portuguese guesthouse with simple rooms of various sizes and styles of furnishing.

of the building are separated almost imperceptibly by three delicate columns. The choir is vaulted with a coffered barrel ceiling. António Pereira, the bishop of the Algarve from 1704 to 1715, had his final resting-place set up in the Capela de Santo Lenho to the right of the chancel. A climb up the church steeple is rewarded with an unusual view of the lagoon.

Faro *Plan*

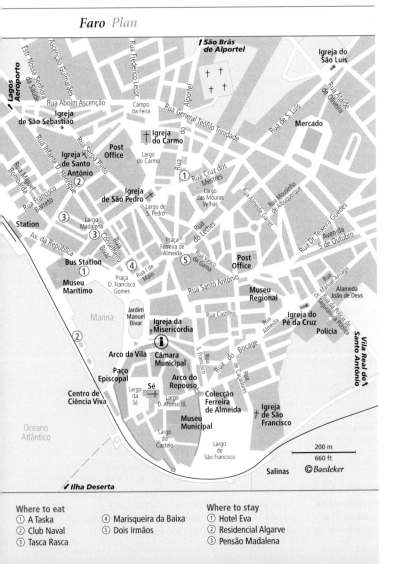

Where to eat
① A Taska
② Club Naval
③ Tasca Rasca
④ Marisqueira da Baixa
⑤ Dois Irmãos

Where to stay
① Hotel Eva
② Residencial Algarve
③ Pensão Madalena

In the square in front of the cathedral (Largo da Sé) stand the town hall and the bishop's palace (Paço Episcopal). The long west wing was added to the original building in the late 18th century.

Largo da Sé

A few hundred yards south of the cathedral, on the Praça Afonso III, stands the Museu Municipal. It exhibits finds from Roman times, including a beautiful Oceanus mosaic from the second/third century. The museum is housed in the former convent of the Poor Clares of Nossa Senhora da Assunçao, founded in 1518, and has a beautiful two-storied cloister.

Museu Municipal

> **! *Baedeker* TIP**
>
> **Café with tradition**
> The Cafe Aliança on the corner of Praça D. Francisco Gomes/Rua Santo António, which opened in 1908, is one of the oldest cafés in Portugal. Many illustrious guests have sat here, among them Simone de Beauvoir, Fernando Pessoa and Almada Negreiros. The interesting old black and white photographs show views of an Algarve that no longer exists.

The Arco Do Repouso provides access to the broad Largo de São Francisco with the church of the same name (**Igreja de São Francisco**). The 17th-century sacred building is part of a former Franciscan monastery.

The Museu Regional do Algarve, a few hundred yards north of the Franciscan church, affords an interesting insight into former way of life of the inhabitants of the villages of the Algarve. The exhibits include some impressive old townscapes (open: Mon–Fri 9am–12.30pm and 2pm–5.30pm).

Museu Regional do Algarve ☉

The harbour commander's office in the north of the harbour houses a maritime museum. The exhibits provide a brief overview of seafaring and fishing in the Algarve (open: Mon–Fri 2.30pm–4.30pm).

Museo Marítimo ☉

To the north-east of the museum is the Igreja de São Pedro, a 16th-century building located on the square of the same name.

Igreja de São Pedro

To the north it extends into the wide Largo do Carmo, which is dominated by the Igreja do Carmo, a twin towered baroque church. The sacristy provides access to a cemetery and the Capela dos Ossos which was consecrated in 1816. Its vaulted ceiling and walls are composed of pieces of human skeletons (open: Mon–Fri 10am–1pm and 3pm–5pm, Sat 10am–1pm).

Igreja do Carmo, Capela dos Ossos ☉

Around Faro

Beyond the airport north-west of the town, the Praia de Faro, a sandy beach several miles long, stretches out on an offshore island. A small road bridge crosses over to the island. It is the only beach around Faro which is directly accessible (without ferry).

Praia de Faro

Estói

Estói, a typical town of the Algarve hinterland, lies 12km/7.5mi north of Faro. It owes its fame to the Palácio de Estói. The late 18th-century palace is not open to the public; it has been closed for years for reconstruction works, and a pousada is supposedly being established within it. The palace garden also seems a little neglected at the moment. If the gate to the park is open, there is a good opportunity to take a short stroll. The gardens, which were laid out in the 18th and 19th centuries, are on several levels and decorated with azulejos and busts. A tiled perron leads down to the lower part of the garden with a grotto, which is completely covered with mosaics from the nearby Milreu.

Milreu

On the western edge of Estói, on the road leading to Santa Bárbara de Nexe, is the ruin site of Milreu(open: Tue–Sun 9.30am–12.30 and 2pm–6pm, in winter until 5pm). In Roman times Milreu was a summer residence for well-to-do families from Faro, then known as Ossonoba (Milreu is also sometimes called by this name). Archaeological excavations have been undertaken here since 1877. The remains of a villa with thermal baths and a water shrine have been exposed, along with beautiful mosaics which probably date from the first century AD. The walls of an early Christian basilica are relatively well preserved.

In the garden of the Palácio de Estói: steps decorated with azulejos

Fátima

Historical province: Ribatejo
District: Santarém

Altitude: 800m/2,625ft
Population: 8,000

Hundreds of thousands of believers from Portugal and abroad make an annual pilgrimage to the world-famous town of Fátima to ask forgiveness for their sins or to be healed.

Fátima should not be missing on any organized pleasure trip or bus tour of central Portugal. The main pilgrimages – on 13 May and 13 October – are accompanied by great light processions on the nights of the 12th and 13th of the month respectively.

The three shepherd children **Lúcia de Jesús dos Santos** and **Francisco and Jacinta Marto**, who are now saints, are said to have seen the »Virgem do Rosário« (Virgin of the Rosary) on 13 May 1917 and then on the 13th of each month until October of the same year near the then insignificant village of Fátima. At first the Church was doubtful with regard to these visions. Over 70,000 people nevertheless made a pilgrimage to the site of the last appearance in Fátima on 13 October 1917. They allegedly not only witnessed the appearance of the Virgin but also an amazing natural spectacle: during pouring rain the sun suddenly began to revolve on its axis and throw out multicoloured rays of light. In addition, a number of miraculous cures are said to have taken place in the days that followed. The Church's authorities investigated the incidents for several years before finally officially recognizing the Fátima cult of the Madonna in 1930.

Miracle of Fátima

Of the three revelations that the Virgin made to them on 13 July 1917 – according to the children who were seven, nine and ten years old at the time – two have been public knowledge for a long time. The first prophesy states that God chose Lúcia as a mediator and that the two other children would soon die – and Jacinta and Francisco did indeed die in the Spanish influenza epidemic in 1919 and 1920 respectively. The second prophesy announced the impending end of the First World War, but also foretold a dreadful war to come if the world did not cease offending God. The third prophesy was confided in writing to the Vatican in 1942 by Lúcia, who had entered a convent in 1928, asking that it should not be made public before 1960. Pope John Paul II eventually revealed the third revelation of the Mother of God in the year 2000, which includes mention of the assassination attempt on him in 1981, according to the interpretation of the Vatican.

◄ The three revelations

Lúcia died in Coimbra on 13 February 2005 and was moved to Fátima a year after her death to find her final resting place next to Jacinta and Francisco.

▶ VISITING FÁTIMA

INFORMATION

Avenida D. José Alves Correia da Silva
2495-402 Fátima
Tel. 249 531 139
www.rt-leiriafatima

WHERE TO EAT

▶ Moderate
Tia Alice
Rua do Adro
Tel. 249 531 737
Very popular restaurant, offering well
prepared home cooking.

WHERE TO STAY

▶ Mid-range
Pousada Conde de Ourém
2490-481 Ourém
Tel. 249 540 920
Fax 249 542 955

Located in the medieval city centre of
Ourém near Fátima. The location of
Ourém is advantageous, and accord-
ingly the hotel makes a good starting
point for visits to the monastery of
Tomar and Batalha.

▶ Budget/Mid-range
Hotel São José
Av. D. José Correia da Silva
2495-402 Fátima
Tel. 249 530 120
Fax 249 530 129
hotel.s.jose@clix.pt
The Hotel São José lies only 100m/
109yd from the pilgrimage church.
The 65 rooms are decently furnished.
A restaurant is also part of the hotel.
Make reservations well in advance
during the main pilgrimages.

What to See in Fátima

A miniature train runs through Fátima; it provides information on the place of pilgrimage in five languages.

Miniature train

At 150,000 sq m (37 acres), the assembly area of Fátima is absolutely gigantic. Many believers move across it on their knees. It is domi- nated by the neo-Baroque basilica with its 65m/215ft-high central tower, whose construction began on 13 May 1928. Inside the basilica are the tombs of Francisco and Jacinta Marto and their cousin Lúcia dos Santos. Porticoes on both sides connect the basilica with the ex- tensive cloister and hospital buildings. The site of the Virgin Mary's alleged appearance to the children in the branches of an oak in 1917 is marked by the Capela das Aparições (Chapel of the Apparitions) in front of the cathedral. A chapel was first built here as early as 1918, but it was later destroyed by a bomb attack.

Assembly area

A museum was opened in 1984 west of the assembly area. Fátima's miraculous events are retold in 29 scenes with wax figures.

Museu de Cera

← *Tens of thousands come to Fátima to the main pilgrimages which take place on 13 May and 13 October every year.*

Museu de
Arte Sacra e
Etnologia

Leaving the assembly area to the east, there is the Museum of Sacred Art and Ethnology after a short distance. It tells the story of the Redemption in pictures, crucifixes, cribs and other exhibits. The ethnological department focuses on those cultures that have influenced the gospels.

Around Fátima

★
Ourém

About 10km/6mi north-east of Fátima, on a hill over the basin, is the little medieval walled town of Ourém with narrow alleys and picturesque twists and turns. Above the town towers the castle, bearing the same name, of the margraves of Ourém (15th century). In the crypt of the originally Gothic collegiate church, which was reconstructed in the 18th century, is the magnificent tomb of Dom Afonso de Ourém, a descendent of Joao I, who rebuilt and enlarged the originally Moorish castle and added a palace.

The town also has a beautiful Gothic fountain as well as a pillory, both from the 15th century. The pousada offers attractive overnight accommodation.

Surrounding area ►Alcobaça, ►Batalha, ►Leiria, ►Tomar

Figueira da Foz

E 16

Historical province: Beira Litoral
District: Coimbra

Altitude: sea level
Population: 40,000

Figueira da Foz means »fig tree on the estuary«. As charming as the name may sound, the Figueira da Foz is actually a small seaside town consisting of high rises – and one of the most important ports for cod fishing in Portugal.

Municipal
swimming resort

With its broad 3km/2mi beach of fine sand, Figueira da Foz is also one of the most popular swimming resorts on the western coast of Portugal. The range of sports and recreational pursuits on offer is correspondingly large, and includes a yacht harbour and a casino. Near the harbour is the old town centre, whose houses often still date from the 19th century, while the coastal road is lined predominantly with rows of high rises.

What to See in Figueira da Foz

Forte Santa
Catarina

The fortress of Santa Catarina was built on the outermost part of the estuary in the 17th century. It has a functioning lighthouse and a small 17th century chapel.

The city museum (Museu Municipal do Dr. Santos Rocha) is housed in a building surrounded by a park. It displays prehistoric finds as well as Roman exhibits, decorative art, pottery, furniture, sacred art and overseas folk art.

Museu Municipal do Dr. Santos Rocha

The Santo António monastery is a few hundred yards east of the museum. The Franciscan monastery was founded in 1527 and considerably altered in the 18th century. Quite a few depictions of the life of St Anthony decorate the walls on the inside.

Convento de Santo António

Around Figueira da Foz

North-west of Figueira da Foz, the Portuguese mainland ends abruptly at the Atlantic Ocean at Cabo Mondego. The drive there

Cabo Mondego

▶ VISITING FIGUEIRA DA FOZ

INFORMATION
Avenida 25 de Abril
3081-501 Figueira da Foz
Tel. 233 407 200
www.figueiraturismo.com

WHERE TO EAT
▶ Moderate
① *Forte de Santa Catarina*
Rua Bernardo Lopes 85-87
Tel. 233 426 930
Good, simple restaurant in the centre of town. Grilled dishes and a large selection of fish.

▶ Inexpensive/Moderate
② *Caçarola Dois*
Rua Bernardo Lopes 85-87
Tel. 233 426 930
Pleasant, simple restaurant in the town centre. The fish dishes are especially recommended.

③ *Teimoso*
Avenida Dom João II
(district of Buarcos)
Tel. 233 402 720
Popular with the locals. Good food at average prices.

④ *Plataforma*
Praia de Buarcos (district of Buarcos)
Tel. 233 413 500
View of the ocean, good fish dishes.

WHERE TO STAY
▶ Budget
① *Hotel Costa de Prata*
Largo Coronel Galhardo 1
3080-150 Figueira da Foz
Tel. 233 426 620; fax 233 426 610
www.costadeprata.com
Relatively plain hotel in a superb location: almost all rooms offer a beautiful view of the sea.

② *Hotel Wellington*
Rua Dr. Calado 23/27
3080-153 Figueira da Foz
Tel. 233 426 767; fax 233 427 593
Recommended small hotel in the centre of town.

③ *Pensão Aviz*
Rua Dr. Lopes Guimarães 16
3080 Figueira da Foz
Tel. 233 422 635; fax 233 420 909
A friendly guesthouse set up in a beautiful old town house.

Figueira da Foz Plan

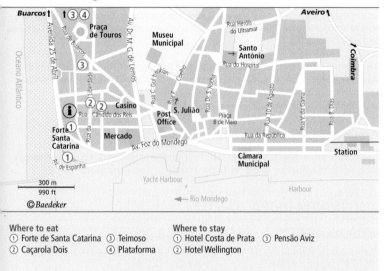

Where to eat
① Forte de Santa Catarina   ③ Teimoso
② Caçarola Dois   ④ Plataforma

Where to stay
① Hotel Costa de Prata   ③ Pensão Aviz
② Hotel Wellington

passes through Buarcos, once a fishing village, which has in the meantime merged completely with Figueira da Foz.

Serra da Boa Viagem   Walks in the Serra da Boa Viagem, a park-like wooded region rising up to 258m/846ft which extends to the north of Figueira da Foz, are very rewarding.

✶ Guarda

P 13

Historical province: Beira Alta	**Altitude:** 1,057m/3,468ft
District: Guarda	**Population:** 20,000

Guarda lies on a plateau in the north-east of the Serra da Estrela and was once an important stronghold of the Beira Alta province. Portugal's highest town has a very pleasant, healthy climate and is visited as a climatic health resort.

»Cold, ugly, rich and strong«   Guarda is supposed to be »Fria, feia, farta e forte«: cold, ugly, rich and strong. At least according to an old Portuguese proverb. »Cold« – especially in winter; »rich« – Guarda is located in a fertile region; and Guarda's fortress once held »strong« against the hostile Spaniards. The residents of Guarda did not want their town to be known as »ugly« however and thus did not hesitate to change the proverb

▶ VISITING GUARDA

INFORMATION
Praça do Município
6300-854 Guarda
Tel. 271 205 530
www.rt-serradaestrela.pt

WHERE TO EAT
▶ **Inexpensive/Moderate**
① *Belo Horizonte*
Rua de São Vicente
Tel. 271 211 454
Game dishes are included on the menu here; the wild boar (javali) is especially good. Your meal is accompanied by a beautiful view.

WHERE TO STAY
▶ **Budget/Mid-range**
① *Hotel Turismo da Guarda*
Praça do Município
Tel. 271 223 366
Fax 271 223 399
www.hturismoguarda.com
Elegantly furnished mid-range hotel in an impressive old building.

---

into »fria, farta, forte, formosa e fiel« – since then, the town has been »cold, fertile, strong, beautiful and faithful«!

The strategically important site of today's town was strongly fortified **History** as early as Roman times. In 80 BC its citizens sided with Quintus Sertorius in an attempt to break away from Rome and afterwards withstood sieges by Roman troops for many years. After the Moors destroyed the town, its inhabitants fled and the buildings fell into dereliction. It was not until the 12th and 13th centuries that Guarda was rebuilt by the kings Sancho I and Dinis I and fortified against impending attacks from the Arabs and Castilians. Today Guarda is the district's capital and the see of a bishop.

The many granite houses lend Guarda a rather sombre appearance; **»Granite town«** but a closer look reveals beautifully decorated old burgher houses in the cathedral square and Rua de Dom Luis I. The castle keep, three town gates and parts of the town walls remain of the 12th and 13th century fortifications – so there is still something to see of the »strength« of the town.

What to See in Guarda

The cathedral, a granite building designed in 1390 in the Gothic style ★ and completed in the 16th century, gives an almost fortified impres- **Catedral** sion with its closed battlements. The doorway on the northern aisle of the transept is still Gothic. The Manueline additions, notably on the western façade, were built in the style of the Abbey of ▶Batalha by Boytaca, the master builder of Manuel I.

The interior of the cathedral is harmoniously proportioned.

The magnificent **interior**, with a nave and two aisles, achieves its effect through its harmonious proportions as well as the simplicity of the design.

The stone retable from 1550 is the work of João de Rouão (Jean de Rouen); the gilding was added in the 18th century. The more than 100 figures on the retable depict scenes from the life of Christ. A climb up to the roof terrace of the cathedral, spanned by flying buttresses, is also very rewarding. It offers a magnificent view of the roof, whose construction principle is easily recognized; there is also a good view across the roofs of the town up to Serra da Estrela.

In front of the northern cathedral façade is the Praça de Luís de Camoes, also called Praça da Sé, with a modern monument to King Sancho I. The town owes its economic and cultural advancement of the Middle Ages to him.

The former bishop's palace from the 15th/16th centuries is now home to the municipal museum, the **Museu da Guarda**, among other things. An interesting collection of archaeological finds, graphical documents, paintings and sculptures are on display.

The 17th-century **Igreja da Misericòrdia** with a splendid Renaissance tomb and a Baroque altar is also worth a visit.

Ermida de Nossa Senhora da Póvoa de Mileu
About 1km/0.6mi outside of the town centre stands the Romanesque Ermida de Nossa Senhora da Póvoa de Mileu. It was allegedly founded by the spouse of Afonso Henriques in the year 1150. The beautiful capitals particularly stand out from the otherwise fairly simple interior.

Around Guarda

Both ► **Serra da Estrela** south-west of Guarda and the little town of ► **Belmonte** south of Guarda are rewarding destinations.

About 30km/18.8mi north of Guarda at an elevation of 880m/2,886ft is the town **Trancoso**. The circular wall, which was extended several times up until the 16th century, bears witness to Trancoso's former significance as a fortified town. In 1282, King Dinis I married Isabel, the eventual Rainha Santa Isabel (► Coimbra, ► Estremoz) in Trancoso Castle, of which only ruins remain.

In very rugged countryside some 45km/28mi north-east of Guarda lies the town of Almeida.It is surrounded by some well preserved Vauban style fortified buildings,erected according to a floor plan of a twelve-point star. Almeida remained impregnable until the 19th century, when the French succeeded in entering it in 1810.

✶ **Almeida**

Guarda Plan

© Baedeker

Porta d' el-Rei · M. Bombarda · São Vicente
Porta da Erva
Praça Luís de Camões
Catedral · Torre dos Ferreiros
Torre de Menagem
Rua Vasco da Gama · Misericórdia
Museu da Guarda
Largo General Humberto Delgado
Coimbra, Lisboa ↙

Where to eat
① Belo Horizonte

Where to stay
① Hotel Turismo da Guarda

Another excursion takes visitors from Guarda north-east to **Pinhel** and further on to Freixo de Espada à Cinta. Pinhel is a small town surrounded by defensive walls with six towers. Inside the decayed castle, built by King Dinis I, stands the 14th-century church of Santa Maria do Castelo. In the interior, a fourteen-part picture cycle with depictions of the life of Mary (17th century) is of note.

Excursion to the north-east

17km/10.6mi north-east of Pinhel to the right of the road stands the small, fortified town of **Castelo Rodrigo**, which was important in the Middle Ages. Remains of the 15th-century castle complex, including fortified tower, the palace and a cistern, have been preserved. The view from the castle is beautiful.

The larger **Figueira de Castelo Rodrigo**, situated 3km/2mi to the north on a plateau, is covered by fruit cultivations. To some degree, the small town has been able to maintain its medieval townscape. There are several gilded and carved altars inside the 18th-century Baroque church.

Some 20km/12.5mi north of Figueira de Castelo Rodrigo, the N 221 crosses the Douro, following the course of the river for a while – that here forms the border to Spain – and after another 25km/15.6mi reaches **Freixo de Espada á Cinta**. This is the birthplace of the seafarer Jorge Álvares and the poet Guerra Junqueiro (1850–1923), to whom a small museum in town has been dedicated.

✶ ✶ Guimarães

J 8

Historical province: Minho
District: Braga

Altitude: 200m/656ft
Population: 55,000

Because of its well preserved historic centre and a wealth of historical buildings and important art treasures, the northern Portuguese Guimarães – the »cradle of the nation« – was declared a World Cultural Heritage Site by UNESCO in 2001.

Guimarães owes its nickname »berço da nação« (cradle of the nation) to the fact that it was the first capital of the newly established kingdom of Portugal and also the birthplace of the first king, Afonso Henriques. Another famous son of the town is the celebrated poet and playwright Gil Vicente. Guimarães, with its many parks, has a very friendly atmosphere. The focal point of urban life is the Largo do Toural, surrounded around by business and residential buildings and banks, which is also the exit point of the main shopping street in the town, Rua de S. António. Tourists, however, tend to be drawn more to the picturesque historic centre with its stately granite houses, many of which have wrought iron balconies and rich floral decoration. The most beautiful houses can be found around the Largo da Oliveira as well as in Rua de Santa Maria and to the west of it.

Guimarães Plan

200 m
660 ft
©Baedeker

Capela de São Miguel do Castelo
Paço Ducal
Convento do Carmo
Praça de Mumadona
Amarante
Rua Francisco Agra
Rua Serpa Pinto
Av. E. D. Pacheco
Rua Dr. A. Pimenta
Rua Gil Vicente
Post Office
Town Hall
Rua de Santa Maria
Av. Dr. Sampaio
Museu de Martins Sarmento
Rua de S. António
Paço do Conselho
Praça de São Tiago
Largo da Oliveira
Nossa Senhora da Oliveira
J. Sampaio
Museu de Alberto Sampaio
R. Dr.
Rua da Rainha
Largo do Toural
Largo da República do Brasil
R. D. João
Rua de Camões
Alameda São Damaso
Santos Passos
Braga
Porto
São Francisco
Porto

Where to eat
① Solar do Arco
② Cozinha Regional
③ Recantos

Where to stay
① Hotel de Guimarães
② Hotel Residencial do Toural
③ Hotel Residencial Fundador

What to See in Guimarães

The sombre, mighty 10th-century **fort**, crowned by high, slender battlements, rises above the town. It is one of the most self-contained castles in Portugal, and is very impressive thanks to its state of preservation. On 24 June 1110 this became the birthplace of the first Portuguese king, Afonso Henriques,which lends the building its character of a nationally

Portugal's first king Afonso Henriques was christened in the Capela de São Miguel do Castelo.

significant holy place. In the middle of the oval courtyard rises the massive Torre de Menagem, a keep that could also be defended as an independent fortress in the case of an emergency. The circular walls, fortified with eight towers, afford a magnificent view.

Below the castle entrance stands the small castle chapel of São Miguel do Castelo from 1105, layered with massive blocks of stone, in which Afonso Henriques was baptized. A Mass is given here annually on the king's birthday to commemorate the event.

Capela de São Miguel do Castelo

Only a few yards below the castle is the extensive Paço Ducal, also called Paço dos Duques de Bragança, the palace of the dukes of Bragança. Afonso, first Duke of Bragança, had the Gothic palace built in the French style which was fashionable in his day. The magnificent building, completed in 1442, lost its importance after the seat of the Bragança family was moved to ▶ Vila Viçosa in the early 16th century, and became dilapidated over the course of the centuries. It was extensively restored and rebuilt in 1933 under Salazar and became the official residence of the Portuguese presidents in northern Portugal. The interior rooms are open to the public. The 16th–18th century interior was decorated with Flemish tapestries and valuable porcelain (open: daily 9.30am–12.30pm and 2pm–5.30pm).

✱ Paço Ducal

★★
Largo da Oliveira

In the heart of the historic centre, the Largo da Oliveira is full of atmosphere and has been particularly successful in maintaining its medieval flair. There is a legend concerning the square and the church of the same name (»oliveira« means »olive tree«): the Visigoth Wamba, who was appointed king, refused to accept the position unless a dry olive twig stuck into the sand would sprout green shoots again. No sooner was the twig in the ground – presumably in the location of the Gothic portico – that it began to turn green. The little museum housed in the old **town hall** on the northern side of the square shows naive paintings (Museu de Arte Primitiva Moderna). The construction, with its pointed arcades, was started in the 14th century under the reign of João I, though it was fundamentally altered in the 17th century. The adjacent building houses a **pousada**. A Gothic-

▶ VISITING GUIMARÃES

INFORMATION

Alameda de São Dâmaso 86
4810-286 Guimarães
Tel. 253 412 450
www.guimaraesturismo.com

WHERE TO EAT

▶ Inexpensive/Moderate

① *Solar do Arco*
Rua de Santa Maria 50
Tel. 253 513 072
Recommended restaurant in the historic centre serving typical dishes from the Minho. Good, friendly service.

② *Cozinha Regional*
Praça de São Tiago
Tel. 253 516 669
There are several good restaurants on the Praça de São Tiago – of them, this is probably the most typical.

③ *Recantos*
Largo dos Laranjais
Tel. 253 419 020
Pretty, well-kept restaurant. There is a large selection of appetizers as well as fine fish and meat dishes.

WHERE TO STAY

▶ Budget

① *Hotel de Guimarães*
Rua Eduardo de Almeida
4801-911 Guimarães
Tel. 253 424 800, fax 253 424 899
www.hotel-guimaraes.com
Modern, large hotel with 72 rooms. Next to the pousada one of the best places to stay in town.

Baedeker recommendation

② *Hotel Residencial do Toural*
Largo do Toural (entrance: Largo A. L. de Carvalho)
4800-153 Guimarães
Tel. 253 517 184, fax 253 517 149
www.hoteltoural.com
Well-kept hotel in a beautiful old town house. Central location.

③ *Hotel Residencial Fundador*
Avenida D. Afonso Henriques
4810-431 Guimarães
Tel. 253 422 640, fax 253 422 649
Very pleasant rooms are found in this high-rise hotel with a correspondingly good view.

Manueline **pillared gallery** was erected in the centre of the square to commemorate the battle on the Rio Salado in 1340, during which the allied defence forces of Portugal and Spain were able to drive back the strong troops of the Sultan of Morocco.

As early as the 10th century there was apparently a monastery, donated by the Countess Mumadona, on the Largo da Oliveira where the collegiate church of Nossa Senhora da Oliveira now stands. The church, built by Afonso Henriques in the 12th century in thanks of the successful battle of Ouriquem, was considerably enlarged from 1387 to 1400 by Joao I to commemorate the battle of Aljubarrota. The church as it appears today is largely from the 16th century; the Manueline tower was added in 1523.

✱ **Igreja de Nossa Senhora da Oliveira**

The cloister of the collegiate church, and parts of the former monastery, house the Museu de Alberto Sampaio. The museum's contents include sculptures by Portuguese artists of the 14th–16th centuries, magnificent gold works, and a valuable collection of historical costumes – including the cloak worn by King João I over his suit of armour during the battle of Aljubarrota (open: Tue–Sun 10am–12.30pm and 2pm–6pm).

✱ **Museu de Alberto Sampaio**

🕐

The long Largo da República do Brasil stretches from the Largo da Oliveira to the twin-towered 18th-century Baroque church of Santos Passos. The façade is impressive because of its rich azulejo decoration and sculptures which show Italian influence.

Igreja dos Santos Passos

Further west stands the church of São Francisco, founded by Joao I around 1400 and remodelled in the Baroque style. The spacious interior is entirely clad with azulejos.

Igreja de São Francisco

The Museu Arqueológico Martins Sarmento, housed in a former 14th-century Dominican monastery in the west of the town centre, is well worth a visit. This archaeological museum's exhibits include finds from the prehistoric settlements of Citânia de Briteiros and Castro de Sabroso (► p.338) (open: Tue to Sat 9.30am–12.30pm and 2pm–5pm, Sun as of 10am).

Museu Arqueológico Martins Sarmento

🕐

Around Guimarães

The rocky hill known as Penha or Serra de Santa Catarina (617m/2,024ft), on which stand a pilgrimage church from 1898 and a statue of Pope Pius IX, is located about 5km/3mi south-east of Guimarães. The view from the summit extends to Serra do Marão (►Amarante) in the south-east, and, in clear weather, north to Serra do Gerês (► Peneda-Gerês National Park) and to the Atlantic Ocean in the west. A cable railway (Teleférico) starts from Largo das Hortas in the south-east of the city centre and ascends to Penha.

Penha de Santa Catarina

Caldas de Vizela The spa of Caldas de Vizela, already popular in Roman times, lies about 10km/6.3mi south of Guimarães on both sides of the Rio Vizela. The temperature of its 55 sulphurous springs range from 16°C/61°F to 65.6°C/150°F and provide relief for rheumatism and joint problems, infections of the upper respiratory tract and skin conditions. The spa gardens by the river are pretty, and at the end of August host the annual »bathing week«, becoming the setting for numerous events including folklore performances, various competitions, and clay pigeon shooting.

From Caldas de Vizela, it is worthwhile taking excursions to the 17th-century pilgrimage church of São Bento (4km/2.5mi) and to the 12th-century Romanesque church of São Miguel de Vilarinho (3km/1.9mi) with its Gothic cloister.

Santo Tirso Santo Tirso lies south-west of Guimarães in a pleasant, wooded landscape on the left bank of the Rio Ave. It is a popular starting point for trips into the beautiful surrounding countryside. The town's inhabitants make a living from the textiles industry, the manufacture of arts and crafts, and pottery. The most important building is the former monastery of São Bento. The Benedictines founded a monastery here as early as the 10th century. Today's building, with its remarkable Baroque façade, was constructed between the 14th and 18th centuries. The monastery church is richly furnished with talha and sculptural decorations; in the cloister there are elaborate figurative capitals from the 14th–17th centuries. Archaeological exhibits from early history and the Middle Ages are displayed in the small Museu do Abade Pedrosa attached to the monastery.

Caldas das Taipas The spa of Caldas das Taipasca, 7km/4.4mi north-west Guimarães, was also already known to the Romans. The warm sulphurous springs (30°C/86°F) promise relief from respiratory and digestive problems as well as rheumatism and joint trouble. The spa gardens, through which the Rio Ave flows, are charming.

★ ★
Citânia de Briteiros North of Caldas das Taipas, the prehistoric Citânia de Briteiros lies on the Monte São Romão. Discovered in 1874, this Celtiberian settlement is, along with Castro de Sabroso, the **oldest known settlement in Portugal** and the **largest of its type on the Iberian Peninsula**. It is thought that it originated around 800 BC and experienced its heyday in 4 BC; archaeological finds confirm that it was inhabited until late Roman times. Excavation of the site began in 1875 under the leadership of the archaeologist Francisco Martins Sarmento (1833–1899). The pieces of pottery, mostly painted, as well as the artfully carved stones, weapons, jewellery and tools discovered in the ruins are now on display in the Museu de Martins Sarmento in Guimarães.

Visitors should take their time to view the Citânia de Briteiros: from the entrance, climb to the two reconstructed houses and then on to the small hilltop chapel of São Romão. From up here, there is a superb overview of the archaeological site. The ancient town was enclosed by three circular walls and included about 200 one-room houses, some with a round or oval floor plan, some rectangular. The houses were built from hewn stones which were so precisely stacked one on top of the other that they formed a stable structure without the use of mortar. Even today, water pipes are clearly recognizable, as are roads and paths that were paved with stone slabs. Two of the round houses have been reconstructed, it being assumed that the round shape with a conical roof is the archetype of human architecture, although these reconstructions remain in some senses problematic. It is thought that a much larger house (diameter approx. 11m/36ft) served as an assembly point. At the lower edge of the settlement, archaeologists stumbled upon a bathing complex. An isolated building outside the circular wall (near the Guimarães–Braga road) probably served as a crematorium.

About 15km/9.4mi south-west of Citânia de Briteiros, also on a hill, lie the less well preserved remains of the prehistoric settlement of Castro de Sabroso. Sabroso, also excavated by Francisco Martins Sarmento, is smaller than Briteiros and was abandoned earlier. In the centre of the round houses there is often a block of stone; it is assumed that it once served as the base for the roof support.

Castro de Sabroso

One of the reconstructed round houses in the Citânia da Briteiros

✶ Lagos

F/G 34

Historical province: Algarve	**Altitude:** sea level
District: Faro	**Population:** 22,500

Lagos is situated midway along the Algarve cliff coast on the edge of a wide bay. To the south and west of Lagos, the coast is marked by bizarre rock formations and small sandy bays framed by towering cliffs, making it an attractive destination for tourists.

Holiday resort on the Algarve cliff coast

The outskirts of Lagos are unattractively built up with skyscrapers and large apartment blocks, but this makes the centre seem all the prettier. The town caters for tourists, yet at the same time it has managed to retain a very pleasant life of its own. At several points around the heart of the historic centre, sections of the medieval town wall are still visible. It is worth leaving the main thoroughfares for a while to take a walk through the side streets: here, Lagos is not picturesque, but simply a town where people live. A central area around the Praça Gil Eanes and the Praça da República has been made into a pedestrian zone. There are many small shops and any number of restaurants and cafés where visitors can sit outdoors. These do not cater for tourists alone; locals sit here alongside the holidaymakers, getting on with their daily lives.

The **tourist infrastructure** in and around Lagos is excellent. There are innumerable apartment blocks, hotels, and guest houses, as well as private accommodation and camp sites. There are plenty of restaurants and cafés in the town and along the nearby beaches. Northeast from Lagos the Meia Praia, a broad, flat beach, extends for several miles; to the south and west of the town are the famous cliff-framed bays.

Trade

Some of the inhabitants still make a living from trade and fishing – especially for tuna and sardines. In addition to its fishing port, Lagos has a yacht harbour. The Ribeira de Bensafrim flows into the Atlantic here; the river has been made into a canal in the area of the town, just before it reaches the sea.

History

The Romans called the town Lacóbriga; under Moorish rule it was called Zawaya. The fortifications built by the Moors were not a lasting defence against the Portuguese kings: in the mid-13th century Sancho II succeeded in conquering the town for good. In the following centuries it developed into an important port and shipyard, a development promoted not least by **Henry the Navigator**.

A native of Lagos, **Gil Eanes** set sail from the town's port to become the first to sail round the West African Cape Bojador in 1434. The voyages of discovery brought wealth and renown to Lagos; trade flourished, including the trade in people. In a building on what is

Lagos Plan

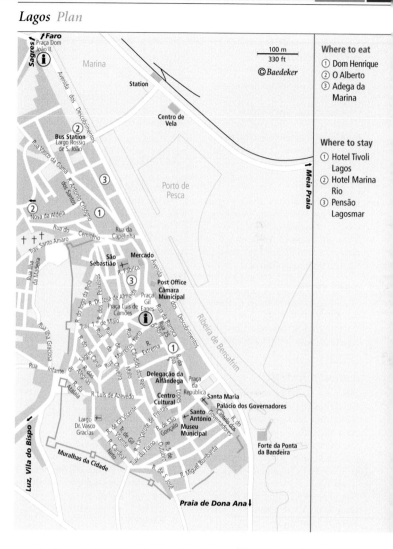

Where to eat
① Dom Henrique
② O Alberto
③ Adega da Marina

Where to stay
① Hotel Tivoli Lagos
② Hotel Marina Rio
③ Pensão Lagosmar

now the Praça da República, the first slaves from Africa were put on show in 1444, and then trading began: one horse, for instance, was worth ten slaves. In 1577 Lagos became the capital of the historical Algarve province. It kept this status until 1756 – one year after an earthquake had destroyed most of the town. Thereafter it sank into insignificance. It owes its revival to the tourism that began in the 1970s.

▶ VISITING LAGOS

INFORMATION

Turismo
Rua D. Vasco da Gama (São João)
Tel. 289 803 604
www.turismodoalgarve.pt

Municipal tourist information
Largo Marquês de Pombal
Tel. 282 764 111

PARKING

It takes some luck to find a parking spot in the Avenida dos Descobrimentos; if unsuccessful, look near the town gates west of the historical district, e.g. in front of the town gate on Rua Infante de Sagres.

BOAT TRIPS

From Lagos, boat trips go to Ponta da Piedade, and along the rocky coast to several grottoes. It is also possible to take boats out to sea to watch dolphins.

ENTERTAINMENT

There are plenty of bars and pubs in Lagos, most of them in the historical district; the bars on the marina stay open late into the night.
The Stones Bar and Bar Zawaia are both on Rua 25 de Abril; listen to jazz at Stevie Ray's (Rua Senhora da Graça 9).
The Phoenix Club on Rua de São Gonçalo/Rua 5 de Outubro is a well-known discotheque.

WHERE TO EAT

▶ **Moderate/Inexpensive**
① **Dom Henrique**
Rua 25 de Abril 75
Tel. 282 763 563
Typical Portuguese cuisine, international dishes also on the menu.

② **O Alberto**
Largo Convento Sra. da Glória
Tel. 282 769 387
In the centre, a little outside the town walls. Frequented by the Portuguese. Good wine list.

Baedeker recommendation

③ **Adega da Marina**
Avenida dos Descobrimentos 35
Tel. 282 764 284
The atmosphere is nothing special here, but the food is good and the helpings generous. Also popular with the locals.

WHERE TO STAY

▶ **Mid-range**
① **Hotel Tivoli Lagos**
Rua António Crisógono dos Santos
8600-678 Lagos
Tel. 282 790 000, fax 282 790 345
Large hillside hotel with a good view. Some smaller rooms; swimming pool and sunbathing with a view.

▶ **Mid-range/Budget**
② **Hotel Marina Rio**
Avenida dos Descobrimentos
8600-645 Lagos
Tel. 282 769 859, fax 282 769 960
Cosy little family-owned hotel, simple rooms, well looked after.

▶ **Budget**
③ **Pensão Lagosmar**
Rua Dr. Faria e Silva 13
8600-734 Lagos
Tel. 282 763 722
fax 282 767 324
Pleasant, well-kept guest house, central yet quiet location. Small, modern rooms. Beautiful roof terrace.

Evening illuminations: the historic centre of Lagos

What to See in Lagos

Praça Gil Eanes is one of the two main squares in the centre of La- **Praça Gil Eanes**
gos. In the middle of the square stands a well-known statue of King
Sebastião (»the long awaited«). In 1578, Sebastião set off from Lagos
to conquer North Africa; he never returned from this brave enter-
prise, and to this day has been regarded as missing. The disappear-
ance of the young king was a grave loss at the time since he left no
heir, and Portugal fell into Spanish hands for 60 years. The statue,
erected in 1973, is by the well-known Portuguese sculptor João Cuti-
leiro. On the east side of the square stands the town hall, built in
1798.

From the Praça Gil Eanes the small Praça Luís de Camões curves **Igreja de São**
around to reach the Igreja de São Sebastião a little further north. **Sebastião**
Steps ascend to the pretty courtyard in front of the church. Construction started in the 15th century, but considerable alterations
were undertaken at a later date. A bone house adjoins the church.

A second central square is the Praça da República at the southern **Praça da**
end of the pedestrian zone. The square opens onto the Avenida dos **República**
Descobrimentos and the port canal. Henry the Navigator is en-
throned on a stone pediment (► Famous People). The monument
was erected in 1960 to commemorate the 500th anniversary of his
death.

Igreja de Santa Maria	On the south side of the square stands the Igreja de Santa Maria, on the site of an older church dating from the 14th century. It was rebuilt after the earthquake of 1755. Henry the Navigator was buried in the earlier church in 1460; his body was later re-interred in the Capela do Fundador in ▶Batalha.
Palácio dos Governadores	Behind the church stands the former Governors' Palace, partially integrated into the old city wall. Until 1756 the Algarve provincial administration was located here.
Delegação da Alfândega	Black African slaves were put up for auction for the first time beneath the arcades of the Delegação da Alfândega (Customs House) in 1444, on the north side of the square. They were tied up under the arcades and initially put on show as a kind of curiosity. Later they were sold as labourers.
Forte da Ponta da Bandeira	The wide Avenida dos Descobrimentos (Avenue of the Discoveries), with palm trees planted along each side, was officially opened in 1961. It leads along the bank of the port canal to the Forte da Ponta da Bandeira. The fortress with four small corner towers was built in the 17th century in order to protect the harbour. The narrow drawbridge gives access to the interior, where there is an exhibition dedicated to the Age of Discovery (open: Tue–Sun 9.30am–12.30pm and 2pm–5pm).
Museu Municipal	A collection put together on decidedly original lines has been housed here since 1934. Alongside azulejos (blue-and-white tile work), coins, sacral exhibits and a number of curiosities, there is a small archaeological section (open: Tue–Sun 9.30am–12.30pm and 2pm–5pm).
✷ **Igreja de Santo António**	The baroque chapel of Santo António (entrance via the Museu Municipal) is worth a visit; it was built in 1769 on the site of an earlier church. Its interior is almost entirely clad with **talha dourada (gilded woodcarving)** (▶Arts and Culture).
Centro Cultural	A visit to the Cultural Centre is recommended for anyone interested in modern art. In addition to exhibitions of contemporary art the centre offers theatre, dance and concerts (open: daily 10am–midnight, in winter until 8pm).

Around Lagos

Meia Praia	The beaches around Lagos are spectacular, but also very full in the holiday season. North-east from Lagos the Meia Praia curves gently for several miles round the Baía de Lagos. Here there are various opportunities for watersports. Take a bus to the beach, get a boat from Lagos, or go on foot, past the Lagos railway station.

The Praia de Dona Ana, one of the most popular beaches of the Rocky Algarve

In the south of the town are two small beaches, **Praia do Camilo** and the famous Praia de Dona Ana, with little rock islands opposite. Praia de Dona Ana is said to be the most beautiful of all the bays in the vicinity, but during peak season it is very busy.

★

Praia de Dona Ana

From Praia de Dona Ana it is just 2km/1.2mi south by car or on foot to Ponta da Piedade. At times the footpath goes directly along the cliff-top. These are the loveliest **rock formations on the Algarve coast**. They can be seen on land, but the water is an even better vantage point. Boats go from Lagos to Ponta da Piedade and to several nearby grottoes. Ponta da Piedade is a superb promontory at the southern end of the Baía de Lagos, with steep cliffs going straight down into the sea. At their highest point the cliffs are 20m/66ft high. There is a profusion of rocky outcrops, single crags and tors, natural arches and gateways, and together they create a bizarre and wonderful fantasy landscape. A lighthouse guides ships passing in and out of the Lagos bay.

★ ★

◀ Ponta da Piedade

Photo p.218

The village of Odiáxere, 6km/3.6mi north of Lagos, has suffered greatly from the traffic on the busy N 125 which passes right through its centre. There is a pretty village church in Odiáxere, which was rebuilt after the earthquake of 1755. The Manueline main portal is all that survives of the pre-earthquake church.

Odiáxere

In Odiáxere a road branches off north from the N 125 to the Barragem da Bravura. It is a 10km/6.5mi drive through glorious countryside to the reservoir.

Barragem da Bravura

★ Lamego

M 10

Historical province: Beira Alta	**Altitude:** 490m/1,620ft
District: Viseu	**Population:** 12,000

Lamego is a modest little town, which has preserved a few handsome burgher houses from the 16th–18th centuries. The sparkling wine of Lamego is well known – the Caves da Raposeira 2km/1.2mi south of the town are open to visitors.

Pleasantly located amongst vineyards and fields on the slopes of Monte Penude, approx. 70km/44mi east of Porto, this small Episcopal seat has been an important trading centre for the agricultural products of the fertile surrounding region since the middle ages. In 1143 Portugal's Estates-General gathered in Lamego for the first time in order to proclaim Dom Afonso Henriques king of the new state.

What to See in Lamego

Sé In the centre of the town is the Gothic cathedral, a massive building founded in 1129 by Afonso Henriques, and much altered in the 16th and 17th centuries. The massive square tower is all that remains of the original building. The interior was refurbished in the 18th century; the ceiling frescoes from this time are particularly striking. Don't miss the Santo António chapel lined with talha dourada (gilded woodcarvings) in the Renaissance cloisters with the small rose garden.

Museu de Lamego The regional museum (Museu de Lamego) is worth a visit; it is in the former bishop's palace, dating from the 18th century, on the round Largo de Camões diagonally opposite the cathedral. Exhibits

▶ **VISITING LAMEGO**

INFORMATION
Av. Visconde Guedes Teixeira
5100-074 Lamego
Tel. 254 612 005
www.douro-turismo.pt

WHERE TO EAT
▶ **Moderate**
Parque
Santuário de Nossa Senhora dos Remédios – Sul
Tel. 254 609 140

This agreeable restaurant in the Santuário park serves traditional dishes.

WHERE TO STAY
▶ **Mid-range**
Casa de Santo António de Britiande
5100-360 Britiande
Tel. 254 699 346; fax 254 699 346
www.turihab.pt
Small, delightful rural establishment; south of Lamego (4 rooms).

include 16th-century Flemish tapestry, used from earliest times to decorate the bishop's palace, 16th–18th century Portuguese painting, 13th–17th century sculpture, and sacral art.

South of the cathedral, on the main road to Guarda, the Capela do Desterro is noteworthy. A renaissance portal affords entry to this chapel, which was built around 1640; the interior is richly adorned with 17th-century talha (woodcarving) and azulejos (blue-and-white tile work), and has a beautifully painted coffered ceiling.

Capela do Desterro

On a hill above the town stand the remains of an originally Moorish castle; only the 13th-century keep and a few remnants of the wall have survived.

Castelo

Below the castle, to the west, is the Romanesque Igreja de Almacave with beautifully moulded capitals. The interior has a 16th-century Renaissance chancel.

Igreja de Almacave

From the Largo de Camões, in the centre, it is possible to see the Santuário Nossa Senhora dos Remédios on the Monte de Santo Estêvão, on the edge of the town. Baroque steps with 14 »station« chapels on various levels lead up from the town to this pilgrimage church. It is also possible to reach the Santuário by car, following the signs to the hotel. The church, with its two-tower façade, was built in the 18th century. Every year, in early September, thousands of the faithful come here in search of solace and healing. On the terrace below the church are statues of kings and biblical figures; in the centre is an obelisk decorated with relief work. The view from up here extends well beyond Lamego to the fertile surrounding region.

**★
Santuário Nossa Senhora dos Remédios**

A painstakingly designed Baroque flight of steps leads up to the pilgrimage church of Nossa Senhora dos Remédios.

Around Lamego

The drive west along the N 222 is very rewarding. This little road twists and turns, sometimes directly above the **Douro**, and there are many wonderful views down into the ► Douro Valley. For those interested in Romanesque architecture, there are several notable churches in this area, which was

Delightful wine-growing countryside in the Douro Valley

Christianized at an early date. In the charming village of **Barrô** above the Douro Valley 16km/10mi north-west of Lamego, is a 12th-century Romanesque church.

São Martinho de Mouros

Another 5km/3mi along the N 222 lies São Martinho de Mouros. The Romanesque church on the edge of the village was originally built in the ninth century; subsequent extensions continued well into the 11th century. The rich moulding of the capitals is noteworthy here, as is a painting of St Martin attributed to Vasco Fernandes in the interior.

Resende

8km/5mi further west lies Resende. The Romanesque church of São Salvador stands above this handsome little town; from up here there is a good view into the distance. In Anreade, 2km/1.2mi west of Resende, a little road branches off and leads after 8km/5mi to the Manueline church of **Santa Maria de Cárcere**, which once belonged to a monastery founded in the 11th century.

Caldas de Aregos

On a wooded hill 5 km/3.2mi west of Anreade lies Caldas de Aregos. The 50–61°C/122–142°F sulphur springs are beneficial for ailments of the joints and respiratory system. The spa gardens are very pleasant, as is the view from the Penedo de São João cliffs above the town.

Cinfães

Cinfães, another 15km/9.6mi further west, is known for its excellent Vinho Verde. The 18th-century estate Quinta da Fervença is worth a visit. 15km/9.6mi west of Cinfães is **Tarouquela**. The well-preserved Romanesque church of Santa Maria Maior stands on a hilltop. It once belonged to a 12th-century Benedictine monastery. Directly adjacent to it is the Romanesque-Gothic chapel of São João Baptista.
It is another 10km/6.4mi from Tarouquela to **Castelo de Paiva**, otherwise known as Sobrado de Paiva. This little town encircled by hills

is famous for its wine, and is a good base for walks. In the town itself, pay a visit to the 18th-century estate, Quinta da Boa Vista.

Around 3km/1.8mi north-east of Lamego, in the Rio Balsemão valley, is the Visigothic church of São Pedro de Balsemão. This hall church dates from the seventh century, and is probably the **oldest church in Portugal**. It was restored in 1643, and a coffered ceiling was added.

São Pedro de Balsemão

Along the IP 3 north from Lamego, it is 13km/7.8mi to Peso da Régua, or Régua for short, situated on the right bank of the Douro and inhabited by 6,000 people. Here, the small rivers Corgo and Baroso flow into the Douro, and boat trips from Porto come up this far. In spite of its pleasant location directly on the river, the little town is industrial in character and not particularly attractive. Régua is the heart of the area where grapes are grown for port (▶Douro Valley), and it is a busy trading centre. The busiest time is during the grape harvest, from late September to late October, when many helpers arrive, both from the immediate neighbourhood and from further afield.

Peso da Régua

◀ Where to stay see p.301

A good 10km/6.4mi south of Lamego lies the pretty village of Tarouca at the end of a valley enclosed by cliffs. In the church of the Cistercian monastery of São João de Tarouca, thought to have been founded in 1171 by Afonso I, is the mighty stone coffin of Conde Pedro de Barcelos (died 1354), the illegitimate favourite son of King Dinis I, and author of the aristocracy register *Livro das Linhagens*. The stone coffin of Condessa de Barcelos, wife of Pedro, was also once here; it is now preserved in the Lamego regional museum.

Tarouca

✴ Leiria

F 18

Historical province: Beira Litoral
District: Leiria

Altitude: 30–113m/99–373ft
Population: 34,000

Leiria is a lively regional capital in central Portugal. High above the town tower the ruins of the castle built by Afonso Henriques in 1135. Pretty burgher houses and aristocratic palaces from the 16th and 17th centuries still stand in the old town centre.

The small country town, called Collipo by the Romans, was at times a noble residence under Dinis I; from 1545 it was a lively diocesan town, with the Praça de Rodrigues Lobo at its centre. In the middle of the square stands a monument to Rodrigues Lobo (1579–1621), who drew inspiration from this idyllic little place, as did various fellow poets after him. Through the town flows the Rio Liz.

What to See in Leiria

★
Castelo

In 1135 Afonso Henriques had a castle built on the ruins of fortifications originally constructed by the Romans and later used by the Moors. When it became possible for Portugal's frontier to be moved further south, in 1147, the fortress lost its strategic significance, and fell into decay. In the early decades of the 14th century, King Dinis built it up again, and added a palace as well.

Parts of the castle walls and the keep of 1324 are still well preserved, and provide a magnificent vantage point. Restoration work has been undertaken on the remains of the royal castle, for instance on some rooms deliberately left unadorned, and the loggia with its Gothic pillars; they, too, offer a good view of Leiria. The castle church of Nossa Senhora da Pena, dating from 1314, is impressive even as a ruin; it has a lovely Gothic portal.

Igreja de São Pedro

Below the castle stands the church of São Pedro. It is Romanesque in origin, and dates from the 12th century, but has been substantially altered several times.

Sé

Leiria's cathedral, in the historic centre, is a simple Renaissance building of the 16th century, which was renovated in the 18th century. Adjacent to it is a small museum where paintings, furniture, ceramics, glass and so on are on display.

Santuário de Nossa Senhora da Encarnação

Opposite the castle hill, on a wooded slope, is the Santuário de Nossa Senhora da Encarnação of 1588. Steps dating from the 18th century lead up to it.

▶ VISITING LEIRIA

INFORMATION
Jardim de Luís de Camões
2401-801 Leiria
Tel. 244 848 770
www.rt-leiriafatima.pt

WHERE TO EAT
▶ Moderate
Tromba Rija
Rua Professores Portela 22 (Marrazes)
Tel. 244 855 072
In the Tromba Rija there is no printed menu: a wide range of traditionally prepared dishes is available from the buffet. This long-established traditional establishment is very popular in the area.

WHERE TO STAY
▶ Budget/Mid-range
Hotel D. João III
Avenida D. João III
2400-164 Leiria
Tel. 244 817 888
Fax 244 817 880
www.bestwestern.com/pt/
hoteldomjoaoiii
Reliable central hotel with 64 rooms.

The hilltop castle ruins of Leiria are visible from far and wide.

Around Leiria

7km/4.2mi north of Leiria lies Milagres , a pretty place with an 18th-century pilgrimage church that receives many visitors.

Milagres

Busy Pombal in the valley of the Rio Soura, approx. 27km/16.2mi north-east of Leiria, owes its fame to the once powerful **Minister Sebastião José de Carvalho e Mello, Marquês de Pombal** (▶ Famous People), who died here in exile in 1782. There is a monument to him in the main square. Up above the town is the castle, renovated in the 16th century, alongside the 12th-century church of Santa Maria do Castelo.

Pombal

Around 8km/5mi east of Leiria is the impressive canyon of the Rio Caranguejeira with cliffs that reach a height of 100m/330ft in places.

Rio Caranguejeira

12km/7.2mi west of Leiria lies Marinha Grande, amidst the pine woods – Pinhal de Leiria – which King Dinis I planted with beach pines from the south of France as protection against flying sand from the sea. Today they yield resin and turpentine. Marinha Grande experienced an economic in the mid-18th century, when a glass foundry was built there which is still one of the most important in the country.

Marinha Grande/ Pinhal de Leiria

✶ ✶ Lisboa • Lisbon

Historical province: Estremadura
District: Lisboa (Lisbon)

Altitude: 23–112m/76–370ft
Population: 680,000
(Greater Lisbon: approx. 2.1 million)

The capital of Portugal for more than 700 years, Lisbon is considered one of the most beautiful cities in Europe, not least because of its attractive situation on the Tagus. Many pens have written and voices sung of the special Atlantic light and ramshackle charm of the once glittering metropolis.

Lisbon, or Lisboa (pronounced Lishboa), is the seat of government and the administrative centre of thedistrict of the same name, one of three districts in the historical province of Estremadura. Many centuries of centralized organization in the country have led to a concentration of the most important administrative, economic and cultural functions in the city. Lisbon is very hilly, and lies approx. 12km/7.2mi from the Atlantic on the north shore of the Tagus bay Mar da Palha (»sea of straw«), which is like a large lake; it is approx. 7km/4.2mi wide, and forms a very well protected natural harbour. As it approaches the Atlantic, the Tagus narrows to an estuary just 2km/1.2mi wide. The **panoramic view** of the »white city« enjoyed by those who **approach Lisbon by ship** is justly acclaimed.

The »white city« – Portugal's capital

> **!** *Baedeker* TIP
>
> **»Sea view«**
> Those who do not arrive in Lisbon by sea can still relish the splendid view of the city from the water by taking the ferry from Cais do Sodré across to Cacilhas, and back again. The panoramic view can be enjoyed for a small sum.

In ancient times the Phoenicians founded a settlement on the tranquil harbour bay in the Tagus estuary, and called it Alis Ubbo. It was taken over as a Lusitanian harbour, **Olisipo**, by the Romans. Fortified and re-named **Felicitas Iulia**, it was elevated to become the administrative capital of the province of Lusitania. Thus what had started as a modest settlement became the second most important city on the Iberian Peninsula, after Mérida.
It fell to the Alani in 407, and was then under Visigothic rule from 585 to 715, before falling into the hands of the Moors after the battle of Jerez. The Moors called it **Al Oshbuna** or **Lishbuna**, and under their rule (until 1147) there was a flowering of culture and the economy.

History

← *Looking from the Praça do Comércio toward the streets of the lower city through the Arco Triunfal*

The Ponte Vasco da Gama, the 17km/10.6mi-long bridge over the Tagus near Lisbon

Lisbon gained new significance under Afonso III, who made the city his residence in 1260. The capital was a prime beneficiary of the **great discoveries** of the late 15th century and the conquest of the East Indies, and it soon became **one of the wealthiest cities in Europe**.

On 1 November 1755 a terrible **earthquake** reduced most of the city to rubble. Re-building began almost immediately, with the very active participation of the Marquês de Pombal: he had the city re-designed by master builder Manuel da Maia on the magnificent scale still visible today, retaining what was left of the earlier Gothic-Manueline buildings.

At the time of the French invasion of 1807/1808 the royal residence was moved to Rio de Janeiro (until 1821), and this, coupled with the loss of Brazil as a colony, proved a severe setback for the city, from which it could only gradually recover during the second half of the 19th century.

In the course of the 20th century Lisbon became a modern, open metropolis, while retaining for the most part its distinctive characteristics. The city hit the headlines in August 1988, when a **great fire** ravaged an area of approx. 2ha/5ac in the Chiado quarter. The gutted buildings were re-built, and such historic façades as were still standing were retained. From the point of view of city architecture, the eastern part of the town is particularly interesting. In a large scale operation for Expo 98 a dilapidated industrial area was first decon-

Highlights Lisbon

taminated after which construction work began on the **Expo site** on the Tagus as well as in the adjoining part of the town, **»Expo-Urbe«**. A station, Estação Oriente, and the gigantic Tagus bridge **Ponte Vasco da Gama** were built in preparation for Expo 98.

Lisbon's sea of whitish-grey houses extends over hilly terrain down to the banks of the Tagus. The differences in altitude can be considerable, and this is one of Lisbon's charms: there are many wonderful vantage points, and numerous terraces have been constructed, the so-called **»miradouros«**, with views out over the city and the river. Various means of transportation, such as lifts and cable-cars, help to overcome the differences in altitude.

✶ ✶
City of hills

 The different **areas of the city** play a very important role in Lisbon. The centre of Lisbon is the **Baixa** area, the lower city, which is all on one level just above the Tagus. This area was destroyed by the earthquake of 1755, and everything had to be built anew. Here, visitors find several imposing squares and wide promenades, but there are also narrow streets with old workshops. Much of the area is given over to business premises and shops. To the east of Baixa, the oldest areas of Lisbon spread around the hill on which the castle stands: **Alfama** and **Mouraria**. These parts were hardly affected at all by the earthquake of 1755, so that a charming tangle of medieval alleys has been preserved. Another old area, to the west of Baixa, **Bairro Alto** (upper city), also survived the earthquake almost unscathed. West of

Lisboa Plan

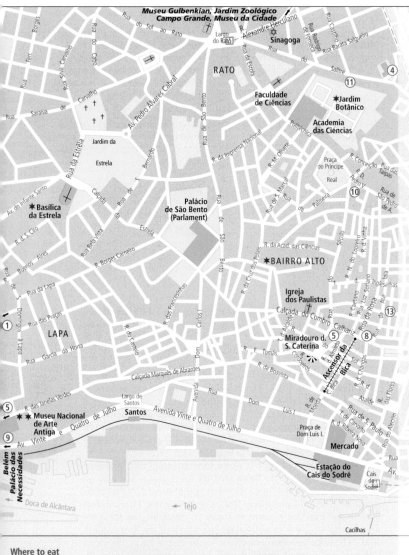

Museu Gulbenkian, Jardim Zoológico, Campo Grande, Museu da Cidade

RATO

Sinagoga

Faculdade de Ciências

★Jardim Botânico

Academia das Ciências

Jardim da Estrela

Praça do Príncipe Real

★Basílica da Estrela

Palácio de São Bento (Parlament)

★BAIRRO ALTO

LAPA

Igreja dos Paulistas

Miradouro d. S. Caterina

Ascensor da Bica

Calçada Marquês de Abrantes

Largo de Santos

Santos

Avenida Vinte e Quatro de Julho

★★ Museu Nacional de Arte Antiga

Praça de Dom Luís I.

Mercado

Belém Palácio das Necessidades

Estação do Cais do Sodré

Cais do Sodré

Doca de Alcântara

← Tejo

Cacilhas

Where to eat

1. Casa do Leão
2. Clara
3. Tágide
4. Adega de São Roque
5. Adega Dantas
6. Cervejaria da Trindade
7. Mestre André
8. Primeiro de Maio
9. Cosmos Café
10. Casa do Alentejo
11. Os Tibetanos
12. Restô Chapitô
13. Cravo e Canela
14. Café Nicola
15. Café Suíça
16. A Brasileira
17. Pastelaria Benard
18. Confeitaria Nacional
19. Cerca Moura

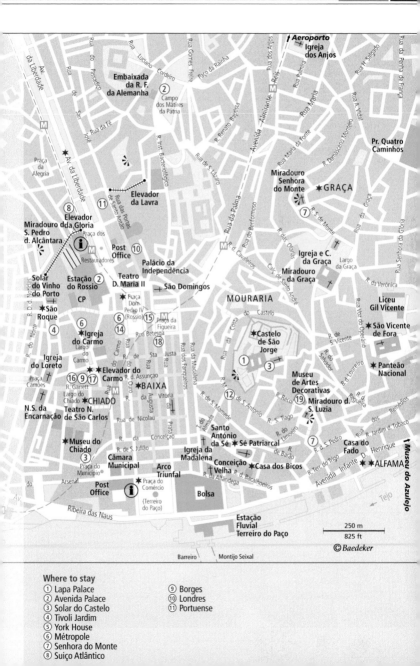

Where to stay
① Lapa Palace
② Avenida Palace
③ Solar do Castelo
④ Tivoli Jardim
⑤ York House
⑥ Métropole
⑦ Senhora do Monte
⑧ Suiço Atlântico
⑨ Borges
⑩ Londres
⑪ Portuense

▶ VISITING LISBON

INFORMATION

Turismo Palácio Foz
Praça dos Restauradores
1250-187 Lisbon
Tel. 213 463 314
www.visitlisboa.com

Turismo Praça do Comércio
Tel. 210 312 810

Turismo Airport
Tel. 218 450 660 (arrivals)

TRANSPORT

Try to avoid driving in Lisbon. In the rush hour the main roads into the city are totally blocked, and cars come to a halt in the centre, too. It is difficult to park, and charges are high.

It is possible to reach most of the sights on foot, and there is also an efficient and varied public transport network, with trams, cable cars, buses, a lift, ferries and an underground metro system. So far there are four metro lines, which will be extended further.

LISBOA CARD

The »Lisboa Card« is valid for free rides on buses, trams and lifts, and also gives free or much reduced entry to around 25 museums. Valid for one, two or three days, the »Lisboa Card« is obtainable from the tourist information office, the ticket office at the foot of the Elevador de Santa Justa, and various other outlets.

A evening out in Bairro Alto: at the weekend night becomes day here.

SHOPPING

The central shopping area encompasses the streets between the Rossio and the Praça do Comércio in Baixa. One elegant shopping street is Rua Garrett in Chiado. In the central area there are small shopping centres everywhere. The large Lisbon shopping centres are Amoreiras, Colombo, Vasco da Gama and El Corte Inglés.

ENTERTAINMENT

Lisbon is one of the great European cities for an evening out. Nightlife begins late – the bars and taverns start to fill up from 11pm. The most important areas are Bairro Alto, the Docas de Santo Amaro and the Docas de Alcântara on the Tagus river bank. There are many fado venues in Bairro Alto, and a few in Alfama and Bica.

WHERE TO EAT

► Expensive

① *Casa do Leão*
Castelo de São Jorge
Tel. 218 875 962
High up within the castle walls. In fine weather it is possible to sit in the open air and enjoy a splendid view of the city below.

② *Clara*
Campo dos Mártires da Pátria 49
Tel. 218 853 053
One of the top places to eat in Lisbon, located in a small park up on the Campo dos Mártires da Pátria.

③ *Tágide*
Largo da Academia de Belas Artes 18
Tel. 213 471 880
Elegant interior decoration with antique tile pictures. Good view of city and river. Portuguese and international cuisine.

► Moderate

⑦ *Mestre André*
Calçadinha Santo Estêvão 6
Tel. 218 871 487
Tiny restaurant with good atmosphere on the edge of Alfama. Seating outside on the street in summer. Good food, ample helpings – almost always crowded.

⑧ *Primeiro de Maio*
Rua da Atalaia 8
Tel. 213 426 840
Popular with journalists, politicians and intellectuals. Good food and pleasant, unpretentious ambience.

⑨ *Cosmos Café*
Doca de Santo Amaro
Tel. 213 972 747
On the Tagus riverside, almost underneath the bridge. Mediterranean food. There are plenty more restaurants in the old warehouses round about – mostly rather expensive.

⑪ *Os Tibetanos*
Rua do Salitre 117
Tel. 213 142 038
Long-established restaurant with good vegetarian food. Those with a window seat enjoy a good view over the Avenida da Liberdade towards the castle.

⑫ *Restô Chapitô*
Rua da Costa do Castelo 7
Tel. 218 878 225
On the castle hill, very pleasant outdoor seating in summer. Good international cuisine.

⑬ *Cravo e Canela*
Rua da Barocca 70
Tasteful décor and international cuisine. Good selection of starters, wide range of side dishes.

Eat in a former monastery: Cervejaria da Trinidade

▶ Inexpensive

⑤ *Adega Dantas*
Rua Marechal Saldanha 15
Tel. 213 420 329
Popular, simple venue in Bica. Patronized especially by young Portuguese. Good food, inexpensive.

⑥ *Cervejaria da Trindade*
Rua Nova da Trindade 20
Tel. 213 423 506
Established in a former monastery, pleasant tile pictures on the walls, two dining halls and pretty little inner courtyard. Especially good for seafood. Hot meals served till late evening.

⑩ *Casa do Alentejo*
Rua das Portas de Santo Antão 58
Tel. 218 956 116
Typical Alentejo dishes, »Carne do Porco à Alentejana« highly recommended: pork with mussels.

Baedeker recommendation

④ *Adega de São Roque*
Rua da Misericórdia 120
Tel. 213 432 167
A very agreeable restaurant, always well frequented. The whole menu is worth trying. Get there early – or book a table.

CAFÉS

⑭ *Café Nicola*
Praça Dom Pedro IV (Rossio) 24

⑮ *Café Suiça*
Praça Dom Pedro IV (Rossio) 99

⑯ *A Brasileira*
Rua Garrett 120 (▶Tip p.373)

⑰ *Pastelaria Benard*
Rua Garrett 104-106

⑱ *Confeitaria Nacional*
Praça da Figueira 18 B/C

⑲ Cerca Moura
Rua Largo das Portas do Sol 4

Pastelaria Versailles
Av. da República 15 A

Confeitaria dos Pastéis de Belém
Rua de Belém 84/86

WHERE TO STAY
► Luxury
① Hotel Lapa Palace
Rua Pau da Bandeira 4
1249-021 Lisbon
Tel. 213 949 494, fax 213 950 665
www.orient-expresshotels.com
Member of the Leading Hotels of the
World. All 94 rooms in this old city
palace have Arraiolos rugs. Quiet
location, perfect service. Pool, sauna,
fitness studio.

② Hotel Avenida Palace
Rua 1° de Dezembro
1200-359 Lisbon
Tel. 213 460 151, fax 213 422 884
www.hotel-avenida-palace.pt
Traditional Lisbon luxury hotel,
mentioned in Thomas Mann's *Confessions of Felix Krull*. A high-class,
elegant establishment.

③ Solar do Castelo
Rua das Cozinhas 2
1100-181 Lisbon
Tel. 218 870 909
www.epoquehotels.com
A special place to stay in Lisbon:
lovely little hotel with 14 rooms up in
the castle area. Tastefully decorated.

► Mid-range
④ Hotel Tivoli Jardim
Rua Júlio César Machado 7
1250-135 Lisbon
Tel. 213 591 000, fax 213 591 245
www.tivolihotels.com

*Old established Lisbon luxury hotel: the Avenida Palace
at the lower end of Avenida da Liberdade*

Central and quiet, adjacent to Tivoli
Lisboa; Tivoli garden and pool available
to guests. 119 rooms with air-
conditioning, TV and safe.

⑤ York House
Rua das Janelas Verdes 32
1200-691 Lisbon
Tel. 213 962 435, fax 213 972 793
www.yorkhouselisboa.com
Exclusive establishment in 16th-century
monastery, a short distance from
the centre in the Belém direction. 48
lovely rooms, and a beautiful monastery
garden with fountain.

⑥ Hotel Métropole
Rossio 30
1100-200 Lisbon

Tel. 213 219 030, fax 213 469 166
www.almeidahotels.com
Handsome hotel located on the central
Rossio. The front rooms are nicer, but
rather noisy. View of the Rossio from
the lounge.

*Central and comfortable: the
Métropole on the Rossio*

⑦ **Senhora do Monte**
Calçada do Monte 39
1170-250 Lisbon
Tel. 218 866 002
Fax 218 877 783
www.maisturismo.pt/sramonte
Spectacular location – some way out –
on a hill in the Graça area, with a view
over the entire city centre. 28 comfortably appointed rooms.

▶ **Budget**
⑧ **Hotel Suiço Atlântico**
Rua da Glória 3-19
1250-114 Lisbon
Tel. 213 461 713
Fax 213 469 013
www.grupofbarata.com
Simple, well-run hotel; 88 small rooms
with bath and TV. Very central
position.

Baedeker recommendation

⑨ **Hotel-Pensão Borges**
Rua Garrett 108
1200-205 Lisbon
Tel. 213 461 951
Fax 213 426 617
Venerable old hotel-pension in a central
location. Most rooms are very spacious, with
bath and TV, and most have been renovated.
The old breakfast room with a crystal
chandelier is charming. Pleasant clientele,
and a very friendly atmosphere.

⑩ **Pensão Londres**
Rua Dom Pedro V 53
1250-092 Lisbon
Tel. 213 462 203
Fax 213 465 682
Pleasant guesthouse in Bairro Alto.
Some rooms have been well renovated,
others are still in the old Portuguese
pension style. Rooms with and with-
out bath.

⑪ **Pensão Portuense**
Rua das Portas de Santo Antão 153
1150-267 Lisbon
Tel. 213 464 197, fax 213 424 239
The Portuense is a friendly, long-
established family guesthouse right in
the centre, simple and well looked
after. Renovated rooms, both with and
without TV; some rooms with several
beds.

the upper city is **Lapa**, one of the grandest residential areas in Lisbon, and also the diplomats' area. The embassies of numerous countries are here, as are the residences of their staff. Further west again is **Belém**, where impressive buildings recall the former greatness of Portugal.

For decades the **decaying city centre** of Lisbon was totally neglected. Since rents were frozen at a very low level, property owners were not interested in renovation; the houses deteriorated, and some are still in a catastrophic state. Yet since the mid-1980s there have been attempts to remedy the problem. An improvement and modernization programme in Alfama aimed to preserve its traditional communities. In Bairro Alto, on the other hand, modernization resulted mostly in luxury dwellings.

Problems of a metropolis

In recent decades, vast **suburbs** have grown up around the city centre. Many residents prefer to live in one of these modern skyscraper residential areas rather than in the unmodernized houses in the centre.

A large number of inhabitants have also been moved to the suburbs from the **»bairros da lata«**, sprawling areas of corrugated iron shacks, which usually had no mains water, drainage or heating. In the »bairros da lata« lived the poorest of the poor, predominantly those returning from the former Portuguese colonies, but also immigrants from the colonies or from other parts of Portugal.

Those without much time to spend in Lisbon should at least have a look at the Rossio, stroll through Alfama, and take a trip to Belém.

Whistle-stop visit

Baixa – Lower City

The Praça dos Restauradores is a good starting-point for a walk through the lower city. The tourist information office is here, too. The square is embellished by the Monumento dos Restauradores de Portugal, erected in 1886. The obelisk is almost 30m/99ft high, and commemorates the uprising of 1 December 1640, when the storming of the royal palace ended 60 years of Spanish rule.

Praça dos Restauradores

The Estação do Rossio at the south-west end of the Praça dos Restauradores seems more like a theatre, or some other grandiose building, than a railway station. The suburban trains to ► Sintra are among those that depart from here, leaving the city via a 2,600m/2,850yd tunnel. Repair work on the tunnel has now been completed and normal services have been resumed.

Estação do Rossio

Diagonally across from the station is the huge side façade of the national theatre; the main façade faces the Rossio. The classical building of 1846 burnt down in 1964, and did not re-open until 1978 – newly equipped with a revolving stage.

Teatro Nacional de Dona Maria II

Rossio

The Rossio, or **Praça de Dom Pedro IV** as the square is officially called, is the real centre of Lisbon. It is worth lingering in one of the street cafés here to watch the passers-by, lottery ticket vendors, shoe-cleaners and street hawkers. In the middle of the square is a 23m/80ft marble pillar, erected in 1870, crowned by a bronze statue of Pedro IV. The square has jacaranda trees all around it, and two nice fountains.

! **Baedeker** TIP

Ginjinha

Why not enjoy a little glass of ginjinha, a delicious kirsch liqueur, at the northern end of the Rossio, in a one-room shop just around the corner to the right. Order it with (»com«) or without (»sem«) cherries and quaff it on the spot – no sitting down.

The main streets **between the Rossio and the Praça do Comércio** were designed in a checkerboard pattern at the behest of Marquês de Pombal after 1755. The streets were each assigned to particular guilds: for instance, Rua da Prata (Silver Street) and Rua Aurea (Gold Street) to the silversmiths and goldsmiths, and Rua Augusta to the cloth merchants. Although there are no visible traces of this system nowadays, these streets still constitute Lisbon's business and shopping centre.

Elevador do Carmo

The Santa Justa elevator (or Carmo elevator) still forms a bizarre link between the lower city and Bairro Alto to the west (see also the 3D image on p.367). The ironwork construction is often attributed to Gustave Eiffel, but in actual fact it was built around 1900 from designs by Mesnier de Ponsard, a Portuguese engineer of French descent. It is still worth going up the Elevador de Santa Justa, even though there is no longer any access to the upper city from the top. There is a café on the upper platform, with a wonderful view of the Rossio and lower city. From up here the checkerboard pattern of the streets below is clearly discernible.

Praça do Comércio

Before the earthquake of 1755, the royal palace (Paço da Ribeira) stood on the Praça do Comércio, which is therefore also called the Terreiro do Paço. The square opens onto the water, so it is referred to from time to time as **Lisbon's »arrival point«**. In the middle is the equestrian statue of José I, erected in 1775. The Praça do Comércio is flanked by arcades and public buildings – largely ministries – which Santos de Carvalho built after 1755. A striking feature of the north side is the triumphal arch completed in 1873, with statues of famous national worthies.

Boat trip to Cacilhas

From the landing-stage at the south-east end of the square there are regular ferries to Cacilhas (▶Around Lisbon) on the opposite bank of the Tagus; from the boat there is an excellent view of the gently rising swathes of houses that make up Portugal's capital.

Alfama

From the north-east corner of the Praça do Comércio runs Rua da **Igreja da** Alfândega; on it stands the church of Conceição Velha, newly built **Conceição Velha** after 1755. A side portal is all that remains of the much larger church that preceded it. Today this splendid portal in rich Manueline style serves as the main entrance.

> **!** *Baedeker* TIP
>
> ### The legendary 28
> It's no longer a secret tip, but still a wonderful little adventure: a trip on the no. 28 tram, up and down the hills, through Lisbon's city centre. The loveliest stretch is through the streets of Alfama, which at times are so narrow that the tramcars only just get through.

A little further east is the noteworthy **Casa dos Bicos**. The »pointed house« owes its name to the striking pattern of diamond-shaped stones on the façade. This palace was built in the 16th century, and only the ground floor survived the earthquake of 1755 intact. The upper floors were restored according to old plans, but with deliberately modern building materials. It is now used for exhibitions.

Sé Patriarcalis Lisbon's cathedral, and the city's oldest ecclesiastical **★** building. For the most part it was newly built in 1344, on the site of **Sé Patriarcal** an older church which is said to have been converted from a mosque in 1150. The fortress-like main façade was restored in the 1940s to look as it did in 1380.

The **interior of the cathedral with a nave and two aisles** is predominantly Romanesque, the choir and ambulatory Gothic. St Anthony, Lisbon's patron saint, is supposed to have been baptized in 1195 in the font to the left of the entrance. The lovely Baroque terracotta crib in the first side chapel is by Joaquim Machado de Castro. The body of Afonso IV (1325–1357) rests here in the choir, as does that of his

Sé Patriarcal Plan

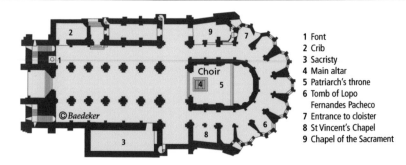

Choir

4

© Baedeker

2

9

7

1

5

3

8

6

1 Font
2 Crib
3 Sacristy
4 Main altar
5 Patriarch's throne
6 Tomb of Lopo
  Fernandes Pacheco
7 Entrance to cloister
8 St Vincent's Chapel
9 Chapel of the Sacrament

wife. Relics of St Vincent used to be venerated in St Vincent's Chapel. In another of the ambulatory chapels is the sarcophagus of Lopo Fernandes Pacheco, a retainer of Afonso IV.

While going round the cathedral, be sure to take a look at the 14th-century **cloisters**. Excavations in the cloister courtyard have exposed remains of Phoenician and Roman walls.

Igreja de Santo António da Sé

Below the cathedral to the west is the church of Santo António da Sé, which was newly built after the earthquake, between 1757 and 1812; it is supposed to mark the erstwhile location of the house where St Anthony of Padua was born. A monument and a small museum next to the church commemorate the saint, whom Padua and Lisbon both claim as their own.

★ ★ Alfama

To the east of the cathedral, the famous area of Alfama extends up the hill, a thoroughly picturesque old area of the city, with steep alleyways and atmospheric squares.

The name »Alfama« is derived from **Arabic »al-Hama«**, and means **»warm springs«**. In the middle ages, the nobility and wealthy bourgeoisie lived in this part of Lisbon. Later on, craftsmen, fishermen and seafarers settled here, and in the 18th century Alfama was known as the prostitutes' district, too. Today it is mostly the poor that inhabit Lisbon's old city, and it is doubtful that life here is as picturesque as tourists may think. A renovation programme has included modernization of some of the houses in the centre. At the same time, some high-class condominiums have been built here.

The best way of seeing the area is to stroll through the network of narrow alleys, steep steps and hidden courtyards. Though poverty is clearly visible, the area is never dreary: the houses have flowerpots in front of them, and canaries sing in every little alley. The liveliest of the small streets is Rua de São Pedro, with shops, taverns and street hawkers.

Casa do Fado e da Guitarra Portuguesa
🕐

The fado museum is housed in a former waterworks on the Largo do Chafariz do Dentro. The history of fado (► Baedeker Special, p.118) is presented with examples of the music. The tour culminates in a reproduction fado tavern (open: Wed–Mon 10am–6pm).

Miradouro de Santa Luzia

From Rua do Limoeiro at the upper end of Alfama, the lovingly designed terrace of Miradouro de Santa Luzia offers a beautiful view of the city's tangled mesh of rooftops and narrow streets. It also has an interesting large azulejo picture, showing the Praça do Comércio before the earthquake.

Museu de Artes Decorativas

Opposite the viewing terrace, in what was once the city palace of Visconde de Azurara built in the 17th century, is the Museu de Artes Decorativas. Adjoining it are an applied arts school and

Alfama Plan

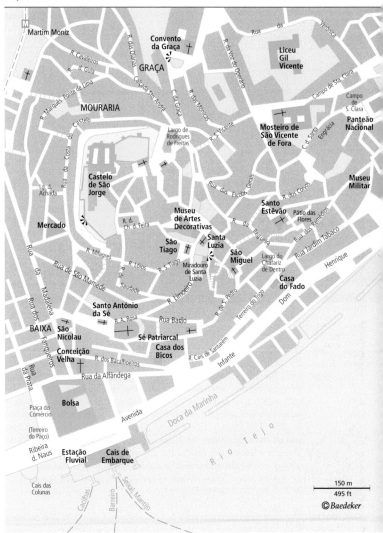

workshops. The museum houses Portugal's most important furniture collection, from the 16th to the19th century. Further exhibits include woven carpets, silver, and china (open: Mon–Sat 10am–5pm). The workshops have developed an excellent reputation and created furnishings for clients all of the world.

View from Castelo de São Jorge of the Ponte 25 de Abril and the Tagus estuary

★

Castelo de São Jorge

On the castle hill, once the centre of the Moors' city, stands the Castelo de São Jorge, visible from afar. The oldest parts of the castle date from the 6th century; in the 12th century the Moorish fortifications were altered and extended to become the king's palace. Well into the 16th century it served as a royal residence; it was then used as a weapons store and prison. It was severely damaged by the earthquake of 1755. The remains of the castle walls were restored in 1938–1940, and at the same time the inner courtyard was made into a park. There is a fascinating view of the city and Tagus bay from the terrace on the south side, and from the ramparts and towers. An azulejo information board helps visitors to find their way around (open: daily 9am–9pm, in winter until 6pm).

Convento da Graça

The church of the Convento da Graça was built in 1556 and restored after 1755. Miracles are attributed to the revered figure of Christ in the southern transept, »Nosso Senhor dos Passos«. There is a good view from the Miradouro da Graça outside the church.

Ermida Nossa Senhora do Monte

From a hill-ridge further to the north rises the Ermida de Nossa Senhora do Monte (100m/330ft), built in 1243. The terrace offers another splendid view of the city.

Around 500m/550yd east of the castle hill is the tall church of São Vicente de Fora, built by the Italian Filippo Terzi during the years 1582–1627. There is a sharp contrast between the severe façade, with its two soaring towers, and the lavish Baroque ornamentation of the interior. Adjacent to the church is the former Augustinian convent, with 18th-century azulejo pictures in entrance hall and cloisters. Since 1855 the former refectory has housed the Panteão Real – the burial vault of the Bragança royal family, from João IV (died 1656) to Queen Amalia (died 1951).

São Vicente de Fora

Below São Vicente de Fora stands the church of Santa Engrácia, also known as Panteão Nacional. The building has an unusual history: an earlier church was demolished in 1630, after it had been desecrated by the theft of altar bread. A new church was immediately constructed, but it collapsed in 1681. Building started on the present-day church in 1682, but it took almost three hundred years to complete. It took until 1966 for the last phase to be finished, with the construction of the cupola.

Santa Engrácia / Panteão Nacional

The ground plan is based on a Greek cross, and the interior has **tombstones** recalling famous Portuguese figures: Vasco da Gama, Henry the Navigator, Luís Vaz de Camões, Afonso de Albuquerque (viceroy of India) and Pedro Álvares Cabral (discoverer of Brazil). Among the less prominently displayed tombs is that of fado singer Amália Rodrigues, so far the only woman given a place of honour in the national pantheon.

The military museum on the Tagus riverside is housed in the former army arsenal (Arsenal do Exército). Weapons were produced here until the beginning of the 20th century. Nowadays an extensive collection of weapons and trophies is on display; and some of the rooms have lavish Baroque decoration. Exhibits include 14th-century guns and a sword belonging to Vasco da Gama (open: Tue–Sun 10am–5pm).

Museu Militar

Santa Apolónia station, to the east of the military museum, is the departure and arrival point for trains to and from the direction of Porto and France.

Estação de Santa Apolónia

In Rua da Alviela, about halfway between Apolónia station and the azulejo museum, a municipal waterworks museum opened in 1987. In the former pumping-station the history of the city's water supply is shown, with numerous displays (open: Mon–Sat 10am–6pm).

Museu da Água da EPAL

About 500m/550yd east of Apolónia station, in part of the Madre de Deus, a former Franciscan nunnery of the Order of the Poor Clares dating from 1509, is the Museu Nacional do Azulejo. Like many others, this building was largely destroyed in 1755, and re-built during the second half of the 18th century. The richly ornamented main

✶ Museu Nacional do Azulejo / Madre de Deus

doorway of the church was reconstructed in 1872, in keeping with the original Manueline style.

The interior decoration of the **church** dates almost entirely from the second half of the 18th century. Only the two cloisters survived the earthquake largely unscathed; the larger was built in Renaissance style, while the smaller is Manueline.

The two cloisters and further conventual buildings house the **azulejo museum**, a very extensive collection of Portuguese and foreign ceramic tiles. A huge azulejo picture gives an impression of Lisbon prior to 1755; on it the royal palace and the Casa dos Bicos, that still survives today, are clearly discernible(open: Tue 2pm–6pm, Wed–Sun 10am–6pm).

Bairro Alto – Upper City

Chiado

Chiado is the name given to the quarter that lies on the slopes west of Baixa, forming a link between the upper and lower city. Frequently the name is also used for the **elegant shopping street, Rua Garrett** in the centre of the quarter. The name derives from António Ribeiro (c1520–1591), who made a name for himself in Lisbon as

Tram route 28 emerges from the narrow alleyways and rumbles across the Largo do Chiado – past the monument to the poet Chiado.

»Chiado« – a disrespectful, satirical poet. At the turn of the 20th century and during the following decades, Chiado was a meeting-point for literati and artists. Political and cultural discussions took place in the local cafés.

Chiado hit the headlines all over the world when a **great fire** destroyed part of the area on 25 August 1988. »Only« 2ha/5ac were burnt down – primarily buildings on Rua do Carmo – yet Chiado was wounded to the quick. Long-drawn-out discussions about rebuilding yielded two main alternatives: reconstruction of the destroyed area in a manner as close as possible to the original, retaining the outer façades; or a completely new design with modern buildings. In the end, Álvaro Siza Vieira (►Famous People), an architect from Porto, got the contract: reconstruction was to take into account the original character of the area.

The centre of the upper city is Largo do Chiado. Where Rua Garrett leads into the square, there is a bronze monument to the poet and actor known as »Chiado«. It shows him as a satirical, and not exactly deferential, orator. The square owes its second name, Largo das duas Igrejas, to the two churches that stand here: on the southern side, Nossa Senhora da Encarnação, built in 1784; on the north side, the Loreto church, dating from 1517.

Largo do Chiado

The Largo do Chiado opens onto the **Praça de Camões**, a leafy square, with a statue erected in 1867 to commemorate Portugal's national poet, Luís Vaz de Camões (►Famous People).

> ! **Baedeker TIP**
>
> **»A Brasileira« – The Brazilian Girl**
> Definitely worth a visit: the »A Brasileira« café on the Largo do Chiado (daily 8am–2am). It began as a retail coffee shop in 1905. »The Brazilian Girl« became a well known meeting place for literati, journalists and artists. The bronze sculpture outside the café shows one of them: Fernando Pessoa.

Further north-east on the Largo do Carmo, which features a dolphin fountain built in 1796, lies the former Convento do Carmo. The convent was built during the years 1389–1423; it was destroyed for the most part in 1755, and never rebuilt, yet the ruin of what was once the largest church in Lisbon is still an impressive monument of Gothic architecture.

✳ *Convento do Carmo*

The interior of the nave, which has lost its roof, is now used as an archaeological museum. Antique and medieval tombstones and fragments of architecture are on display (open: Mon–Sat 10am–6pm, in winter until 5pm).

The Igreja de São Roque, north-west of the Convento do Carmo, has the most sumptuous interior of any church in Lisbon. The Jesuits commissioned the building; work started in 1566, and Filippo Terzi played a part in it. Whereas the external façades are simple and so-

✳ *Igreja de São Roque*

ber, the interior is ornamented with azulejos, paintings, marble and gilded woodcarving. The fourth side chapel on the left, the Capela de São João Baptista, is the most splendidly adorned. It was commissioned by King João V in Rome in 1742, made from the most costly materials – marble, alabaster, semi-precious stones, gold and silver – and sent by ship to Lisbon in 1747. The **Museu de São Roque** next door, a museum for sacred art, has excellent Italian gold artefacts as well as other exhibits (open: Tue–Sun 10am–5pm).

Miradouro São Pedro de Alcântara

Heading north, Rua de S. Pedro de Alcântara leads to a terrace which offers a splendid view of the city and Tagus bay.

Elevador da Glória

From this point, the Calçada da Glória descends to ► Baixa. Those who do not want to go on foot can take the cable car system, the Elevador da Glória.

Praça do Príncipe Real

Further north-west, at the end of Rua de Dom Pedro V, is the Praça do Príncipe Real, the highest point of the upper city. There is a good view from the west side of the square.

Jardim Botânico

There is a glorious display of plants in the Jardim Botânico, which was laid out in 1873. With its tropical and subtropical vegetation this is considered one of the most beautiful botanical gardens in Europe. It belongs to the Faculdade das Ciências, the Natural Sciences faculty of the university, which is located in the classical building on the west side of the park (open: Sat–Sun 10am–6pm, Mon–Fri 9am–8pm, in winter until 6pm).

Teatro Nacional de São Carlos

In the southern part of Bairro Alto is the famous Teatro Nacional de São Carlos. This opera house was built during the years 1792–1795 in classical style.

Museu do Chiado

The Museu do Chiado houses works by Portuguese painters from 1850 to 1950 (more recent works are displayed in the Gulbenkian foundation's Centro de Arte Moderna). The collection includes paintings by Marquês de Oliveira, Silva Porto, José Malhoa, Alfredo Keil, Columbano Bordalo Pinheiro, Carlos Reis, Eduardo Viana, Francisco Smith and Carlos Botelho, among others; it also has sculpture by Soares dos Reis, Teixeira Lopes and Diogo de Macedo. In addition, the museum has a small international art collection, with drawings by Rodin and French sculpture from around 1900 (open: Tue 2pm–6pm, Wed–Sun 10am–6pm).

West of Bairro Alto

Palácio de São Bento

The Palácio de São Bento was converted from a 17th-century monastery in 1834, and has been renovated several times since then. It is the seat of the Portuguese parliament.

Towering behind the subtropical vegetation: the dome and a tower of the Basílica da Estrela

The Casa-Museu Amália Rodrigues is at Rua de São Bento 193, the home of the great fado singer who died in 1999; memorabilia recall her life (open: Tue–Sun 10am–1pm and 2pm–6pm).

Casa-Museu Amália Rodrigues

It is well worth taking a look at the puppet museum below the Palácio de São Bento to the south in Rua da Esperança. The collection includes puppets, props, posters and other items.

Puppet museum

On the north-west edge of the city centre stands the Basílica da Estrela. The »star basilica« was built during the years 1779–1790. With its grand two-tower façade and cupola rising high above the central intersection, it is a distinctive feature of the cityscape. From the cupola there is a good view of the city. Maria I, who died in Brazil in 1816, is buried in the church. She arranged for the building of the

Basílica da Estrela

church after the birth of an heir to the throne; he, however, died before it was completed.

Jardim da Estrela Opposite the church is an inviting and restful place, the Jardim da Estrela with a rich array of flowers, little lakes, fountains and grottoes.

Cemitério dos Prazéres Lisbon's best known cemetery is the Cemitério dos Prazéres, the »cemetery of pleasures«. It is laid out like a miniature town with streets, and graves and mausoleums that look like houses.

Casa Fernando Pessoa A few hundred yards north-west of the Jardim da Estrela, in Rua Coelho da Rocha 16/18 (Campo de Ourique area), is the last residence of the writer Fernando Pessoa (▶Famous People). The house, in which Pessoa lived from 1920 until his death in 1935, was restored in 1993 and made into a library.

Lapa South-west of the Jardim da Estrela is one of the smartest residential areas in Lisbon and the centre of diplomatic life – Lapa.

Northern Quarters of the City

Avenida da Liberdade Lisbon's main traffic artery is Avenida da Liberdade, which starts from the Praça dos Restauradores in Baixa. This splendid street is 1.5km/1mi long and 90m/100yd wide; it has ten rows of trees, and attractive green spaces; on either side are hotels, banks, administrative offices and commercial premises.

Praça do Marquês de Pombal To the north, Avenida da Liberdade leads into the Praça do Marquês de Pombal, where a great deal of traffic circulates. In the centre of the »Rotunda«, as it is also called, stands the monumental statue of the Marquês (▶Famous People).

Parque Eduardo VII Parque Eduardo VII rises gently from the Rotunda. It was named after Edward VII, king of England, who paid a state visit in 1903. In the upper part of the park are glass-houses for tropical plants, the so-called »Estufa Fria«. Those who climb still higher can enjoy an extensive view of the city and Tagus bay from the terrace.

★ ★
Fundação Calouste Gulbenkian Around 1km/0.6mi north of the Parque Eduardo VII lies the Fundação Calouste Gulbenkian, the Gulbenkian Foundation's cultural centre with theatres, concert and conference halls, a library containing some 400,000 volumes and the Calouste Gulbenkian Museum containing one of the largest private collections in the world. The museum was opened in the 100th anniversary year of the birth of the founder, Armenian **oil magnate Calouste Sarkis Gulbenkian** (▶ Famous People), who lived in Lisbon from 1942 until his death in 1955.

Fundação Calouste Gulbenkian *Plan*

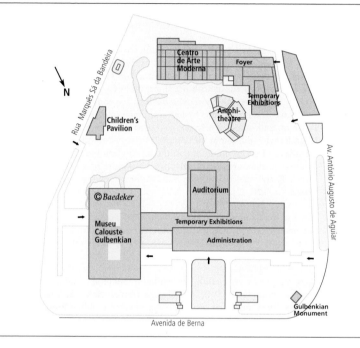

The 25,000 sq m/270,000 sq ft of the Gulbenkian Museum were constructed in the years 1964–1969 from plans by architects Alberto Passoal, Pedro Cid and Ruy Athouguia. The focal points are the outstanding and extensive **collections of oriental art**, especially the art of Egypt, Mesopotamia, and Islamic countries, as well as of the Far East (China and Japan); an unusually rich collection of ceramics; and important works from Greek and Roman antiquity – the collection of Greek coins deserves special attention.

The **picture gallery** includes works by German masters; the Flemish painters Rubens, Thierry Bouts, Van Dyck and Gossaert; Frans Hals and Rembrandt from Holland; Fragonard, Corot, Manet, Monet, Renoir and Degas from France; Hoppner, Gainsborough, Romney, Lawrence and Edward Burne-Jones from England; the Venetian Carpaccio; and Ghirlandaio and Guardi from Florence. In addition there are sculptures by Houdon (*Diana*) and Rodin (*The Burghers of Calais*, in the inner courtyard), textiles, French furniture of the 18th century, and more recent jewellery, including Art Nouveau pieces by **René Lalique** which should not be missed (open: Tue–Sun 10am–6pm).

The foundation buildings are set in the attractively landscaped **Parque Gulbenkian**, where there is a small amphitheatre for concerts and a range of other events organized by the foundation.

Centro de Arte Moderna

The Centro de Arte Modernain the south-west corner of the Gulbenkian Foundation grounds opened in 1984. It is a lively cultural centre; its museum of modern art rounds off Gulbenkian's original collection, which ended with the Impressionists. The museum is especially interesting for those who want to see **contemporary Portuguese art**. There are works by Jaime Azinheira, Jorge Pinheiro, Costa Pinheiro, and others. There are also several pieces by **José Almada Negreiros**. In addition to the comprehensive collection of Portuguese art, the centre has numerous works by modern artists from other countries. Adjoining the museum are a sculpture park, a multi-purpose hall, and studios (opening times as for Museu Calouste Gulbenkian).

Campo Grande

The Campo Grande park begins about 1km/0.6mi north-east of the Gulbenkian Foundation, and is around 1.2km/0.7mi long and 200m/220yd wide. There is a small lake with rowing-boats for hire, and a pleasantly situated café.

Cidade Universitária

West of the Campo Grande are university buildings. The university itself was founded in 1911. The Cidade Universitária was built here between 1955 and 1960. An imposing modern building houses the national archive, Torre do Tombo. The oldest of its holdings is a document dating from 882.

Museu da Cidade

At the northern end of the Campo Grande is the city museum, which provides a good historical overview of Lisbon's development. It is located in the Palácio Pimenta, given long ago as a gift by João V to his mistress. Of particular note is a model of Lisbon, true to scale, which shows the city before the earthquake of 1755 (open: Tue–Sun 10am–1pm and 2pm–6pm).

Museu Rafael Bordalo Pinheiro

The Museu Rafael Bordalo Pinheiro is opposite the Museu da Cidade. It is dedicated to the artist Rafael Bordalo Pinheiro (1846–1905), who made his name with ceramics and caricatures (open: Tue–Sun 10am–1pm and 2pm–6pm).

Museu Nacional do Traje

The traditional costume museum is worth a visit. It is situated north of the Campo Grande, in the Lumiar area of the city (Estrada do Lumiar 12), and is housed in the Palácio do Monteiro-Mor, surrounded by an extensive park. Costumes from different eras are displayed in appropriate settings (open: Tue–Sun 10am–6pm).

Museu Nacional do Teatro

The theatre museum is also in the Parque do Monteiro-Mor (Estrada do Lumiar 10). Theatrical costumes, scenery, tickets, and many other items, tell the story of theatre (open: Tue 2pm–6pm, Wed–Sun ☉ 10am–6pm).

The Amoreiras Shopping Centre in the north-west of the inner city **Amoreiras** was built in the early 1980s. The initially very controversial design **Shopping Centre** was by Tomás Taveira. In the coloured high-rise towers are apartments, offices and gallery-shops (open: daily 10am–midnight).   ☉

Since 1997 the Amoreiras Shopping Centre has had competition in **Centro Colombo** the form of the Centro Colombo, situated close to the metro station Colégio Militar. The Centro Colombo has 420 shops spread over three floors; in addition, there is a gigantic amusement arcade (open: daily 10am–midnight).

About halfway between the Amoreiras Shopping Centre and the **Jardim Zoológico** Centro Colombo is the zoological garden. It was founded in 1884, and had to relocate twice before moving here in 1905 (open: daily 10am–8pm in summer, 10am–6pm in winter).

Going West from the Centre

West of the Praça do Comércio is the Praça do Município (city hall **Praça do** square). Because of the 18th-century pillory in the middle, it is also **Município** called the Largo do Pelourinho. The city hall on the east side of the square was built in the years 1865–1880.

The Estação do Cais do Sodré, the station for trains in the Cascais di- **Cais do Sodré** rection and the point of departure for ferries, is located west of the Praça do Município. Opposite is the market hall. The wide Avenida 24 de Julho extends along the river to the Museu Nacional de Arte Antiga.

The palace built by Count Alvor in 1690 has been home to the Na- **★ ★** tional Museum of Ancient Art since 1884. An occasional sobriquet is **Museu Nacional** »Casa das Janelas Verdes« (house of green windows), because it used **de Arte Antiga** to have green shutters. The original palace was altered several times, and eventually a new extension was added. A small chapel that belonged to the Carmelite monastery of St Albert, founded in 1584, was in the way, and was integrated into the new buildings. The museum has a **collection** of Egyptian, Greek and Roman sculpture, ceramics, and porcelain, as well as outstanding artefacts in silver and gold. Ecclesiastical vestments, Portuguese furniture, carpets, tapestries, Indo-Portuguese arts and crafts, and Namban art are also represented. The collection of **European painting** from the 14th–19th centuries includes numerous masterpieces: among them are works by Hans Memling (*Virgin and Child*), Piero della Francesca (*St Augustine*), Dürer (*St Jerome*), Cranach (*Salome*), Holbein the older (*Virgin with Child and Saint*), Bassano (*Virgin and Child*), Pieter

Brueghel the younger (*The Boy*), Velázquez, van Dyck, Reynolds, Hoppner and Romney. The **altarpiece *Temptation of St Anthony* by Hieronymus Bosch** is one of the museum's most precious works. It is sensibly displayed in a way that makes it possible to see the black-and-white Golgotha scenes on the reverse as well.

Museu Nacional de Arte Antiga Plan

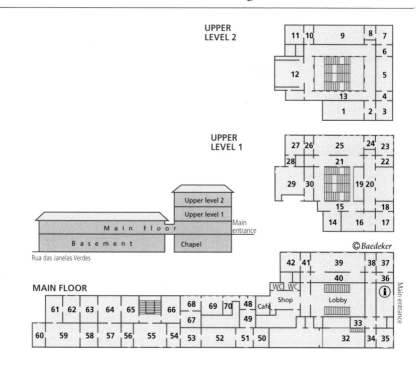

© Baedeker

Rua das Janelas Verdes

1-11 Portuguese painting (15th–19th century)	**22** Portuguese porcelain (19th c.)	**33-35** Textiles
12/13 Sculpture (16th–19th c.)	**23-25** Portuguese ceramics (17th–19th century)	**36-42** Furniture (15th–19th c.)
14-19 Oriental art	**26-30** Gold- and silversmithery (12th–19th century)	**48** Sculpture
20/21 Chinese porcelain (12th–19th century)	**32** St Albert's Chapel	**49-70** European painting (14th–19th century), applied art (17th–19th century)

BASEMENT

The most significant of the Portuguese paintings is undoubtedly the **St Vincent altar polyptychon**, found in the São Vicente de Fora monastery and restored in 1910. The origin of the ***Veneration of St Vincent*** (Veneração a São Vicente) is still unclear. Neither the precise date nor the artist could be identified with certainty to date; but it is widely assumed that Nuno Gonçalves, court painter (1450–1467) under Afonso V, painted the 6-part altarpiece. The work is regarded as an important testimony to cultural history, since it portrays several prominent 15th-century personalities. Yet art historians sometimes also disagree as to the identity of those portrayed (open: Tue 2pm–6pm, Wed–Sun 10am–6pm).

Around 1km/0.6mi north-west of the National Museum of Ancient Art is the Palácio das Necessidades, built during the years 1743–1750 on the site of the Ermida Nossa Senhora das Necessidades. It was a royal residence until 1910, and now houses the foreign ministry. Around the palace is a pleasant little park, Tapada das Necessidades.

Palácio das Necessidades

Further west, the street passes along the river under the Ponte 25 de Abril. A slip-road that rests on massive pillars, and is 945m/1040yd long, takes the traffic up to the Tagus bridge (a toll bridge). This suspension bridge was opened in 1966, and named at the time »Ponte de Salazar«; it is 2,277m/2,500yd long, the deck is 70m/230ft above water level, the two pillars are 190.5m/360ft high, and the span width is 1,013m/1,115yd.

★
Ponte 25 de Abril

In Rua 1° do Maio (Santo Amaro area), beneath the Ponte 25 de Abril, is the tram museum with exhibits recalling the history of the popular »eléctricos« (open: Mon–Sat 10am–1pm and 2pm–5pm).

Museu da Carris

On the edge of Belém, right on the riverside, stands the electricity museum. It is located in the red-and-white headquarters of the power station, the »Central Tejo«.

Museu da Electricidade

Belém

Situated directly on the banks of the Tagus on the western edge of Lisbon, Belém's historic buildings document the most important epoch of Portuguese history. It was in the monastery here that the Portuguese application to EU membership was signed. The name »Belém« is short for »Bethlehem«; this kind of short form is typical of the Portuguese language. The town's significance originated in the former harbour of Restelo, which was the Portuguese seafarers' **point of departure for voyages of discovery**. Here, too, they disembarked at the end of their journeys, with their booty gained in distant lands. Belém was independent until 1885, and was largely untouched by the earthquake of 1755, so its historic buildings are some of the oldest in the Portuguese capital.

Brimming with history

Praça do Império

A good starting-point for a walk around Belém is the Mosteiro dos Jerónimos on the Praça do Império. From here a mini-railway also goes to Belém's most important sights. The »imperial square« was created for the **world exhibition of 1940**. It consists of a small park with neatly clipped hedges which represent Portugal's various city emblems. The fountain is also decorated with coats of arms; on special occasions it is turned on, and illuminated in colour.

✶ ✶
Mosteiro dos Jerónimos

The world-famous former Hieronymite Monastery on the north side of the Praça do Império is of unparalleled splendour. The Mosteiro dos Jerónimos de Belém is considered to be the most important example of Manueline architecture and the most impressive **symbol of Portugal's colonial power and wealth**.

The founding of the monastery is attributed to Henry the Navigator, who had a place of prayer for seafarers built here, close to the harbour of Restelo which was the point of embarkation for the great voyages of discovery. He entrusted it to the Order of the Knights of Christ. Tradition has it that in 1497 **Vasco da Gama** spent the nights before his departure for India praying in this chapel; here, too, the king received him with honours on his return. In gratitude for the glorious voyage of discovery, Manuel I had the monastery built in 1502 on the site of the small house of prayer, from plans drawn up by master builder Boytaca, who had also played a crucial part in the extension of the Abbey of ▶Batalha. Details were completed between 1517 and 1522 under the supervision of João de Castilho, who also created the cloisters. After the dissolution of the monastery in 1834, the orphanage »Casa Pia« was moved here. At the south-east corner stands the **church of Santa Maria** with a nave, two aisles and a beau-

Belém Plan

tiful south facing façade. The south entrance by João de Castilho is impressive, as is the west entrance by Nicolas Chanterène. The high Renaissance choir was added in 1571/1572. The spacious **interior of the church**, with wonderful reticulated vaulting, has the most imposing dimensions: it is 92m/300ft long, 22.6m/75ft wide, and 25m/82ft high. The octagonal columns are richly ornamented with relief work. In the transept and choir apse are the graves of Manuel I and his successors and relatives, borne by elephants – all in all, five kings, seven queens and 19 infantas of the house of Aviz. Beneath the organ loft are the **sarcophagus of Vasco da Gama** (► Famous People) and the **cenotaph for Luís de Camões** (► Famous People). In the high choir (access to the cloisters) there is an impressive Renaissance stall from 1560.

Adjoining the monastery church are the **cloisters**. This two-storey architectural masterpiece by João de Castilho is constructed on a square floor plan, each side 55m/180ft long. A lion fountain, which once adorned a small island in a central pool, is now in the north-west corner of the cloisters. From this point there is access to the former refectory, with beautiful 17th-century reticulated vaulting and decorative wall tiles. On the north-east side of the cloisters is the former chapter house; those buried here include the poet and historian Alexandre Herculano (1810–1877). In the middle of the north cloister arcade a tombstone was erected in 1985 for Fernando Pessoa (► Famous People; open: Tue–Sun 10am–5pm, in summer until 6.30pm).

In the southern wing of the monastery, never completed, is the former dormitorium; today it houses the National Museum of Archaeology. Themed temporary exhibitions focus largely on metalwork products, agriculture and fishing. Of exceptional interest are a separate display of jewellery and a collection of Egyptian exhibits (open: Tue 2pm–6pm, Wed–Sun 10am–6pm).

Museu Nacional de Arqueologia

The marine museum is in the monastery's west wing. Here, and further west in the new building opposite, a series of marine models tells the story of Portuguese navigation. Two grandiose 18th-century ships are particularly impressive (open: Tue–Sun 10am–5pm, in summer until 6pm).

Museu da Marinha

Between the west wing of the monastery and the marine museum's new building is the Planetário Calouste Gulbenkian, built in 1965.

Planetarium

On the west side of the Praça do Império is the Centro Cultural, which was opened in 1993. It has a conference centre and two concert or performance halls, one with 400 and the other with 1500 seats. Most of the centre's space is used for art exhibitions. There is a rewarding **Museu do Design**, which provides an overview of design products from 1937 onwards (open: daily 10am–6.15pm).

Centro Cultural de Belém

Praça de Afonso de Albuquerque

★ ★

East of the Jerónimo Monastery lies the Praça de Afonso de Albuquerque, with the memorial to Afonso de Albuquerque (1450–1515), viceroy of the Portuguese Indies.

Palácio de Belém

On the north side of the square stands the former royal palace, built by Count Aveiro in 1700. Today it is the residence of the president of the republic.

Museu Nacional dos Coches

★

The carriage museum is located on the ground floor of the east wing, in the former riding hall which was added in 1726. This is one of the best and most comprehensive museums of its kind, with around 60 gala carriages and state coaches from the 17th to 19th centuries (open: Tue–Sun 10am–6pm).

Padrão dos Descobrimentos

South of the Praça do Império, on the Tagus riverbank, stands the huge Padrão dos Descobrimentos (Monument of the Discoveries). It was unveiled in 1960, on the occasion of the 500th anniversary of the death of Henry the Navigator. The monument is 54m/180ft high, and has the **shape of a ship's bow**. It commemorates the Portuguese explorers of the 15th century. First among the personalities in the bow is **Henry the Navigator**, who carries a model ship in his hands. Inside the monument there is a conference room, and several smaller rooms for temporary exhibitions. There is a lift to the viewing platform (temporarily closed). On the ground in front of the Padrão dos Descobrimentos is a large mosaic compass and map of the world.

Museu de Arte Popular

West of the Monument of the Discoveries stands the Museu de Arte Popular, a good collection of Portuguese popular art organized according to province. It includes costumes, furniture and ceramics (open: Tue–Sun 10am–12.30pm and 2pm–5pm).

Torre de Belém

★ ★

Around 500m/550yd further west, on the Tagus, stands the Torre de Belém. The tower was built at the entrance to the Tagus in pure Manueline style during the years 1515–1521, in order to protect the harbour of Restelo. It originally stood on an island in the river, but the river changed its course over the years and now it stands on a spit of land. In 1983 it was **designated a World Heritage Site by UNESCO**. For a long time the Torre de Belém was a state prison. After the capture of Lisbon in 1807, French troops destroyed the two upper storeys, but in 1845 the tower was restored to its original dimensions. Between the tower and the Tagus is a bastion with embrasures. Here, there were storerooms below water level for food and ammunition. Inside the tower, one above the other, are the Governor's Hall, the King's Hall, and the Audience Hall; at the very top there was once a small chapel. From the tower platform there is a good view of Belém and the Tagus(open: Tue–Sun 10am–5pm, May–Sept until 6.30pm).

Could almost be from »The Arabian Nights«: Torre de Belém, the emblem of Lisbon

East of the Palácio de Belém, the Calçada da Ajuda passes the botanical garden of Ajuda, in which there is a dragon tree (»dracaena draco«) dating from 1598. Another 1km/0.6mi further on, up above Belém, stands the massive Palácio Nacional da Ajuda. Construction of this former royal palace started in 1802, but has never been entirely completed. The building now houses the office for the protection of monuments and historic buildings.

Palácio Nacional da Ajuda

The ethnology museum is found about 600m/660yd west of the Palácio Nacional da Ajuda in Avenida Ilha da Madeira. Although the museum was only opened in 1985, space constraints make it impossible to display more than a selection of the most important exhibits at any one time; in consequence, temporary exhibitions are organized under various themes (open: Tue 2pm–6pm, Wed–Sun 10am–6pm). ⊙

Museu de Etnologia

In the western suburb of Algés, the Aquário Vasco da Gama exhibits the oceanographic collection of King Carlos I, and also numerous fish species from the Portuguese coastal waters and former overseas territories (open: daily 10am–6pm). ⊙

Aquário Vasco da Gama

Built from 1728–1748, the Aqueduto das Águas Livres runs through the north-west of the Monsanto park. This aqueduct is 18km/11mi long, and crosses the Alcântara valley with arches up to 65m/215ft high. Until 1880 most of the city's water supply came via the aqueduct. Increasing demand for water meant that a new supply system was built, although the aqueduct could still be viable today.

Aqueduto das Águas Livres

One of the recurring motifs of Manueline ornamentation: the cross of the Order of the Knights of Christ

MANUELINIC: BUILDING STYLE OR DECORATION?

Art historians argue about whether Manuelinic architecture, named after Manuel I (1495–1521), counts as its own building style or whether it is just a form of decoration marking the transition from Gothic to Renaissance. Whatever the case, the style definitely reflects a new attitude of mind.

After a visit to the Hieronymite monastery, Prince Felix Lichnowsky wrote in his *Recollections from the Year 1842*: »The monastery is built in half Moorish-Byzantine, half Norman-Gothic style; a confusing mixture from which here and there, as if triumphing over all the other apposing elements, some piece of the named architectural styles stands out in its original purity.«

Architectural novelty

Many years later the German writer Karl August Varnhagen von Ense (1785–1858) coined the term which is still valid for this style today: »arte manuelina«, Manueline style – named after Manuel I, during whose rule from 1495 until 1521 building work flourished. Nearly every Portugal travel guide speaks of Manuelinic as Portugal's own style, but the academics treat the term with scepticism. Many art historians take the view that the style is not actually original but **merely a decoration** that marks the transition from Gothic to Renaissance in Portugal. This argument is not to be rejected out of hand: the plain and monumental basic structure of the buildings is in keeping with late-Gothic architecture as was usual in many places in Europe at that time; and on the arcades, balconies, canopies, towers and columns influences from the early Renaissance, the Moorish Mudejar style and the oriental-Indian world are recognizable.

But it is clearly the **ornamentation** that dominates the picture in Manueline buildings. Decorating single building elements so abundantly that the construction almost became almost invisible was **a novelty in European architecture**. Oriental art, too, did not yet feature the exotic and ocean motifs carved into stone with much attention to detail: sea creatures, such as octopuses, starfish, corals and mussels; nautical instruments, like armillary spheres and wind roses; ship's equipment, such as anchors, nets, knotted and twisted ropes;

Completely new for the Portuguese: a stranger who nourishes himself from the fruits of nature. Decoration in the cloister of the Hieronymite Monastery

blooms, leaves and plants from the tropics; the cross of the Order of the Knights of Christ, the symbol of the Portuguese discoverers, the crown, and the »M« for Manuel; as well as mythical creatures and sea monsters – details that all tell of Portugal's time of greatness, and of the discoveries and conquests overseas which bestowed upon the country a short economic and cultural flowering.

Royal passion

King Manuel the Fortunate, as he was also known, was a **squanderer** par excellence. The riches that came to him thanks to the overseas conquests allowed him, his entire court and the upper echelons of society to live in consummate luxury while the rest of the people starved. The king displayed an extravagance that was unparalleled – when he went out riding for example, he was escorted by elephants, hippopotamuses and other exotic creatures that Indian and African rulers had given him.

But Manuel was also an art lover, and a large part of the state budget was spent on his own special passion: the construction of churches, monasteries, convents, palaces and castles. The stories of seafarers – their experiences, dreams, fears and fantasies – were picked up on by master builders and sculptors who transformed them into stone, in the course of which the European building forms that they had learned mixed with decorative forms from other cultures. This is beautifully illustrated on the Torre de Belém at the mouth of the Tagus, which with its flat domes and fine loggias seems almost Arabic-Moorish. Only rarely are the named buildings wholly Manueline; much more often the style is expressed in the details.

The **heyday of the Manuelinic** lasted only a few decades – from 1490 to 1540. The most important master builders of this era were Diogo de Boytaca, Diogo de Arruda, Francisco de Arruda and João de Castilho. By the reign of João III, the successor of Manuel I, the Renaissance had replaced the Manueline style. Whether it can be viewed as a original Portuguese style or not, one thing is certain: the new attitude of mind of a nation was carved in stone; a nation that for a short time between 1495 and 1521 rose to be the most powerful country of the Occident and which – spurred on by success and optimism – set out continually to discover, conquer and eventually colonize new worlds.

Expo-Urbe in the East

Expo-site, Expo-Urbe

Expo 98, the last world fair of the 20th century, was held in Lisbon in the summer of 1998; its theme was »The Oceans – a Heritage for the Future?«. In five pavilions the oceans, their history, the dangers to them, their possible uses and their future were highlighted.

At an early stage, planners started to think about what to do with the site once the world fair was over. In fact the 70ha/175ac space is part of a riverside district totalling around 330ha/825ac, on which a whole new city area is developing, the »Expo-Urbe«. Back in 1993 there were oil refineries here, along with rough accommodation blocks, disused quays, and wastelands full of weeds. The **Doca dos Olivais**, the central harbour, and a refinery tower which has been converted into an observation tower, the **Torre Vasco da Gama**, still testify to the area's one-time usage as a petroleum harbour. The Expo-Urbe development plan foresees up to 2010 dwellings for 25,000 residents, and space for 18,000 workplaces, covering an area around 5km/3mi long and 800m/880yd wide. There will be schools, kindergarten facilities, and a hospital. At the heart of the new city area will be the **park of the nations** (Parque das Nações), the Expo 98 site. The halls on the northern part of the Expo site are now used for trade fairs,

A few exhibition pavilions still stand on the Expo '98 site, including the Pavilhão Atlântico, which is now a multi-event venue.

or the **Pavilhão Atlântico**, are available for exhibitions or events. One of the site's main attractions is the Tagus promenade with the **Teleférico Lisboa**, a cable car that starts from the Torre Vasco da Gama and runs parallel to the riverbank, hovering over the water (cable car opening hours: Mon–Fri 11am–8pm, Sat– Sun 10am–9pm, in winter until 7pm or 8pm).

The enormous aquarium, designed for Expo 98 by American Peter Chermayeff, consists of a central pool with four smaller pools around it. Flora and fauna from the Atlantic, Pacific and Indian Oceans, as well as from the Antarctic, are on view. Altogether there are 15,000 fish, birds and mammals in the Oceanário (open: daily 10am–8pm, in winteruntil 7pm; last admission 1hr before closing time).

✷ Oceanário

The east station was designed by Spaniard Santiago Calatravas; well illuminated, it conveys an overall feeling of lightness. The station was constructed close to the world fair site as part of the preparations for Expo 98, and functions as the main intersection point for rail, bus and underground (metro). It is linked to the former Expo site by the **Vasco da Gama shopping centre**.

Estação Oriente

The Ponte Vasco da Gama arches up from the northern edge of the former Expo site in an easterly direction. Six lanes carry around 90 million vehicles across to Alcochete every year. Its length of 17km/ 10.2mi makes it one of the longest bridges in Europe.

Ponte Vasco da Gama

Benfica

In recent decades, rapid expansion has affected the once-elegant suburb of Benfica on the north-west edge of the Portuguese capital. High-rise buildings and shopping centres now dominate the scene, rather than the villas of former times.

Benfica is famous in Portugal and beyond as home to **Benfica Lisbon football club**, a team steeped in tradition. Its new stadium on Avenida General Norton de Matos was completed in 2003.

Estádio do Benfica

On the Largo de São Domingos stands the church of the Dominican monastery; the monastery was founded in 1399 and renovated in 1755. The azulejo paintings in the interior of the church are by António de Oliveira. Take a look at the elegant marble work in the Capela de São Gonçalo.

Igreja São Domingos

Not far from the church is the Palácio dos Marqueses de Fronteira, a lordly 17th-century mansion. In the splendid gardens is a large pool surrounded by blind arcades, which are decorated with wonderful azulejo pictures. The Palácio is in private ownership, but there are

✷ Palácio dos Marqueses de Fronteira

⊙ tours of both house and gardens (tours: Mon–Sat 10.30am, 11am, 11.30am, 12 noon; Oct–May 11am, 12 noon; up-to-date information from Lisbon »turismo«, or by telephone: 217 782 023).

Around Lisbon

Tagus south bank The town of Almada is situated on the south bank of the Tagus, opposite Lisbon. On a promontory down below is the little port of **Cacilhas**, served by ferries from Lisbon. It is a popular destination, especially because of its fish restaurants; it also provides an excellent view of Lisbon on the north bank of the Tagus.

Clearly visible from the centre of Lisbon, the towering **Monumento Cristo Rei** stands on the south bank of the Tagus. Erected in 1959, it has a plinth 82m/270ft high, in which there is a chapel; it is crowned by a ferro-concrete statue of Christ, 28m/93ft high. Take the lift to the platform for a marvellous view (open: daily 9.30am to 6pm).

> ### ! Baedeker TIP
>
> **Walk along the water**
> Need a rest from the city? Enjoy an easy and rewarding walk from Estoril to Cascais along the waterfront. Take the suburban train from Cais de Sodré in the direction of Cascais; get out at Estoril station, by the river; a pedestrian underpass leads to the esplanade, which has a good surface to walk on, and runs all the way to Cascais.

Destinations around Lisbon Further destinations south of the Tagus worth a visit are ►Costa de Lisboa, with the coastal resort Costa da Caparica; the Serra da Arrábida (►Costa de Lisboa); and the small towns of ►Setúbal and ►Sesimbra.

From Lisbon city centre it is a relatively quick trip on the suburban train to the ►Costa do Sol, west of the city, with the popular resorts of ►Estoril and ►Cascais.

►Sintra is definitely worth seeing, as are the palace of ►Queluz and the monastery palace of ►Mafra.

Loulé

K 34

| **Historical province:** Algarve | **Altitude:** 170m/560ft |
| **District:** Faro | **Population:** 10,000 |

Loulé – a busy centre in the Algarve hinterland – is an attractive little town, with almost metropolitan avenues and squares and a pretty historic centre full of nooks and crannies. At times the smart, whitewashed houses make the old parts of the town look like stage-sets.

▶ VISITING LOULÉ

INFORMATION
Av. 25 de Abril, 9
8100-506 Loulé
Tel. 289 463 900
www.turismodoalgarve.pt

SHOPPING
Market
Saturday is market-day, 9am–1pm;
kitsch and bric-a-brac are on sale, but
also nice ceramics, textiles, leather
goods and souvenirs.

Workshops
Metalwork, pottery and leather
workshops can still be found on Rua 9
de Abril and Rua da Barbaça, between
Praça Afonso III and Largo Bernardo
Lopes.

WHERE TO EAT
▶ Moderate
Avenida Velha
Avenida José C. Mealha 13
Tel. 289 416 474
Friendly service, good Portuguese
cuisine.

Bica Velha
Rua Martim Moniz 17
Tel. 289 463 376
Upmarket; rustic decor.

WHERE TO STAY
▶ Mid-range/Budget

Baedeker recommendation

Hotel Loulé Jardim
Praça Manuel de Arriaga
8100-665 Loulé
Tel. 289 413 094
Fax 289 463 177
www.sdias.pt/jardim
Very pleasant hotel with 52 rooms in a
lovely old town house.

▶ Budget
Pensão Dom Payo
Rua Dr. F. Sá Carneiro
8100-578 Loulé
Tel. 289 414 422
Fax 289 416 453
Well-kept guesthouse, modern fittings
and furniture, with 26 rooms.

Casa Beny
Rua São Domingos 13
Tel. 289 417 702
Private rooms, well kept with nice
fittings and furniture, bath and TV,
central location.

The small town is 15km/9mi north-west of Faro, in the so-called
Barrocal, the foothill region of the Algarve mountains. It nestles in
hilly, country-garden landscape, with many fig, almond, olive and
fruit-trees. In spring the meadows are full of poppies. The region's
natural beauty has led both Portuguese and foreigners to build weekend or holiday houses here. This means that in recent decades the region, long untouched, has seen increasing development.
A well-known market is held every Saturday, with booths around the
market halls in the centre; this draws people from a great distance.

Carnival, almond blossom festival

Loulé is especially worth visiting at carnival time, when the place is transformed into colourful confusion – the little town is famous throughout Portugal for its elaborate carnival ceremonies. The almond blossom festival is celebrated at the same time; the carnival floats are covered over and over with paper almond blossom.

What to See in Loulé

Castelo

The ancient castle probably goes back to the Moors. Only a few sections of castle wall remain, marking the centre of the earlier settlement. Next to the tourist information office, stone steps lead up to the remaining walls. In a room beside the steps, a traditional Algarve kitchen is displayed with various pieces of equipment. In the **Museu de Arqueologia** in the same buildings, archaeological finds from Silves and the surrounding area are exhibited (open: Mon–Fri 9am–5.30pm, Sat from 10am).

Ermida de Nossa Senhora da Conceição

Opposite the monastery is the plain façade of the Ermida de Nossa Senhora da Conceição. This chapel was built in the mid-17th century in gratitude for the restoration of independence from Spain.

Convento do Espírito Santo

Today the tastefully restored Convento do Espírito Santo houses a municipal gallery. The monastery was founded in the late 17th century, partially destroyed by the earthquake of 1755, and dissolved in 1836. The gallery often shows very interesting modern art by Portuguese artists.

Igreja Matriz de São Clemente

Loulé's main church is in the historic centre, between the Largo da Silva and the Largo da Matriz. Its origins go back to the second half of the 13th century.

Around Loulé

Capela de Nossa Senhora da Piedade

2km/1.2mi west of Loulé, above the road to Boliqueime, is the 16th-century Capela de Nossa Senhora da Piedade. A pilgrim route goes up the hill. From in front of the church there is an excellent view of the hilly Algarve landscape to the north, and of a great expanse of sea to the south. Beside the old chapel is a modern church with cupola, in which pilgrim Masses are celebrated.

✱ Alte

In the midst of relatively unspoilt, hilly countryside lies the truly pretty village of Alte, around 25km/15mi north-west of Loulé. This picturesque place attracts increasing numbers of tourists. Alte's location is enchanting, as is the village itself, with its small whitewashed houses, narrow streets and flower gardens.

Salir

Almost as pretty as Alte, and much less busy, is the village of Salir, 15km/9mi to the east, stretching over two small hills. On the western one, there are traces of a Moorish castle. The vicinity of the castle with its tiny white houses and abundance of flowers is really idyllic. Most of the village is situated on the second hill, topped by a water-tower and the simple village church.

★ ★ # Mafra

B/C 23

Historical province: Estremadura
District: Lisbon

Altitude: 237m/780ft
Population: 13,500

Approximately 30km/18mi north-west of Lisbon lies Mafra – famous far and wide for its enormous National Palace, the most extensive architectural complex of its sort on the Iberian Peninsula.

Mafra is in itself a simple little town; the enormous monastery palace dominates its centre. The carefully restored Gothic church of Santo André is also worth visiting; it dates from the 13th/14th century, and contains the sarcophagi of Dom Diogo de Sousa and his wife.

King José I founded the »Mafra School« in the town. It is a **sculpture school** of national importance whose teachers have included José Almeida and Joaquim Machado de Castro.

Mafra School

★ ★ # Palácio Nacional de Mafra

Mafra's monastery palace is often compared to the Escorial in Madrid, but was intended by its founder to outdo the Escorial in size and splendour. The dimensions abound in superlatives: the palace is laid out on a largely symmetrical ground plan that almost forms a square, 251m/825ft long and 221m/730ft wide; the total space is 40,000 sq m/440,000 sq ft; there are 900 rooms, said to have a total of 4,500 windows and doors. The series of rooms on the first floor of the west side extends without interruption for 250m/825ft. 300 monks and 150 nuns inhabited the monastery.

Architectural superlatives

More than any other building in Portugal, the Mafra palace represents cool Baroque splendour; it epitomizes extravagance and the demonstration of absolute power.
Ownership of the **goldmines in Brazil** provided the necessary funds. The basilica is open to visitors, and there are tours of some parts of the royal palace and monastery (open: basilica, daily 10am to 13pm and 2pm–5pm; and the monastery-palace Wed–Mon 10am to 5pm).

▶ MAFRA

INFORMATION
Palácio Nacional de Mafra
2640-492 Mafra
Tel. 261 817 170
www.cm-mafra.pt

Mafra's Palácio Nacional was founded by João V and his wife Maria **History**
Anna of Austria in fulfilment of a pledge made in 1711, and in
thanksgiving for the birth in 1717 of an heir to the throne, later King
José I. It was built by Regensburg architect **Johann Friedrich Ludwig**
(trained in Rome, and known in Portugal as Frederico Ludovice),
and by his son, Johann Peter Ludwig. More than 45,000 people
worked on the building; some were forced labourers, watched over
by soldiers. The monastery was
dedicated after a mere 13 years of
building, in 1730; the complex was
extended considerably during the
subsequent 20 years.

The monastery was occupied first
by Franciscans, and then, at certain
periods, by Augustinians. It was
closed in 1834, when all the religious orders were dissolved; some
of the accommodation was assigned to the military.

! **Baedeker TIP**

Memorial do Convento
The ambitious building project of the Mafra
monastery palace is described in José Saramago's novel *Memorial do Convento* (English
translation *Baltasar and Blimunda*, Jonathan
Cape, 1988).

The royal quarters were hardly ever used as such. King João V and
Maria Anna of Austria only ever spent a few days here. At the beginning of the 19th century there was a brief period of brilliance: João
VI resided in Mafra in 1806/1807. When French troops drew near,
however, the royal family hastily abandoned the palace, and moved
to Lisbon, and later to Brazil; most of the valuable furnishings and
works of art went with them. Nor did later rulers spend much time
here; when they did pay brief visits, it was usually in order to hunt
in the vicinity.

The basilica occupies the central space of the severe, scarcely orna- **Basilica**
mented main front of the building. Its façade is flanked by two bell-
towers, 68m/225ft high, from which there is an almost seamless transition to the palace frontage. The carillon of 114 bells was created by
the bell-founder Lavache of Antwerp.

In the **vestibule** stand 14 large statues of saints in Carrara marble, by
the Italian Alexandre Giusti. The limestone **interior** of the basilica
has no aisles. The ground plan of the church is in the form of a Latin
cross. The total length is 58.5m/190ft; the widest point, at the intersection, is 43m/140ft. It took two years to construct the intersection
cupola, with a height of 65m/215ft, 13m/42ft diameter, and the 2m/
6.6ft-wide lantern. The interior has a coffered barrel-vault ceiling;
the 62 fluted columns give a sense of structural clarity. Different
sorts of marble in pink, white, black, grey, blue and yellow are combined into a geometrical pattern. Echoes of German Baroque and
Italian classicism are evident; Johann Friedrich Ludwig is said to
have been influenced by St Peter's Basilica in the Vatican, and by the

← *The monastery palace that breaks all the records*

Palácio Nacional de Mafra Plan

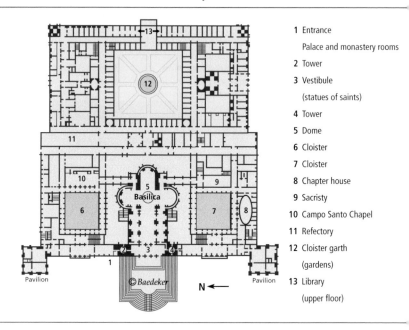

1 Entrance
  Palace and monastery rooms
2 Tower
3 Vestibule
  (statues of saints)
4 Tower
5 Dome
6 Cloister
7 Cloister
8 Chapter house
9 Sacristy
10 Campo Santo Chapel
11 Refectory
12 Cloister garth
   (gardens)
13 Library
   (upper floor)

© Baedeker N ←

Pavilion Pavilion

Church of Jesus in Rome. A striking feature is the six **organs**, commissioned by João V in the years 1792–1807 from plans by organ builders Joaquim António Peres Fontanes and António Xavier Machado.

The basilica has eleven **chapels**. Oil paintings by Portuguese and Italian painters hung in the church until the 18th century; they were damaged by high humidity to such an extent that they had to be replaced by bas-relief works in Carrara marble. The reliefs were created by artists from the school of sculpture, and are still in place. The altar paintings in the large chapels at the intersection are collaborative works by Alexandre Giusti and his pupil Machado de Castro. The marble statues in the side-chapels are of various saints; they were made in Italy and then transported to Mafra. With the statues on the façade and in the entrance, they constitute Portugal's most important collection of Italian sculpture.

Monastery building, royal apartments

The tour of the palace takes in some parts of the monastery building and the royal apartments. There is a stark contrast between the spartan monastery cells and exquisitely furnished royal living quarters which are in close juxtaposition. On the monastery side it is possible to see an old pharmacy and kitchen, as well as the hospital, with cells for the sick. The hard wooden bed-boards are curved in the middle, in order to ease pressure on the sick person's spine. Artefacts and furnishing in the royal apartments date from the 18th and 19th centuries. One suite of rooms includes several bedrooms, the throne room, the Hall of Discoveries, the music room and a drolly furnished hunt room. The games room has **two antique billiard-tables** and **predecessors of modern-day gaming machines**. In the vestibule is a bust of the founder of the palace, João V, with a laurel wreath.

In the east wing of the palace is the 88m/290ft-long royal-monastic library. It contains approximately 40,000 volumes, including numerous incunabula and manuscripts. Among the most valuable items are **first editions of Camões'** *Lusíadas*, the plays of Gil Vicente, a trilingual Bible of 1514, and the earliest edition of Homer in Greek. **Library**

Beyond the palace is the Tapada de Mafra, a game park enclosed by a 20km/12mi-long wall – the ruling family's hunting grounds until the early 20th century. **Tapada de Mafra**

★ ★ Marvão

O 20

Historical province: Alto Alentejo
District: Portalegre

Altitude: 862m/2,850ft
Population: 500

Thanks to its authentically medieval appearance, Marvão attracts a great number of visitors. Its castle high up on the Serra de São Mamede offers a fine view right into Spain.

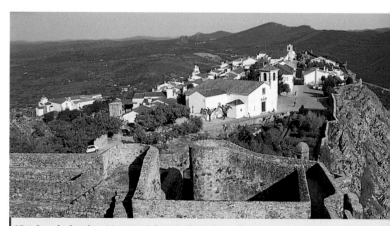

View from the fort above Marvão and the Serra de São Marmede

▶ VISITING MARVÃO

INFORMATION
Largo de Santa Maria
7330-101 Marvão
Tel. 245 993 886
www.rtsm.pt

WHERE TO EAT
▶ Moderate
Pousada de Santa Maria
Tel. 245 993 201
Traditional food and a panoramic view
of the mountains.

Albergaria El-Rei D. Manuel
Largo do Terreiro
Tel. 245 909 150
Regional dishes served in very pleasant
ambience.

WHERE TO STAY
▶ Mid-range
Pousada de Santa Maria
7330-122 Marvão
Tel. 245 993 201
Fax 245 993 440
The pousada is situated inside the old
town walls of Marvão. It has 28 rooms,
with a splendid panoramic view of the
village and surroundings.

▶ Budget
Albergaria El-Rei D. Manuel
Largo do Terreiro
7330-104 Marvão
Tel. 245 909 150
Fax 245 909 159
www.turismarvao.pt
Pleasant accommodation in a typical
mountain village house.

Pensão-Residencial Casa D. Dinis
Rua Dr Matos Magalhães
7330-121 Marvão
Tel. 245 993 957
Fax 245 993 959
Simple, well-run guesthouse in the
centre of Marvão.

In Roman times this little place was called Herminio Minor. King
Dinis had it strongly fortified because of its strategic position close
to the Spanish border. During the civil war in 1833 it was an important Liberal base.

★★
**Picture-book
medieval village**

The village lies on a steep slope of the Serra de São Mamede, and is
still entirely enclosed by its medieval walls. The steep, narrow streets
are paved with flagstones, and some are spanned by arches. Some of
the houses are covered in flowers, and some have lovely 17th-century
cast-iron lattice-work.

The way to the castle weaves up through the little streets. The village
has been restored, on the whole successfully, in order to establish a
moderate amount of tourism. There was a serious risk of obsoles-
cence, and there are few job opportunities in the area.

What to See in Marvão

The castle towers above the village. It was founded in the 13th century, and extended in the 15th and 17th centuries. Several circular walls surround the keep. A beautiful little garden has been planted up on this windy spot, and is lovingly looked after.

Castelo

Just outside the town lay the monastery of Nossa Senhora da Estrela, dating from the 15th century; today the premises are occupied by a hospital. The monastery church has a Gothic doorway.

Convento de Nossa Senhora da Estrela

A stay in Marvão may well be combined with a visit to ►Castelo de Vide and ►Portalegre.

Around Marvão

✷ Mértola

N 31

Historical province: Baixo Alentejo
District: Beja

Altitude: 85m/276ft
Population: 7,000

Mértola stretches in picturesque fashion up the right bank of the Guadiana. Its narrow winding streets give it an almost Moorish feel.

This pretty little town lies 50km/30mi north-west of the coastal frontier town of Vila Real de Santo António, at the point where the Oeiras flows into the Guadiana. In Roman times a town called Myrtilis was located here (mentioned by Ptolemy, 2nd century AD); later it gave way to a Moorish fortress.

What to See in Mértola

The Gothic parish church, with crenellation and a handsome Renaissance doorway, was converted from a mosque in the 16th century. There are traces of its Islamic origin in the almost square ground plan, the clustered pier construction, the **mihrab** (Islamic prayer-niche in the wall) behind the altar, and the horseshoe arch above the sacristy door.

Igreja Matriz

It is only a few steps from the parish church up to the **Castelo dos Mouros**. The castle was greatly extended at the end of the 13th century. There is a splendid view from the keep.

❗ Baedeker TIP

Mina de São Domingos

It is worth visiting the Mina de São Domingos, approx. 15m/9mi east of Mértola, close to the village of Vaqueiros. For a long time the copper mine was the most important employer in this remote area. In 1965 it was closed because the copper was exhausted; now this interesting industrial landscape is open to visitors.

▶ VISITING MÉRTOLA

INFORMATION
Rua Alonso Gomes 18
7750-324 Mértola
Tel. 286 610 109
www.rt-planiciedourada.pt

WHERE TO EAT
▶ Moderate
O Nautico
Rua Dr. Serrão Martins
Good, simple restaurant; situated
above the Guadiana.

WHERE TO STAY
▶ Mid-range
Estalagem São Domingos
Mina de S. Domingos
7750-171 Mértola
Tel. 286 640 000
Fax 286 640 009
www.hotelsaodomingos.com
Unusual accommodation: located in
Mina de São Domingos, approx.
15km/9mi east of Mértola, in an old

English mining company. Very elegant
classical design. The affiliated restaurant is stylish.

▶ Budget

Baedeker recommendation

Beira Rio
Rua Dr. Afonso Costa 18
Tel. 286 612 340
A pleasant little guesthouse with a nice view
of the river.

Casa das Janelas Verdes
Rua do Dr. Manuel F. Gomes, 38
7750 - 354 Mértola
Tel. 286 612 145
Three rooms are let in this lovely
house, amidst the old streets in
Mértola's historic centre.

One of the few testaments to the Moorish era in Portugal can be seen in the church of Mértola: behind the altar an Islamic mihrab (prayer niche) has been preserved.

Archaeological excavations have been undertaken between the castle and the church since 1980. The archaeologists have found Roman foundations and mosaics, and Islamic ceramics. The oldest pieces, dating from the 10th century, come from Andalusia. These finds, and other exhibits, are on show in a little display in the castle, as well as in the Museu Romano on the Praça Luís de Camões. In the more recent part of the town, it is worth visiting the Museu Paleocristão, which displays the remains of an early Christian basilica.

Minho

E-M 4-8

Historical province: Minho
Districts: Braga, Viana do Castelo
Principal city: Braga

Area: 4,928 sq km/1,971 sq mi
Population: 966,000

The north-western province of Minho is the »garden of Portugal«. The green Minho landscape seems northern European rather than southern – quite different from Portugal's south.

The espigueiros are characteristic of the landscape in Minho.

VISITING MINHO

INFORMATION
▶ Braga, ▶Viana do Castelo

WHERE TO STAY •
WHERE TO EAT
▶ **Mid-range/Luxury**
Pousada do Dom Dinis
4920-296 Vila Nova de Cerveira
Tel. 251 708 120; fax 251 708 129
Lovely pousada in a palace commissioned by King Dinis in 1321. Excellent restaurant, with a nice view of

the Minho flowing gently by. 29
rooms; fishing and watersports.

▶ **Budget**
Quinta de Parada do Vez
Parada
4970-261 Arcos de Valdevez
ParadaVez@solaresdeportugal.pt
5210-210 Miranda do Douro
Quinta with splendid view of the
Peneda-Gerês National Park. Dinner
must be booked in advance.

The country's north-western historical province takes its name from the border river of Minho. From the river in the north it extends east to Trás-os-Montes, and south to the neighbouring province of Douro Litoral. In the west it meets the Atlantic, at the so-called ▶ Costa Verde. Historically the Minho countryside, once part of Castile, forms an **ethnic and cultural unit with Galicia**, and there are linguistic similarities.

Lush, green landscape

The lush, green vegetation here gives the area a central European look. With 1,000–3,000mm/40–120in annual rainfall, Minho has more rain than any other region of the Iberian Peninsula. The three rivers Minho, Lima and Cávado run parallel to one another through the province in wide valleys. They enable the moist Atlantic atmospheric conditions to permeate far into the hinterland. Rich deposits of granite have led to an architectural style that gives the towns and villages a rather sombre look.

Inhabitants and the economy

The people of Minho are said to be very devout and mindful of tradition. There are many Catholic feasts and romarias – commemorations of saints or miracles – which are gaily celebrated with music and dance. Because of its fertile soils, the Minho countryside has always been densely populated. Yet the farms are often very small, and not run on economical lines, so they could never support the inhabitants. Therefore many of the young are forced to earn their living elsewhere. In the fertile, well watered valleys there are two harvests each year – wheat and maize in succession. Wine-growing is also very important. **Vinho Verde** is much in demand. Autumn sets in early, so the grapes are harvested and pressed early; the wine has a certain tartness, and a dry, tangy freshness.

Typical of the region are small storage buildings for grain and maize, known in Portuguese as »espigueiros«. The walls consist of stone slabs with slits in them. The wind is supposed to get in, but not birds or large insects, so the slits are only 5mm/0.2in wide. The stone supports on which the storage boxes stand are designed to protect the interior against moisture. Between the supports and the boxes, flat stones are pushed in – a barricade against mice. The stores were used mainly for grain in earlier times; now they are used mostly for maize.

Espigueiros

Worthwhile sights in Minho are the towns of ►Braga and ►Guimarães, the Celtiberian settlement of Citânia de Briteiros (►Guimarães), ►Viana do Castelo on the coast, the small fortress towns of ►Caminha, ►Valença and ►Monção on the border river Minho, the pretty destinations of ►Ponte da Barca and Ponte de Lima (►Ponte da Barca) on the Lima, and the ►Peneda-Gerês National Park.

Sights in Minho

Miranda do Douro

V 8

Historical province: Trás-os-Montes
District: Bragança

Altitude: 690m/2,280ft
Population: 2,000

Miranda do Douro is worth a visit if only for its splendid location: it is remotely situated in the north-east on the rocky heights above the Douro, which is dammed at this point and forms the border between Portugal and Spain. The region around Miranda do Douro is one of the most sparsely populated in Portugal.

The remoteness of the region has made cultural and linguistic development very slow, so that numerous archaic characteristics have been preserved. A dialect survives that is close to Vulgar Latin, called **»Mirandês«**. In recent years it has become possible to study Mirandês as an optional subject at school.

Miranda do Douro has a rather gloomy air to it, but there are handsome burgher houses around the marketplace, with coats-of-arms and Manueline ornamentation.There is no industry in Miranda do Douro and the city depends on trade and local tourism, especially from Spain.

! *Baedeker* TIP

Pauliteiros

In the remote Miranda do Douro region, men perform a very special dance, reminiscent of the Roman sword dances – except that it is performed with wooden sticks, »paulitos«, rather than with swords. The »pauliteiros« are becoming a rare tourist attraction – but they are sure to dance every year on the third weekend in August at the town festival, dedicated to St Barbara.

▶ VISITING MIRANDA DO DOURO

INFORMATION
Largo do Menino Jesus da Cartolinha
5210 Miranda do Douro
Tel. 273 431 132
www.rt-nordeste.pt

WHERE TO STAY

▶ **Mid-range**
Pousada de Santa Catarina
5210-183 Miranda do Douro
Tel. 273 431 005
Fax 273 431 065
From the Pousada de Santa Catarina
(12 rooms), there is a magnificent
view of the river valley.

▶ **Budget**
Pensão Vista Bela
Rua do Mercado, 63
5210-210 Miranda do Douro
Tel. 273 431 054; fax 273 431 054
Guesthouse in the new part of Miranda do Douro. Several rooms with a
good view of the river.

What to See in Miranda do Douro

Castelo   Once the 12th-century castle dominated the town, but it was destroyed by an explosion in 1760. Today only the keep is impressive.

Sé   The cathedral, dating from 1522, stands on a rock spur above the Douro. Its Renaissance façade is flanked by two towers. The main altar in the beautiful, spacious interior displays scenes from the life of the Virgin Mary, and from the crusades. A curiosity is the »Christ Child with top hat«, a mid-19th-century votive offering that emanates from local popular culture. The terrace in front of the cathedral offers an imposing view of the grey, rocky Douro Valley.

Archbishop's Palace   The archbishop's palaceonce stood close to the cathedral. It was destroyed by fire in 1706; all that remains is the Baroque courtyard.

Regional Museum   In the small regional museumit is possible to gain some idea of daily life in these remote parts. The exhibits include everyday items that are, or were, often used in the region.

Mirandela

P 8

Historical province: Trás-os-Montes
District: Bragança

Altitude: 250m/825ft
Population: 8,000

The attractive little town of Mirandela lies in the middle of no-where, approximately 50km/30mi south-west of Bragança on the bank of the Rio Tua. Parts of the small historic centre seem almost medieval.

What to See in Mirandela

There was already a crossing over the Rio Tua in Roman times. It was replaced by a 232m/765ft medieval bridge with 17 arches, which still spans the river today. There is a pleasant park by the river, and a simple café encourages visitors to linger.

Bridge

On a little hill in the town centre is the 18th-century Paço dos Távo-ras, now occupied by the town's administrative offices.

Paço dos Távoras

A museum of modern art has been set up in a civic and cultural centre; the collection includes about 400 paintings.

Museu de Arte Moderna

Around Mirandela

Murça, about 20km/12mi south-west of Mirandela, was granted town status in 1224 by Sancho II. It is famous for its granite sculpture of a wild boar, which was once believed to have originated in the Ice Age, but is now thought to date from the 7th century. Many a tale has been woven around it. It is worth taking a look at the 17th-century Igreja da Misericórdia; on the handsome marketplace, the parish church with its classical granite façade and a Manueline pillory are also worth seeing.

Murça
✱
◄ The wild boar of Murça

⊙ VISITING VISITING MIRANDELA

INFORMATION
Rua D. Afonso II – Praça do Mercado
5370 Mirandela
Tel. 278 200 272
www.rt.nordeste.pt

WHERE TO STAY
► **Budget**
Grande Hotel D. Dinis
Av. Nossa Senhora do Amparo

5370-126 Mirandela
Tel. 278 260 100
Fax 278 260 101
A simple but recommended hotel: central, directly on the river. Respectable, somewhat austere furnishings; swimming-pool and garage.

Monção

H 4

Historical province: Minho
District: Viana do Castelo

Elevation: 98m/322ft
Population: 3,000

The old fortified border town of Monção lies on the left bank of the river Minho opposite Salvatierra de Minho in Spain. The thermal springs of Monção are beneficial for those suffering from rheumatism, skin conditions and illnesses of the upper respiratory tract.

Specialities — Salmon and »lampretes« (lamprey) caught from the waters of the Minho are local specialities found on the menus of most of the restaurants in the area.

What to See in Monção

Townscape — Monção is surrounded by a 17th-century circular wall. Adorned with flowers, the Praça Deu-la-Deu is the town's focal point, named after local hero **Deu-la-Deu Martins** who distinguished himself in the battle against the Castilians; a monument has been erected in his honour. Just as in the Largo do Loreto bordering the town to the north, attractive houses with pretty balconies stand around the Praça Deu-la-Deu. From the northern end of the Largo do Loreto there is an extensive view across the countryside around Rio Minho. Above the town stand the ruins of a medieval castle.

Igreja Matriz — The originally Romanesque parish church Santa Maria dos Anjos (»holy Mary of the angels«), which was redesigned in the 16th century, features a beautiful Manueline doorway. In the interior are sev-

▶ VISITING MONÇÃO

INFORMATION

Casa do Curro
4950-480 Monção
Tel. 251 652 757
www.rtam.pt

WHERE TO STAY

▶ **Budget**

Quinta da Portelinha
4950-852 Cortes
Tel. 251 652 911
Fax 251 652 911
www.portugalquinta.com

Beautiful old quinta west of Monção near the Spanish border. Guests stay either in the main building or in one of the small outbuildings.

Albergaria Atlântico
Rua General Pimenta de Castro, 15
4950-498 Monção
Tel. 251 652 355
Fax 251 652 376
Simple guesthouse with 24 rooms in the centre of Monção.

eral old tombs, including that of Deu-la-Deu Martins, in addition to which the magnificent talha dourada, the azulejos in the choir and a Manueline side chapel are worth taking a look at.

Around Monção

About 24km/15mi east of Monção lies Melgaço (180m/590ft). A 12th-century castle stands above the village; the Romanesque parish church originates from the same time.

Melgaço

► Valença do Minho

Other sights

✴ Montemor-o-Velho

F 15/16

Historical province: Beira Litoral
District: Coimbra

Elevation: 51m/197ft
Population: 2,500

In the Middle Ages Montemor-o-Velho, situated on a hill above the right bank of the Mondego, was an important defence post against the Moors who were advancing on Coimbra from Estremadura. Today it is characterized by farming; rice in particular is cultivated in the surrounding areas.

Montemor-o-Velho lies about half way between Figueira da Foz and Coimbra. It is the birthplace of the seafarer Cavalheiro Diogo de Azambuja (1432–1518), the author and world traveller **Fernão Mendes Pinto** (around 1510–1583) and the poet Jorge de Montemor (1520–1561).

What to See in Montemor-o-Velho

The ruins of the mighty castle, once one of the most strategically important fortifications in the country, tower over Montemor-o-Velho. The first references to the castle are from the year 716, when it was in the possession of the Moors. There is now nothing left of the castle from this time. The ruins visible today, with the double oval castle wall, towers and ring of battlements, are from the 11th and 12th centuries. Visitors can ascend some of the towers and enjoy the view of the surrounding landscape.

✴ Castelo

The very small **Gothic-Manueline Santa Maria de Alcáçova church** within the oval castle wall is well worth taking a look at; it dates from the 16th century, the work of the famous master builder Boytaca.

▶ MONTEMOR

INFORMATION

Castelo
3140 Montemor-o-Velho
Tel. 239 680 380
www.turismo-centro.pt

Pregnant Madonna in the Santa Maria de Alcáçova church

In the interior, take a look at the impressive twisted columns which are typical for that epoch, the beautiful wooden ceiling, the pregnant Madonna, »Nossa Senhora de O«, on the side altar to the left, azulejo decoration in the Moorish style of the 16th century and the two-part baptismal font.

The former monastery church **Nossa Senhora dos Anjos** (»our lady of the angels«) is also Manueline, but it is the contents concealed in the spacious interior that are the real treasure: the Renaissance sculptures of the Coimbra school include the resplendent sarcophagus of Diogo de Azambuja, completed by Diogo Pires-o-Moço during Azambuja's lifetime.

Around Montemor-o-Velho

The popular **»Pastéis de Tentúgal«**, small, filled rolls of puff pastry, come from Tentúgal about 10km/6.3mi north-east of Montemor-o-Velho. In the town, take a look at the 15th-century Igreja da Nossa Senhora do Mourão, the 16th-century Igreja da Misericórdia, and the attractive burgher houses.

Moura

O 28

Historical province: Baixo Alentejo	**Elevation:** 180m/590ft
District: Beja	**Population:** 8,500

Moura is a pretty little town, lying about 60km/37.5mi north of Beja in the midst of the expanses of the Alentejo. It is a thermal spa – primarily, the alkaline bubbling springs in the spa gardens promise relief from rheumatism.

»The Moor« The name Moura (Moor) and the municipal coat of arms showing a dead woman at the foot of the castle refer to a Moor by the name of **Salúquia**. Salúquia was the daughter of the highest town official, and she is said to have jumped from the castle battlements after her betrothed and his entourage were caught in an ambush by Christians

► VISITING MOURA

INFORMATION
Largo de Santa Clara
7860 Moura
Tel. 285 251 375
www.rt-planiciedourada.pt

WHERE TO STAY
► **Budget**
Hotel de Moura/Residencial
Praça Gago Coutinho, 1
7860-010 Moura
Tel. 285 251 090; fax 285 254 610

www.hoteldemoura.com
Very attractive hotel with 35 rooms in
an old town palace.

Herdade da Negrita
7875-101 Santo Aleixo da Restauração
– Moura
Tel. 285 965 136; fax 285 965 135
http://herdadedanegrita.com
A beautifully furnished country estate
situated in the middle of the countryside south-east of Moura.

and killed. The Christians were then able to outwit the castle guards
by donning the clothes of their victims, and captured the castle.

What to See in Moura

The Gothic-Manueline Igreja de São João Baptista is located at the
central Praça de Sacadura Cabral. Azulejo depictions of the Virtues
are to be found in the church's side chapel on the right hand side.
The town hall on the other side of the road houses a small regional
museum in which archaeological finds are displayed. In front of the
town hall stands the fountain »Três Bicas« (»three jets of water«)
with a Latin inscription. The entrance to a small spa garden, with a
brilliant display of flowers, is also situated at the Praça de Sacadura
Cabral. There is a pretty view from the terrace at the end of the
green.

Praça de Sacadura Cabral

The Convento de Nossa Senhora do Carmo in Moura is **the oldest
Carmelite convent in Portugal**; it was founded around 1250. The
small, dainty cloister was built in the 16th and 17th centuries; a notable fresco has been preserved in the choir of the church.

Convento de Nossa Senhora do Carmo

In the old quarter Mouraria, near the main square, quite a number
of features are characteristic of the Moorish past. Many of the low,
white houses are ornamented with azulejos and small chimney
stacks. One of the houses on the Largo da Mouraria has been reconstructed in oriental style, including its courtyard.

Mouraria

The ruins of the originally Moorish castle, which was renovated at
the end of the 13th century by King Dinis, tower above the town
centre. Within the circular castle wall stands the Igreja da Nossa Se-

Castelo

nhora da Assunção; the mortal remains of the conquerors Álvaro and Pedro Rodrigues have been laid to rest in the Capela dos Rolins in the church.

Nazaré

D 19

Historical province: Estremadura
District: Leiria

Elevation: 0–110m/361ft
Population: 13,000

Now a well known seaside resort, Nazaré is one of the most visited towns on the Portuguese Atlantic coast. Wonderful long, sandy beaches have contributed to the one time fishing village's transformation into a large tourist centre.

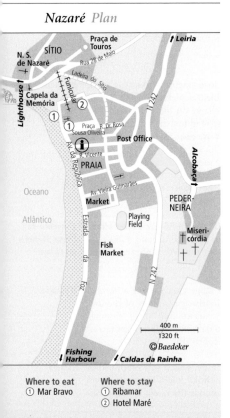

Nazaré Plan

Where to eat
① Mar Bravo

Where to stay
① Ribamar
② Hotel Maré

Founded in all probability by the Phoenicians, Nazaré lies on a bay, today sandy, which is protected to the north by Monte Sítio. The harbour was built in the 1980s at the southern end of the town. Due to the lack of a quayside in former times, the **typically colourful ships with raised, pointed stem posts** had to be pushed into the water by hand; on their return they were **pulled onto dry land by oxen** to be unloaded by the fishermen and the women waiting on the shore. In addition, a method of fishing known as »**arte xávega**« was practised, in which a net was cast out from the coast and later pulled in from the beach. Tourism may be the main source of income these days, but a proportion of the population still lives from fishing. One attraction for tourists are the fish auctions which are held every day on the fishermen's return.

On special occasions or during organized folklore events the people of Nazaré still wear their characteristic **traditional costume**: the men wear a checked shirt and

Nazaré beach at twilight. In the background are the steep slopes on which the quarter Sítio lies.

trousers with a different check pattern; they also wear a black, pointed cap which functions like a bag for keeping all sorts of odds and ends in, including coins. The women wear dresses whose billowing skirts are supported by up to seven underskirts and richly decorated with lace.

There are no historical monuments in Nazaré – what is attractive **Bustling seaside** about this extremely lively resort is primarily its hustle and bustle **resort** and the aura of a tradition-conscious town. Although since the construction of the harbour the typical working day of the fishermen plays out at the southern edge of the town, visitors still see one or two fishermen amongst the tourists on the beach, laying out their catch on wire racks to dry. Especially at weekends, when numerous day trippers arrive from Lisbon, Coimbra and Porto, the beaches can get rather crowded. In the lower part of town in the Pederneira area there is a good view from the forecourt of the 16th-century Misericórdia church across the beach and all the way to Monte Sítio.

Sítio

There is an outstanding view from Sítio (110m/360ft), the small part **✱** of town located on the top of the Monte Sítio foothills. The hills can **View** be reached by car; alternatively make the ascent using the funicular or climb the steps.

Capela da Memória According to legend, the foundation of the Capela da Memória goes back to the councillor Dom Fuas Roupinho. Taking part in a hunt in 1182, he is said to have pursued a stag here. As it jumped from the cliff and Roupinho's horse got ready to do the same, the Virgin Mary is said to have answered the rider's prayer: her apparition dazzled Roupinho's mount so that he held himself back from the abyss. To thank the Virgin for miraculously coming to his aid Dom Fuas Roupinho had the chapel built directly on the edge of the cliff. It is decorated with pretty azulejos and is definitely worth a visit; have a look at the interior to see the walls and the tent-like roof which are completely covered with tiles. Next to the chapel stands a column which commemorates the fact that **Vasco da Gama** made a pilgrimage here before and after his travels to India in order to pray to Nossa Senhora de Nazaré (our lady of Nazaré).

Nossa Senhora de Nazaré The pilgrimage church Nossa Senhora de Nazaré was built in the 17th century opposite the Capela da Memória. In the interior there is a picture of the Virgin Mary which is said to perform miracles. Every year on 15 August and in the second week of September pilgrimages attract visitors from far and wide.

Museu de Nazaré The small town museum in Sítio displays predominantly folkloristic exhibits, most of which are connected with fishing. There are also archaeological finds.

São Miguel About 0.5km/0.3mi west of Sítio stands the former fort São Miguel, which now operates as a lighthouse (farol).

▶ VISITING NAZARÉ

INFORMATION
Avenida da República
2450-100 Nazaré
Tel. 262 561 194
www.rt-leiriafatima.pt

WHERE TO STAY
▶ **Budget/Mid-range**
① *Ribamar*
Rua Gomes Freire 9
2450 Nazaré
Tel. 262 55 11 58
Fax 262 56 22 24
Guesthouse by the sea – a little antiquated, but the rooms are really quite nice and typically Portuguese. There is also a pleasant restaurant.

② *Hotel Maré*
Rua Mouzinho de Albuquerque 8
2450 Nazaré
Tel. 262 561 226, Fax 262 561 750
Central location near the beach. There are 36 modern rooms; the hotel also runs a restaurant serving regional dishes.

WHERE TO EAT
▶ **Inexpensive/Moderate**
① *Mar Bravo*
Praça Sousa Oliveira 67-A
Tel. 262 569 160
Good fish and seafood with a view of the ocean. It is also possible to rent rooms here.

Around Nazaré

Approx. 12km/7.5mi south of Nazaré, the seaside resort of São Martinho do Porto lies on the north-east edge of a protected lake-like bay known as »concha« (mussel) because of its curious shape. The popular town is a particular favourite for families with small children.

São Martinho do Porto

It is worth visiting the coastal towns and resorts on the ► Costa de Prata.

Costa de Prata

✶✶ Óbidos

D 20

Historical province: Estremadura
District: Leiria

Elevation: 70m/230ft
Population: 1,500

The whole of the particularly picturesque town of Óbidos has been declared a national monument thanks to its pretty, well-tended appearance. As one of Portugal's greatest tourist magnets, it is often overcrowded in summer.

Not least to preserve the original character of the town, no large hotels have been built in Óbidos, but there are several luxurious smaller establishments within the old buildings. However, there is an extremely limited number of beds and in the summer months it is virtually impossible to get a room without booking well in advance. For the most part visitors to Óbidos are day trippers, so that the town is a little quieter in the evening – it is therefore advantageous to stay overnight.

Lagoa de Óbidos, a large lagoon with a narrow opening to the sea, is located about 10km/6.3mi north-west of Óbidos; in former centuries it almost reached the town. Because of the proximity of the Atlantic, Óbidos was strategically important and accordingly well fortified as far back as Moorish times. For Portugal's kings Óbidos must have been an attractive place: since the late 13th century it has repeatedly been presented as a gift to the brides of kings on the morning after the wedding night and was the favourite place of residence of **St Isabel**, as well as other subsequent monarchs. Among others, **Queen Leonor** spent some years here, after her only son was killed in a riding accident on the banks of the Tagus.

The old town centre of Óbidos is surrounded by a 13m/43ft-high wall, crowned with battlements and fortified with towers. Visitors can walk all the way around this 1,570m/1,718yd-long wall.

There are numerous pretty nooks and crannies to be discovered in the picturesque old town with its beautiful patrician houses from the

✶✶
Pretty little town

▶ VISITING ÓBIDOS

INFORMATION
Rua Direita
Apartado 42
2510-914 Óbidos
Tel. 262 955 060
www.rt-oeste.pt

Porta da Vila (car park)
2510-089 Óbidos
Tel. 262 959 231
www.rt-oeste.pt

WHERE TO EAT
▶ Moderate
Dom João V
Largo da Igreja do Senhor da Pedra
Tel. 262 959 134
Popular restaurant next to the Igreja
Senhor Jesus da Pedra outside the
walls of the town. Large selection of
dishes, half-portions provided.

*The Casa d'Óbidos. Living
room with billiard table*

▶ Inexpensive
Café-Restaurante 1° Dezembro
Largo 1° Dezembro
Café and bar somewhat removed from
the hurly burly. Simple and very small,
with tables outside. Only light meals
and snacks are available here, for
example salads.

WHERE TO STAY
▶ Mid-range
Pousada do Castelo
Paço Real
2510-999 Óbidos
Tel. 262 955 080
Fax 262 959 148
www.pousadas.pt
A lovely old pousada established in the
castle of Óbidos.

Albergaria Rainha Santa Isabel
Rua Direita
2510-060 Óbidos
Tel. 262 959 323, fax 262 959 115
Small hotel with 20 rooms right in the
centre of Óbidos. The rooms are
comfortably furnished; four have a
balcony. There is a lift.

Baedeker recommendation

▶ Budget
Casa d'Óbidos
Quinta de São José
2510-135 Óbidos
Tel. 262 950 924
Fax 262 959 970
www.casadobidos.com
Located somewhat outside the town's historic centre, there is a view of the castle from
this very nice »Turismo de Habitação«
establishment. A lavish breakfast is served
for all guests at a large table.

Renaissance and Baroque periods. Most of the houses are lavishly adorned with flowers. The yellow and blue stripes on the façades are regularly renewed; they are said to keep insects away. Besides this, Óbidos is a place for art, with numerous galleries and shops.

What to See in Óbidos

From the Porta da Vila, the town gate, whose inner side is decorated with 18th-century tiles, Rua Direita leads to the main square with a very pretty fountain and a 15th-century pelourinho (pillory column). The pillory bears the emblem of Queen Leonor, a **fishing net**. It became part of the queen's coat of arms from the day that the body of her dying son was brought to her by fishermen who had recovered it from the Tagus in a net.

Pelourinho

The town museum is found in Rua Direita. Alongside sculpture and paintings from the 15th to the 17th century, archaeological finds are also exhibited.

Museu de Óbidos

The Santa Maria parish church also stands on the Praça de Santa Maria. It was originally a Gothic building; later it was redesigned in Renaissance style. In the interior the church is completely lined with 17th-century azulejos; take a look at the tomb of João de Noronha, the governor of the fortress, who died in 1575 (by Jean de Rouen), and the painting *The Mystic Betrothal of St Catherine* by Josefa de Ayala Figueira (17th century).

Igreja de Santa Maria

Just a few steps from the parish church stands the Igreja da Misericórdia with its impressive Baroque doorway.

Igreja da Misericórdia

From Moorish times a fort had stood at the town's highest point, and in 1148 it was renewed and reinforced by Afonso Henriques after he conquered Óbidos. The one time palace within the castle walls was converted into the Pousada do Castelo in the mid-20th century. There is a magnificent view over the town and its surroundings from the keep.

Castelo

Outside the city wall, the Senhor Jesus da Pedra church stands on the road to Caldas da Rainha. In the 18th century, a farmer found a cross at this point that originated from the 2nd century. Funded by the farmers, the church, an impressive Baroque building with a hexagonal floor plan, was constructed here between 1740 and 1747. The cross is preserved inside the church.

Senhor Jesus da Pedra

Around Óbidos

The Aqueduct of Amoreira, whose construction was ordered by Catherine of Austria in 1575, runs south of the town.

Aqueduct

<table>
<tr><td>Foz do Arelho
Lagoa de Óbidos</td><td>The coast near Óbidos is beautiful, though it is surrounded by high cliffs making access difficult. A trip to Foz do Arelho, where the Lagoa de Óbidos flows into the Atlantic, is worthwhile.</td></tr>
</table>

Nearby destinations Other destinations in the area are ►Caldas da Rainha to the northeast and ►Peniche to the west.

Olhão

L/M 34

Historical province: Algarve	**Elevation:** sea level
District: Faro	**Population:** 37,000

Olhão is different from all other towns in the Algarve, both in terms of its appearance and its atmosphere. It is often referred to as the most North African town in the Algarve.

The town – largely untouched by tourism – lies a few miles east of Faro. The most important local industry is fishing, the catch consisting mainly of sardines and tuna. The fishing harbour is located on the eastern edge of the town and is the largest in the whole region; in the district of Faro, only Portimão has a comparable turnover. The freshly caught fish are processed in a canning factory in the harbour.

Influence of North Africa It is said from time to time that Olhão bears many similarities to the towns of North Africa. This impression stems primarily from the construction of the **characteristic white, cubic, flat-roofed houses**. The fishing quarter in particular, located down by the sea, consists of two or three-floor cubic houses of this kind, arranged in a maze-like pattern. All the houses are similar, but none is exactly the same as any other. All have one feature in common, the »açoteias«, flat roofs used for drying fruit and fishing implements. On almost every roof there is a small turret from which, it is said, the wives of the fishermen look out for their husbands' boats. The North African influence on the architecture can be traced back to the trade between Olhão and North African coastal towns; the construction methods used there were effective in Olhão because of the similarity in climate. Further parts of the town were built in the 19th century, and newer buildings stand further inland towards the N 125.

What to See in Olhão

There is not a great deal to see in Olhão; its attraction lies in its atmosphere. Those wishing to take a look at the town's buildings are best advised to follow the main thoroughfare, Avenida da República, in the direction of the sea.

▶ VISITING OLHÃO

INFORMATION

Largo Sebastião Martins Mestre 6 A
8700-349 Olhão
Tel. 289 713 936
www.visitalgarve.pt

PARKEN

With luck, parking spaces can be found on Avenida da República, otherwise down by the water in Avenida 5 de Outubro or a little further east on Avenida das Forças Armadas at the harbour.

SHOPPING

There are numerous little stores in the pedestrian zone where you can shop quite cheaply. Every Saturday a large market is built up around the market halls down by the water, where shoppers find not only fresh food but also everything from music cassettes to clothes, flowers, dried fruit and toys.

WHERE TO EAT
▶ Moderate/Inexpensive
O Tamboril
Avenida 5 de Outubro 160
Tel. 289 714 625

On the menu here are good fish and mussel dishes, prepared in a manner typical for the region.

WHERE TO STAY
▶ Budget
Hotel Ria Sol
Rua General H. Delgado 37
8700 Olhão
Tel. 289 705 267
Fax 289 705 268
The only hotel in town: simple, central, but also very quiet; 52 rooms.

Pensão Bela Vista
Rua Teófilo Braga 65
8700-520 Olhão
Tel. 289 702 538
This small, renovated guesthouse with nine rooms is located in the centre of the old town.

Pensão Bicuar
Rua Vasco da Gama 5
9700-522 Olhão
Tel. 289 714 816
www.pension-bicuar.net
Pleasant guesthouse in the centre of town. There is a good view of Olhão from the roof terrace.

Construction of the Igreja Matriz, funded by the town's fishermen, began in the late 17th century: the foundation stone was laid in 1698. The connection between the church and fishing as well as sea-faring still exists today: until recently there was a **red navigational light** on the main façade facing the water, visible in the evening from the lagoon to help the fishermen get their bearings. Meanwhile the buildings in the town have become taller, and the red light has been placed on the top of the church.

The aisle-less church, whose interior is covered with barrel vaulting, gives a rather sober impression; the Baroque high altar decorated with talha dourada is the only striking feature. On no account should visitors miss the ascent of the church tower, from which there

Igreja Matriz de Nossa Senhora do Rosário

is a magnificent view over the roofs of Olhão out to the lagoon and the open sea.

Capela de Nossa Senhora dos Aflitos At the back of the Igreja Matriz is the Capela de Nossa Senhora dos Aflitos. The chapel consists of a room which is open on one side – although fitted with bars – and lined with tiles. Candles burn constantly, flowers are on display and **votive offerings** such as waxen arms, legs, feet and heads are stacked up. In stormy weather in winter, the wives of fishermen go to the popular little chapel to pray for their husbands.

Museu da Cidade On the Praça da Restauração next to the Igreja Matriz there is a small museum with a nicely presented exhibition of archaeological finds, artworks and handicraft items. Visitors can also learn something about fishing and seafaring here (open: Tue–Fri 10am to 12.30pm and 2pm–5.30pm, Sat 10am–1pm).

Olhão by night: in the pedestrian area the lights reflect in the sparkling pavement mosaic

Rua do Comércio (commercial street) is the main street and a pedestrian zone and shopping area. The shops are simple; some of them are very cheap.

Rua do Comércio

The long Avenida 5 de Outubro runs parallel to the shoreline. Coming from the town centre, the two covered markets are straight ahead, and between them a passageway leads directly to the lagoon. The large market halls each have four corner turrets, in which little shops and cafés are to be found. A large open-air market takes place around these halls on Saturdays.

Market halls

> ## ! *Baedeker* TIP
>
> ### Balmy summer nights in Olhão
> In summer in Olhão there is a buzz around the covered markets late into the night. People enjoy sitting outside and looking over the lagoon towards the light of the lighthouse on the offshore islands.

East of the market halls stretches the **Jardim Patrão Joaquim Lopes**, where visitors can sit down on the benches and enjoy the view onto the mud flats. A little further outside the town is the jetty from which ships sail to the islands of Culatra and Armona. To the west of the market there is a small yacht harbour.

Around Olhão

A visit to the grounds of the Quinta de Marim, situated about 1km/0.6mi east of Olhão, is definitely worthwhile. This environment and nature conservation centre is part of the Parque Natural da Ria Formosa. In a small information centre, you can find out about the Ria Formosa area around the lagoon, the fauna and flora that live here, and general issues concerning nature protection and the environment.

Parque Natural da Ria Formosa/ Quinta de Marim

During a stroll around the grounds, visitors can view a **tide mill** (moinho de maré), the last preserved mill of its kind which were used extensively in the Middle Ages.

In addition, the »cão de água« or **Portuguese Water Dog**, a threatened breed, is bred on the quinta's grounds. The poodle-like dog was once used to help with fishing. In the east of the area, the ruins of Roman salt plants have been discovered (open: daily 9am–noon and 2pm–5pm).

⊕

Both of the islands in the lagoon are flat dune islands with very good beaches. There are a few simple summer houses, restaurants and cafés. Ships sail to the islands from Olhão: from June to September several times a day, in winter somewhat less often.

✴
Culatra, Armona

On Culatra island the ships put into the harbours at Culatra and Farol, and another ship goes to Armona in the east, at the island's western tip. It is also possible to reach Armona from Fuzeta, east of Olhão.

✳ Palmela

Historical province: Estremadura
District: Setúbal

Elevation: 238m/781ft
Population: 18,000

Palmela is a small, simple mountain town with few sights of particular note. The small wine producing area, located 10km/6.3mi north of Setúbal on a ridge of the Serra da Arrábida, is well known. At the time of the grape harvest in September and October quite a number of festivals take place here.

The single important sight is the castle. Walking through Palmela, visitors will come to the 18th-century church of São Pedro, below the castle near the Largo do Município. The beautiful azulejo pictures in the interior show scenes from the life of St Peter. Diagonally opposite stands the 17th-century town hall whose banqueting hall is decorated with portraits of Portuguese kings. The name of the town in the Serra de São Luís stems from the Roman praetor of the province of Lusitania, Aulus Cornelus Palma.

✳ Castelo

Mighty fortress of the Moors

In the time of the Moors the strongest fortress in the south of Portugal stood here. Afonso Henriques managed to capture the castle, first in 1147 and then, after a renewed Moorish intermezzo, conclusively in 1165. He had the castle reinforced and handed it over to the knights of the Order of São Tiago who based themselves here in the 15th century. In the 18th century the fortress was further strengthened and safeguarded against artillery fire.

From the **keep** (Torre de Menagem), built in the late 14th century, there is a view of the entire castle site; in conditions of good visibility it is also possible to see the mouth of the Tagus and Lisbon in the distance. The Bishop of Évora, Garcia de Meneses, was incarcerated in the well with other captives and reputedly poisoned because of his involvement in a conspiracy in the year 1484. The ruins of the **Igreja de Santa Maria do Castelo** stand within the fortress site. This is a Renaissance

▶ PALMELA

INFORMATION
Castelo de Palmela
2950-997 Palmela
Tel. 212 332 122
www.costa-azul.rts.pt

WHERE TO STAY • WHERE TO EAT

▶ **Budget**
Pousada do Castelo de Palmela
Castelo de Palmela
2950-997 Palmela
Tel. 212 351 226; fax 212 330 440
www.pousadas.pt
Known throughout the region, this is a beautiful pousada in the castle at Palmela.

church which was built on the site of a Moorish mosque; it collapsed during the earthquake of 1755.

The 15th-century **São Tiago monastery** takes up the outermost western part of the castle, though it was radically altered in later centuries. Today the pousada is on the monastery premises. The monastery church, built in the transitory Romanesque-Gothic style, is lined inside with beautiful azulejo decoration from the 17th and 18th centuries and holds the tomb of Jorge de Lencastre (1481–1550), a son of João II.

Around Palmela

Near Quinta do Anjo 3km/1.9mi west of Palmela, chambers for graves were hewn into the rock face around 5,000 years ago and served as burial sites until the Middle Ages. Coming from Palmela, turn left in the centre of Quinta do Anjo, and then left again behind the houses onto a track across the fields to find them.

Quinta do Anjo

►Setúbal, ►Serra da Arrábida, ►Costa de Lisboa

Other destinations

✶ ✶ Peneda-Gerês National Park

H–L 4–6

Historical provinces: Minho, Trás-os-Montes
Elevation: up to 1,545m/5,069ft

Districts: Viana do Castelo, Braga, Vila Real
Area: 72,000 ha/177,840ac

Peneda-Gerês National Park extends along the Portuguese-Spanish border in the north of Portugal. It features expansive, completely untouched areas with wonderful woods, mountain scenery and calm reservoirs.

It is possible to explore the national park by car, but it is rewarding to go on a few walking trips, too. There is a limited choice of accommodation; a wider range of guesthouses is found only in the small **Gerês spa**. Camping is only allowed on the small number of camp sites. Apart from that, Ponte de Lima or ► Ponte da Barca are good starting points for tours of the area. Information about the national park is available from visitor centres in Arcos de Valdevez, Gerês and Montalegre, as well as at the head office in Braga.

The **highest elevations** are found in the Serra do Gerês, the Nevosa reaching 1,545m/5,069ft and the Altar de Cabrões 1,538m/5,046ft on the Portuguese side.

There are large, strictly protected areas within the Parque Nacional da Peneda-Gerês, whose boundaries were officially defined in 1971. Due to the varied landscape, zones with different microclimates have

Fauna and flora in the national park

Parque Nacional da Peneda-Gerês Map

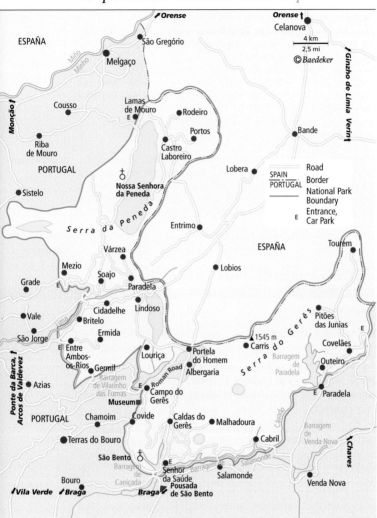

produced an unusual variety of flora. At the same time, the seclusion of the area has spared many endemic species from human interference, so that several kinds of plants which have become **extinct in the rest of Europe** are to be found here. Alongside extensive coniferous forest there are oak trees which are several hundred years old – especially in the vicinity of Pincães and São Lourenço – as well as cork oak forests, eucalyptus, and rocky landscapes with heather. Red deer and wild boars, rabbits, partridges, **feral horses**, lizards, snakes and golden eagles live in the mountains of the national park. In addition the park is the habitat of approximately 80 **wolves**.

Numerous archaeological digs show that the area covered by the Peneda-Gerês National Park was the site of ancient settlements. The dolmens from Mezio, Paradela, Cambezes, Pitões and Tourém from the 3rd millennium BC are still preserved. Pre-Roman, probably Celtic castros have so far been excavated near Pitões, Tourém and Cidadelhe, and it is likely that several more prehistoric settlement sites remain untouched under the ground. Today, around 15,000 people live in over 100 villages in the area of the national park.

Ancient settlement area

▶ VISITING PENEDA-GERÊS NATIONAL PARK

INFORMATION
Av. Manuel Ferreira da Costa
4845-067 Gerês
Tel. 253 391 133
Fax 253 391 282

WHERE TO EAT
▶ Moderate
Pousada de São Bento
4850-047 Caniçada/Gerês
Tel. 253 647 190
Diners enjoy a splendid view from the pousada's own restaurant.

Beleza da Serra
Lugar do Bairro 25
Vilar da Veiga
4845-065 Gerês
Tel. 253 391 457
Beautifully situated restaurant, which serves delicious regional dishes.

WHERE TO STAY
▶ Mid-range
Pousada de Santa Maria do Bouro
4720-688 Amares
Tel. 253 371 971
Fax 253 371 976
A pousada with 32 rooms has been set up in a Cistercian monastery from the

12th century: located between Braga and the Gerês mountains, it offers a swimming pool and tennis courts.

Pousada de São Bento
4850-047 Caniçada/Gerês
Tel. 253 647 190
Fax 253 647 867
An old hunting lodge with 29 rooms on the edge of Peneda-Gerês National Park. Most of the rooms have a lovely view onto the wooded valleys and the reservoirs.
Those who are keen on sport can choose from angling, water sports, tennis and swimming in the pool.

▶ Budget
Hotel Universal
4845-067 Gerês
Tel. 253 391 143
Fax 253 391 102
Venerable old spa hotel with 50 rooms on the small main street of Gerês. Somewhat more modern and stylish interior décor is found in the Termas hotel opposite; the contact is the same for both establishments.

By no means a rare sight in the Peneda-Gerês National Park: animals roaming free on the roads

Trips through the National Park

As all the roads are winding, plenty of time should be planned for tours. Signposting is not always good, and it is not uncommon that a road which initially inspired confidence comes to a sudden dead end. Because the protected areas are the habitat of numerous animal species, there are often animals on the roads. Incidentally, it is strongly advised to follow the rules on parking, as they are regularly enforced.

Serra da Peneda From the departure points ▶Ponte da Barca or Ponte de Lima the N 203 near Entre-Ambos-os-Rios leads 13km/8.1mi east from Ponte da Barca into the national park. This road, busy with through traffic, runs in an easterly direction above the Rio Lima, which is for the most part dammed in this area. Passing through the mountain villages Britelo and Cidadelhe, whose dark, granite houses give them a rather gloomy atmosphere, the route leads to **Lindoso** (468m/ 1,536ft) just before the Spanish border. The town is dominated by the fort built in 1287 by King Dinis; silos (espigueiros) typical for the ▶Minho region are also to be seen here. Lindoso is a good starting point for various walking trips, for example to the Vilarinho das Furnas reservoir; to Miradouro Leira do Canto with beautiful views into the Rio Lima valley; to the top of the pass at Portela do Homem (822m/2,697ft) on the Spanish border from which there is a magnificent view into the rocky valley of the Rio Homem; and south to the Cabril wood.

North of the Lima lies **Soajo**, whose houses are built from raw granite blocks laid one on top of the other without mortar. The 10th-century pillory is the oldest stone column in Portugal. Again, more »espigueiros« stand on a small cliff directly adjacent to the through road. It is worth continuing on through this particularly delightful landscape to the **pilgrimage church Nossa Senhora da Peneda**, whose remote location – in the middle of the countryside beneath a rock face from which a waterfall descends into the valley below – is truly enchanted. Steps with statues of saints lead up to the church.

Castro Laboreiro lies further north. A track leads from here to the in all likelihood originally Roman Castro Laboreiro, which was newly fortified by Afonso Henriques and further extended by King Dinis. The castle buildings were almost completely destroyed by an explosion in the powder tower caused by a lightning strike.

The Serra do Gerês lies in the eastern part of the national park. The road most people probably take exits near Senhor da Saúde in the south-west of the park at the Caniçada reservoir. This is also the main access road to the picturesque **Caldas do Gerês spa** (400m/ 1312ft), known as Gerês for short and located in a basin. The thermal springs are especially sought out by those suffering from liver and gall bladder problems; moreover, the spa is a good starting point for walking trips in the Serra do Gerês. A well made road runs from Caldas do Gerês north to the border crossing of Portela do Homem.

Serra do Gerês

The reservoir **Vilarinho das Furnas** lies north-west of Gerês. When it was created at the end of the 1960s the village Vilarinho da Furna disappeared underwater and the inhabitants were relocated. At low water levels it is still possible to see the remains of the houses in the reservoir. A small road leads from the Barragem de Vilarinho das Furnas via Germil further into the Serra da Peneda.

> ## ! *Baedeker* TIP
>
> ### Flooded village
> The Museu Etnográfico de Vilarinho das Furnas on a crossroads near Campo do Gerês is dedicated to the disappearance of the old mountain village of Vilarinho das Furnas and the fate of its inhabitants. The small exhibition is put together using the simplest of methods but still reflects the mood of the villagers and the desire to keep the memory of the lost village alive.

Around Campo do Gerês there are still numerous traces of the Romans: the Roman road, constructed from AD 79–353 runs along the south-east bank of the Barragem Vilarinho das Furnas, leading to the top of the pass at Portela do Homem on the Portuguese-Spanish border; it has the highest number of preserved Roman milestones on the whole Iberian Peninsula.

Near Paradela and Covelães it is possible to enter the eastern part of the park. Narrow roads with little traffic lead to the prehistoric archaeological sites of **Pitões** and **Tourém**.

Peniche

B 20

Historical province: Estremadura
District: Leiria

Elevation: 0–15m/49ft
Population: 17,000

The bustling fishing town of Peniche lies on a rocky peninsula that is only about 3km/1.9mi long 2km/1.3mi wide. Tourism is held within reasonable limits in Peniche, and there are hardly any larger hotels in the centre of the town.

Peniche is connected with the mainland by a natural sandbank (»Istmo«). The town is one of the most significant trading locations in Portugal for lobster, sardines and tuna. Beach life takes place on the extensive sandy stretches on both sides of the »Istmo«. The next good beach is near Baleal. In Peniche there is a state school for **lace making**, a traditional handicraft here.

Peniche *Plan*

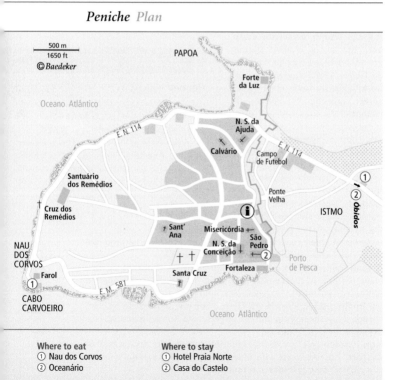

Where to eat
① Nau dos Corvos
② Oceanário

Where to stay
① Hotel Praia Norte
② Casa do Castelo

The castle walls and moat, intended to defend the town on the inland side, run from the castle in the south of the town up to the northernmost point of the peninsula. It is very lively down at the harbour which is protected by two moles. The entry of the fishing boats makes an especially fascinating spectacle, as they hurry to be quickly unloaded of their perishable freight. The catch is then auc-

Fortified fishing town

▶ VISITING PENICHE

INFORMATION
Rua de Alexandre Herculano
2520-676 Peniche
Tel. 262 789 571
www.rt-oeste.pt

TRIP TO THE ILHA DA BERLENGA
Boats leave for the Ilha da Berlenga from Peniche harbour; the journey takes about an hour. At high season there are two connections per day.

ESSEN IN PENICHE
▶ Inexpensive
① **Nau dos Corvos**
Cabo Carvoeiro, Nau dos Corvos
This restaurant is sought out not for its culinary delights, but rather for its special location at the outermost end of the peninsula above the sea at Cabo Carvoeiro.

② **Oceanário**
Largo da Ribeira
Tel. 262 785 697
A good selection of fish and meat dishes. Diners look onto the harbour area from the veranda.

ÜBERNACHTEN IN PENICHE
▶ Budget/Mid-range
① **Hotel da Praia Norte**
Avenida Monsenhor Bastos
2520-206 Peniche
Tel. 262 780 500
Fax 262 780 509

A little way outside Peniche: a large, detached, rather sober building. The rooms with balconies are spacious and comfortable.

Baedeker recommendation

② **Casa do Castelo**
Estrada Nacional 114
2525-025 Atouguia da Baleia
Tel. 262 750 647
Fax 262 750 937
www.solares-de-portugal.com
Beautiful old manor house in the village of Atouguia da Baleia a short distance southeast of Peniche directly opposite the church.

WHERE TO STAY ON THE ILHA DA BERLENGA
▶ Budget
Pavilhão Mar e Sol
Tel. 262 750 331
Simple double rooms with bathroom; breakfast provided.

Casa-Abrigo/Forte São João Batista
Tel. 262 785 263, 262 750 244
Very plain and simple accommodation in the style of a youth hostel in Forte São João Batista.

Área de Campismo da Berlenga
Tel./fax 262 789 571
Simple camp site

Anglers on the cliffs of Cabo Carvoeiro

tioned off in a large hall from a conveyor belt. In the summer months, ships leave from the harbour to sail to the off-shore Berlenga islands.

What to See in Peniche

Fortaleza

At the harbour stands the well-preserved fortress, built in the 16th century by Filippo Terzi, and further extended in the style of Vauban in the 17th century. During the dictatorship of Salazar it served as a notorious jail for political prisoners. Part of the former prison – cells, a visiting room, and other facilities – can be viewed. An impression of the resistance and the mechanisms of repression during the Salazar dictatorship is given in both words and pictures. Visitors to the municipal museum can also see exhibits on fishing, ship building and the history of the region.

Other sights

The Baroque Misericórdia church is located in the centre of the town near the ramparts. Scenes from the New Testament are depicted on the wooden ceiling in the interior. Another Baroque church is the Igreja de São Pedro just a few hundred metres south whose choir is adorned with 18th-century talha dourada. Also noteworthy is the Igreja Ajuda in the far north of the town with sumptuous azulejo decoration and ceiling frescoes in the choir.

Around Peniche

Several roads lead from Peniche to the lighthouse (farol) 2km/1.3mi west on Cabo Carvoeiro, a cape with rock needles and caves. Excellent fishing grounds are found in this area, including areas rich in lobster. Off the cape is the cliff Nau dos Corvos (raven ship). The Berlenga Islands, among others, are visible in the distance. A few hundred yards north of the cape stands the pilgrimage chapel of Santuário dos Remédios, which is completely lined with azulejos.

★
Cabo Carvoeiro

◀ Santuário dos Remédios

About 12km/7.5mi north-west of Cabo Carvoeiro, the bizarre Ilhas Berlengas jut out of the shimmering green sea. The granite islands form a small archipelago with the 4.5km/2.8mi-long and up to 800m/875yd-wide main island, Ilha da Berlenga, and the smaller islands of Estelas, Forcadas and Farilhões. In addition there are numerous reefs and cliffs, highly prized as diving areas. The number of visitors to the islands is limited. For those staying overnight, there is a camp site, basic accommodation in the fort and a simple guesthouse.

★
Berlenga Islands

On the highest elevation of the **main island** stands a lighthouse, visible for miles around. Below lies the protected harbour bay with the Forte de São João Baptista from the time of King João IV.
A signposted **circular route** (1.5hr) leads from the fort to picturesque grottoes, tunnels, ravines and coves filled with thundering surf. The Blue Grotto beneath the fort bears comparison with the one on Capri. South of the fort, the 70m/77yd-long natural tunnel Furado Grande leads to the small Cova do Sonho.

★ Ponte da Barca

Historical province: Minho
District: Viana do Castelo

Elevation: 178m/584ft
Population: 2,000

Ponte da Barca – about 30km/18.8mi north of Braga in a beautiful, lush landscape on the banks of the Rio Lima – is a popular starting point for excursions into the Peneda-Gerês National Park.

What to See in Ponte da Barca

The view of the village from the old 15th/16th-century bridge which spans the Rio Lima here is particularly picturesque.

View of the village

The most important building in the centre of the village is the impressive 15th-century church whose interior features a beautiful coffered ceiling and a special ornament in the form of a silver Passion Cross, reputedly a gift from Manuel I.

Igreja Matriz

VISITING PONTE DA BARCA

INFORMATION
Rua D. Manuel
4980-637 Ponte da Barca
Tel./fax 258 452 899
www.rtam.pt

WHERE TO EAT
▶ **Inexpensive**
Tulha
Rua Formosa
Tel. 258 942 879
Frequently visited by the locals. Good
value, rustic, hearty meals.

Grill Costa do Vez
Estrada de Monção
4970-483 Arcos de Valdevez
Tel. 258 516 122
Good traditional cooking in comfort-

able, rustic surroundings; north of
Ponte da Barca.

WHERE TO STAY

Baedeker recommendation

▶ **Budget/Mid-range**
Casa da Várzea
Beiral do Lima
4990-545 Ponte de Lima
Tel. 258 948 603; fax 258 948 412
casa.varzea@netc.pt
Located in the midst of vineyards between
Ponte de Lima and Ponte da Barca, this well-
kept and tastefully furnished manor house
has a friendly atmosphere.

Around Ponte da Barca

Bravães
About 5km/3.1mi west of Ponte da Barca, on the edge of Bravães,
stands the plain **Romanesque Igreja de São Salvador** from the 12th
century. It owes its fame to the highly artful sculptured portals; along
with animal and plant motifs there are also geometrical patterns and
human figures. In the aisle-less in-
terior, also richly decorated with
stone friezes and reliefs, there are
remains of 14th-century frescoes;
nowadays the best of them are exhibited in the Museu Nacional de
Soares dos Reis in ▶Porto.

! Baedeker TIP

Square at the riverside
The Largo de Camões in Ponte de Lima is not a
particularly spectacular square, but it enjoys a
marvellous location directly on the bank of the
river with a view of the old bridge. The cafés
here are an inviting place to spend some time.

The extremely pretty Ponte de Lima lies directly at the riverside
about 15km/9.4mi west of Bravães.
An extended stay is worthwhile;
moreover it is a good starting point for journeys into the ▶Peneda-
Gerês National Park. In Ponte de Lima a medieval bridge spans the
Ponte de Lima
Rio Lima. The small, historical town features very beautiful old patrician houses from the 16th century; it is also worth taking a look at
the Manueline doorway of the former monastery church Santo

View over the Rio Lima to Ponte da Barca

António dos Frades. The Torre de São Paulo is a leftover from the medieval fortifications of the town.

The particularly picturesque village Arcos de Valdevez, with about 3,000 inhabitants, lies on both sides of the Rio Vez approximately 5km/3.1mi north of Ponte da Barca. There is a handsome 14th-century parish church, which was remodelled in the 17th century. In front of the church stands a remarkably beautiful pelourinho in Manueline style, and behind it the 16th-century Casa do Terreiro. It is also worth taking a look at the Baroque façade of the Nossa Senhora da Lapa church as well as the monolithic memorial column outside the Church of the Holy Ghost in the upper part of town, which commemorates the assistance provided to Afonso Henriques by the town's citizens in the war against the Spanish.

✶
Arcos de Valdevez

Portalegre

O 21

Historical province: Alto Alentejo
District: Portalegre

Elevation: 477m/1,565ft
Population: 16,000

Portalegre is located at the foot of the Serra de Portalegre. With its white houses, some of which are built on a steep incline, and its numerous impressive palaces, it is considered a stronghold of the Portuguese Baroque.

● VISITING PORTALEGRE

INFORMATION

Palácio Póvoas – Av. da Liberdade
7300 Portalegre
Tel. 245 331 359
www.rtsm.pt

WHERE TO STAY •
WHERE TO EAT

▶ Mid-range/Luxury
Pousada de Flor-da-Rosa
7430-999 Crato
Tel. 245 997 210
Fax 245 997 212
A castle, a monastery and a duke's

palace were the origins of this pousada about 20km/12.5mi west of Portalegre bei Crato, in which 24 rooms are available. A certain medieval flair.

▶ Budget/Mid-range
Pensão Restaurante Quinta da Saúde
Quinta da Saúde
7300-085 Portalegre
Tel. 245 202 324
Fax 245 207 234
Located next to the camp site with a lovely view over the plateau. Good hotel with its own restaurant.

The district capital and old diocesan town Portalegre (»merry gate«), located near the Spanish border, became prosperous in the 16th century through wool weaving and in particular tapestry making, enjoying its greatest heyday at the end of the 17th century with the emerging art of silk weaving. Today, Portalegre is still a centre for wool processing, but also for the wood and cork industries. Because the industry based in the area make Portalegre a rather hectic place, it tends to be only briefly visited by tourists who are passing through on their way to the delightful ▶Castelo de Vide and ▶Marvão about 20km/12.5mi north.

Portalegre's old town centre is surrounded by medieval walls. At the highest point stand the ruins of the mighty fort from 1290. The most interesting buildings in the town are concentrated around the Praça do Município. The modern-day centre of Portalegre is north of this: the traffic streams around the Rossio, which is splendidly decked out with greenery. The busy square is lined with attractive residential and municipal buildings as well as the Misericórdia hospital, with an 18th-century façade and a nice patio.

What to See in Portalegre

Praça do
Município

The western end of the Praça do Município is formed by the **Sé**. The cathedral was first erected in the 16th century and altered considerably in the 18th century, at which time the main façade, flanked by two towers, was rebuilt. The interior however still displays the unaltered Renaissance style of the time the cathedral was founded. The retable with scenes from the life of the Virgin Mary in the second chapel on the right is worth taking a look at, as is the tile decoration in the sacristy. The cloister is from the 18th century.

The small **Museu Municipal** is situated north-east of the cathedral on the opposite side of the square. Along with a collection of sacral art, the museum displays Chinese porcelain, as well as ivory and wood carvings.

On the same square the **Câmara Municipal**, the town hall built in the 18th century, is also worth seeing.

Pass through the alley between the cathedral and the town museum and turn right to reach the Palácio Amarelo 200m/219yd away. The palace, actually called the Palácio dos Albrançalhas, owes its current name to its yellow paint job.

Palácio Amarelo

South-east of the Praça do Município on the Rua Santa Clara stands the 14th-century Convent of the Order of St Clare with a fine cloister.

Convento de Santa Clara

Rua do 19 de Junho, lined with attractive burgher houses from the 17th and 18th centuries, runs in a south-easterly direction from the Praça do Município to the Praça da República. There are very impressive palaces here too, including the Palácio dos Condes de Avilés and the Palácio do Fonseca Acciolo. The former Franciscan monastery, founded in the 13th century and extensively altered in the 18th century, is also on the Praça da República.

Praça da República

Fans of sacred sculpture are well advised to pay a visit to the museum in the former home of José Régio (1901–1969) on Rua de José Régio, just south of the Praça da República. Among other things the famous Portuguese poet's unusual private collection of Christ figures and religious statues are on display.

Casa de José Régio

North of the Praça do Município stands the Museu da Tapeçaria de Portalegre, which informs its visitors about tapestry making. The process itself is explained and there are also interesting wall hangings, some of which bear motifs by famous artists such as Le Corbusier, Sonia Delaunay, Almada Negreiros and Júlio Pomar (open: Thu–Tue 9.30am–1pm and 2pm–6pm).

Museu da Tapeçaria de Portalegre ⊙

The Manufactura de Tapeçarias north-east of the old town near Jardim da Corredoura goes back to one of the silk weaving and rug workshops founded by the Marquês de Pombal in 1772. It is housed in the 17th-century former Jesuit monastery.

Manufactura de Tapeçarias

Not far north of the park stands the former São Bernardo monastery, today a barracks. It was founded in 1518 and later remodelled in a Baroque style. In the monastery church, the magnificent marble tomb (16th century) of Dom Jorge de Melo, the Bishop of Guarda

Convento de São Bernardo

Alentejan rural idyll: the ringing of sheep and goat bells is often to be heard.

and monastery founder, is attributed to the French sculptor Nicolas de Chanterène. Take a look at the two cloisters, one in Manueline, one in Renaissance style; in the larger one there is a beautiful marble fountain. The cross vault in the chapter house is impressive.

Around Portalegre

Vantage points As far as scenic beauty is concerned, Portalegre lies in an unusually charming region. There are magnificent views from Penha de São Tomé, the rock overhang 2km/1.3mi north-west of the town, as well as from the highest elevation of the Serra de São Mamede, the towering Pico São Mamede (1,025m/3,363ft) located 13km/8.1mi east.

Medóbriga About 12km/7.5mi north of Portalegre, near the village of Aramenha, lie the ruins of the Roman settlement Medóbriga; the finds from the excavations here are today exhibited in the Archaeology and Ethnology Museum in Belém (►Lisbon).

Crato Crato, the **former base of the order of the Knights of Malta**, lies about 20km/12.5mi west of Portalegre. Only sparse remains of the once mighty monastery complex still exist; it was destroyed in 1662 by Spanish troops.

The former Maltese monastery, 2km/1.3mi north of Crato in Flor da Rosa, is much better preserved. Part of the complex, built in 1350 and extended in the 16th century, now houses a pousada. The monastery church exhibits impressive austerity; plain marble columns adorn the late Gothic cloister. **Flor da Rosa**

Alter do Chão, located a good 30km/19mi south-west of Portalegre, is known for its state-run stud farm. It was founded as the »Coudelaria Real« (royal stud) as early as 1748. There is much of the original atmosphere here, and the 18th-century manor houses, the 14th-century castle crowned with battlements, a pretty Renaissance fountain from 1556, and the palace of the Vasconcelos family from 1732 are all worth seeing. **Alter do Chão**

►Castelo de Vide
►Marvão

Other destinations

Portimão

G 34

Historical province: Algarve
District: Faro

Elevation: 0–35m/115ft
Population: 40,000

Along with Faro und Olhão, Portimão one of the Algarve's biggest towns. For centuries it was the centre of Portuguese sardine fishing and the highly subsidized fish processing industry. Tourism plays only a secondary role in Portimão – visitors are predominantly day trippers from the nearby tourist centres who come here to shop.

Until the mid-1970s more than 70 trawlers regularly set off for the fishing grounds from Portimão, and fish were processed in a total of 61 factories. Then the subsidies were reduced considerably; today there is only one fish canning factory, few trawlers head out to sea, and disused sardine factories line the river banks. In the north of the town there are a few shipyards. **Fishing industry**

Portimão is a very lively town. On the banks of the Rio Arade with their prettily set out large squares, tourists and locals alike while away their time in cafés. In the centre north-west of the Praça Manuel Teixeira Gomes stand row upon row of shops. **Bustling Algarve town**
The area near the old road bridge conveys a bit of harbour atmosphere; there are quite a number of bars here, small family-run establishments, which offer excellent fresh fish – primarily sardines of course. In the north a railway bridge, an imposing expressway bridge and an old road bridge cross the Arade, over which you come directly into the town centre.

 **VISITING PORTIMÃO**

INFORMATION
Avenida Zeca Afonso
8500-516 Portimão
Tel. 282 470 732
www.visitalgarve.pt

SHOPPING
There are good shops in the streets
north of the Largo 1° de Dezembro.

BOAT TRIPS
Information and bookings down by
the water: trips to the grottoes on the
coast; also trips up the Rio Arade to
Silves (water level permitting).

WHERE TO EAT
▶ Moderate
Taberna da Maré
Travessa da Barca 9
Tel. 282 414 614
Family-run, small and simple restau-
rant, offering good, simple, Portuguese
cuisine. Speciality: various dried cod
dishes.

Cervejaria Lúcio
Largo Francisco A. Maurício 2
Tel. 282 413 962
Very good seafood, many Portuguese
are regular guests.

Dinamarca
Rua de Santa Isabel 14
Tel. 234 422 072
International cuisine, numerous spe-
cialities from the grill, Argentinean
steaks.

WHERE TO STAY
▶ Mid-range
Hotel Casabela
Ferragudo, Vale de Areia
Tel. 282 461 580, fax 282 461 581
High-class, mansion-like hotel with 53
rooms some distance from the town
near the beach; hardly any planned
activities on offer, more somewhere
for those seeking peace and quiet.

▶ Mid-range/Budget
Hotel Globo
Avenida 5 de Outubro 26
8500-581 Portimão
Tel. 282 416 350, fax 282 483 142
Respectable town hotel with 62 rooms.
Centrally located and rather loud.

▶ Budget
Pensão do Rio
Largo do Dique 20
8500 Portimão
Tel. 282 423 041, fax 282 411 895
Small guesthouse with 11 rooms
situated on a lively square on the bank

What to See in Portimão

Praça Visconde de Bívar
The Praça Visconde de Bívar, located at the riverside, is set out as a
pretty little park. From here there is a pleasant view over the Arade
to the opposite bank and the town of Ferragudo.

Largo 1° de Dezembro
The special feature of the pleasant Largo 1° de Dezembro are the ten
benches with azulejo pictures on which important events in Portuguese history are represented.

Postcard motif: the picturesque coastal town of Ferragudo at the mouth of the Rio Arade on the Atlantic coast

North of Largo 1° de Dezembro towers the Igreja Matriz. Before the earthquake in 1755, a 14th-century church stood at this location, and the Gothic portal is still preserved from this precursor. The small, meanwhile very weathered capitals showing various heads are of particular note. In the interior there are depictions of saints, some of which come from the destroyed church.

Igreja Matriz

Around Portimão

On the side of the Rio Arade opposite Portimão lies the fishing village of Ferragudo. It is the stuff of picture postcards, with its alleys lined with fishermen's houses, guesthouses and bars. Up in the village stands a pretty church as well as the Fortaleza de São João, built in 1622 to protect the entrance to the river. Today the fort is in private ownership.

✱
Ferragudo

South of Ferragudo stretches the **Praia Grande**, a large beach as the name suggests. A breakwater ensures that it is safe to swim here; besides this, the Praia Grande is primarily prized by surfers. The various restaurants offer refreshment.

The tourist hotspot ▶ Praia da Rocha is a neighbouring town to the south of Portimão. The former Moorish capital ▶ Silves, about 15km/9.4mi north-east of Portimão, still seems very antiquated. A number of other destinations, along the coast to the west and east of Portimão as well as inland, can be found under the section ▶ Algarve.

Other destinations near Portimão

✶ ✶ Porto

Historical province: Douro Litoral
District: Porto

Elevation: 0–140m/459ft
Population: 400,000 (Greater Porto: 1.6 million)

Porto is the second largest city in the country after Lisbon – an interesting, lively metropolis that some prefer to the capital. The city is world famous for its port wine – which actually comes from Vila Nova de Gaia on the southern banks of the Douro, where the wine dealers have their so-called port lodges.

Porto's name speaks for itself – »o porto« means harbour. In Portugal, the northern Portuguese metropolis is often referred to as **Oporto**, a moniker which almost reduces the city to its traditional function as harbour and trading city.

»o porto«, the harbour

There has always been a certain competition between the two Portuguese metropolises. While the Lisbonites refer disparagingly to the townsfolk of Porto as »tripeiros« (tripe eaters, see below), in Porto the residents of the capital are given the equally derogatory nickname of »alfacinhas« (lettuce eaters). In many respects the lively northern Portuguese metropolis is relegated to second place. It is the second largest city with about 400,000 inhabitants (1.6 million people live in Greater Porto); in economic and cultural terms, too, Porto has to be content with second place. That is especially painful because the people of Porto believe they are considerably more business-minded than their compatriots further south. A much-quoted saying claims that money is earned in Porto, and spent in Lisbon.

Tripe eaters versus lettuce eaters

> ### ! Baedeker TIP
>
> #### Do as the »tripeiros« do?
> Be brave and try it: »tripas à moda do Porto« (tripe with haricot beans) – a dish with history: when the Porto-born Henry the Navigator sent a ship off on a journey to conquer Ceuta, the inhabitants of Porto slaughtered all their livestock in order to provide the ship's company with meat. They themselves were content to eat the offal, and since then have been known throughout the land as »tripeiros« (tripe eaters).

The harbour has always played a fundamental role in the economy of the city. Leixões, today's harbour, lies just north of the city in Matosinhos. The »Francisco de Sá Carneiro« airport 13km/8.1mi north of the city connects Porto to the international air network. A remodelling for the 2004 European football championships have made it one of the most modern in the world.

Air and sea

← *An old ship loaded with barrels of port on the Douro. On the opposite bank lies the old town of the north Portuguese seaport and metropolis.*

History Porto's historical significance is undisputed: the city didn't only give the famous alcoholic beverage its name – the whole country is named after it. In antiquity a Hellenistic trading post existed in the area of today's city, and in Roman times the settlement Portus Cale was here. Later, the existence of a Suevian castle and afterwards the presence of the Visigoths has also been confirmed. After becoming a diocesan town, in 716 it was captured by the Arabs; it was destroyed in 825. After being reconquered in the 10th century the region between Minho and Douro, with the meanwhile newly built capital Porto, **became the county of Portucalia, the heartland of the later kingdom of Portugal**.

Traditionally, Porto is a liberal city. On several occasions in its history the inhabitants resisted authoritarian dictatorships with bloody revolts, as in the years 1628, 1661, 1757 and 1927. In 1808 Napoleonic troops under the command of Junot were beaten back here for the first time. In addition, the battle of the liberals against absolutism began in Porto; Dom Miguel I besieged the city in 1832/1833 and destroyed parts of it.

★ ★
City centre under UNESCO protection The houses in Porto's centre are crowded together on steep rock faces – often densely packed one above and behind the other – and form extremely picturesque terraces. Brilliance and misery lie side by side here. The heart of the city centre was declared a UNESCO World Cultural Heritage Site in 1996. But the observant visitor walking through Porto's old town will notice that there are problems: a large proportion of the houses stand partly or completely empty; whole streets are uninhabited. Restoration is expensive, and because the houses are listed buildings, they cannot be demolished. Rents for inner city flats are high despite their poor condition – **many people from Porto prefer living in modern quarters at the periphery of the city** where there is also sufficient parking space. Meanwhile, those remaining in the deserted inner city feel increasingly unsafe. In spite of all that Porto's centre is no ghost town, and at first glance visitors notice nothing of the emptiness, because in nearly all the houses there is a shop on the ground floor doing normal business. In this way the city centre is full of hustle and bustle during the daytime, though in the evenings – similar to many other cities – it seems rather desolate.

> ! **Baedeker TIP**
>
> **A bar with a panoramic view**
>
> On the top floor of the high-rise Dom Henrique hotel there is a bar from which you can enjoy a magnificent view over Porto at night (Hotel Dom Henrique, Rua Guedes de Azevedo 179).

European City of Culture In 2001 Porto was European City of Culture. To mark this special year several large construction projects were initiated, including the new underground system.

Highlights Porto

Avenida dos Aliados
A broad thoroughfare from the 1920s with several representative buildings

Torre dos Clérigos
The symbol of Porto. Marvellous view from the tower

Palácio da Bolsa
Especially impressive: the Sala dos Arabes

Ribeira
Interesting quarter in the old town. Relax in one of the cafés down by the river.

Sé
Cathedral with a well-fortified character and two beautiful cloisters.

Solar do Vinho do Porto
Sip on a glass of port in cosy surroundings with a view of the river.

Museu Nacional de Soares dos Reis
Cultural full house: furniture, textiles and porcelain from various centuries, as well as a comprehensive collection of Portuguese paintings

Museu dos Serralves
Outstanding museum for modern art

Foz do Douro
Suburb of Porto on the Atlantic coast

Vila Nova de Gaia
Visit a port lodge and take part in a tasting

The most important sights of Porto can be comfortably visited in one day, and a good starting point is the busy Praça da Liberdade. Those who also plan to see the important museums or wish to travel to the mouth of the Douro on the Atlantic coast should allow rather more time. In any case you should definitely take the opportunity to visit one of the port lodges in Vila Nova de Gaia.

Sightseeing in the city

What to See in Porto

On the spacious Praça da Liberdade stands an equestrian statue of King Pedro IV (died 1834), who from 1822 to 1831 was also Pedro I, Emperor of Brazil, and who to a large degree supported the liberal revolution that started in Porto in 1820.

✷
Praça da Liberdade

From the north side of the square runs the broad Avenida dos Aliado which was built from 1923–1929 after the demolition of an old residential quarter and, lined with banks and shops, climbs to the **city hall**. The granite building with its high tower originated in the first decades of the 20th century and is reminiscent of the government buildings in Flanders.

Avenida dos Aliados

VISITING PORTO

INFORMATION

Porto
Rua do Clube dos Fenianos 25
4000-172 Porto
Tel. 223 393 470

Airport
Tel. 229 412 534

Rua do Infante D. Henrique 63
Tel. 222 009 770
www.portoturismo.pt

Vila Nova de Gaia
Av. Diogo Leite 242
4400-111 Vila Nova de Gaia
Tel./fax 223 790 994
www.cm-gaia.pt

CAR/PUBLIC TRANSPORT

Driving and looking for a parking space in Porto can become a real strain. As the most important sights are in close proximity to one another, the car should be left behind at least during the week in favour of going on foot or using public transport – in the form of buses, trams or the underground.

PASSE PORTO

The Passe Porto allows you to use nearly all buses, trams, the metro, some suburban train services and the AeroBus free of charge.

SHOPPING

Porto's main shopping street is Rua de Santa Catarina along which there are numerous shops, cafés and restaurants – the same applies to the adjoining side streets. It is best to go to the nearby Mercado do Bolhão for fruit and vegetables.

ENTERTAINMENT

Good places for the evening's entertainment are the Ribeira down by the Douro and the »Food & Flirt-Zone« on the opposite river bank in the newly designed Cais de Gaia in Vila Nova de Gaia. Alternatively, it is pleasant to take a trip to Foz on warm summer evenings and visit the beach bars there.

WHERE TO EAT

▶ Expensive

① *Portucale*
Rua da Alegria 598
Tel. 225 370 717
Renowned restaurant on the 13th floor of a high-rise with a panoramic view over the roofs of Porto.

▶ Moderate

Baedeker recommendation

⑤ *Real Indiana*
Cais de Gaia, Loja 360
Tel. 223 744 422
On the opposite bank of the Douro in Vila Nova de Gaia. Excellent Indian cuisine. Terrace with a view of the river and the centre of Porto.

② *O Escondidinho*
Rua Passos Manuel 144
Tel. 222 001 079
Very good food, typical of the region, for example »tripas à moda do Porto« (a traditional tripe dish). The restaurant is small; reservation recommended.

③ *Tripeiro*
Rua Passos Manuel 195
Tel. 222 005 886

Typical restaurant for the region, centrally located. Good fish and meat dishes, also popular at lunchtime.

④ *Filha da Mãe Preta*
Cais da Ribeira 40
Tel. 222 055 515
This is one of the best of the numerous restaurants on the banks of the Douro. Nice furnishings and wonderful decorated tiles on the walls.

WHERE TO STAY
► Mid-range/Luxury
① *Hotel Infante de Sagres*
Praça D. Filipa de Lencastre 62
4050-259 Porto
Tel. 223 398 500; fax 223 398 599
www.hotelinfantedesagres.pt
The exclusive, old luxury hotel of which dreams are made, with valuable furnishings and impeccable service. Beautiful patio.

► Mid-range
② *Hotel Dom Henrique*
Rua Guedes de Azevedo 179
4049-009 Porto
Tel. 223 401 616; fax 223 401 615
www.hotel-dom-henrique.pt
Good hotel in a not especially attractive high-rise in the city centre. Comfortable rooms. The bar on the top floor has a magnificent view of the city.

► Budget
④ *Pensão Universal*
Avenida dos Aliados 38
4000-064 Porto
Tel. 222 006 758
Pleasant, spacious guesthouse with rather antiquated appeal in the city centre.

⑤ *Residencial O Escondidinho*
Rua Passos Manuel 135

The charm of bygone days: a lounge in the Grande Hotel do Porto

4000-385 Porto
Tel. 222 004 079; fax 222 026 075
Simple, newly-furnished guesthouse; rooms with one to four beds – reliable, friendly, centrally located.

Baedeker recommendation

► Budget/Mid-range
③ *Grande Hotel do Porto*
Rua de Santa Catarina 197
4000-450 Porto
Tel. 222 076 690
Fax 222 076 699
www.grandehotelportocom
An old, well-kept hotel with about 100 mostly rather small rooms, with a central quiet location. The lounges and the breakfast room still possess the charm of bygone days. Very good restaurant; own car park.

Porto *Plan*

Rua de Miguel Bombarda

Rua Boa Nova

Rua Adolfo Casais Montero

Rua Rosário

Museu Nacional Soares dos Reis

Tv. do Rosário

R. Clemente Menéres

R. Dr. Tiago de Almeida

R. de Cedofeita

R. de

Teatro

Praça Carlos Alberto

Tv. Sá Noronha

Rua José Falcão

Igreja do Carmo

Solar do Vinho do Porto

Rua de D. Manuel II

Igreja das Carmelitas

Rua Carmo

Rua Alberto Gouveia

Hospital de Santo António

Palácio de Cristal

Rua Jorge Viterbo

Praça Gomes Teixeira

Rua Carmelitas

Universidade

Praça de Lisboa

Rua da Restauração

R. Lage

Campo Mártires da Pátria

R. Felipe Nery

R. da Assunção

Torre dos Clérigos

Rua de Trás

Rua dos Caldeireiros

Bandeirinha

Rua A. Albuquerque

MIRAGAIA

R. Monte Hudere

R. Dr. B. Castro

Cadeia da Relação

Mosteiro S. Bento da Vitória

Mosteiro de S. Bento

Rua de Miragaia

R. da

Cais da Alfândega

Rua de Monchique

Largo da Alfândega

Igreja de Miragaia

R. C. Cima
R. C. Baixo
R. Armazém

R. S. Pedro
C. Virtudes
R. Atafona

R. Francisco Rocha

R. Virtudes

R. S. Miguel

R. de S. Bento da Vitória

Vitória

Igreja da Misericórdia

Rua Mouzinho

Rua

R. T. Gonçaga

R. da Armênia

R. de Miragaia

Rua Nova da Alfândega

Alfândega Nova

R. de Belmonte

R. Comércio do Porto

Rua da Bolsa

R. Ferreira Borges

Mercado Ferreira Borges

Palácio da Bolsa

Praça do Infante D. Henrique

Casa do Infante

Rua da Alfândega

R. S. Nicolau

R. Fonte

Rua Cais de Gaia

Rio Douro

Igreja de S. Francisco

Igreja de S. Nicolau

Rua da Reboleira

Rua S. Marcos

Rua Castelo

Lg. do Castelo

CASTELO

R. S. Lourenço

Rua Vitorio Campos

Rua do Prior

Rua Rua Porto

Muro dos Bacalhoeiros

Cais da Estiva

Cais dos Barcos R.

Rua Cais de Gaia

Avenida Ramos Pinto

150 m
495 ft

©Baedeker

(5)

VILA NOVA DE GAIA

Cais de Gaia

Avenida

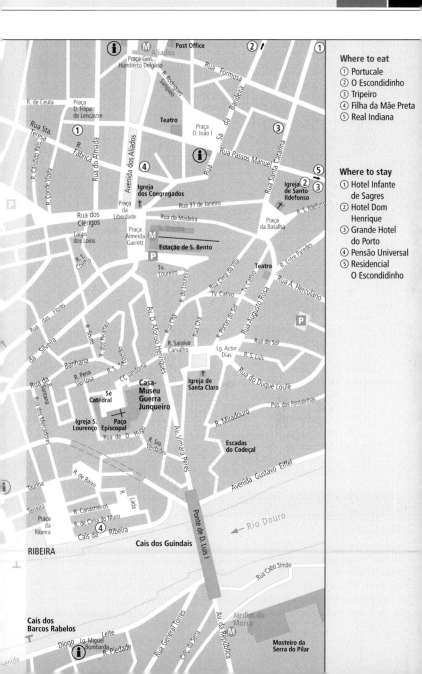

Where to eat

① Portucale
② O Escondidinho
③ Tripeiro
④ Filha da Mãe Preta
⑤ Real Indiana

Where to stay

① Hotel Infante
   de Sagres
② Hotel Dom
   Henrique
③ Grande Hotel
   do Porto
④ Pensão Universal
⑤ Residencial
   O Escondidinho

An absolute must-see: São Bento station with its marvellous azulejo pictures. Various modes of transport from the different eras are depicted.

Estação São Bento

✳ São Bento station located directly south-east of the Praça da Liberdade was built in the early 20th century. Take a look inside the station concourse: it is clad with **azulejo pictures** showing historical motifs and the history of the development of various means of transport.

Igreja dos Congregados

Diagonally opposite the station stands the Igreja dos Congregados, flanked on both sides by residential and commercial buildings. The façade of this church, built around 1700, is partly covered with azulejos.

Torre dos Clérigos

✳ From the south-west corner of the Praça da Liberdade, the busy Rua dos Clérigos leads up to the Igreja dos Clérigos, built in 1732–1748 according to plans by Italian architect Nicolo Nasoni. The Baroque church was constructed on an oval floor plan. There is a connecting building between the church and the Torre dos Clérigos. The 75m/246ft-high tower, considered an emblem of Porto, was erected between 1755 and 1763 and financed by the clergy of the city. It is possible to climb to the top from which there is a view of the city panorama and the Douro Valley over to the Atlantic coast.

The **concert glockenspiel** with 49 bells can be heard daily at around 11.30am and 6pm.

! *Baedeker* TIP

Lello bookshop

A minor sight: the Livraria Lello (Rua Carmelitas 144, next to the university), the most beautiful bookshop in Porto – probably for that matter in the whole of Portugal. The wide range of books is of course mostly in Portuguese, but that aside, the old interior of the shop is nothing short of breathtaking.

A little further north – beyond the Praça de Lisboa – extends the white, elongated building of the university, which until 1911 was a polytechnic.

University

On the Praça de Gomes Teixeira to the north-west and opposite the university, two churches stand side by side: the **Igreja do Carmo** (right hand side; built 1756), whose eastern side is clad with blue 19th-century azulejos; and the **Igreja das Carmelitas** (left hand side; 1619–1628). Inside both churches is a richly gilded altar.

There are some old, tall trees in the green area, the **Campo dos Mártires da Pátria**, on the southern side of the university. From the square, the streets of the old town and steps lead down towards the river.

> ! **Baedeker** TIP
>
> **A Sunday in Porto**
> A single Sunday in Porto reveals all the variety that Portugal has to offer: in the morning a visit to the livestock market at São Bento station, then on to the Museu de Serralves. While the market gives an almost medieval impression, visitors to the museum are surrounded by Portugal's most modern art and architecture.

It is a short detour to Rua das Flores, once the street of goldsmiths and cloth merchants, in which jeweller's shops and other very exclusive stores are still to be found today.

Rua das Flores

Also on Rua das Flores stands the Igreja da Misericórdia, built in the first half of the 18th century by Nasoni, the architect responsible for the Clérigos church.

Igreja da Misericórdia

The large square in the old town is the Praça do Infante Dom Henrique with a monument to **Henry the Navigator**, who was born in Porto.
The north side of the square borders on the Mercado de Ferreira Borges. The market hall, built in 1883, now hosts temporary exhibitions.

Praça do Infante Dom Henrique

The most important controlling authority for the cultivation and production of port is the Instituto do Vinho do Porto whose offices are opposite the market hall.

Instituto do Vinho do Porto

The stock exchange, the seat of Porto's trade association, was built in 1842 on the site of a Franciscan monastery which burnt down. A hall with a glass roof was erected where the cloister once stood. The interior of the building, including the Nation's Courtyard, the Commercial Court and the President's Salon, can be visited in organized tours taking place several times a day. The »Arab hall«, used for official receptions, is particularly interesting (open: Nov–March 9am–1pm and 2pm–6pm; April–Oct 9am–7pm).

Palácio da Bolsa

★
◄ Sala dos Arabes
🕐

View of the opposite river bank on the nightly illuminated Ribeira

Igreja de São Francisco It is definitely worth taking a look at the former church of the Franciscan monastery, the Igreja de São Francisco, situated just south of the stock exchange. Originally Gothic, the church was later remodelled in Baroque style and is decorated by a rose window. The interior is interesting: it is clearly visible how the golden **talha dourada decoration** was added to the plain medieval building in the 17th/18th centuries. The small museum for sacred art adjoining the church is just as interesting. From here it is possible to enter the **catacombs** – in the 17th and 18th centuries they served as tombs for the Franciscan monks.

Alfândega Nova A little further along the river bank stands the former customs building, which today houses a museum for transport and telecommunications.

Museu do Vinho do Porto Some distance further out from the city, also on the bank of the river, is the Museu do Vinho do Porto. It shows a small, attractive exhibition on the history of port wine, complete with original documents and photographs.

Casa do Infante Rua Alfândega Velha leads from the Praça do Infante Dom Henrique down to the river. Until recently it was considered highly unlikely that the Casa do Infante in Rua Alfândega Velha was in fact the **birthplace of Henry the Navigator**. However during investigations in 1992, traces from the 15th century fitting that theory were indeed discovered; indications of the Roman era were also found under the foundations of the house. The Casa do Infante served as a customs house until the 19th century.

The Ribeira is the **quarter of the old town directly beside the Douro**. Although the one time harbour quarter has in the meantime become a tourist attraction and excursion boats are now moored at the quays, this part of Porto has kept its charm to a large extent. The focal point of the hustle and bustle is the Praça da Ribeira. Here and in the surrounding streets there is a colourful jumble of houses. While it may appear picturesque to tourists, it is less attractive for the people who live here: the quarter is in urgent need of development, but the necessary funds for investment are not available. Only a few of the houses and the buildings directly at the edge of the Douro have been renovated and decorated attractively: galleries, boutiques and restaurants in the upper price bracket are found here today. From the Ribeira there is a good view of the Ponte de Dom Luís I (► p.456) and the port lodges in Vila Nova de Gaia on the other side of the river.

★ ★
Ribeira

West of the Praça da Ribeira in Rua da Reboleira 37 is the Centro Regional de Artes Tradicionais, in which arts and crafts from northern Portugal are sold.

Centro Regional de Artes Tradicionais

The twin-towered cathedral was originally a Romanesque building from the 12th century which was later remodelled in the Gothic style and almost completely restored in the 17th and 18th centuries. It has, however, retained its fortified character. The rosette over the doorway on the west façade still dates back to Roman times; the loggia on the north façade was created by Nasoni in 1736. In the plain and simple interior there are several richly furnished altars, including the carved and gilded wooden altar in the choir from the first half of the 18th century. The silver altar in the chapel of the sacrament in the left transept is even more magnificent; it was created by several Portuguese artists from 1632–1732. The statue of **Nossa Senhora de Vendoma, the patron saint of Porto** is also in the left transept. The right aisle leads to the Gothic **cloister** from 1385 whose azulejo decoration is from the first half of the 18th century, adjoining which are remains of a Romanesque cloister.

★
Sé

There are extensive views onto the jumbled houses and streets of Porto from the terraces on the north and west façades of the cathedral. The neo-Manueline pillar, modelled on a medieval pelourinho, was created at the end of the 19th century.

The Igreja de São Lourenço, seen from the terrace on the west façade of the cathedral, is one of Portugal's first Baroque churches and was built in the early 17th century as a Jesuit seminary church. Its second name, Igreja dos Grilos, is due to the barefoot Augustinian monks

Igreja de São Lourenço

who took ownership of the church in 1780: the monks were known as »Grilos« (crickets) because of their brown and black habits.

Adjoining the cathedral to the south is the former bishop's palace, a mighty building begun in 1771 with an elegant stairwell. Today, the palace serves as the headquarters of the municipal authorities.

Paço Episcopal

The reconstruction of a medieval tower in the immediate vicinity of the cathedral created something of a stir. The chosen spot – 15m/16.5yd from the original location – and the manner of the reconstruction annoyed many residents of Porto.

Medieval tower

The writer Abílio Manuel de Guerra Junqueiro (1850–1923) lived east of the cathedral in an 18th-century Baroque building which is also attributed to Nasoni. In his verse, the politically active poet vehemently advocated the founding of a republic. Amongst the exhibits in the Casa-Museu Guerra Junqueiro are pieces of furniture and ceramics as well as the death mask of the poet (Rua D. Hugo 32; open: Tue–Sat 10am–12.30pm and 2pm–5.30pm, Sun 2pm–6pm).

Casa-Museu Guerra Junqueiro

Further east, beyond the wide approach road to the Ponte de D. Luís I, stands the originally Gothic Santa Clara church, on which considerable alterations were carried out during the Renaissance period. The interior is richly decorated with talha dourada.

Igreja de Santa Clara

Those wishing to enjoy a magnificent view should go from the Igreja de Santa Clara to the **Passeio das Fontainhas**, a narrow promenade high above the Douro with a view onto the river and towards Vila Nova de Gaia on the other side.

✱ View

Rua Augusto Rosa leads north-east from the Santa-Clara church to the Praça da Batalha, busy with traffic. The Igreja de Santo Ildefonso is an impressive building; its Baroque façade is adorned with blue-and-white azulejos. Set slightly further back on the corner of Rua Augusto Rosa stands the Teatro Nacional São João, built in 1920.

Praça da Batalha

Rua de Santa Catarina, Porto's main shopping street which is in part a pedestrian zone, exits at the northern end of the Praça da Batalha. The shops here and in the surrounding side streets are not only good, many of them also offer excellent value for money.

! Baedeker TIP

Café Majestic

This café is on no account to be missed: the Majestic at Rua de Santa Catarina 112 is an Art Nouveau coffee house with an ambience all its own; open daily until 2am (except Sundays).

← *Café Majestic: mirrors, decoration, lamps, furnishings – finest Portuguese Art Nouveau*

North-west of the City Centre

Jardim do Palácio de Cristal

South-west of the Museu Nacional de Soares dos Reis lies the Jardim do Palácio de Cristal. The Pavilhão dos Desportos was built in the midst of the park grounds in 1952 on the site of the former crystal palace. The round stadium, which can seat about 10,000 people, is also used for other big events. From the south side of the park there is a magnificent view of the city, river and ocean.

In the **Romantic Museum** (Museu Romântico), to the west outside the Jardim do Palácio de Cristal, there is a house completely furnished in the Portuguese style of the 19th century (open: Tue–Sat 10am–12.30pm and 2pm–5.30pm, Fri and Sat until 6pm, Sun 2pm–6pm).

Casa Tait

Temporary exhibitions are shown in the Casa Tait, a beautiful residential building near the Museu Romântico. A small permanent exhibition displays coins from various countries and eras.

✷ Museu Nacional de Soares dos Reis

About 500m/550yd north-west of the Jardim de João Chagas is the Museu Nacional de Soares dos Reis, housed in the Palácio dos Carrancas on Rua de Dom Manuel II. The building was built as a royal palace in 1795. The collections in the museum include prehistoric and Roman antiquities, medieval and modern sculpture, painting, ceramics and porcelain, wrought gold items, furniture and textiles.

The extensive **art collection** is worth seeing, with works by the sculptor Soares dos Reis (1847–1899) from Porto as well as Teixeira Lopes and Diogo de Macedo. As far as paintings are concerned, the Portuguese school of the 16th century is represented with pictures by Vasco Fernandes and Frei Carlos; from the 19th and 20th centuries there are works by the painters Henrique Pousão, Columbano Bordalo Pinheiro, António Carneiro, António Carvalho da Silva Porto, Marquês de Oliveira, Aurélia de Sousa, Eduardo Viana and Dordio Gomes, as well as paintings by Jean Clouet and Jean-Baptiste Pillement from France. The museum café with tables in the inner courtyard is a good place to relax (open: Tue 2pm–6pm, Wed–Sun 10am–12.30pm and 1.30pm–6pm).

Casa da Música

At the Rotunda da Boavista and the Praça de Mousinho de Albuquerque north of the Jardim do Palácio de Cristal stands the Casa da Música, Porto's new concert hall. The crystal-shaped structure was built to a design by the Dutch architect Rem Koolhaas and is highly praised for its **excellent acoustics**. The Casa da Música is also open to the public when concerts are not being played.

The monument on the Praça de Mousinho de Albuquerque, erected in 1929, commemorates the war of 1808/1809 against France.

Monument

Not far east of the square stands the small, Romanesque Igreja de Cedofeita dating back to the 12th century, the oldest place of worship in the city. The name of the church (»cedo feita« = »quickly done«) points to the fact that it was built within a very short period of time.

Igreja de Cedofeita

A visit to the Fundação Serralves with the Museu Serralves, a museum for modern art, and a spacious park is definitely worthwhile. The whole complex grew around the Casa de Serralves (Rua Serralves 977), an architecturally interesting Art Déco house which was owned by the Conde de Vizela. At the same time the count had the park landscaped as a garden with meadows, avenues and citrus fruit plantations, to which today a school garden and a farm have been added.

★
Fundação Serralves

The Museu Serralves was built by **Álvaro Siza Vieira** (►Famous People) in the late 1990s. Temporary exhibitions of modern art by artists from all over the world are shown here. The greatest aesthetic treat – the exhibitions notwithstanding – is the passageway through the functionalist building (opening hours for museum: Tue–Sun 10am–7pm, April–Sept: Fri, Sat 10am–10pm, Sun 10am–8pm; park: Tue–Sun 10am–7pm, April–Sept: Sat, Sun 10am–8pm).

★
◄ Museu Serralves

Further out of town is Foz, actually Foz do Douro. »Foz do Douro« means something like the mouth of the Douro – and the Porto suburb indeed lies at the point where the river flows into the Atlantic. The atmosphere of Foz is completely oriented to the ocean. There are rather urban beaches, and a few nice cafés, restaurants and bars in the summer months. From the mole at the lighthouse there is a wide view of the estuary and the coast, once defended by the Castelo da Foz from 1570. The 17th-century Castelo do Queijo stands on the road to Matosinhos further north-west; it was built to defend the coast against pirates from North Africa.

Foz do Douro

> **!** *Baedeker* TIP
>
> **Sunset on the Douro estuary**
>
> In Foz do Douro there are a few good street cafés and bars on the Praia dos Ingleses, serving coffee, drinks and also food. Here, you can sit and look out at the sea – exactly in the direction of the setting sun.

A somewhat bizarre local relic can be found in the cemetary of Foz: the body of the priest and abbot José dos Santos Ferreira Moura was embalmed and preserved as a mummy. It is on display there because he is venerated as a saint by local people.

Vila Nova de Gaia

Centre of the port trade
The storage and trade in port is concentrated in the town of Vila Nova de Gaia on the south bank of the Douro. The name »Gaia« is a variation of the ancient »cale« (beautiful). Several bridges connect Vila Nova de Gaia with Porto.

✱ Ponte de Dom Luís I
The Ponte de Dom Luís I leads from the centre of Porto directly to Vila Nova de Gaia. Built between 1881 and 1885 by the Belgian company Willebroek, the bridge spans the Douro with an iron arch 172m/564ft long. The lower roadway runs 10m/33ft over the river, the upper one – along which a metro line now runs – is 68m/223ft high. From the southern bridgehead there is a wonderful view of Porto's city centre and the river with its steeply rising banks.

Ponte de Dona Maria Pia
Rail traffic rolls across the Ponte de Dona Maria Pia east of the centre. The bridge, which was put into service in 1877, is the work of **Gustave Eiffel**: an iron construction with a height of about 60m/197ft above the water and a length of 344m/376yd. In order to deal with the increasing volume of traffic, another rail bridge was built immediately beside it.

Ponte da Arrábida
The Ponte da Arrábida to the west outside the centre was first opened in 1963; some of the traffic now uses a new motorway bridge outside the city centre to the east.

Mosteiro da Serra do Pilar
On a hill east of the Ponte de Dom Luís I stands the 17th-century former Augustinian monastery of Serra do Pilar. A perfectly circular cloister adjoins a similarly round church, which is crowned by a

Vila Nova de Gaia *Plan*

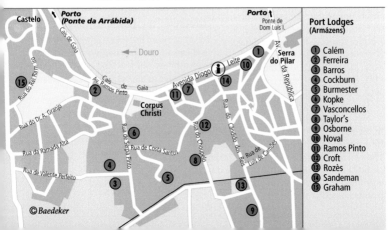

Port Lodges (Armázens)

① Calém
② Ferreira
③ Barros
④ Cockburn
⑤ Burmester
⑥ Kopke
⑦ Vasconcellos
⑧ Taylor's
⑨ Osborne
⑩ Noval
⑪ Ramos Pinto
⑫ Croft
⑬ Rozès
⑭ Sandeman
⑮ Graham

© Baedeker

Flat-bottom boats, the so-called »rabelos«, carrying port on the Douro near Porto

»DO YOU KNOW DR WRIGHT OF NORWICH?«

Tawny, red, ruby, late bottled vintage, white port – with such terms, it is no wonder that many people believe port is an English product. It is true that without England Portugal's best-known export would surely never have been created. Port is almost the English national drink, and woe betide anyone who abuses it – like Lord Nelson!

Wine grapes thrived in the upper reaches of the Douro as early as Roman times. Though the wine was traded in Porto, it was not called port but »vinho de Cale«. In the local vernacular it came to be known as »vinho para nobres« (wine for the nobility). This grape juice, an ordinary red wine, was also exported.

English preferences

It is said that the English developed a preference for »red Portugal« as early as the Middle Ages; during the War of the Roses, the Duke of Clarence was captured by his brother, Richard III, and allegedly **drowned by him in a barrel of wine** – Malmsey wine from Porto. The export of wine from the region around Porto to England increased markedly after Charles II (1630–1685) married Princess Catarina from the House of Bragança. In 1666 a »Factory House« was founded in Porto, a kind of English trade guild; it survives today as the British Association.

Shortly afterwards the families whose names still stand on port bottles moved in: the **Crofts**, the **Osbornes**, the **Taylors**. The Dutch (the **Kopkes**) and the Germans (the **Burmesters**) came too, but the English formed by far the largest colony. Port wine, vinho do Porto, was born in the form it is known today as an aperitif or digestif in 1680. English merchants began to add up to 25 % brandy to the wine from the Douro in order to make it keep longer on the sea voyage to England. From the early 19th century the cease in fermentation achieved by adding 76% proof spirits was valued as a means of producing a very special drink – from the once very rough alcoholic plonk came the delicate, sweet nectar with 20% alcohol that we know today.

England's profit – Portugal's loss

The export of port resulted in Portugal becoming very **economically dependent on England**. On 17 December 1703 the Portuguese and the English signed a trade agreement, the so-called Methuen Treaty named after the English ambassador in Lisbon, John Methuen, whose father and father-in-law were in the textile business. This trade agreement comprised the exchange of English textiles and Portuguese wine: England received export relief for its woollen goods; in return Portugal could introduce wine to the British Isles under favourable conditions and potentially profit by filling the gap in the market created since 1667, when the British crown had prohibited the importation of French wine in protest against the protective duty and taxation policies of Louis XIV. The agreement was directed against the French economy, but the actual loser was – despite the resulting port boom – Portugal. The country was flooded with woollen goods from England, which destroyed the domestic wool industry. In addition many farmers and land owners changed from grain and vegetable growing to wine production. The wine, produced in greater and greater quantities, became increasingly cheap; on the other hand the insufficient grain had to be supplemented by imports – from England. The English were rubbing their hands with glee as the imported grain

» *...many farmers and land owners changed from grain and vegetable growing to wine production.*«

No chance for the successors of Dr Wright – in Portugal, port is served in glasses.

and textiles had to be paid for with two-thirds of the gold that the Portuguese crown received from the colonies. In 1757 the Marques de Pombal created a Portuguese monopoly company for the trade in port, known as the Old Wine Company and later as the Royal Oporto Wine Company; it still does business under the latter name and is one of the largest port companies. Only aristocratic landowners benefited from the lucrative trade in port wine, not the small traders and wine growers, many of whom lost everything they owned. The wine growers formed a **protest group**, forced their way into the offices of the hated trading company in Porto and burnt it to the ground. Pombal reacted quickly. Of the several thousand revolting farmers, 442 where sentenced in court, 26 to death; 17 did in fact end up at the gallows. Pombal's goal to dismantle the supremacy of the English was only partly achieved. The largest English companies remained in existence and developed into the most respected port producers, as names such as Sandeman, Dealforce and Croft show.

Nelson's faux pas and Dr Wright

In the 18th and 19th centuries port was considered the drink of the English gentleman; many patriotic individuals were of the opinion that it held the British Empire together. And woe betide anyone who violated the rules! Even **Lord Nelson** was never forgiven for drawing up the plans for a sea battle on the table top with vintage port. For a while, it seemed, port was better known in the British Isles than in its land of origin; at least, English travellers to Lisbon in the 18th century are said to have sorely missed the port they were used to at home. The drinking of port also brought about **customs and etiquette** which some may find a little odd. One rule is that the decanter should be passed clockwise from guest to guest. If a particular guest fails to do this, he will be asked the traditional question »Do you know Dr Wright of Norwich?« and thereby gently reprimanded. Dr Wright was a gentleman from the 1850s who was well known for being an inveterate talker who omitted to pass on the port.

Under the roofs of Vila de Gaia fine port is stored in barrels.

magnificent dome. The cloister's barrel vaulting is supported by 36 Ionic columns. The monastery terrace boasts what is probably the very best view of Porto and the Douro Valley with its bridges.

Port lodges The wine dealers from Porto – many companies were founded by the British – have their long, low storage facilities west of the Ponte de Dom Luís I. They are referred to as »armazéns« or »lodges« and are often hewn deep into the granite. Almost all port producers offer guided tours through their lodges. Wine tastings are part of the tours, and there is the possibility to buy port(basic wine vocabulary ►Food and Drink).

Around Porto

Matosinhos Matosinhos, lying at the mouth of the small Leça river not quite 10km/6.3mi north of Porto, is an industrial seaport. The fish canning factories are important economic factors. The Portuguese, unfazed by the industrial feel, visit the town with its good beaches as a seaside resort.

Porto de Leixões At the mouth of the Leça lies the modern port of Porto de Leixões with a harbour protected by two pincer-like breakwaters projecting into the sea, one 1,597m/1,747yd and one 1,145m/1,252yd long, serving as an outer harbour for Porto. It was built in 1884 and continually extended during the course of the 20th century; today Porto de Leixões is one of the largest commercial trading ports on the Iberian Peninsula.

It is necessary to travel out of Porto almost as far as Esposende or Ofir south of the mouth of the Cávado to find nice beaches with an acceptable hinterland (▶Barcelos, ▶Costa Verde). All the places closer to Porto are plainly characterized by the city and the surrounding industry. Even the towns Póvoa de Varzim and ▶Vila do Conde are not particularly suitable for excursions.

Coast north of Porto

The coast south of Porto is somewhat more appealing (▶Costa de Prata). The beaches of Granja and Miramar are within easy reach, as is the rather urban Espinho.

Coast south of Porto

Praia da Rocha

G 34

Historical province: Algarve
District: Faro

Elevation: 20m/66ft
Population: 2,000

Praia da Rocha is one of the large, unappealing tourist centres of the Algarve. Today, nothing remains of the flair of the once stylish seaside resort that Praia da Rocha must have been in the first half of the 20th century.

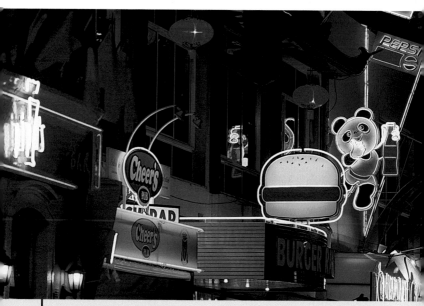

Praia da Rocha's party promenade

VISITING PRAIA DA ROCHA

INFORMATION
Avenida Tomás Cabreira
8500-802 Portimão
Tel. 282 419 132
www.visitalgarve.pt

WHERE TO EAT
▶ **Moderate**
Falésia
Avenida Tomás Cabreira
Tel. 282 412 917
Pleasant restaurant with a nice terrace.

Safari
Rua António Feu 8
Tel. 282 423 540
The speciality here is seafood as well as African dishes.

WHERE TO STAY
▶ **Luxury**
Hotel Algarve
Av. Tomás Cabreira
8500-802 Portimão
Tel. 282 402 000
Fax 282 402 099
www.solverde.pt
Old, established luxury hotel on the promenade with 220 rooms. Nicely furnished, excellent service, playground, casino.

> ## Baedeker recommendation
>
> ▶ **Mid-range**
> *Hotel Bela Vista*
> Av. Tomás Cabreira
> 8500-802 Portimão
> Tel. 282 450 480,
> Fax 282 415 369
> www.hotelbelavista.net
> One of the traditional Algarve hotels. The painstakingly renovated building on the promenade with 14 rooms exudes atmosphere. Good service and amenities.

As far as the municipal authorities are concerned, the holiday town of Praia da Rocha is a suburb of the seaport ▶Portimão 3km/1.9mi to the north. There is a good tourist infrastructure here, with quite a lot of possibilities for sport and recreation and numerous restaurants, cafés and bars.

Townscape With its faceless apartment and hotel buildings, Praia da Rocha counts as one of the absolute blots on the landscape of the Algarve. Above the approximately 2km/1.3mi-long and almost 100m/110yd-wide main beach runs Avenida Tomás Cabreira, lined with hotels, restaurants, cafés, boutiques and shops. At the east end of the Avenida the Fortaleza de Santa Catarina, a 17th-century fortification, stands guard over the mouth of the Rio Arade. From here there is a nice view over to Ferragudo (▶Portimão) and the marina directly below the fort.

Beaches Praia da Rocha's main beach with its unusual boulders is the holiday resort's capital. Once it must have been very picturesque; today it is very crowded in the peak season. To the west, a row of idyllic bays adjoin the Praia da Rocha, separated from one another by rocky reefs and arches in the rocks. However because of the large number of holiday camps here, especially in the vicinity of Alvor (► Algarve), visitors can hardly expect to find a secluded spot on the beach.

✳ Queluz

C 24

Historical province: Estremadura
District: Lisboa

Elevation: 125m/410ft
Population: 48,000

Located immediately north-west of Lisbon, the town of Queluz owes its importance and fame to the pretty Rococo palace and summer residence of the same name – meaning »what a light!« – still used today for state receptions.

Apart from the palace, Queluz has no sights whatsoever. The small town, whose concrete residential blocks provide housing about 30,000 people, lies in the capital's catchment area.

✳ Palácio Nacional de Queluz

The palace and gardens are usually open from Wed–Mon 10am–5pm; because they are used for official receptions however, it is advisable to ask if the palace complex is accessible at the tourist information office. **Opening times**

The palace of Queluz was built from 1747 to 1794 on the orders of Pedro III and his wife, later Queen Maria I. Construction work was first carried out according to the plans of the Portuguese master builder Mateus Vicente de Oliveira (1706–1785) – a student of the Regensburg architect Johann Friedrich Ludwig, whose creations included the monastery in ►Mafra. The middle section of the building was completed in 1758. From 1760 onwards, under the leadership of the French architect Jean Baptiste Robillon, the west wing of the pal- **History**

 VISITING QUELUZ

WHERE TO EAT

► **Expensive**
Cozinha Velha
Largo do Palácio
Tel. 214 356 158
Gourmet restaurant in the former palace kitchen. Exquisite cuisine.

WHERE TO STAY

► **Budget**
Pousada de Dona Maria I
2745-191 Queluz-Lisboa
Tel. 214 356 158; fax 214 356 189
Very stylish pousada (26 rooms) opposite the Rococo palace.

A summer palace as if from the pages of a book: the light and airy Rococo Palácio Nacional de Queluz, requested by Queen Maria I.

ace was built, numerous rooms furnished and the gardens designed. Work was completed in 1794.

Palace square The spacious Largo do Palácio opens out in front of the palace; a monument to Maria I stands here. The buildings for the royal guard and the domestic staff as well as the palace church built in finest Rococo style are today separated from the other palace buildings by a road.

Palace site The three-winged palace radiates a cheerful, bright atmosphere. The French influence is visible in the palace's interior. There is gold painted stucco ornamentation almost everywhere in rocaille and garland patterns as well as wall panelling made of tiles and ceiling frescoes which illustrate the original function of the individual rooms. The **throne room**, still often used for state receptions or balls, was decorated with Rococo wood carvings by Faria Lobo. In the otherwise empty room, the allegorical ceiling frescoes and heavy crystal chandeliers are striking. Between 1759 and 1768, work was carried out on the **music room**. The surroundings are perfect for the small chamber concerts that frequently take place here even today. The **Corredor das Mangas** (corridor of the shirtsleeves) connects two parts of the building. It was given its second name, the azulejo corridor, because of the tile pictures (from 1784) with depictions of the seasons, the continents and hunting scenes.

The pousada has been opened in one of the palace wings. The luxury restaurant »Cozinha Velha« has now been established in the former palace kitchen (entry from the square in front of the palace).

Pousada Cozinha Velha

The gardens are well worth seeing. They are landscaped according to plans by **Jean Baptiste Robillon**, who designed them in Rococo style based on the work of the French landscape gardener Le Nôtre. Allegorical figures, vases and azulejos are integrated into the garden plants which consist of box tree hedges, geometric flower beds and herbaceous borders. Some of the lead sculptures were cast in England. The plants are interspersed with fountains and water courses; the reflective surfaces of the calm pools were consciously included as an original design element. In the lower part of the garden the waters of the Jamor stream are dammed, forming a 115m/377ft-long pond decorated with azulejos. Members of the royal family would linger in this corner of the garden to fish, go out on boats, play games or take meals in a summer house. The broad **Lion Staircase**, so-called because of the lion sculptures, connects the garden with the palace buildings considerably higher up.

Palace gardens

Ribatejo

D–L 18–24

Historical province: Ribatejo
District: Santarém
Principal city: Santarém

Area: 6,747 sq km/2,605 sq mi
Population: 460,000

The meadows on the flood plains of the Ribatejo are excellent areas for cultivating cereals and rice; these pastures are also used for traditional horse breeding and cattle farming. Most Portuguese fighting bulls come from the Ribatejo countryside.

The historical province of Ribatejo (»bank of the Tagus«), whose principal city is Santarém, approximately covers today's district of Santarém. The very fertile 600 sq km/230 sq mi alluvial basin of the lower Tagus Valley in the east of the province of Estremadura is part of the Ribatejo, but the hilly country bordering to the south and north and the plateau in the east through which the Tagus flows also belongs to the province. The Ribatejo is the centre of horse breeding and cattle farming in Portugal, and many fighting bulls come from here, in particular from **Vila Franca de Xira** and the surrounding areas.

Centre of horse breeding and cattle farming

The drier hilly zones in the north are densely populated and intensively cultivated with mixed crops on predominantly small-scale farms: wheat, olives, wine, citrus fruits, and figs are grown here. In contrast, the south is thinly populated and exhibits the typical agri-

Population and agriculture

● VISITING RIBATEJO

INFORMATION
►Santarém

WHERE TO EAT
► **Moderate**
Al Foz
► Where to stay

WHERE TO STAY
► **Mid-range**
Palácio de Rio Frio
Rio Frio
2955-014 Pinhal Novo
RioFrio@solaresdeportugal.pt
Early 20th-century palace-like quinta

in which three rooms are available.
Attractive decorations characteristic
of the Ribatejo.

► **Budget/Mid-range**
Hotel Al Foz
Avenida D. Manuel I
2890-014 Alcochete
Tel. 212 341 179
www.al-foz.pt
Small, pleasant hotel with 32 rooms
directly on the southern bank of the
Tagus, reliable and well-run. The
hotel restaurant has a wonderful view
of the river.

cultural structure of the ►Alentejo adjoining it further south, with
latifundia and the transition to monocultures. The meadows which
form an approximately 50km/30mi strip alongside the Tagus flood
every year in spring.

✶ Sagres

E 34/35

Historical province: Algarve   **Elevation:** 35m/115ft
District: Faro   **Population:** 3,000

**Sagres' fame is primarily rooted in history. Located in the far
south-west of the Algarve, the town played an important part in
the Portuguese ocean voyages of the 15th and 16th centuries. Even
today, the whole region continues to live off this historical role.**

Located only 5km/3.1mi from Cabo de São Vicente, the south-west-   **Magical place:**
ernmost point of the European mainland, Sagres is a magical place –   **Europe's south-**
and not just for the Portuguese. It was here that Henry the Navigator   **westernmost**
is said to have founded his scientific centre, in which the most im-   **point**
portant geographers, cartographers and astronomers in the country
gathered in the 15th century (►Baedeker Special, p.469).
Both Sagres and Cabo de São Vicente lie on a rocky plateau that
comes to an abrupt end at the coast and forms 150m/490ft cliffs.

← *One bull, many heroes: »Largada de Touros« in Vila Franca de Xira
in Ribatejo*

▶ VISITING SAGRES

INFORMATION

Turismo de Sagres
Rua Comandante Matoso
Tel. 282 624 873
www.visitalgarve.pt

Turinfo
Praça da República
Tel. 282 620 003

EXCURSIONS

Organized excursions are offered into the unspoilt landscape of the Costa Vicentina; in addition it is possible to go on trips along the coast by ship (information from Turinfo).

WHERE TO EAT

▶ Moderate

Vila Velha
Rua Patrão António Faustino
Tel. 282 624 788
A very pleasant, well-run restaurant serving excellent fish and meat dishes.

A Tasca
Porto da Baleeira
Tel. 282 624 177
A popular restaurant, also with the Portuguese; delicious seafood and fish.

WHERE TO STAY

▶ Mid-range/Luxury

Pousada do Infante
8650-385 Sagres
Tel. 282 620 240, fax 282 624 225
www.pousadas.pt
Modern pousada in a marvellous location above the Praia da Mareta with a view of the cliffs on the coast.

▶ Mid-range

Hotel da Baleeira
Baleeira
8650-357 Sagres
Tel. 282 624 212
Fax 282 624 425
www.sagres.net/baleeira
Pleasant hotel in a nice location above the harbour.

Like the climate, the landscape around Sagres is harsh, and low macchia plants are the only vegetation to cover the ground. Tourism is until now only moderately developed, no doubt because of the cooler climate. Though it is true there are some hotels and private lodgings in and around Sagres, so far the tourist infrastructure is in no way comparable to the holiday destinations further east and the sections of the Algarve which were – originally – more charming.

On a windy plateau
The modest houses of the port and fishing town are scattered across a barren, windy plateau. Visitors will search for a proper central point of the town in vain. The main street ends at the busy fishing harbour.

Beaches
The beaches in the vicinity of Sagres are only partially suitable for swimming and sunbathing. The Praia do Martinhal, located 4km/2.5mi north-east of the town, is the best protected from the wind and is prized not least by surfers.

IN SEARCH OF NEW WORLDS

As discoverers and conquerors the Portuguese pulled no punches: those who didn't wish to trade with them felt the force of their military strength. Trade, the acquisition of colonies and the dissemination of Christianity led Portugal on bold journeys in unknown realms.

The Portuguese landed with 19 ships crewed by 1,400 men. Afonso de Albuquerque, commander of the armed forces and governor of the Portuguese king in the East Indies was absolutely determined to take revenge for the ignominious flight of his countryman Diego Lopes de Sequeira. On 1 September 1509, with only a few ships, Sequeira had put into the **Southeast Asian city of Malakka** situated opposite Sumatra on the peninsula of the same name. Never before had a European succeeded in advancing so far east. But Sequeira's goal to establish trading relations with the seaport had not been achieved. Resident traders – concerned about their own livelihoods – had persuaded the ruler of Malakka to issue a call to arms against the unwanted competition. Militarily the weaker, Sequeira was forced to set sail back to Portugal, leaving 19 of his men behind. Two years later Albuquerque attempted to atone for Sequeira's humiliating sins. When the Malayans agreed only to his demand to set the 19 prisoners free but not to bear the costs of Sequeira's

trading losses or to establish a Portuguese base, he let his weapons do the talking. The Malayans stood no chance against the superior strength of the Portuguese; within a short time Malakka was conquered. Many inhabitants of the city were literally slaughtered; even women and children were shown no mercy.

The **conquest of Malakka in 1511** is typical of the Portuguese voyages of discovery. Should cities, countries or peoples discovered on the sea route to India not be prepared to agree to trading relations with Portugal, they were made to feel Portugal's superior military strength – instead of becoming trading partners, they were **subjugated as colonies.**

The allure of distant shores

The Portuguese undertook their first voyages of discovery and conquest 100 years before the capture of Malakka – in 1415 they conquered the North African city of Ceuta, today still a colony of Spain. But what in fact were their motives? The country's resources were dwindling, but the

population was growing. Above all, though, the kingdom lacked grain and gold. Portugal had to look for new sources of income. What was more obvious than taking to the high seas? After all, Portugal had had a seafaring tradition for a long time. But in which direction should the Portuguese ships head?

At that time there was only one possibility: **Africa**. The Mediterranean was dominated by the Genoese, Florentines and Venetians; the Turks increasingly hindered the European connection to the lands of gold and other wonders, China and India. The Portuguese conjectured that by circumnavigating the African coast they

»Portugal had to look for new sources of income. What was more obvious than taking to the high seas?«

could create a direct trade connection with the gold and slave markets of east Africa; furthermore, if it were possible to discover a sea route to India they could break the spice monopoly of the Islamic travelling merchants and the trading cities in

northern Italy. Religion also played a fundamental part. The **medieval crusading spirit** had in no way disappeared on the Iberian Peninsula; the Islamic world was after all still just next door – the neighbouring Moorish kingdom of Granada would only cease to exist in 1492. In this way the circumnavigation of Africa also served the battle against Islam. If the Christian priest-king John, thought to be in Ethiopia, could finally be found, then with his help the Holy Land could be conquered and Islam destroyed.

»The Navigator«

But the age of discovery would surely have started later had it not been for one man: **Henry the Navigator**. Referred to as »o Navegador«, Henry actually went to sea only once, in 1415 to take part in the conquest of Ceuta. As the fourth son of João I he had almost no chance of the crown; perhaps for this reason he saw his life's work as being in another sphere and therefore developed a markedly scientific pioneering spirit. In Sagres, in the far south-west of the province of the Algarve of which his father appointed

The Japanese called the Portuguese intruders »Namban-jin«. Large-scale screen paintings and lacquer ware depicted the conquerors from the Japanese artists' point of view – a real Namban art form came into being. This detail of a screen painting shows the arrival of Portuguese merchants.

him governor, he built a base: a kind of scientific centre in which all knowledge from the fields of astronomy, geography, cartography, mathematics and nautical science – partly inherited from the time of Arab rule – was collected. It was here that the plans for the caravel were allegedly drawn up.In contrast to the Hanseatic cog, the caravel was a fast and nimble ship (though it only had a limited loading capacity) that with its square sails on both of the front masts and the triangular sail at the stern – the so-called Latin sail – or alternatively with three large Latin sails, was well suited for voyages across the Atlantic, primarily because it could take a zig-zag course against the wind. That it was at all possible to leave coastal waters was due to new technical inventions such as the **astrolabium,** an instrument used to measure the positions of the stars with which it was possible to calculate distances with some certainty, as well as other astronomical navigational instruments such as the Jacob's staff, the armillary sphere, the quadrant – the predecessor of the sextant – and the compass.

Losing the terror of the sea

Instructed in the newest knowledge about the stars and the sea, equipped with new technical aids and financed by the wealthy Order of the Knights of Christ (in which Henry held the position of Grand Master) – as well as by risk-taking businessmen from the increasingly powerful bourgeoisie, the nobility and overseas creditors – Portuguese seafarers set sail and explored the west African coast. Their experiences were evaluated and used for further expeditions.

But there was still one obstacle: **Cape Bojador,** in today's western Sahara, 1,500km/940mi south of Gibraltar. For it was here that the »mare tenebrosum« began: the place where the ocean gurgled and foamed, where horrible sea monsters lay in wait for unsuspecting seamen, where magnets pulled out the nails in planks of wood, and where ships fell vertically into the void.

Henry did not believe in such **medieval horror stories**. Captain Gil Eanes, after his return to Sagres from Cape Bojador, was therefore welcomed by his lord and master with a severe ticking off. Again he set sail on the Prince's orders, and in 1434 successfully circumnavigated the so-called »Cape of Fear«. With this deed the irrational terror of the high seas ended. Now began the race to discover distant shores, the conquest of foreign lands, and the consequent creation of a completely new world order.

Fortaleza de Sagres

A road leads from Sagres in a southerly direction to the Ponta de Sagres 2km/1.3mi away, on which stands the Fortaleza de Sagres. Even today the fortress is considered to be the centre of Portugal's history of discovery and conquest in the 15th and 16th centuries. Sagres harbour however always remained insignificant, as the expeditions set out from Lagos.

Not much remains of the original **fortress** built in the time of Henry the Navigator; it was to a large extent destroyed during an attack by Sir Francis Drake as well as in the earthquake of 1755. During the course of the 18th century however the fortress complex was rebuilt. The date 1793 above the entrance of the fortress walls, which have been restored with concrete, gives the year of completion. Within the fortress only scant remains from the time of Henry the Navigator have been preserved.

Just behind the fortress gateway on the left hand side is the so-called **Rosa dos Ventos** (wind rose), a circle on the ground with a diameter of 43m/141ft composed of stones. Over centuries it remained covered and overgrown with grass; it was not brought to light until the 20th century. It is thought the wind rose originates from the 15th century, though its function at that time remains unclear. Wind roses normally only feature 32 fields, but the geometrical figure in Sagres has 48 lines, running from the centre to the edge of the circle.

On the other side stands the small, 16th-century **Igreja de Nossa Senhora da Graça**. It is supposed that a church dedicated to the Virgin Mary once stood at this point. In 1960 a memorial stone was erected directly adjacent to it to mark the 500th anniversary of Henry the Navigator's death.

A small **museum** has been opened in the former stables and adjoining fortress buildings in which temporary exhibitions on the history of the fortress and the geological conditions at the cape are shown. A plateau stretches beyond the visitor centre on which it is possible to stroll to the edge of the cliffs.

Cabo de São Vicente

The western point of the Algarve coast forms the Cabo de São Vicente, a 60m/200ft-high headland towering out of the sea which is the south-westernmost point of the European mainland. A 22m/72ft-high lighthouse stands on the cape whose navigational light is visible from a distance of 33 nautical miles. The small fortification dates back to the 16th century, when the Bishop of Silves had the first lighthouse, fortified walls and monastery built here. The buildings were largely destroyed in 1587 during an attack by the fleet of Sir Francis Drake; the complex as it stands today was built in 1846 at the instigation of Maria II. It is said that in the 12th century a ship carrying the body of St Vincent –martyred in 304 – accompanied by two ravens, was stranded at the cape. The mortal remains of the saint of seafarers and wine growers were brought to Lisbon and buried in a silver coffin in the Sé Patriarcal.

✳ Santarém

F 21

Historical province: Ribatejo
District: Santarém

Elevation: 105m/345ft
Population: 25,000

The low, whitewashed houses of Santarém are situated high above the right bank of the Tagus in a once strategically important location. With its numerous Gothic churches, Santarém is considered the »capital of the Portuguese Gothic«.

Santarém is the capital of the historical province of Ribatejo. The beautiful Gothic monuments and the fine view over the Tagus make it worthwhile visiting this pleasant little town, which exudes a certain pride.

Santarém is the centre of an agriculturally important area: primarily cereals, fruit and vegetables are cultivated in the surrounding countryside. A highly regarded agricultural fair (Feira Nacional de Agricultura) takes place here every year at the beginning of June. It is interesting for tourists on account of the accompanying folkloristic programme; among the events, bullfights are an attraction. *(Agriculturally important area)*

As early as Roman times Santarém, then known as Iulianum Scalabitanum, was the most important trading centre in Lusitania, alongside Braga and Beja. During the Moorish period the town was fortified with a castle. After its recapture by Afonso Henriques in 1147, Santarém became the residence of several kings. Dinis I received the papal bull here in 1319 in recognition of the Order of the Knights of Christ which he founded. *(History)*

What to See in Santarém

The attractively landscaped Jardim da República in the north of the town is a good starting point for a tour of Santarém. The east side of the park borders on the Convento de São Francisco. The former Franciscan convent, founded in the mid-13th century – the cloister still dates back to this time – functions today as a barracks. *(Jardim da República)*
North of the Jardim da República stands the 18th-century town hall, and to the west are the buildings of the market; the azulejo pictures on the outer façade show the most important buildings in the town as well as rural motifs.

The Praça de Sá da Bandeira south of the Jardim da República is steeped in history: in 1357 it was the scene of the gruesome **execution of Álvaro Gonçalves and Pedro Coelho, the murderers of Inês de Castro**, ordered by Pedro I (►Baedeker Special, p.284). They are said to have been skinned alive. The Igreja do Seminário stands *(Praça de Sá da Bandeira)*

▶ VISITING SANTARÉM

INFORMATION
Rua Capelo Ivens 63
2000-039 Santarém
Tel. 243 304 437
www.rtribatejo.org

WHERE TO EAT
▶ Moderate
① *Quinta da Ribeirinha*
R. Bispo D. António de Mendonça 17
Póvoa de Santarém
Tel. 243 428 200
This lovely quinta is situated outside Santarém to the north, on the other side of the motorway. Tasty regional

dishes are on the menu. A good selection of wines. Products from the region such as jam or wine are also sold.

▶ Inexpensive
② *Restaurante Portas do Sol*
Portas do Sol
Local Santarém bar with a splendid view. It is possible to sit outside. Typical food of the Ribatejo is served here.

WHERE TO STAY
▶ Mid-range
① *Hotel Alfageme*
Avenida Bernardo Santareno 38
2000-153 Santarém
Tel. 243 377 240
Fax 243 370 850
www.hotelalfageme.com
Very pleasant three-star hotel with parking.

▶ Budget
② *Pensão Muralha*
Rua Pedro Canavarro
2000 Santarém
Tel. 243 322 399
Relatively simple little guesthouse in the town centre.

on the square. The Baroque façade of the seminary church was built in 1676 by Baltasar Álvares.

Capela de Nossa Senhora da Piedade Opposite the Igreja do Seminário stands the Capela de Nossa Senhora da Piedade. Afonso VI had the chapel built in 1665 in gratitude for his victory over Juan de Austria and the Spanish army.

Igreja de Marvila From the Praça de Sá da Bandeira, Rua Serpa Pinto runs south-east to the Igreja de Marvila, a church with a beautiful 16th-century Manueline doorway and polychrome azulejo decoration from the 17th century.

Santarém *Plan*

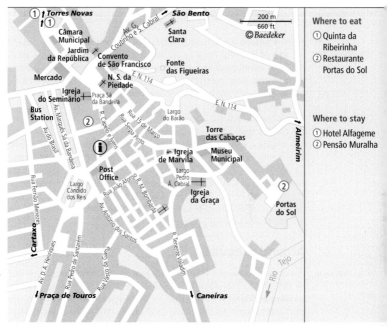

Where to eat

① Quinta da
  Ribeirinha
② Restaurante
  Portas do Sol

Where to stay

① Hotel Alfageme
② Pensão Muralha

Not far away to the south-east stands the Igreja da Graça, which has been declared a **Monumento Nacional**. The late Gothic convent church was built at the end of the 14th century, possibly by the master builder of the abbey at ►Batalha. The large rose window on the outer façade catches the eye; it was made from a single stone slab. The Graça church is the burial place of the Meneses family. The founders of the lineage, João Afonso Teles de Meneses and Dona Guimar de Vila Lobos, were laid to rest in the choir under stone slabs bearing their coats of arms; beside them is their daughter's tomb. To the right of the choir is the tomb of **Pedro Álvares Cabral** (1467/1468–1520) – seafarer and discoverer of Brazil – and his wife. Outside the church stands a monument to Pedro Álvares Cabral.

★
Igreja da Graça

From Igreja da Graça it is only a few yards' walk to the Museu Municipal de Santarém, housed in the Romanesque and Gothic São João de Alporão church. In addition to the fine stellar vaulting in the choir and numerous sculptures, a Gothic cenotaph is of particular interest. It was created for Duarte, son of Pedro I, who fell in a battle in North African Alcazar-Sequer in 1458 and of whose body only a tooth was brought back to his homeland. The museum shows rotating exhibitions on archaeological subjects.

Museu
Municipal

Torre das Cabaças Opposite the archaeological museum stands the Torre das Cabaças, the **emblem of Santarém**. Possibly the tower was once a minaret.

✱

Portas do Sol A few hundred yards further south-east stands the Portas do Sol. At the end of the 19th century, on the site of a Moorish fort, the small park was landscaped and a viewing terrace built from which there is an extensive view over the Tagus Valley. The Tagus is spanned here by the 1,200m/1,312-long Ponte Dom Luís, built from 1876 to 1881.

Igreja de Santa Clara Somewhat outside the old town – in the north of Santarém – stands the Gothic Igreja de Santa Clara from the 13th century. The church was affiliated to one of the convents founded by the Infanta **Leonor**. The mortal remains of the queen were transported here in 1634 and lie in a tomb decorated with a coat of arms. Another sarcophagus from the first half of the 14th century intended for the queen is empty. South of the Igreja de Santa Clara stands the Fonte das Figueiras, a Gothic fountain house; around 500m/550yd further east is the São Bento lookout point.

Around Santarém

Almeirim It was near Almeirim, about 6km/3.8mi south-east of Santarém, that in 1491 the Infante **Afonso**, son of João II und Leonor, **was killed in a riding accident**. It is said that his body was laid in a net by fishermen and brought to his mother (▶Óbidos). Afonso had married Isabella of Castile shortly before, a partnership from which it was hoped that a closer relationship would form with the Spanish royal family. After the death of the heir to the throne, Manuel I, as the brother of Leonor, became king. In order to strengthen the bond with Spain, he for his part married Isabella of Castile.

Alpiarça From here it is another 7km/4.4mi north-east to Alpiarça, where it is worthwhile visiting the museum in the Casa dos Patudos, the former country seat of the Portuguese statesman and art-lover José Relvas (1858–1929). The collection contains important paintings from all parts of Europe and tapestries from the 17th to 19th centuries, as well as porcelain and faience.

Golegã Another 25km/15.6mi away lies Golegã. The highlight of the year here is the large horse show which takes place in the second week of November. The Manueline doorway of the parish church from around 1500 is of interest: it is attributed to Diogo Boytaca.

Almoster A good 10km/6.3mi west of Santarém lies the village of Almoster with the church of a monastery founded in the late 13th century. The 17th-century azulejos are worth taking a look at. In the traditional Portuguese style, they imitate the gold fringe of an altar cloth in the yellow border tiles.

★★ Serra da Estrela

M–P 13–15

Historical province: Beira Alta   **Districts:** Viseu, Guarda, Coimbra, Castelo Branco

You can ski in Portugal! In winter, snow falls in the highlands of the Serra da Estrela, Portugal's only skiing area. The 100km/62.5mi-long and 30km/18.8mi-wide mountain range extends from Guarda to the region south of Coimbra.

The highest mountain in the country is found in the Serra da Estrela: the **Torre or Malhão da Estrela** (1,991m/6,532ft). With its bizarrely shaped cliffs and gorges, its mountain streams and lakes, its lovely woods and constant spectacular views, the Serra da Estrela – the »mountain range of the star« – is one of Portugal's great areas of out-standing natural beauty. Pastural agriculture with sheep and goats, and wool processing in the valleys are of economic significance here.

Portugal's highest mountain

Hiking is a good way to get an impression of the raw beauty of the mountains. The national park authorities of the Serra da Estrela have created an extensive network of footpaths in recent years. Detailed information is available from the offices in Covilhã, Manteigas or Gouveia. Between November and April hikers must be prepared for snowstorms and mist; during this period of the year long walking tours are inadvisable.

Hikes

A Tour through the Serra da Estrela

The sights of the Serra da Estrela will be described within the frame-work of a tour which also takes in the scenic beauty of the mountain range. The starting point of the tour is Covilhã; the final destination, after about 140km/87.5mi, ►Belmonte.

Touring

The small hill town of Covilhã is a popular point of departure amongst the Portuguese for excursions into the Serra da Estrela. The appearance of the town is disturbed somewhat by the industry around Covilhã: the town is the focal point of the Portuguese cloth industry.

Covilhã

The town's steep and winding alleyways create an idyllic impression. The traffic hub is the **Praça do Município** where the town hall stands. The town's main place of worship, the 15th-century **Santa Maria church**, stands above the square; the azulejo cladding on the façade shows scenes from the life of the Virgin. The Romanesque Capela de São Martinho is worth taking a look at, as is the 16th-century Capela de Santa Cruz which contains paintings and wood carvings. There is a municipal garden within the walls of the former Franciscan monas-tery. A fine view can be enjoyed from the Monumento de Nossa Se-

VISITING SERRA DA ESTRELA

INFORMATION

Av. Frei Heitor Pinto
6200-113 Covilhã
Tel. 275 319 560
www.rt-serradaestrela.pt

WHERE TO EAT

▶ **Moderate**

Pousada de São Lourenço
6260-200 Manteigas
Tel. 275 982 450
Perfect restaurant with a splendid view
into the mountains.

Serra da Estrela
6200-073 Covilhã
Tel. 275 310 300
Well-run and comfortable – restaurant
outside Covilhã to the north-west.

WHERE TO STAY

▶ **Mid-range**

Pousada Convento do Desagravo
3400-758 Vila Pouca da Beira
Tel. 238 670 080
Fax 238 670 081
Pousada in an old monastery in a
wonderful location on the edge of the
Serra da Estrela (28 rooms).

Pousada de São Lourenço
6260-200 Manteigas
Tel. 275 982 450
Fax 275 982 453
This pousada with 21 rooms in a
beautiful old granite house is a suitable
base and starting point for exploring
the Serra da Estrela.

nhora da Conceição. South of the town, between the Serra da Estrela and the Serra da Gardunha (▶Castelo Branco) stretches the fertile **Cova da Beira valley** formed by the Rio Zêzere. Woods, cornfields, fruit and vegetable gardens and above all the production of wool are the basis for the visible prosperity of the region.

Penhas da Saúde   Leave Covilhã on the N 339 in a north-westerly direction: the road leads uphill to the right from the Praça do Município by the town hall in Covilhã. It first runs through an area of dense forest and climbs rapidly. Penhas da Saúde(1,453m/4,767ft), a mountain health resort and area for winter sports, is about 10km/6.3mi away. The February temperatures of –10°C/14°F provide very good conditions for winter sports.

Torre   The route runs past a reservoir, and then 10km/6.3mi outside Penhas da Saúde passes the Torre(1,991m/6,532ft). An observation tower and a granite monument crown Portugal's highest mountain.

Seia   Seia (532m/1,745ft) lies about 52km/33mi further to the north-west. The parish church stands on a hill overlooking the town. About 2km/1.3mi outside Seia, follow the major road coming from Coimbra on the left, the N 17, in a north-easterly direction.

After 13km/8mi leave the major road and join the N 232; Gouveia
(650m/2,133ft) lies 5km/3mi along this road. The small town on the
Mondego is popular as a convenient starting point for excursions into the Serra da Estrela. The façade of the parish church is clad with
blue-and-white azulejos. Beautiful azulejos are also preserved in the
Misericórdia church, which belongs to a former Jesuit monastery
from the 18th century.

Gouveia

Behind Gouveia the road twists and turns upwards on a rocky
mountain slope with increasingly extensive views of the mountain
landscape. After about 20km/12.5mi a signpost points to Penhas
Douradas (1,496m/4,908ft). This settlement with its observatory und
holiday villas is known as the »golden rocks«; it is the starting point
for worthwhile walking trips, for example to the mighty rock faces of
the same name.

Penhas Douradas

Beyond Penhas Douradas the road runs through a wooded area to
the Pousada de São Lourenço (1,450m/4,757ft), from which there is
a splendid view of Manteigasand the Zêzere valley. The twists and
turns of the road later lead down into the Zêzere valley. Since it has
become barely possible to earn money in the textile industry, the
720m/2,362ft-high Manteigas is in-
creasingly turning to tourism.
2km/1.3mi further south in the
upper Zêzere valley lies the spa
Caldas de Manteigas, whose 43°C/
109°F springs contain calcium car-
bonate and sulphur.

Manteigas

Another 3km/1.9mi further up the
valley lies the **Poço do Inferno**.
Here at the »hell's well« a waterfall
cascades down into a hollow.

From Manteigas, the route leads
downwards through the wooded
slopes, fields and gardens of the
Zêzere valley, and crosses the river
just outside Valhelhas. A good
25km/15.6mi from Manteiga the
houses of ►**Belmonte** appear.

Those wishing to extend the tour
should not first drive – as described – to Penhas de Saúde, but
should leave Covilhã on the N 230
in a southerly direction. The first
destination on this route is Unhais

*A refreshing foot bath while hiking in the Serra da Estrela.
The Torre towers in the background.*

da Serra, known for its sulphurous springs and situated in the valley of the Rio Alfora. The road then winds up the mountain in a stretch by no means short on fine views, and about 20km/12.5mi beyond Unhais da Serra it leaves the N 230 and continues north on the N 231 to Loriga (740m/2,428ft). Behind Loriga the road climbs steeply at first, and then snakes downhill to Valezim. Later there is a fine view from the Ponte da Jugais onto the Rio Alva, and shortly afterwards the route reaches São Romão (590m/1,936ft). The town is the departure point of a lane leading to the Ermida Senhora do Desterro (790m/2,434ft) from 1650, located 12km/7.5mi distant in a southeasterly direction; the area's scenic beauty is unfortunately somewhat impaired by a power station. In Seia 4km/2.5mi to the north the route described above can be resumed.

✴ Serra de Monchique

F–H 32/33

Historical province: Algarve   **District:** Faro

The Serra de Monchique is charming hilly country with a diverse and lush flora. Expansive woods with eucalyptus, cork oaks, spruce and mimosas spread over the slopes, and rhododendrons and shrubs grow up in the highlands. In the foothills of the Serra to the south there are extensive orchards.

The Serra de Monchique extends like a protective wall in the northwest of the Algarve. Its highest peaks, Fóia and Picota, reach 902m/2,959ft and 774m/2,539ft respectively. The Serra holds back all of the cool Atlantic influence on the weather and in this way ensures a coastal climate that is North African in character. Thanks to the low permeability of the ground, precipitation is collected in streams and rivulets which flow to the coastal plain. In the orchards, which adjoin the Serra in the direction of the coast, lemons, figs, almonds and olives thrive. For the last few years more and more **fires in both forested and open areas** have been raging in the Serra de Monchique; large areas of forest have been destroyed in this way.

Climate barrier: warmth for the Algarve

What to See in Serra de Monchique

The small hill town of Monchique (458m/1,503ft) located on the slopes of the Serra de Monchique is the region's principal residential area with around 8,000 inhabitants. Steep streets and alleys run through the centre of the town. Everywhere there are views of the surrounding mountains. The central square is the **Largo 5 de Outubro**; the modern fountain here represents a »Nora«, a component of

Monchique

← *The delightful hilly landscape of the Serra de Monchique*

VISITING SERRA DE MONCHIQUE

INFORMATION

Monchique
Largo dos Chorões
Tel. 282 911 189
www.visitalgarve.pt

SHOPPING

Tiles, wickerwork and wooden articles are sold in Monchique. A typical product is the wooden folding stool. The Serra de Monchique is known for »Medronho«, a high-alcohol spirit made from the fruit of the strawberry tree.

HIKING

Various companies and individuals offer hiking holidays in the Serra de Monchique. Enquire at travel agents.

WHERE TO EAT

► **Moderate**

Paraíso da Montanha
Estrada de Fóia
Tel. 282 912 150

Ideal stopover for those on a trip through the mountainous Algarve hinterland.

WHERE TO STAY

► **Mid-range**

Estalagem Abrigo da Montanha
Estrada de Fóia, Corte Pereira
8550-257 Monchique
Tel. 282 912 131, fax 282 913 660
abrigodamontanha@hotmail.com
Very well-kept, pleasant hotel located slightly outside Monchique on the road up to Fóia, the highest mountain of the Serra de Monchique.

Albergaria do Lageado
Caldas de Monchique
Tel. 282 912 616
Fax 282 911 310
Comfortable, reliable guesthouse with 19 rooms in the idyllic centre of the village of Caldas de Monchique. Absolute peace and quiet!

the irrigation system introduced by the Arabs to the Algarve. From the square, alleys lead upwards in a 15-minute climb to the **Convento de Nossa Senhora do Desterro**. The ruins of the convent are not particularly spectacular, but there is a fine view of Monchique from here.

Fóia From Monchique a winding road leads 6km/3.8mi uphill to Fóia (902m/2,959ft), the highest peak of the Serra de Monchique. The road first passes pretty houses and several tourist cafés. Gradually the vegetation becomes sparser and, after a bend, the Alentejo to the north suddenly comes into view. The barren peak is relatively inhospitable: there is a real forest of aerials here, installed by the Portuguese telecommunications companies, among others. There is however a café and a souvenir shop for day-trippers. The view of the whole coastal strip of the western Algarve is spectacular.

★

Caldas de Monchique Because of volcanism there are several hot springs in the Serra de Monchique. In fact Monchique owes its fame to the Caldas de Monchique, the »warm springs« (caldas) 6km/3.8mi further south. They are said to help with rheumatism, and liver, urinary tract and intestinal complaints. The healing water is bottled and sold all over Portugal. Caldas de Monchique is one of the most idyllic places in the Algarve hinterland. A turn of the century charm has been preserved here, a phenomenon that could hardly be thought possible a few hundred miles away at the coast. In the meantime everything in Caldas de Monchique has been renovated, but the tiny centre of the village in the shade of high trees – a quiet square with a café and a restaurant – remains a good place to linger.

Sesimbra

D 26

Historical province: Estremadura
District: Setúbal

Elevation: 0–249m/817ft
Population: 23,000

Sesimbra, located on the southern slopes of the Serra da Arrábida, is a small fishing town and a seaside resort at the same time. Simple white houses and small hotels line the promenade; outside the town centre, large and well-appointed hotel complexes are being built.

The inhabitants of Sesimbra make a living from tourism, though fishing still remains significant. On the town beach fishermen are to be seen repairing their nets and boats enter and leave the harbour at the west end of the town. Freshly caught fish and seafood are served in the restaurants.

▶ VISITING SESIMBRA

INFORMATION
Largo da Marinha 26
2970-657 Sesimbra
Tel. 212 288 540
www.costa-azul.rts.pt

WHERE TO EAT
▶ Moderate
Do Mar
Rua General Humberto Delgado 10
Tel. 212 288 300
Excellent fish dishes and various kinds of seafood are served in the hotel restaurant. Diners enjoy a sea view.

WHERE TO STAY
▶ Mid-range
Hotel do Mar
Rua Gen. Humberto Delgado 10
2970-628 Sesimbra, Tel. 212 288 300
Hotel complex with rather plain rooms; balconies with sea view.

▶ Budget
Pensão Náutico / Residencial
Av. dos Combatentes, 19
2970-636 Sesimbra
Tel. 212 233 233, fax 212 233 233
Well-run guesthouse without many extras.

What to See in Sesimbra

Fortaleza de Santiago
In the centre of town right next to the beach stands the Fortaleza de Santiago. The small 17th-century fortress with a lighthouse was used as a prison for a time.

Museu Municipal
A few hundred yards further north stands the municipal museum in which archaeological finds, a coin collection and sacred exhibits are on display.

Castelo
The castle, built in the 12th and 13th centuries, towers high above the town. It was almost completely rebuilt in the early 17th century by the Flemish Jesuit and master builder Cosmander for João IV.

Surrounding areas
From Sesimbra it is possible to take trips along the ▶Costa de Lisboa and into the Serra da Arrábida (▶Costa de Lisboa).

Setúbal

E 25

Historical province: Estremadura	**Elevation:** sea level
District: Setúbal	**Population:** 90,000

For an industrial town Setúbal has a really appealing townscape. Harbours for freight, yachts and fishing boats extend along the bank of the Rio Sado, and the atmospheric old town a little way inland consists mostly of pedestrian areas with small shops.

The industrial town and district capital of Setúbal on the broad estuary of the Sado boasts Portugal's third largest harbour. Fish canning factories, shipyards, salt works and car manufacturing – Ford and VW have a joint factory here – shape the economy.

Narrow old town
Parallel to the river bank runs one of the main traffic axes of the town, the Avenida de Luísa Todi, named after the **celebrated singer Luísa Todi** (1753–1833). Beyond the Avenida stretches the narrow old town, whose centre is the Praça do Bocage with a statue of the poet.

History
It is suspected that Setúbal came into being in the 5th century, after the Roman town **Cetóbriga** on the Tróia peninsula was destroyed in a catastrophic flood. In the 15th century Setúbal served temporarily as the **royal seat**. The harbour became the starting point for many voyages of discovery and contributed to its importance. Setúbal is the birthplace of the satirist and literary figure Manoel Maria de Barbosa do Bocage (1765–1805); in the house in which he was born on Rua do São Domingo, a small museum is dedicated to him.

Setúbal *Plan*

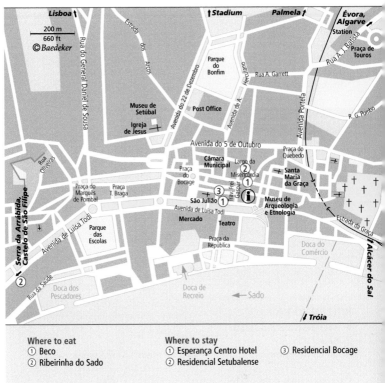

Where to eat
① Beco
② Ribeirinha do Sado

Where to stay
① Esperança Centro Hotel
② Residencial Setubalense
③ Residencial Bocage

What to See in Setúbal

In the west of the old town stands the Igreja de Jesus, which has earned a certain amount of fame as the **first church built in the Manueline style** in Portugal. Work on the sacred building began in 1490/1491 under the leadership of **Diogo de Boytaca**, who later became known for his work on the abbey at ►Batalha and the monastery at Belém (►Lisbon). From the outside, the hall church with a nave and two aisles is relatively plain; but in the interior the twisted columns, the stellar vaulting in the choir and the azulejo scenes depicting the life of the Virgin are impressive.

✱ Igreja de Jesus

The bordering former Monastery of Jesus now houses the municipal museum. The exhibits include paintings by Portuguese, Flemish and Catalan masters as well as archaeological finds from the region around Setúbal.

Museu de Setúbal

▶ VISITING SETÚBAL

INFORMATION
Tv. Frei Gaspar 10
2900-388 Setúbal
Tel. 265 539 120
www.costa-azul.rts.pt

Baedeker TIP

Dolphin watching

The region of the Sado estuary was declared a protected area in 1980. Alongside rare species of bird, dolphins live here. Through the »Reserva Natural do Estuário do Sado« tours are offered during which dolphins are sighted from time to time (Vertigem Azul, Edifício Marina Deck, Rua Praia da Saúde II D, loja 10, tel. 265 238 000, www.vertigemazul.com).

WHERE TO EAT
▶ **Inexpensive/Moderate**

① *Beco*
Largo da Misericórdia 24
Tel. 265 524 617
Fine food; such dishes as fish stew or »duck rice« are on the menu.

② *Ribeirinha do Sado*
Avenida Luísa Todi 586

Tel. 265 238 465
Of the numerous grill rooms on Avenida Luísa Todi this one is especially popular with the locals. Very good grilled fish.

WHERE TO STAY
▶ **Budget**

① *Esperança Centro Hotel*
Avenida Luísa Todi 220
2900-452 Setúbal
Tel. 265 521 780
fax 265 521 789
Pleasant mid-range hotel on Setúbal's main avenida.

② *Residencial Setubalense*
Rua Major Afonso Pala 17
2900 Setúbal
Tel. 265 525 790
fax 265 525 789
Well-run guesthouse in the very centre of Setúbal. Functionally furnished, clean rooms.

③ *Residencial Bocage*
Rua de São Cristovão 14
2900-611 Setúbal
Tel. 265 543 080
fax 265 543 089
Simple guesthouse, all rooms with their own bathroom and satellite TV.

Igreja de São Julião   It is worthwhile visiting the Igreja de São Julião at the Praça do Bocage a little further south-east. The original 16th-century building was heavily damaged in the earthquake of 1755 and had to be almost completely rebuilt.

Igreja de Santa Maria da Graça   The Igreja de Santa Maria da Graça in the east of the old town goes back to a 13th-century church building which was almost completely remodelled in the 16th century. Its carved and richly gilded altars are from the 16th and 17th centuries, the azulejos from the 18th century.

Still choc-a-block with boats: the fishing harbour of Setúbal

South of the church there is a small **archaeology and ethnology museum** whose exhibits include models of boats and tools which were used in agriculture and fishing around Setúbal.

The Castelo de São Filipe towers above Setúbal to the west; today, part of it is a pousada. It was built in the late 16th century by the Italian master builder Filippo Terzi. From here there is an extensive view over the town onto the funnel-shaped mouth of the Rio Sado and over to Tróia (►Costa de Lisboa).

Castelo de São Filipe

Around Setúbal

About 15km/9.4mi west of Setúbal lies the village of **Vila Fresca de Azeitão** with the São Simão church and the **Quinta das Torres**, surrounded by lovely gardens, in which a hotel has been established.

> ## Baedeker TIP
>
> **A café with a view**
> The airy pousada café is a pleasant spot, established within the castle walls. Sipping on a drink, you can enjoy the wonderful view in total peace and quiet.

The **Palácio da Bacalhoa** on the road to Setúbal a little distance from the town features Moorish domed towers and was built in the last quarter of the 15th century. It was altered fundamentally in the 16th century. In the lovely park stands the Casa de Prazer, a pretty mid-16th century summer residence with an azulejo picture *Susanna at her Bath*.

Vila Nogueira de Azeitão Vila Nogueira de Azeitão 2km/1.3mi west of Vila Fresca de Azeitão is famous for its wineries which are open to the public. The palace of the dukes of Aveiro, built from 1520–1523 by Jorge de Lencastre, is one of the first Renaissance buildings in Portugal.

Costa de Lisboa Excursions from Setúbal into the Serra da Arrábida as well as to the Tróia peninsula are very worthwhile. Ferries sail from Setúbal to Tróia (both ▶Costa de Lisboa).

✷ Silves

H 33

Historical province: Algarve	**Elevation:** 85m/279ft
District: Faro	**Population:** 11,000

Once, Silves was capital of the Moorish province of Al-Gharb. There is little sign of its former importance however. Today, Silves is a very appealing but somewhat sleepy little town which neverthe-less has something to offer the visitor in the form of a pretty townscape, old burgher houses and a few buildings which are steeped in history.

Old Moorish town The small town in the Algarve hinterland was supposedly founded by the Phoenicians. As of the first half of the 8th century it came under Moorish rule and was not reconquered until 1242, by Afonso III. As the spiritual and cultural centre of the Moorish Al-Gharb (▶ Algarve) Silves, which at that time was called **Xelb**, competed in terms of splendour and influence with Granada – Silves is said to have had 40,000 inhabitants. The status as the capital of the province was handed over to Lagos, but Silves remained an episco-pal see until 1577, after which this function was transferred to Faro. The destruction wrought by the earthquake in 1755 did the rest: the town descended into complete insignificance.

What to See in Silves

✷ Castelo dos Mouros Visible from a great distance, the mighty red sandstone Moorish cas-tle towers over the town, crowned by battlements. Its appearance to-day goes back to the restoration work in 1940. It is possible to stroll along the circular wall and enjoy extensive views of the surrounding countryside. The inner courtyard of the castle with its old stock of trees is used for open-air performances in the summer months. The Moors dug enormous wells up to 60m/197ft deep and installed ven-tilation systems here.

✷ Sé Below the castle stands the cathedral. It was built in the 13th century on top of a mosque but was subject to multiple alterations in subsequent centuries. The Sé is one of the few buildings in the Algarve in which **Gothic elements are preserved**; in other places they were largely destroyed by the earthquake. In the interior of the building, which has a nave and two aisles, several tombs of crusaders are still to be seen.

The Igreja da Misericórdia alongside the cathedral was built in the 16th century. On the side facing the cathedral a Manueline window frame from this time is still visible.

Igreja da Misericórdia

In Rua das Portas de Loulé south of the cathedral there is an interesting archaeological museum. The exhibits originate in large part from Silves and the surrounding areas. An Arabic well is integrated into the museum building.

Museu Municipal de Arqueologia

▶ VISITING SILVES

INFORMATION

Posto de Turismo Municipal
Praça Al-Mutamid
8300 Silves

Posto de Turismo –
Região de Turismo do Algarve
Rua 25 de Abril
8300-184 Silves; Tel. 282 442 255
www.visitalgarve.pt

WHERE TO EAT
▶ Expensive
Marisqueira »O Rui«
Rua Comandante Vilarinho 23/25
Tel. 282 442 682
Nice bar with good Portuguese food; the menu offers plenty of fish and shellfish.

▶ Moderate
Casa Velha de Silves
Rua 25 de Abril
Tel. 282 445 491
Very good food and excellent service.

Café Inglês
Below the castle
Tel. 282 442 585
Very nice café and restaurant.

WHERE TO STAY
▶ Mid-range/Budget
Hotel Colina dos Mouros
Pocinho Santo
8300-999 Silves
Tel. 282 440 420; fax 282 440 426
A very pleasant hotel on the south side of the river. Some of the rooms at the back have a splendid view of Silves's old town with the castle. It is rather loud on the street side.

▶ Budget
Quinta da Figueirinha
8300-028 Silves
Tel. 282 442 671; fax 282 444 226
www.qdf.pt
Quinta in the middle of the countryside under friendly management. Several holiday flats and rooms for rent.

Quinta do Rio
Santo Estevão
8300-999 Silves
Tel. 282 445 528
The Quinta do Rio lies north-east of Silves in the countryside: very pleasant »Turismo Rural« accommodation.

✳ **Cruz de Portugal** The Cruz de Portugal standing at the eastern exit of the town is a rare example of 16th-century Manueline stonemasonry. Christ on the cross is depicted on the front side of this 3m/9.8ft-high wayside cross; on the back a Pietà is shown.

! *Baedeker* TIP

Interesting industrial museum

In Portugal around 1930 approximately 10,000 people were employed in the production of corks. The cork museum, the Museu da Cortiça, reminds its visitors of those times. It illustrates vividly the history of cork harvesting and processing, a very important branch of industry for Portugal. Open: daily 10.30am–1pm and 2pm–9.45pm; in winter 9.30am–12.45pm and 2pm–6.15pm.

A closed-down English **cork factory**, that until 1995 was in operation as the largest cork production site in southern Portugal, is today a **gastronomy and cultural centre**. Several restaurants, cafés and bars have now been established on the former factory site. The official date of the founding of the factory, originally in English ownership, hence the name »Fábrica do Inglês«, is 1894. The factory's primary product was corks for port bottles.

Sines

E 29

Historical province: Baixo Alentejo
District: Setúbal

Elevation: sea level
Population: 10,000

Sines was once an insignificant fishing town. In the 1970s work began to build the town up into one of the largest harbours and industrial centres in the country. Today only the centre of the old town is really appealing.

Sines lies in a rocky bay on an otherwise dune-rich section of the south Portuguese coast. Even though the far-reaching plans for an industrial park with an oil refinery could only realized in part, Sines is today clearly characterized by industry. By the way, Sines is the **birthplace of the seafarer Vasco da Gama** (1469–1524), who discovered the sea route to India in 1497/1498. West of the town, the 56m/184ft-high **Cabo de Sines**, marked by a lighthouse, rises up from the Atlantic Ocean.

Sights The house where Vasco da Gama was born has been reconstructed and a small museum established inside it. Above the harbour stands the fishermen's chapel, Nossa Senhora das Salas. Vasco da Gama ordered the chapel, originally built in 1335, to be completely renovated after his discovery of the sea route to India. A beautiful Manueline

▶ VISITING SINES

INFORMATION
Castelo de Sines
7520-159 Sines
Tel. 269 634 472
www.costa-azul.rts.pt

WHERE TO STAY •
WHERE TO EAT
▶ **Mid-range**
Pousada de São Tiago
7540-237 Santiago do Cacém
Tel. 269 822 469; fax 269 822 459
Cosy country house 20km/12.5mi

north of Sines. Nice garden, swimming pool, nine rooms available.

Pousada de Quinta da Ortiga
7540-909 Santiago do Cacém
Tel. 269 822 871
Fax 269 822 073
This pousada is suitable for a stop on the journey between Lisbon and the Algarve, but it is also a nice place to stay longer and have a marvellous break; 13 rooms, swimming pool.

doorway decorates the place of worship, and a viewing terrace has been placed in front of it. There is also a fine view from the 13th-century castle; a small museum is found in the castle buildings. In the parish church the mortal remains of St Torpes have found their final resting place; they are said to have been found here in AD 45 on an abandoned ship which had run aground.

Around Sines

The small, tranquil country town of Santiago do Cacém with 17,500 inhabitants lies on a hill in the southern Serra de Grândola about 20km/13mi north-east of Sines. The town is dominated by the castle, a **former Templar stronghold**, to which a road provides access. It is worth wandering around the site outside the circular wall and enjoying the extensive views to Cabo de Sines. The cemetery of the Igreja Matriz, with beautiful cypress trees, lies within the castle complex. The **Igreja Matriz** below the castle dates back to the 13th century but was altered considerably later on. The main façade was redesigned in the 18th century, while the Romanesque and Gothic side doorway has been preserved. In the interior of the church a 14th-century relief depicts St James (São Tiago) in battle, who fell while defending the town against the Moors. In the **Museu Municipal** at the greenery-covered Praça do Município, archaeological finds from the Roman town of Miróbriga (see below) and old coins are on display.

Santiago do Cacém

At the eastern edge of Santiago do Cacém signposts on the road to Beja point to the scant remains of the ancient Roman town of Miróbriga. The ruins of a temple and the remains of a Roman road are recognizable.

Miróbriga

Lagoa de Santo André Lagoa de Santo André 15km/9.4mi further north-west is a small, pleasant place to visit. The country road leads through the dune terrain to peaceful beaches on the Atlantic coast, this section of which is named the ►Costa Dourada. There is hardly any tourist infrastructure in this area.

✶ ✶ Sintra

B 24

Historical province: Estremadura	**Elevation:** 225m/738ft
District: Lisboa	**Population:** 24,000

The small town of Sintra, once a summer residence of the Portuguese royal family, lies at an altitude of some 200m/650ft between Lisbon and the Atlantic Ocean in the wooded Serra de Sintra. Expatriates from various countries have settled in the Sintra region and some occasionally very curious mansions and palaces have been built.

✶ ✶ Glorious Eden Due to its extraordinarily mild and pleasant micro-climate that remains sufficiently rainy in spite of the sub-tropical heat, and the verdant landscape that has resulted from this, Sintra has always been a popular place to stay and a magnet for travellers and those in search of relaxation. **Lord Byron** came to Portugal in the early 19th century

The Palácio Nacional de Sintra with its two kitchen chimneys

and was not particularly enamoured of Lisbon. Sintra, though, he described as a »glorious Eden«. The Englishman's eulogy attracted not only his own countrymen to Sintra: travellers from various countries, including many an eccentric, have made their way to this heralded place.

 VISITING SINTRA

INFORMATION
Praça da República 23
2710-616 Sintra
Tel. 219 231 157
www.cm-sintra.pt

WHERE TO EAT
▶ **Moderate/Expensive**
① *Lawrence's*
Rua Consigliéri Pedroso 38
Tel. 219 105 500
Excellently prepared fish, meat, and pasta dishes.

▶ **Moderate**
② *Tulhas*
Rua Gil Vicente 4-6
Tel. 219 232 378
Very pleasant restaurant serving Portuguese cuisine. A wide variety of fish and meat dishes on the menu.

③ *Cantinho de São Pedro*
Praça Dom Fernando II 12
Tel. 219 230 267
Small but elegant restaurant serving Portuguese cuisine with a French touch.

④ *Páteo do Garrett*
Rua Maria Eugénia R. F. Navarro 7
Tel. 219 243 380
This restaurant is very popular with the locals. It serves Portuguese food with a large selection of soups as well as fish, meat, seafood and even small snacks. A nice spot to sit and relax outside. There is occasionally some fado music.

WHERE TO STAY
▶ **Luxury**
① *Hotel Palácio dos Seteais*
Rua Barbosa do Bocage 10
2710-517 Sintra
Tel. 219 233 200, fax 219 234 277
www.tivoli.pt.com
Hotels don't get much more exclusive than this. It also has its own gourmet restaurant.

▶ **Mid-range/Luxury**
② *Hotel Lawrence's*
Rua Consigliéri Pedroso 38
2710 Sintra
Tel. 219 105 500
Fax 219 105 505
Very pretty, cosy hotel with a fine, rustic atmosphere.

▶ **Mid-range**
③ *Pensão Sintra*
Travessa dos Avelares 12
2710-506 Sintra
Tel./fax 219 230 738
Large hotel established in an old mansion at the edge of the town. The rooms are immense, there is a pool in the gardens and there is plenty of peace and quiet.

▶ **Budget**
④ *Solar dos Mouros*
Calçada de São Pedro 64
2710-508 Sintra
Tel 219 233 216
A small and beautifully kept estalagem with a friendly, private atmosphere. A nice common room with a fireplace.

In 1995 UNESCO added Sintra to its list of **World Heritage Sites**. The town is a first-rate tourist attraction. It is often incorporated into the itinerary of visits to Lisbon and it can get very crowded, especially in the summer months. Since most of the visitors are day trippers, it is worth staying on a little longer in the evening to experience Sintra at your leisure.

The centrepiece of the town is the **Largo Raínha D. Amélia** including the Palácio Nacional de Sintra with its two conical chimneys. In front of the building there is a small fountain with a late Gothic pillory below it. Next to the Largo Raínha D. Amélia is the Praça da República upon which the 12th-century Igreja de São Martinho and the tourist information office both stand. **A steep, rocky mountain with a Moorish castle towers immediately over Sintra**. The castle was wrested from the Arabs by Afonso Henriques 1147. Even higher up than the castle is a ridge called the **Pena** topped by a palace of the same name.

São Pedro

Beyond the Parque da Liberdade, the Igreja de Santa Maria and the Convento da Trindade lies the suburb of São Pedro. Every second and fourth Sunday of the month a large and popular market takes place here.

Sintra festivals

During June and July the castles in and around Sintra host a popular range of concerts that attract a great many people from Lisbon and elsewhere. The concerts exclusively feature works from the Romantic period.

Carriage rides

It is very pleasant to enjoy Sintra's attractions by horse-drawn carriage. There is a rank for drivers and their carriages in front of the Palácio Nacion al de Sintra.

What to See in Sintra

✷ ✷
Palácio Nacional de Sintra

The Palácio Nacional de Sintra or Paço Real was the seat of kings of the Avis dynasty. It has now been determined that a Moorish building was located on the site as early as the 10th century; João I (1385–1433) had a summer palace built on the old foundations. The palace was extended and modified during the reign of Manuel I (1495–1521). The characteristic **conical chimneys** from the kitchens, which can be seen for miles around, were only added in the 18th century. The building was thoroughly restored under Maria II in the 19th century and the interior was redesigned at this time. Luís I made this his favourite residence and Queen Maria Pia retired here after she was widowed.

The palace is not a single edifice but consists of various individual buildings layered one inside another. Its long history means it comprises elements of **Moorish, Gothic and Manueline architecture**, as well as exhibiting some **Renaissance** features. Facing the Largo Raí-

Sintra *Plan*

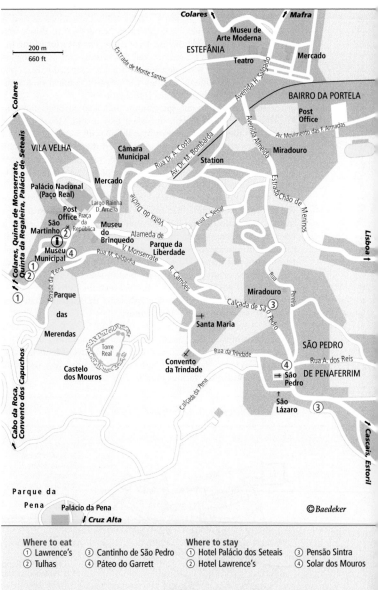

Colares   Mafra

Museu de
Arte Moderna
ESTEFÂNIA
Teatro   Mercado

200 m
660 ft

Estrada de Monte Santos

BAIRRO DA PORTELA

Colares

Post
Office

Av. Movimento das F. Armadas

VILA VELHA

Câmara
Municipal

Rua Dr. A. Costa
Av. Dr. M. Bombarda

Miradouro

Station

Avenida Almeida

Avenida H. Segadas

Palácio Nacional
(Paço Real)

Mercado

Estrada Chão de Meninos

Colares, Quinta de Monserrate,
Quinta da Regaleira, Palácio de Seteais

Largo Rainha
D. Amélia

Post
Office
São
Martinho

Praça
da
Republica

Museu
do
Brinquedo

Alameda de
V. Monserrate

Parque da
Liberdade

Lisboa

Museu
Municipal

Rua M. Saldanha

Volta do Duche

Rua C. Seixal

Rua Camões

R. Camões

Miradouro

Rua Pereira

Estrada da Pena

Parque

das

Merendas

Calçada de São Pedro

Santa Maria

SÃO PEDRO
Rua A. dos Reis

Cabo da Roca,
Convento dos Capuchos

Torre
Real

Castelo
dos Mouros

Convento
da Trindade

Rua da Trindade

São
Pedro

DE PENAFERRIM

Calçada da Pena

São
Lázaro

Cascais, Estoril

Parque da

Pena   Palácio da Pena

©*Baedeker*

Cruz Alta

nha D. Amélia, the palace's façade, with its shallow open stairway and five twin Joanine windows, dates from the earliest period of building. Under Manuel I a great many windows and doors were adorned with typical Manueline decoration. The **interior** of the former royal palace offers a vision of all the various eras of Portuguese history: shady patios with refreshing fountains, carpeted halls, rooms with magnificent coffered ceilings and exquisite azulejo-tiled walls, mostly dating from the 15th and 16th centuries.

Tours ▶ Tours usually start in the guardroom and lead through the huge kitchens to the Arab Room, furnished like an old Moorish palace. Next comes the Coat-of-arms or Stag Room with a ceiling formed in the shape of an octagonal wooden dome. In the centre of the dome is the coat-of-arms of King Manuel I, who commissioned the room. Around the king's coat-of-arms are those of his eight children. The walls are tiled with 18th-century azulejos that depict hunting scenes.

The Magpie Room gets its name from the 136 magpies painted on the ceiling. The banners that emerge from the mouths of each bird feature the motto of João I, »Por bem« (for the good). According to one anecdote, for which there is no historical proof, João's wife caught him kissing one of the ladies in waiting, to which he calmly replied »foi por bem« (»I only meant good by it«). This phrase was then repeated at every opportunity by the ladies of the court. Annoyed at their gossiping, João I commissioned the birds to be painted on the ceiling. The fireplace was fashioned by Nicolas Chanterène from Carrara marble in the 16th century.

The tour now leads through a courtyard to the Swan Room, the largest of the rooms in the palace. The windows and doors of the hall were adorned in the 15th century with rich Moorish/Manueline decoration. The room was formerly used as a banqueting hall and is still utilized as a venue for various events.

Palácio Nacional de Sintra *Plan*

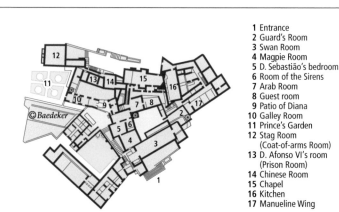

1 Entrance
2 Guard's Room
3 Swan Room
4 Magpie Room
5 D. Sebastião's bedroom
6 Room of the Sirens
7 Arab Room
8 Guest room
9 Patio of Diana
10 Galley Room
11 Prince's Garden
12 Stag Room
  (Coat-of-arms Room)
13 D. Afonso VI's room
  (Prison Room)
14 Chinese Room
15 Chapel
16 Kitchen
17 Manueline Wing

Another of the rooms in the palace was used as a prison for Afonso VI. After his brother Pedro II had systematically excluded him from all royal business before declaring him mad, Afonso was forced to spend the last nine years of his life here until his death in 1683 (open 10am–5.30pm daily except for Wednesdays).

Below the palace on Rua Visconde de Monserrate there is a **toy museum** (Museu do Brinquedo). More than 20,000 exhibits are in the collection (open: Tue to Sun 10am–6pm).

At the northern edge of the city is an imposing 1920s building that houses the **museum of modern art** and the Berardo collection. It has a wide range of European and American artworks from the years after the Second World War. The artists include Andy Warhol, Gerhard Richter, Tom Wesselmann and Dan Flavin (open: Wed–Sun 10am to 6pm).

Palácio Nacional de Sintra: view of the ceiling in the Swan Room

A winding road with some very tight hairpin bends rises steeply from the southern edge of the town. It initially runs through some splendid gardens, then through some wooded parkland. After about 3km/2mi a driveway leads off to the left towards the **Castelo dos Mouros** (429m/1407ft). The castle was originally built in the 8th or 9th century and was conquered by Afonso Henriques in 1147. After that it was much altered but today lays in ruins, although some walls and towers of the fortifications remain. There is a fabulous view of Sintra from Torre Real. Ferdinand von Coburg-Koháry had trees planted in the courtyard of the castle in the middle of the 19th century (open: 1.5.–14.6. 9am–7pm, 15.6. to 15.9. 9am–8pm, 16.9.–31.10. 9am–7pm, 1.11.–30.4. 9.30am to 6pm).

Less than a mile further up the hill from the Castelo dos Mouros is the entrance to the park of the Palácio Nacional da Pena. This palace, built on a steep rocky ridge (528m/1,732ft), also served as a **summer**

★ ★
Palácio da Pena

residence for the royal family. The architect **Wilhelm von Esch-wege** was commissioned to design the elaborate building in the form of a medieval castle by the wife of **Ferdinand von Coburg-Koháry** (Fernando II); it was built from 1840 to 1850. Eschwege was instructed to include elements of an existing 16th-century monastery and to mix in various architectural styles; it is clear that he followed these instructions to the letter. There are Gothic, Manueline, Renaissance and Rococo aspects and even elements of Moorish and Far-Eastern architecture.

The imitation of Portuguese building styles is equally plain to see. The main tower of the castle uses the tower of Belém (►Lisbon) as a template. Art historians continue to harshly criticize this mixture of styles but the remarkable building is nevertheless certainly well worth a visit. The battlements offer what is probably the best view of the Sintra mountains anywhere.

Inside this »fairy-tale castle« there is a collection of furniture, faience pottery, weapons and other curiosities. A chapel and a two-storey Manueline cloister, with azulejo-clad walls, that belonged to the original 16th-century monastery can still be seen. The chapel includes a Renaissance altar that was fashioned by Nicolas Chanterène in 1532. The stained glass windows are German in origin and date from the 19th century.

Parque da Pena
The extensive Parque da Pena around the castle was also laid out for Ferdinand von Coburg-Koháry. On these 200ha/500ac more than 400 types of tree can be seen – including tree ferns – as well as shrubs.

It is particularly lovely in spring when the camellias, rhododendrons and azaleas are blooming. It is possible to climb up to the Cruz Alta (529m/1,735ft), a stone cross that was erected in 1522 to mark the highest point of the Sintra mountains (open: 1.5.–14.6. 9am–7pm, 15.6.–15.9. 9am–8pm, 16.9.–31.10. 9am–7pm, 1 November–30 April 9.30am–6pm).

Palaces in Western Sintra

Quinta da Regaleira
West of the town centre, on the road to Colares, stands the Quinta da Regaleira, a palace built in neo-Manueline style in the early 20th century. It is possible to take part in guided tours of the palace and its extensive parks with their caves and ponds, waterfalls and artificial lakes (open: 10am–5pm; guided tour bookings: tel. 219 106 650).

Palácio de Seteais
Further on towards Colares the road leads past the Palácio de Seteais just beyond the edge of the town. Its name, »the palace of the seven sighs«, derives from the fact that the French army signed the surrender treaty of Sintra here in 1808. The palace was built in the last quarter of the 18th century and was extended in the early

1800s. The triumphal arch from 1802 commemorates a visit of João VI. Nowadays it houses a luxury hotel and gourmet restaurant.

A few miles beyond the Palácio de Seteais where the road comes into Quinta de Monserrate stands a 19th-century villa built in Moorish style. The architect was an Englishman called Francis Cook. This small villa is surrounded by a splendid park. Apart from tall tree ferns, many other types of sub-tropical plants also grow here (open: summer 9am–8pm, winter 9am–7pm; no admission from one hour before closing time; guided tours of the palace can be given if booked in advance, 10am and 3pm daily: tel. 219 237 300).

✱ **Quinta e Palácio de Monserrate**

🕑

Around Sintra

The road finally reaches Colares, which is famous for its port wine. During the last few decades, many of Lisbon's rich have built summer residences here. Less than a mile beyond Colares a road leads off to the left towards the beaches of the ▶Costa do Sol and the most westerly point of the European mainland at Cabo da Roca (▶Costa do Sol). However, the right turn continues another 3km/2mi to Praia das Maçãs and Azenhas do Mar (▶Costa de Prata), two resorts on the steep coast.

Colares

In São Miguel de Odrinhas about 15km/10mi north of Sintra there is an interesting archaeological museum (Museu Arqueológico de São Miguel de Odrinhas) with exhibits from various eras of Portugal's history. The museum complex includes the remains of a Roman village (open: Wed–Sun 10am–1pm and 2pm–6pm).

Museu Arqueológico

🕑

Heading away from Sintra to the south-west is the road to the Palácio da Pena, about 10km/6.3mi along which stands the Convento dos Capuchos. The Capuchin monastery was built in 1560. The monks' cells are so tiny that is neither possible to stand up straight nor to stretch out to sleep. Some of them are carved out of the rock face and insulated from cold and moisture with cork walls (open: 9.30am–8pm in summer; 9.30am to 6pm in winter).

✱ **Convento dos Capuchos**

🕑

A small road leads away from here to Peninha and a hill (489m/1,604ft) that offers a great view of the Serra de Sintra and the sea. The small chapel was built in 1711 and is tiled with azulejos.

Peninha

A few miles south of Sintra lie the popular seaside towns of ▶Cascais and ▶ Estoril. Some 20km/12.5mi to the north is ▶ Mafra with its enormous monastery palace. It is a good idea to break a drive to ▶ Lisbon at ▶Queluz to see the palace there amid its beautiful grounds. The palace was built in 1747 as a summer residence and is considered the best example of Rococo architecture in Portugal. The well-kept grounds are worth an extended visit.

Other attractions in the area

★ Tavira

Historical province: Algarve
District: Faro

Elevation: sea level
Population: 14,000

Tavira is one of the prettiest towns in the Algarve. It is pictur-esquely situated on the banks of the Rio Gilão. Tavira is often called »Little Venice«, a somewhat daring comparison, though when its typical hipped roofs are reflected in the still waters of the river it can be every bit as delightful.

The town is located in the south-east of the Algarve, only about 20km/12.5mi from the Spanish border. It is built on both banks of the Rio Gilão that flows into the Atlantic here. Tavira itself is not ad-jacent to the open sea; it lies instead in the vicinity of the **Ria Formo-sa lagoon**. Just to the south-west of the town is the Ilha de Tavira, an island in the lagoon primarily characterized by its sand dunes. Fish-ing plays a key role in Tavira – the town was once the centre for the tuna fish catch off the Algarve coast – as does salt extraction. At the mouth of the Rio Gilão there are some extensive salt flats. In spite of the glorious sandy beaches in the neighbourhood, tourism does not yet play as great a role in Tavira as in many places further west along the Algarve coast. There are hardly any large hotels in the area.

Since the town had to be completely rebuilt after an earthquake, there are few buildings less than 250 years old. But the uniformity of the buildings gives the town a very pretty look. One typical feature in Tavira is the **characteristic hipped form of the roofs** on many of the old houses. This shape has since been adopted by modern archi-tects.

★
Uniform
appearance

What to See in Tavira

The centre of Tavira is the Praça da República on the right bank of the river. Next to the square is a park with arrays of flowers and trees. Beyond the park is Tavira's former market hall, now filled with small shops and cafes with seats right next to the river. Around the old market hall there are plenty of restaurants.

Praça da
República

In recent years many bridges have been built across the Rio Gilão which has somewhat altered the character of the town centre around the river. For centuries there was only the one, the seven-arched bridge north of the Praça da República. The bridge goes back to Ro-man times, and the Roman road connecting Faro and Mértola used

Ponte Romana

VISITING TAVIRA

INFORMATION
Rua da Galeria 9
8800-329 Tavira
Tel. 281 322 511
www.visitalgarve.pt

WHERE TO EAT
► **Moderate/Inexpensive**
① *Imperial*
Rua José Padinha
Tel. 281 322 306
Of all the restaurants in the town
centre, this is the most highly recom-
mended. One dish you can try here is
Alentejo-style pork, i.e. with mussels.

② *Ponto de Encontro*
Praça Dr. António Padinha 39
Tel. 281 323 730
Simple local restaurant with a homely
atmosphere specializing in fish.

③ *Beira Rio*
Rua Borda d'Água da Assêca
Excellent location at a peaceful spot by
the river. Vegetarian dishes and pizza
are on the menu.

WHERE TO STAY
► **Luxury/Mid-range**
① *Hotel Vila Galé Albacora*
8800 Quatro Águas
Tel. 281 380 800; fax 281 380 850
www.vilagale.pt
A little way outside Tavira, directly by
the sea. Located in a former tuna fish
landing station.

► **Mid-range/Budget**
② *Hotel Porta Nova*
Rua António Pinheiro
8800-323 Tavira
Tel. 281 329 700; fax 281 324 215
www.hotelportanova.com
Nice, comfortable hotel; the rooms
offer splendid views of Tavira.

Baedeker recommendation

► **Budget**
③ *Princesa do Gilão*
Rua Borda d'Água Aguiar 10-12
8800-326 Tavira
Tel. 281 325 171
Small, simple and well-kept hotel on the
banks of the river.

to lead across it. Today's bridge is a reconstruction built in the 17th
century. During the winter of 1989/1990 it was damaged by flooding
and had to be closed; since then it has been open only to pedes-
trians.

Igreja da Misericórdia
The narrow Rua da Galeria leads off Rua da Liberdade to the Igreja
da Misericórdia. In spite of rebuilding undertaken in 1755 after the
earthquake the church, that originally dates from 1541, remains one
of the finest examples of ecclesiastical Renaissance architecture in the
Algarve. The azulejos inside date from the 18th century.

Castro dos Mouros
The former castle that stands above the town centre is entered via
the Travessa da Fonte. The castle was originally built by the Romans

Tavira Plan

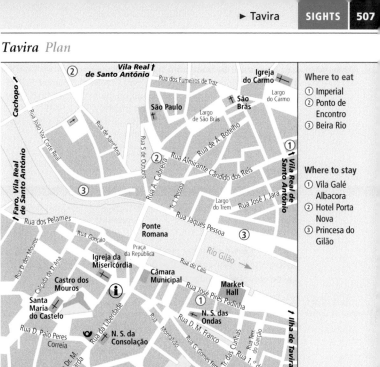

Where to eat
① Imperial
② Ponto de Encontro
③ Beira Rio

Where to stay
① Vila Galé Albacora
② Hotel Porta Nova
③ Princesa do Gilão

© Baedeker

and was taken over by the Moors. It was also rebuilt when Dom Dinis I conquered the town for the Portuguese, but nowadays all that remains of the fortification are a few walls. Part of the castle grounds have now been landscaped as a pretty garden that is privately owned but is still open to the public.

There is a great view of Tavira and the Rio Gilão from the garden and the castle walls.

Igreja Santa Maria do Castelo

Close to the ruins of the castle is the church of Santa Maria do Castelo that was originally built as a mosque. The original Gothic architecture was completely reconstructed after the earthquake. In the choir of the church are the tombs of seven knights who were killed by the Moors in 1242 in spite of a truce having been agreed.

Igreja do Carmo

On the other side of the river in the north of the town stands the 18th-century Igreja do Carmo. It features some beautifully decorated seating in the choir as well as copious talha decoration. The church was originally part of a Carmelite monastery.

✳ **Ilha de Tavira** The Ilha de Tavira lies off the coast to the south-west of Tavira. It can be reached **by boat** from the town. The ferry sets out from the road leading along the bank a little way beyond the market hall; another quay is located near the mouth of the river at Quatro Águas. There is a **pedestrian bridge** to the islands a little further west at Santa Luzia (Pedras d'El Rei). The Ilha de Tavira has a sandy beach 1km/0.6mi long and some shallow dunes.

✳ ✳ Tomar

H 19

Historical province: Ribatejo	**Elevation:** 75–122m/246–400ft
District: Santarém	**Population:** 19,000

The pretty town of Tomar mostly attracts tourists to see its mighty castle, the former seat of the Order of the Knights of Christ. The castle was placed under UNESCO protection in 1983.

Seat of the Knights of Christ Tomar is located on the Rio Nabão in the midst of the fertile Ribatejo region of central Portugal. The little river splits the attractive town into a western and an eastern section. The old centre around the Praça da República lying to the west of the river is now a World Heritage Site. A nice park has been laid out in the centre of town on a sandbank of the Rio Nabão. Looming over the town to the west is the castle of the Knights of Christ; a winding road leads up to the car park outside the grounds of the fortification.

✳ ✳ Convento da Ordem de Cristo de Tomar

History of the order **The Order of the Knights of Christ** (Ordem de Cavalharia de Nosso Senhor Jesus Cristo) was founded in 1319 by Dinis I with an amalgamation of political and religious motives to »defend the faith«, to fight the Moors, and also to extend the power of the Portuguese monarchy. The **Knights Templar** had already established a base in Tomar in 1159. When that order was disbanded in 1314, the Order of the Knights of Christ formed in its wake as a kind of successor: its members were often the same men who simply changed their dress and altered their red crosses. The order was initially based at Castro Marim in the Algarve but it moved to Tomar in 1356 and took up residence in the old Templar castle.

When **Henry the Navigator** (▶Famous People) became grand master of the order, it experienced its first heyday. Money from the order financed expeditions along the west coast of Africa that initiated the colonial acquisitions of the Europeans. In the reign of **Manuel I, who was grand master as of 1484**, the possessions of the Knights of Christ in Africa and the East Indies made it the richest order in Christendom. In 1523 the order of knights was reformed to become

▶ VISITING TOMAR

INFORMATION

Av. Dr. Cândido Madureira
2300-531 Tomar
Tel. 249 322 427
www.rttemplarios.pt

WHERE TO EAT

► Moderate

Chico Elias
Bairro de Algarvias 70
Tel. 249 311 067
The food served in the best restaurant in town is known far and wide.

Bela Vista
Rua Marquês de Pombal 68
Tel. 249 312 870
Right next to the river by the bridge with an excellent view. The menu offers many dishes typical of the Ribatejo region.

WHERE TO STAY

► Mid-range

Pousada de São Pedro
2300-196 Tomar (Castelo de Bode)

Tel. 249 381 1 59/75, fax 249 381 176
Located above the River Zêzere behind the dam at Castelo do Bode on the large reservoir; offers plenty of fishing and opportunities for watersports.

Hotel dos Templários
Largo Cândido dos Reis 1
2304-909 Tomar
Tel. 249 310 100
Fax 249 322 191
www.hoteldostemplarios.pt
Located next to the Mouchão park. The most luxurious and thus the most expensive hotel in town has 84 rooms.

► Budget

Pensão Luz/Residencial
Rua Serpa Pinto 144
2300-592 Tomar
Tel. 249 312 317
Fax 249 312 753
www.residencialluz.com
Small and nicely kept hotel with 14 rooms in the centre of Tomar.

---

an order of monks. It was secularized in 1789 and finally disbanded in 1910.

In defence of the Tagus line the Knights Templar erected a castle above the right bank of the river Nabão in the 12th century. Some remnants of the walls, the keep and the circular Templar church are still in existence. In the early 15th century under Henry the Navigator more buildings were put up around the castle site: the Claustro da Lavagem and Claustro do Cemitério. In the subsequent heyday under Manuel I around 1500, the Claustro de Santa Bárbara, the Knights of Christ church that extends from the Templar church and the new chapter house were all added. Although the political influence of the order diminished during the 16th and 17th centuries, this did not stop further building around the monastery. At this time, the four cloisters of Claustro dos Felipes, Claustro dos Corvos, Claustro da Micha and Claustro da Hospedaria were built, completing an extensive range of buildings dating from the 12th to the 17th centuries.

The building of the castle

The buildings were restored by the Count of Tomar in the mid-19th century. The green parklands that now surround the monastery complex were not added until the 1930s.

Entire complex The castle of the Knights of Christ towers over Tomar. It is entered via two gates that were part of the old Templar castle. Beyond these are some gardens that lead to the circular Templar church that is located next to the monastery entrance.

Claustro do Cemitério The first of the cloisters is the oldest: the Claustro do Cemitério (cemetery cloister). Amongst the tombs is that of Diogo da Gama, brother of the explorer Vasco da Gama.

Claustro da Lavagem To the east of the Claustro do Cemitério is the two-storey Claustro da Lavagem (laundry cloister). Like the cemetery cloister next door it was built during the time of Henry the Navigator.

Templar church The crenellated Templar church (rotunda) was built starting in 1162 using the **Holy Sepulchre in Jerusalem** as its template. The central building has **sixteen sides**. It is supported by massive stone pillars, one of which was later modified to form a bell tower. Inside there is an **octagonal central space** (charola) that was to contain the main altar. When the church of the Knights of Christ was built onto the original Templar edifice in the 16th century, the charola was made into the choir of the new church. All of the fabulous decoration, gilded wood carvings, frescoes and statues date from the 16th century.

Church of the Knights of Christ The church of the Knights of Christ was added onto the original Templar building. It was begun in 1515 to plans drawn up by João do Castilho and is **one of the finest examples of the Manueline style** in Portugal. Three quarters of the interior is taken up by the main choir where the monks once came to pray. The rest of the church was originally planned to be a sacristy but later functioned as a chapter house.

The exterior is richly decorated. The west façade is particularly impressive and, in particular, the magnificent **window of the old chapter house** exhibits the Manueline style in all its splendour and perfection. The best view of the church is from the terrace of the Claustro de Santa Bárbara. From there it is possible to see the variety of the Manueline decoration.

Claustro Principal A resplendently decorated door leads from the Knights of Christ church into the upper storey of the Claustro Principal, the main cloister, a fabulous two-storey building erected between 1557 and 1562 in late-Renaissance style. The upper storey is bordered by a terrace from which the gardens, formerly the monks' vegetable gardens, can be seen. Whereas the lower storey has Tuscan columns, the columns of the upper storey are Ionian. The elegant fountain in the courtyard dates from the 17th century.

On the eastern side of the Claustro Principal stand the impressive ruins of the chapter house that was never completed. Later, the entire roof vaulting collapsed and it is in this ruined form that the chapter house still remains.

Chapter house

From the Claustro de Santa Bárbara it is possible to see the fantastic Manueline window in the west façade of the Knights of Christ church up close. The window is surrounded by two massive cross-beams, with rigging, knots, ropes and a variety of masonry decoration that is all on the theme of the sea. Above the window is the cross of the Knights of Christ with the Portuguese coat-of-arms below it and two stone armillary spheres on either side. Armillary spheres are nautical devices that were of great importance for navigating the oceans at that time. Underneath the window, its builder Diogo de Arruda has apparently immortalized himself.

Claustro de Santa Bárbara/ Manueline window

There are three more cloisters on the site: the Claustro da Hospedaria (guest cloister), where noblemen were once accommodated while visiting the monastery; the Claustro da Micha (bread cloister), where bread was distributed to the poor; and the Claustro dos Corvos (raven cloister). Taking the tour further it is possible to see various monastic rooms such as the corridors of the novices, individual cells, the cross chapel and a room that used to be heated so that the monks could warm themselves.

Other cloisters and monastery buildings

Originally the monastery's water supply came from springs and cisterns, but in the 16th century work began on building an aqueduct to bring water to the monastery from the spring to the north-east. There is a fine view of the aqueduct from the end of the monastery corridor. Another completely different view is to be seen from the small road leading from Tomar to Pegões (a turn-off from the Tomar to Fátima road).

Aqueduto dos Pegões

Other Attractions in Tomar

The Igreja de São João Baptista is situated on the central Praça da República and contains a memorial to the Templar grand master Gualdim Pais, who founded the town of Tomar in 1162. The church was built in 1490 and is entered through an elegant Manueline doorway. The interior features paintings from the Portuguese school of the 16th century.

Igreja de São João Baptista

The 15th-century synagogue is just a few hundred yards south of the Praça da República and now houses a small Jewish museum (open: 10am–1pm and 2pm–6pm daily).

Synagogue ⏲

Museu dos Fosforos
In the former Convento de São Francisco at the southern end of the old town there is now a museum of matches. It has a collection of 43,000 matchboxes from more than 100 countries.

Capela de Santa Iria
Further to the east across the Rio Nabão on the old bridge (Ponte Velha) stands the Capela de Santa Iria on the far bank, with its remarkable Renaissance doorway from 1536.

Igreja de Santa Maria do Olival
The Igreja de Santa Maria do Olival was for many years the **seat of the Knights templar and the mother church for all of the order's churches** in the colonies. Only the vestibule and doorway are left of the original church building from 1160. The interior of the former Templar church dates primarily from the Renaissance period. The church contains the tombs of numerous knights and masters of the order.

Nossa Senhora da Conceição
In the north eastern part of the town near the ascent to the castle is the 16th-century chapel of Nossa Senhora da Conceição whose interior, with a nave and two aisles, is worth taking a look at.

Nossa Senhora da Piedade
Further to the north on a hill overlooking the town, there is a pilgrimage church built in 1613 by the name of Nossa Senhora da Piedade. It is entered via a stairway that has almost 300 steps and is flanked by gardens.
On the way there is an octagonal, shingle-roofed gallery that encircles the Capela de São Gregório, which was originally Manueline but was later modified in the style of the Baroque.

Attractions around Tomar
13km/8mi south-east of Tomar is the Castelo de Bode (▶Abrantes), and about 20km/12.5mi to the south stands the Castelo de Almourol on an island in the Tagus (▶Abrantes). To the west are ▶Fátima, Ourém (▶Fátima), ▶Batalha and ▶Alcobaça.

Trás-os-Montes

K–V 5–10

Historical province: Trás-os-Montes	**Area:** approx. 11,000 sq km/4,250 sq mi
Districts: Bragança, Vila Real, Viseu, Guarda	**Population:** 500,000
Principal city: Bragança	

The remoteness of Trás-os-Montes has led to a great many old customs surviving. Almost without comparison in Europe, the town can seem almost medieval: everyday life here is hard and the modern world quite distant. At times, Trás-os-Montes appears truly ancient.

VISITING TRÁS-OS-MONTES

INFORMATION

►Bragança, ►Vila Real, ►Viseu, ►
Guarda

WHERE TO STAY • WHERE TO EAT

► Mid-range
Pousada do Barão Forrester
5070-031 Alijó
Tel. 259959215, fax 259959304
The pousada situated to the east of
Vila Real was named after the English
baron James Forrester (1809–1862),
who came to Portugal to work in his
uncle's port business, Offley Forrester
& Co. It has 21 rooms and a
restaurant, as well as a swimming
pool, tennis courts and angling.

► Budget/Mid-range
Estalagem do Caçador
Largo Manuel Pinto de Azevedo

5340-219 Macedo de Cavaleiros
Tel. 278 426 354
Fax 278 426 381
An old house situated about 35km/
22mi south-west of Bragança, in
which 25 rooms are available. The
pretty décor is striking: all the rooms
are furnished in the most diverse
styles – most with lovely antique
furniture. There is a swimming pool
and a pleasant in-house restaurant
with plenty of atmosphere.

WHERE TO STAY

► Budget
Quinta do Real
5400-740 Santa Leocádia
Tel. 276 966 253
Fax 276 965 240
This former family home in a small
village south of Chaves has 10 rooms
for rent.

The rugged, mountainous province of Trás-os-Montes – »beyond the mountains« – is in the extreme north-east of Portugal. Spain lies to the north and east while the Portuguese landscapes of Minho and Douro Litoral lie to the west and south-west with Beira Alta to the south. The mountains reach heights of 1,500m/4,900ft.

»Beyond the mountains«

The tempering effect of the Atlantic Ocean hardly makes a difference as far inland as Trás-os-Montes. The climate goes from one extreme to another. The summers are very hot and the winters are fiercely cold – it frequently snows here. Some houses, especially those out in the country, lack any heating or air conditioning, meaning that their inhabitants are directly exposed to the fluctuations in temperature. They keep warm in winter with plenty of layers of clothing and the glowing ashes of the heating stoves that are placed beneath the tables.

Climate

Many archaeological finds have shown that the region of Trás-os-Montes, like neighbouring Minho, has been settled by human beings since ancient times. Then, as now, people were concentrated in the fertile valleys, particularly the upper Douro Valley, where it is possi-

Population and economy

ble to cultivate both wine and fruit. The bleak highlands are used for grazing sheep and goats. In addition to agriculture, there is also a long tradition of craft industries, including the manufacture of cloth, lace and pottery.

✱ ✱ Vale do Côa

Q10/11

Historical provinces: Beira Alta, Trás-os-Montes   **District:** Guarda

The valley of the river Côa came into the public eye when some sensational prehistoric finds were made during preparations for a dam project. The region where the cave engravings were found was declared a national park, the Parque Arqueológico Vale do Côa, in 1996.

✱ ✱
Parque Arqueológico Vale do Côa

Parque Arqueológico Vale do Côa covers a length of 17km/11mi including the regions of Vila Nova de Foz Côa, Muxagata and Castelo Melhor. Many thousands of cave engravings have been discovered here and placed under UNESCO protection. It is possible to see the images carved into the stone in the company of a guide. Guided tours start from the visitor centre at Castelo Melhor, Muxagata and from the main headquarters at Vila Nova de Foz Côa. They last between 1.5 and 2.5 hours, depending on the point of departure. Since places are limited **it is necessary to book a week in advance**. During

▶ VISITING VALE DO CÔA

INFORMATION

Parque Arqueológico do Vale do Côa (main office)
Av. Gago Coutinho, 19 Avila Nova de Foz Côa
Tel. 279 768 260
Fax 279 768 270
www.ipa.min-cultura.pt/coa/

Booking (required a week in advance)
Tel. 279 768 260/1
Fax 279 768 270
e-mail: visitas.pavc@ipa.min-cultura.pt

WHERE TO STAY •
WHERE TO EAT

▶ **Mid-range**
Pousada Senhora das Neves
6350-112 Almeida
Tel. 271574283, fax 271574320
21 rooms established in an old fort.

▶ **Budget**
Estalagem de Penedono
3630-246 Penedono
Tel. 254 509 050, fax 254 509 059
www.estalagempenedono.com
Well-run, respectable hotel without too many frills. Dishes typical of the region served in the restaurant.

the months of September and October boat tours are also offered and it is possible to join tours at night. Further information is available from the headquarters of the archaeological park in Vila Nova de Foz Côa (open: 9am–12.30pm, 2pm–5.30pm, no tours on Mondays). ⏱

Attractions in the Region

The small town of Torre de Moncorvo north-east of Vila Nova de Foz Côa, often simply referred to as Moncorvo for short, is situated on the other side of the Douro set in expansive and arid scenery which is covered in fruit and vegetable fields. The village has many attractive **old houses decorated with coats of arms**. The present town hall, from the 19th century, stands on the site of the former castle that was built under King Dinis. The parish church is a 16th-century Renaissance building with a nave and two aisles; its interior is decorated with fabulous talha decoration and a remarkable Gothic triptych on wood. The Igreja da Misericórdia near Largo do Castelo is also worth seeing. It contains a beautifully worked Gothic pulpit.

Torre de Moncorvo

The small town of Vila Nova de Foz Côa has 2,500 inhabitants and it also caught the public's attention after the discoveries in the valley. Nevertheless, Vila Nova de Foz Côa, situated where the Côa flows into the Douro, has remained the sleepy town it always was, far removed from city life. It has a few minor attractions, though, such as the Manueline church and a fine old pelourinho.

Vila Nova de Foz Côa

In the village of Freixo de Numão south-west of Vila Nova de Foz Côa the attractions include a Romanesque church and the ruins of a castle.

It is worth taking a trip to Marialva situated some 20km/12.5mi south of Vila Nova de Foz Côa. The village has retained an almost medieval atmosphere, with a castle and a pretty centre that has recently been renovated a little.

A little further east towards the Spanish border there are several pretty border villages (▶Guarda).

Marialva – pretty old village in an extremely thinly populated region near to the Spanish border

THE ROCK DRAWINGS IN THE CÔA VALLEY

Was the Côa Valley a sacred place thousands of years ago? During the construction of a reservoir in northern Portugal, hundreds of Stone Age rock drawings were discovered with depictions of animals. Today the Vale do Côa is a tourist attraction.

In the rugged gorges of the Côa, a tributary of the Douro in northern Portugal, a **sensational discovery** was made in the process of damming the river with the intention of creating the second largest reservoir in the country: hundreds of prehistoric rock drawings which no one had set eyes on for thousands of years. Almost every day more of these scratched depictions in the rock were found. Even a tool used to make such art was discovered: a very carefully worked scraper made of quartz. Just about every stone turned in the Côa Valley revealed one of its wonderful secrets. In order to preserve these rock paintings, further work on the reservoir was prohibited by the government, though only after a huge outcry from the people of Portugal, as in the beginning the government insisted that for economic reasons the project should continue regardless of any cultural sensations. The Portuguese electricity company had even known about the drawings years before, and kept the find secret. Under the motto »as gravuras não podem nadar« (the engravings cannot swim) – a line adapted from a popular Portuguese rap by the group Bad Company – a large education and **petition campaign** was launched in support of preserving the drawings.

Preference for animals

No one knows how many drawings are still to be discovered, as the whole reservoir area has not yet been searched. Initial estimates by archaeologists date the bulk of the images in

the shale to that era of the Stone Age stretching from 40,000 to 10,000 BC. Scientists believe that most of the drawings in the Côa Valley were completed **20,000 years ago**. They depict animals that are always shown in side view. Many of the engravings portray movement; some even show perspective. The animals are either being hunted or they are species that were domesticated. Two astoundingly true to life depictions of animals reminiscent of goats with S-shaped horns are scratched into a block of shale whose upper surface is only a little more than half a square metre in size. Of the two goat heads, one is somewhat hidden, probably to express the idea of movement. The most spectacular detail is on the rear of the picture: the hoof and the rump of one animal are almost exactly identical to depictions that were found in the caves at Altamira. On another rock there are two horses which appear to kiss. This strongly expressive image is one of the oldest

that have been found in the valley to date. Alongside these there are many very fine lined drawings that are at first often not recognizable as such.

Invitation to nature

Why did the people of that time, who had a daily struggle to survive in this rugged environment, expend so much effort to leave behind a record of their time? Were they fascinated by the beauty of the animals they hunted? Research, especially into the indigenous people of Australia, has led scientists to believe that, 20,000 years ago, humans made images of animals for **magical or religious reasons**. The depiction of an animal, in the form of a rock drawing or otherwise, meant that it could be dominated and defeated. There are other explanations, based on the idea held by primitive people that the animals come from the soil and will be reborn there. Animal figures which appear to emerge from the rock are a kind of invitation to nature to produce more animals for hunting.

Sacred place?

The region around the Côa river is the only large area of finds from the Stone Age to be discovered in Europe that is in the open air. The Côa, which

»*The core area of the rock art in the Côa Valley could have been a kind of Stone Age ritual site.*«

joins with the Douro in the south, is one of the few rivers on the Iberian Peninsula that flows from south to north. The core area of the rock art in the Côa Valley could have been a kind of Stone Age ritual site. The number of the drawings found along the river has deepened the mystery around the Stone Age art of cave painting. Were this river and valley in some way

sacred? Or was the Douro the great axis of civilization and the Côa, its more remote and inaccessible tributary, the only place that the rock drawings have been able to survive 20,000 years of human history? An answer to these questions will only be possible when other neighbouring valleys of Douro tributaries have been examined.

Tourist attraction

When the government prohibited the further construction of the reservoir in 1995, the region was threatened with financial losses running into the millions. The Portuguese culture minister nevertheless recognized that the cave drawings could prove to be a kind of motor to kick start the development of the region. It is only to be hoped that this prognosis comes true. The **Parque Arqueológico Vale do Côa** makes the prehistoric artworks in the Côa Valley accessible to interested parties – sensibly only in small groups. The preservation of this piece of human cultural heritage many thousands of years old is so far ensured.

✴ Valença do Minho

G 4

Historical province: Minho
District: Viana do Castelo

Elevation: 72m/236ft
Population: 3,000

Valença do Minho is situated on the left bank of the Minho, which forms the border between Portugal and Spain in this region. There is little sign nowadays of the former rivalry between the two nations and some busy small-scale border trade occurs between Valença do Minho and Tui across the river.

A bridge here crosses between Spain and Portugal. The Spaniards travel to Valença do Minho to obtain textiles, especially towelling articles. On market day every Wednesday Valença do Minho is transformed into a bustling small town. Another market takes place the following day in Tui across the border.

In and Around Valença do Minho

Imposing fortified walls surround the centre of Valença do Minho. The town has indeed been fortified from time immemorial; the present **fortress** dates from the 17th century and was built in the **Vauban style**. From the numerous vantage points on the walls there are great views of the lower lying parts of the town, the Minho valley and the Galician mountains. The old centre is threaded with narrow streets of whitewashed houses and everywhere there are traders offering their textiles for sale. Look out for the Capela de São Sebastião,

✴
Townscape

▶ VISITING VALENÇA DO MINHO

INFORMATION
Avenida da Espanha
4930-677 Valença do Minho
Tel. 251 823 374
www.rtam.pt

**WHERE TO STAY •
WHERE TO EAT**
▶ **Mid-range/Luxury**
Pousada do Dom Dinis
4920-296 Vila Nova de Cerveira
►Minho

▶ **Mid-range**
Pousada de São Teotónio
4930-619 Valença do Minho

Tel. 251 800 260
Fax 251 824 397
Pousada inside Valença's fortress, with 18 rooms.

Casa do Poço
Travessa da Gaviarra 4
4930-758 Valença do Minho
Tel. 251 825 235
Fax 251 825 469
A lovely 16th-century building that has been charmingly renovated and reopened as part of the »Turismo de Habitação« project, with six nicely furnished rooms. Evening meals can be provided for guests on request.

the late 13th-century Igreja de Santa Maria dos Anjos, and the Igreja Matriz, founded by João I as a collegiate church around 1400.

Monte do Faro
About 7km/4mi south-east of Valença do Minho, Monte do Faro (566m/1,857ft) towers over the left bank of the Minho. From its summit there is an expansive view over the Minho valley and eastwards towards the mountains of the ▶ Peneda-Gerês National Park or westwards to the Atlantic coast.

Vila Nova de Cerveira
15km/9.4mi south-west along the Minho is the pretty village of Vila Nova de Cerveira, from which there is a ferry connection to Spain. There is stylish accommodation in the pousada (▶ Minho) established inside a castle built in 1321 by Dinis I.

★ Viana do Castelo

E/F 6

Historical province: Minho	**Elevation:** 20m/66ft
District: Viana do Castelo	**Population:** 20,000

Viana do Castelo is situated on the mouth of the Rio Lima at the foot of Monte de Santa Luzia. The town is popular with visitors thanks to its attractive appearance and the beach on the Costa Verde.

The district capital is an important harbour and is also home to various industries including textiles and the processing of wood or fish. There are also a few small boat building yards. The many attractive houses and mansions, some with Manueline or Renaissance granite façades, are testament to the town's glorious past.

History
The town developed from a Greek trading post. It remained a modest harbour town until the Middle Ages, but with the onset of the period of Portugal's great voyages of discovery Viana gained riches and respect. One key factor was the contribution made by highly profitable cod fishing off the coast of Newfoundland. In the 19th century the people of the town took the royalist side in the Liberals' struggle against the monarchy. For this reason Viana do Castelo was granted a municipal charter by Queen Maria II and cast aside its old name of Viana da Foz do Lima.

What to See in Viana do Castelo

Tour
It is good to start a tour of Viana do Castelo from Largo 5 de Outubro down on the river, where there are places to park. From here, go upstream a little along the Rio Lima then head north on the Rua S. Cabral to the cathedral.

⏵ VISITING VIANA DO CASTELO

INFORMATION
Rua do Hospital Velho
4900-540 Viana do Castelo
Tel. 258 822 620
www.rtam.pt

EXCURSIONS
It is possible to take boat trips down the river. They start from the car park at Largo 5 de Outubro at the riverside.

WHERE TO EAT
▶ Moderate
① *Casa d'Armas*
Largo 5 de Outubro 30
Tel. 258 824 999
This stylish hotel is the best in town.

▶ Inexpensive/Moderate
② *Dolce Vita*
Rua do Poço 44
Tel. 258 824 860 Portuguese cuisine supplemented by Italian pastas and pizzas from a charcoal oven.

③ *O Vasco*
Rua Grande 21
Tel. 258 824 665
Good simple Portuguese cooking.

WHERE TO STAY
▶ Mid-range
① *Pousada do Monte de Santa Luzia*
Monte de Santa Luzia

4901-909 Viana do Castelo
Tel. 258 800 370, Fax 258 828 892
This pousada stands up on the hill near the pilgrimage church. There is a splendid view of the town and the confluence of the rivers.

② *Estalagem Casa Melo Alvim*
Avenida Conde da Carreira 28
4900 Viana do Castelo
Tel. 258 808 200
Fax 258 808 220
www.meloalvimhouse.com

A lovely old villa with some rooms featuring antique furniture.

③ *Flôr de Sal*
Avenida de Cabo Verde
4900-350 Viana do Castelo
Tel. 258 800 100
Fax 258 800 110
www.hotelflordesal.com
Hotel on the beach to the west of Viana do Castelo. Nice, modern rooms.

④ *Hotel Rali Resid*
Avenida Afonso III 180
4900 Viana do Castelo
Tel. 258 829 770
Fax 258 820 060
Respectable, well-run hotel in the town centre.

Bridge

From the shore it is possible to see the old bridge spanning the Lima at Viana do Castelo. It was designed by Gustave Eiffel at the end of the 19th century.

Sé

The cathedral was originally built in the first half of the 15th century but saw some extensive rebuilding in the 19th century. The two massive crenellated towers are reminders of the Romanesque period. Inside there are some elegantly worked 17th-century polychromatic wooden sculptures. The illusionist ceiling fresco is another striking feature.

Casa dos Velhos

The Casa dos Velhos alongside the cathedral was built in the 15th century and exhibits obvious Galician influence.

Casa dos Lunas

To the west opposite the cathedral is the mid-16th-century Casa dos Lunas. The decoration of the southern façade may go back to an earlier building.

★

Praça da República

Praça da República is one of the **most impressive squares in Portugal**. The middle of the square features a double Renaissance fountain with a large basin. The most important buildings on the square are the old town hall and the Igreja da Misericórdia.

Antigos Paços do Concelho

The eastern side of the square is bordered by the old town hall (Antigos Paços do Concelho), built from great granite blocks at the beginning of the 16th century. Its colonnades were once open to the public: one of their uses was for the sale of bread.

Viana do Castelo *Plan*

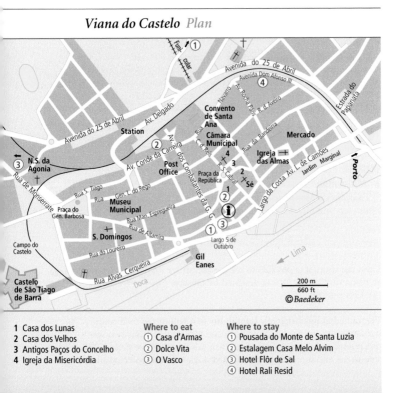

1 Casa dos Lunas
2 Casa dos Velhos
3 Antigos Paços do Concelho
4 Igreja da Misericórdia

Where to eat
① Casa d'Armas
② Dolce Vita
③ O Vasco

Where to stay
① Pousada do Monte de Santa Luzia
② Estalagem Casa Melo Alvim
③ Hotel Flôr de Sal
④ Hotel Rali Resid

The pilgrimage church of Santa Luzia. From up here there is a breathtaking view of the mouth of the Rio Lima and the Costa Verde.

is talk of reopening the long-disused funicular railway, so it may be worth asking if it is in service yet. A short distance to the north of the church are the sparse remains of an old Celtiberian settlement that was populated until the 4th century AD.

Vila do Conde

F 8

Historical province: Douro Litoral	**Elevation:** sea level
District: Porto	**Population:** 21,000

Vila do Conde, the »town of the counts«, is situated about 20km/ 12.5mi north of Porto at the mouth of the Rio Ave. In spite of the industry and commerce that dominates the region, Vila do Conde itself is known as a seaside resort. The old town centre also attracts tourists.

A lot of industry has started up around the town. It earns a living from shipbuilding and cotton processing but its traditional industry is bobbin lace making. All in all, Vila do Conde is nicer than neighbouring Póvoa de Varzim to the north.

To the north of the square is the Igreja da Misericórdia that was re-built in the early 18th century. There is some lovely talha decoration in the interior as well as some 17th-century azulejos. Next to the church is the Misericórdia house, built as of 1589 in Flanders Renaissance style. There is an arcade above which there are two **loggias decorated with caryatids**.

Igreja da Misericórdia

To the north, Rua dos Reis leads first to the town hall, a 16th-century mansion that was completely rebuilt in the early 18th century, then to Convento de Santa Ana, which now houses the Hospital da Caridade. One Manueline tower still remains of the original 16th-century Benedictine monastery. The monastery church is richly adorned with talha decoration and an **impressive ceiling design** featuring individual frescoes.

Convento de Santa Ana

The tour now leads west along Avenida da Carreira and Rua S. Tiago to the pilgrimage church of Nossa Senhora da Agonia. A Baroque stairway leads up to the entrance. Building started as early as the mid-18th century but the bell tower was only added at the end of the 19th century.

Nossa Senhora da Agonia

Castelo de São Tiago da Barra to the south of the pilgrimage church was built in the 16th century to defend the harbour. Two fortified towers were only added in the 18th century.

Castelo de São Tiago da Barra

Igreja de São Domingos was built in Renaissance style in the 16th century and was part of a Dominican monastery. Local brochures describe the **carved and gilded altar** in the Nossa Senhora do Rósario side chapel as the finest in Europe.

Igreja de São Domingos

Diagonally opposite stands the town's museum, housed in the 18th-century Casa dos Barbos Maciel. It includes 17th-century furnishings from the Portuguese Indies and Moorish Spain as well as an important collection of Portuguese ceramics from the 16th to the 19th centuries.

Museu Municipal

Rua de Altamira now leads towards the south-west and the Largo 5 de Outubro, the starting point of the tour, is not far away. The Gil Eanes museum ship can be seen here. It was in use as a hospital ship for the cod fishing fleet around Newfoundland until 1955. Nowadays the ship houses a youth hostel.

Gil Eanes hospital ship

Around Viana do Castelo

About 5km/3mi north-east of the town on Monte de Santa Luzia (250m/820ft) stands the church of the same name that can be seen for miles around. It was built in neo-Byzantine style in the early 20th century. The view alone makes the climb worthwhile, although there

Igreja de Santa Luzia

What to See in Vila do Conde

Visible for miles, the convent of Santa Clara towers over the town. **Mosteiro de** The original convent was established in 1318 but only the fortified **Santa Clara** Gothic church remains from this time. The late 18th-century convent buildings have a palatial appearance. An attractive rose window decorates the western side of the Gothic church, in whose aisleless interior are the fabulous Renaissance tombs of the convent's patrons Dom Afonso Sanches – the illegitimate son of Dinis I – and Dona Tareja Martin and their children, all from the 16th century. The carved coffered ceiling and the grille in front of the choir are also notable.

VILA DO CONDE

INFORMATION

Centro de Artesanato
Rua 5 de Outubro
4480-739 Vila do Conde
Tel. 252 248 473
www.cm-viladoconde.pt

Water was supplied to the convent via an aqueduct 7km/4.3mi in **Aqueduto** length that starts in Póvoa de Varzim. This structure, with its 999 arches, was built in the 18th century.

The fortified parish church towers over the old town. It was built in **Igreja Matriz** the 16th century to a cross-shaped floor plan and has a Manueline doorway. The bell tower was added to the side in the 17th century. Inside there is a pretty gilded wooden pulpit from the 17th/18th centuries, and on the small square in front of the church there is a 16th-century pelourinho with a sword of justice. The northern edge of the square is formed by the 16th-century town hall, adorned with the coat of arms of Manuel I.

The arts and crafts centre (Centro de Artesanato) a few hundred **Centro de** yards east of the parish church shows off the products of Vila do **Artesanato** Conde's traditional lace making industry.

Outside the centre of town, situated directly at the mouth of the Rio **Forte de São** Ave, stands the 17th-century fortress of São João Baptista with its **João Baptista** five bastions.

The small fishing harbour of Azurara is situated on the Rio Ave just **Azurara** 2 km/1.3mi south of Vila do Conde. Its Manueline fortified church is notable. Another pelourinho stands outside the church.

About 6km/4mi east of Vila do Conde – close to the confluence of **Cividade de** the Rio Este and the Rio Ave – there are remains of the Celtic settle- **Bagunte** ment known as Cividade de Bagunte. Excavations have brought to light some fine objects in silver and bronze.

✶ Vila Real

M 9

Historical province: Trás-os-Montes	**Elevation:** 422m/1,385ft
District: Vila Real	**Population:** 14,000

Close to Vila Real, Europe's famous Mateus Rosé wine with its familiar bulbous bottle is made. Vila Real itself is a pretty old episcopal see with some very attractive houses from the 15th to the 18th centuries.

The town is at the confluence of the Rio Corgo and Rio Cabril rivers about 80km/50mi east of Porto amid fruit orchards and vineyards. The black porcelain made in the region is famous, particularly the products made in Bisalhães. Vila Real is now the capital of the eponymous district.

Avenida de Carvalho Araújo
The most important shopping street and main thoroughfare is Avenida de Carvalho Aráujo, along which most of the town's major attractions lie. No. 19, in Italian Renaissance style, is the **birthplace of the seafarer Diogo Cão**, who discovered the mouth of the Congo river. No. 94, where the tourist information office is located, is adorned with a notable Manueline window. The town hall was built in the early 19th century. The 14th-century Gothic **Sé** was originally a Dominican monastery church. Some Romanesque capitals remain from the first church.

View
Both the former castle hill and the Calvário (460m/1,509ft) with the 16th-century Santo António church offer fine views of Vila Real.

▶ VISITING VILA REAL

INFORMATION
Avenida Carvalho Araújo 94
5000-657 Vila Real
Tel. 259 322 819
www.rtsmarao.pt

WHERE TO EAT
► Inexpensive/Moderate
Mira Corgo
Av. 1 de Maio 76
Tel. 259 325 001
Classical and elegant; nicely prepared meals typical of the region.

WHERE TO STAY
► Budget
Casa da Campeã
Sardoeira – Torgueda
5000-072 Vila Real
Tel. 259 979 640, fax 259 979 760
www.casacampea.com
A hotel that resembles a motel right on the IP 4, near an exit to the west of Vila Real. Despite its proximity to the road it is quiet and almost rustic in character. Well located for driving to Vila Real, into the Serra do Marão, to Trás-os-Montes or into the Douro Valley.

Solar de Mateus – reflected in the water. The Baroque palace was built by Nicolo Nasoni.

Around Vila Real

About 4km/2.5mi east of the town is the village of Mateus where the **Baroque residence of the counts of Vila Real** is located. The building is still occupied by members of the Mangualde family but part of the palace is open to the public. Inside there are some exquisite wooden ceilings, as well as furniture, carpets, paintings, silverwork and an interesting collection of porcelain. A small, private museum includes letters the forebears of the present Mangualde family exchanged with kings and other important personages as well as **drawings for *The Lusiads* by Camões**.

★
Solar de Mateus

Even better than the palace itself are the **gardens**. One floral work of art is the old Thuja Avenue in the form of a tunnel (open: June to September: 9am–7.30pm; October, March, April, May: 9am–1pm and 2pm–6pm; November to February: 10am–1pm and 2pm–5pm).

⏱

About 4km/2.5mi beyond Mateus a side road branches off to the sanctuary of Panóias. This was probably a Luso-Roman chapel dedicated to the god Serapis. Six granite rocks once featured Greek and Latin inscriptions but they are no longer decipherable. One of the rocks must have been an altar for sacrifices. It is still possible to see the channels along which the blood of the slaughtered animals

★
Panóias

🕐 drained away (open: 9am–12.30pm and 2pm–5pm daily, closed Monday and Tuesday mornings).

Serra do Marão It is worth taking a drive westward through the terribly romantic Serra do Marão to ▶Amarante.

Peso da Régua About 15km/9.4mi south of Vila Real is Peso da Régua (▶Lamego), a centre for wine-growing and wine trading.

Vila Real de Santo António

O 33

Historical province: Algarve	**Elevation:** sea level
District: Faro	**Population:** 10,000

Vila Real de Santo António is located deep in the south-east of Portugal on the Guadiana river. The small border town is a popular destination for day trippers who like to wander through its bustling centre looking for bargains.

»V.R.S.A.« Signposts to Vila Real de Santo António often have only the abbreviation »V.R.S.A.« , now a commonplace short form of the rather long name of the »royal town«. This small town on the Spanish border is located at the south-eastern tip of the Algarve on the right bank of the Guadiana, the river that forms the border between Portugal and Spain at this point. It is connected to its Spanish counterpart Ayamonte on the opposite bank by means of a regular ferry service, although the ferry has been declining in importance since a motorway bridge was built across the river a few miles to the north. It is interesting to take a day trip down the Guadiana from Vila Real. Vila Real de Santo António is primarily popular with day trippers: both holidaymakers in the Algarve and Spaniards from over the river come to shop for bargains here. Before the 1960s the town had a lot of canning plants producing mainly tinned sardines and tuna fish.

Checkerboard layout The town centre alongside the river has a distinctively uniform appearance. The highly regular layout of the town was the work of the Marquês de Pombal (▶Famous People), who had previously laid out the lower city of Lisbon after the serious earthquake of 1755. Like Baixa in Lisbon, Vila Real de Santo António was conceived as a checkerboard pattern. The town was completely rebuilt in 1774 after the older town of Santo António da Avenilha was destroyed by disastrous floods in the early 18th century. The new town was settled by fishermen from ▶Aveiro. The centre of the town is the Praça do Marquês de Pombal with its star-shaped paving stones and an obelisk built in 1775 as a memorial to José I. Street cafés invite visitors to stop a while.

VISITING VILA REAL DE SANTO ANTÓNIO

INFORMATION

Centro Cultural António Aleixo
Rua Teófilo Braga
8900 Vila Real de Santo António
Tel. 281 542 100
www.visitalgarve.pt

EXCURSIONS

Riosul
Rua Tristão Vaz Teixeira, 15 C
8900-470 Monte Gordo
Various excursions available including
boat trips on the Guadiana from Vila
Real de Santo António to Foz de
Odeleite and back.
Tel. 281 510 200; fax 281 510 209
Mobile 96 20 12 112
www.riosul-tours.com

ENTERTAINMENT

The place for night life in the region is
Monte Gordo. There is also a casino
there.

WHERE TO EAT

▶ **Moderate**
Caves de Guadiana
Avenida da República 89
Tel. 281544498
Excellent Portuguese cuisine makes

the Caves de Guadiana highly popular
with the locals, too.

WHERE TO STAY

▶ **Mid-range**
Hotel Casablanca
8900 Monte Gordo, Praceta Casablanca
Tel. 281 511 444
Fax 081 511 999
www.casablancainn.pt
Small but stylish hotel in the centre of
Monte Gordo, somewhat removed
from the bustling promenades. About
40 rooms, some with a view of the sea.
There are patios around the building,
the furnishings are pleasant, and the
service very good. No organized
entertainment or sport but a guaran-
tee of quiet relaxation.

▶ **Budget**
Hotel Apolo
Av. dos Bombeiros Portugueses
8900 Vila Real de Santo António
Tel. 281 512 448
Fax 281 512 450
Simple but pleasant and well-kept
hotel with 42 rooms.

Around Vila Real de Santo António

It is well worth taking a drive along the Algarve coast to Cabo de São   **Algarve coast**
Vicente. This shows off the varied coastal scenery, first the Sandy Al-
garve then further west to the Rocky Algarve. Right on the coast near
Vila Real de Santo António is Monte Gordo, a rather built-up seaside
resort with a marvellous wide sandy beach. A little bit further west
between Manta Rota and Cacela Velha the lagoon region starts with
many islands off the coast (►Algarve).

About 4km/2.5mi north west of Vila Real de Santo António, the   ★
houses of Castro Marim are scattered across the plain of the Guadi-   **Castro Marim**
ana. The name, meaning »castle on the sea«, indicates that the town

was built, the square was occasionally used as a bullfighting arena. On the eastern side of the square is the church of the former Augustine monastery from the 17th/18th centuries with its richly decorated interior. This is where the dukes of Bragança are interred. Their wives rest in the 16th-century Antigo Convento das Chagas on the southern side of the square. The building is now a pousada.

Porta dos Nós North of the palace, on the road to Borba, it is impossible to miss the Porta dos Nós. The »**knot gate**« is a remnant of the old 16th-century city walls. It was once the gate to the 2,000ha/5,000ac of land that functioned as a game reserve (tapada), where the royal family hunted until the 20th century.

Castelo Standing over the town are the ruins of a mighty crenellated Castelo that was erected under King Dinis in the 13th century before being reinforced and expanded in the 17th century. Nowadays it is a highly atmospheric place. It is possible to circumnavigate the old town on top of the walls. Inside the wall are the Renaissance church of da Conceição and a hunting museum.

Around Vila Viçosa

Borba The attractive and rather quaint old town of Borba, 4km/2.5mi north Vila Viçosa, is known for its marble quarries but also for its wine. The centre of its commercial bustle is the Praça do Cinco de Outubro with the town hall from 1797 and the parish church. The São Bartolomeu church is also worth seeing, a Renaissance building from the 16th century with an attractive doorway, colourfully painted stone vaulting and gorgeous azulejo tiling. In the Convento das Servas there is a fine two-storey cloister, with a tiled fountain in the middle.

Around Vila Viçosa It is well worth going about 50km/31mi south-west past Vila Viçosa to ▶Évora. Other destinations near Vila Viçosa include the rather larger ▶Estremoz and ▶Elvas.

★ Viseu

Historical province: Beira Alta	**Elevation:** 540m/1,772ft
District: Viseu	**Population:** 24,000

Viseu lies in the middle of the famous wine-growing region of Dão. Its attractive houses and palaces date from the Renaissance and Baroque periods. Narrow, granite-cobbled streets and snug nooks and crannies give the town an atmosphere all its own.

The district capital is a major centre for agriculture but it also has an important tradition of craftsmanship: carpets, lace and black porcelain are its most famous products. In the 16th century Viseu **was home to one of the most important schools of painting in Portugal**. The main proponent of the school was **Gaspar Vaz** (died c1568), as well as Vasco Fernandes, known as **Grão Vasco** (died c1542), who was born in the town.

What to See in Viseu

The starting point for any tour of the town must be the central Praça da República (Rossio) with the town hall on its western side.

Praça da República

To the south of the square is the Igreja de São Francisco with its splendid azulejo and talha decoration.

The **Almeida Moreira museum** north of the Praça da República shows of the collection of art enthusiast Moreira. It includes furniture, ceramics, porcelain and paintings.

From here go north through the Porta do Soar, a remnant of the old fortifications, to the centre of the old town, the **Praça da Sé**. It is thought that there was a Celtiberian settlement here in prehistoric times.

To the west of the square stands the **Misericórdia church**, approached by a broad stairway. The church is in pure Baroque style with granite framed windows in walls of white plaster. The interior is characterized by its clear and uniform Baroque design.

Opposite the Igreja da Misericórdia is the 12th-century Romanesque and Gothic cathedral. The two towers that flank the Baroque facade are in Romanesque style. In the central niche above the doorway is a **statue of St Theotonius,**

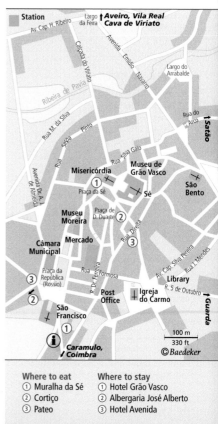

Viseu Plan

Where to eat
① Muralha da Sé
② Cortiço
③ Pateo

Where to stay
① Hotel Grão Vasco
② Albergaria José Alberto
③ Hotel Avenida

© Baedeker

the patron saint of the town. The impressively large and unadorned interior was extended into a hall church in the 16th century, since when the Gothic pillars support a **Manueline vault**. On the massive Baroque altar is a 14th-century statue of the Virgin Mary. The cloister dates from the Renaissance, while the upper section is from the 17th century.

✳
Museu de Grão Vasco

Next to the cathedral stands the **Paço dos Três Escalões**. The Renaissance palace, rebuilt in the 18th century, now houses the Museu de Grão Vasco. The museum exhibits sculptures from the 13th–16th centuries, particularly highlighting the Viseu school (*Saint Peter* and *The Hill of Calvar* by Vasco Fernandes, among others). Also included

▶ VISITING VISEU

INFORMATION

Avenida Calouste Gulbenkian
3510-055 Viseu
Tel. 232 420 950
www.rtdaolafoes.com

WHERE TO EAT
▶ Moderate

① *Muralha da Sé*
Adro da Sé 24
Tel. 232 437 777 Charming restaurant in a lovely old building opposite the cathedral. Good regional fare; the veal dishes are superb. There are also half portions for children.

▶ Inexpensive/Moderate

② *Cortiço*
Rua Augusto Hilário 45
Tel. 232 423 853
Very good regional dishes such as »Vitela à moda de Lafões« (veal in a clay pan with potatoes and carrots), goat or rabbit.

③ *Pateo*
Rua Direita 48
Tel. 232 421 450
Popular restaurant in an old courtyard off Rua Direita.

WHERE TO STAY
▶ Mid-range

① *Hotel Grão Vasco*
Rua Gaspar Barreiros
3510-032 Viseu
Tel. 232 423 511; fax 232 426 444
Located in the centre of Viseu amid well tended gardens. 86 spacious rooms, many including a balcony.

▶ Budget

Baedeker recommendation

② *Albergaria José Alberto*
Rua Cândido dos Reis
423510-057 Viseu
Tel. 232 467 310; fax 232 467 311
Very attractive modern hotel built onto an old town house. Architecturally tasteful both inside and out. Charming rooms, friendly service.

③ *Hotel Avenida*
Avenida Alberto Sampaio
13510-030 Viseu
Tel. 232 423 432; fax 232 435 643
Spartan but pleasant hotel right on the central Rossio. Typical Portuguese ambience.

are works by more recent Portuguese artists (19th und 20th centuries) as well as Spanish, French, Flemish and Dutch masters. There are also some ceramics (16th–18th centuries), carpets and furnishings (17th and 18th centuries).

Some small streets run behind the cathedral towards the main shopping street of Viseu, Rua Direita. This pedestrianized street has many lovely houses from the 16th to the 18th centuries, some of them with wrought iron grilles. Following Rua Direita to the south a right turn down the Rua Formosa leads back to the starting point of this tour. **Rua Direita**

Beyond the centre of the town, a park called Cava de Viriato extends to the north covering a large pentagonal space. The estate once belonged to a Luso-Roman castrum that once occupied the site. A memorial was erected near the park to a **Viriatus of Lusitania**, who led a heroic struggle against the Romans here in the 2nd century BC. **Cava de Viriato**

Around Viseu

It is well worth taking a trip through the picturesque gorges of the **Serra do Caramulo** (up to 1,071m/3,514ft) south-west of Viseu. Amid the mountains lies the health resort of Caramulo (800m/2,625ft). In this remote spot there is a museum that would seem less out of place in a city, **Museu do Caramulo**, displaying medieval art, furniture, tapestries, porcelain and ceramics as well as a remarkable **collection of paintings** by Portuguese and other European masters, mainly works from the 19th and 20th century including pieces by Picasso, Dalí, Miró, Chagall, Léger, Dufy and de Vlaminck. On the ground floor and in the extension there is an exhibition charting the development of the car since 1902 that features about 50 historic vehicles. One of the most important of these **vintage cars** is a Mercedes Pullman from 1937. All of these art treasures and cars were collected by Abel de Lacerda. Since his death the unique museum has been run by his brother (open: 10am–1pm and 2pm–6pm or 5pm in winter). ✱ **Caramulo** ⊙

About 3 km/2mi to the south-west are the hot springs of Termas de São Pedro do Sul, with **hot sulphur and sodium springs** that reach a temperature of 68°C. These were popular as early as Roman times and remains have been found of Roman baths. Even now they are still used by people with rheumatism, skin problems or gynaecological conditions as well as those with breathing difficulties. **Afonso Henriques** also stayed here for some length of time to recover from a broken leg sustained at the battle of Badajoz in 1169. **Termas de São Pedro do Sul**

About 13km/8mi south-east of Viseu is the small town of Mangualde where a 17th-century palace formerly belonging to the counts of Anadia stands amid wild parkland. **Mangualde**

GLOSSARY

Aqueduto Aqueduct

Armillary sphere Nautical instrument that played an important part in 15th and 16th-century seafaring; stylized forms of armillary sphere are often found as ornaments in Manueline architecture.

Artesanato Arts and crafts

Azulejo Tile; azulejos originated in the Arabic and Iberian regions and underwent their own art historical development in Portugal.

Casa House; often found in the term »Casa-Museu«: a small private museum which is established in the house of a famous painter, sculptor or writer.

Castelo Castle, fort; castles were often of Arabic origin and extended or completely rebuilt by the Portuguese for strategic purposes in medieval times.

Chafariz Well system

Cross of the Order of the Knights of Christ Symbol of the Order of the Knights of Christ; a variation on the cross of the Order of the Knights Templar, from which the Order of the Knights of Christ originates. Portuguese sailing ships were adorned with the cross; it is also a commonly used ornament in Manueline architecture.

Claustro Cloister; covered passageway surrounding a small garden or courtyard in a monastery, convent or abbey; it provided monks or nuns access to monastic rooms or the communication room.

Convento Monastery or convent

Descobrimentos »Discoveries«; generally describes the era of the ocean voyages, discoveries and conquests of the 15th and 16th centuries.

Igreja Church

Jardim Garden, park

Chapter house assembly room for members of the monastery or convent

Coffered ceiling flat or arched church ceiling segmented by square or rectangular recesses

Cenotaph Empty tomb

Crypt undercroft of a church used for the storage of relics; at times it serves as a burial site for clerical dignitaries.

Manueline style Specifically Portuguese style of the early 16th century; a style of decoration integrated into the buildings of the late Gothic period or the early Renaissance

Miradouro Vantage point, observation platform

Mosteiro Monastery, abbey

Mouraria Moors' quarter

Reticulated vaulting Gothic church ceiling with network rib pattern

Paço short form of Palácio; e.g. Paço do Concelho (town hall), Paço Real (royal palace)

Palácio Palace

Padrão memorial stone, erected by the Portuguese to mark the first time they set foot in the countries they discovered; sign of discovery and appropriation; a Padrão would usually bear the Portuguese coat of arms and a cross.

Pelourinho Pillory

Pilaster pilaster; essentially intended to aesthetically structure the wall area

Praça Square

Quinta Country residence; has its origin in the Roman country residences in southern Portugal; other terms are »Solar«, »Herdade« or »Monte«, whereby the latter is always situated on a small knoll in the midst of the countryside.

Refectory dining hall for monastery members

Sacristy church room for the storage of liturgical equipment

Sarcophagus monumental tomb, found mostly in churches

Sé Cathedral (derived from »sede« = diocesan town)

Século Century

Século d'Ouro »Golden century« = golden age; 16th century, in which treasures from discoveries and conquests poured into the country.

Talha dourada Gilded wood carvings of the Baroque

INDEX

PHOTO CREDITS

LIST OF MAPS AND & ILLUSTRATIONS

PUBLISHER'S INFORMATION

Illustrations etc:
218 illustrations, 22 maps and diagrams, one large city plan
Text: Rosemarie Arnold, Walter R. Arnold, Monika I. Baumgarten, Prof. Dr. H. Bloss, Birgit Borowski, Achim Bourmer, Werner Fauser, Prof. Dr. Hans-Dieter Haas, Prof. Dr. Wolfgang Hassenpflug, Dr. Eva Missler, Christine Wessely, Reinhard Zakrzewski
Editing: Baedeker editorial team (Dr. Eva Missler, Robert Taylor)
Translation: all-lingua, Robert Taylor, Charity Scott-Stokes
Cartography:
Franz Huber, Munich;
MAIRDUMONT, Ostfildern (city map)
3D illustrations: jangled nerves, Stuttgart
Design: independent Medien-Design, Munich; Kathrin Schemel

Editor-in-chief: Rainer Eisenschmid, Baedeker Ostfildern

1st edition 2008

DEAR READER,

We would like to thank you for choosing this Baedeker travel guide. It will be a reliable companion on your travels and will not disappoint you.

This book describes the major sights, of course, but it also recommends the most attractive beaches, as well as hotels in the luxury and budget categories, and includes tips about where to eat or go shopping and much more, helping to make your trip an enjoyable experience. Our authors ensures the quality of this information by making regular journeys to Portugal and putting all their know-how into this book.

Nevertheless, experience shows us that it is impossible to rule out errors and changes made after the book goes to press, for which Baedeker accepts no liability. Please send us your criticisms, corrections and suggestions for improvement: we appreciate your contribution. Contact us by post or e-mail, or phone us:

▶ **Verlag Karl Baedeker GmbH**
Editorial department
Postfach 3162
73751 Ostfildern
Germany
Tel. 49-711-4502-262, fax -343
www.baedeker.com
E-Mail: baedeker@mairdumont.com

Baedeker Travel Guides in English at a glance:

▶ Andalusia

▶ Dubai · Emirates

▶ Egypt

▶ Ireland

▶ London

▶ Mexico

▶ New York

▶ Portugal

▶ Rome

▶ Thailand

▶ Tuscany

▶ Venice